The Hamlyn Concise Guide to
British Aircraft of World War II

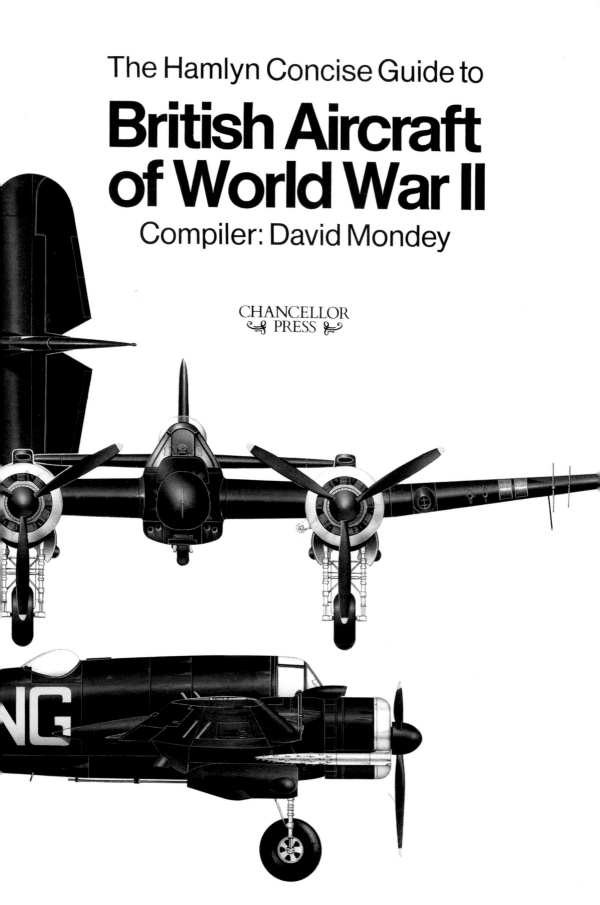

The Hamlyn Concise Guide to
British Aircraft
of World War II
Compiler: David Mondey

CHANCELLOR
PRESS

First published in Great Britain by
Hamlyn Publishing Group Limited in 1982

This edition published in 1994 by Chancellor Press
an imprint of Reed Consumer Books Limited
Michelin House, 81 Fulham Road, London SW3 6RB
and Auckland, Melbourne, Singapore and Toronto

Reprinted 1995

A CIP catalogue record for this book is available
from the British Library

ISBN 1 85152 668 4

Produced by Mandarin Offset
Printed and bound in China

CONTENTS

Airspeed AS.5 Courier **8**
Airspeed AS.6 Envoy **9**
Airspeed AS.10 Oxford **10**
Airspeed AS.30 Queen Wasp **12**
Airspeed AS.45 Cambridge **13**
Airspeed AS.51/AS.58 Horsa **14**
Armstrong Whitworth A.W.38 Whitley **16**
Armstrong Whitworth A.W.41 Albemarle **21**
Avro 621 Tutor/Sea Tutor **22**
Avro 626 Prefect **23**
Avro 652A Anson **24**
Avro 679 Manchester **27**
Avro 683 Lancaster **28**
Avro 685 York **33**
Avro 694 Lincoln **34**
Blackburn B-6 Shark **35**
Blackburn B24 Skua **36**
Blackburn B25 Roc **37**
Blackburn B26 Botha **38**
Blackburn B37 Firebrand **39**
Boulton Paul Defiant **40**
Bristol Type 105 Bulldog **43**
Bristol Type 130 Bombay **46**
Bristol Types 142M, 149 and 160 Blenheim **47**
Bristol Type 152 Beaufort **57**
Bristol Type 156 Beaufighter **61**
Bristol Type 163 Buckingham **68**

Bristol Type 164 Brigand **69**
Bristol Type 166 Buckmaster **70**
Bristol Taylorcraft Auster Series **71**
de Havilland D.H.82 Tiger Moth **72**
de Havilland D.H.89 Dominie **74**
de Havilland D.H.91 Albatross **75**
de Havilland D.H.95 Flamingo **76**
de Havilland D.H.98 Mosquito **77**
de Havilland D.H.103 Hornet **85**
Fairey Fox **86**
Fairey Seafox **87**
Fairey Gordon **88**
Fairey Swordfish **88**
Fairey Battle **96**
Fairey Albacore **100**
Fairey Fulmar **102**
Fairey Barracuda **104**
Fairey Firefly **106**
General Aircraft G.A.L.48 Hotspur **108**
General Aircraft G.A.L.49 Hamilcar **109**
Gloster SS.19B Gauntlet **110**
Gloster SS.37 Gladiator **113**
Gloster F.9/37 **117**
Gloster E.28/39 **118**
Gloster G.41 Meteor **119**
Handley Page H.P.52 Hampden **122**
Handley Page H.P.52 Hereford **124**
Handley Page H.P.54 Harrow **125**
Handley Page H.P.57 Halifax **127**

Hawker Hart **132**
Hawker Osprey **134**
Hawker Demon **135**
Hawker Audax **136**
Hawker Hartebeeste **137**
Hawker Hardy **138**
Hawker Hind **139**
Hawker Hector **140**
Hawker Fury I/II **141**
Hawker Nimrod **144**
Hawker Henley **145**
Hawker Hurricane **146**
Hawker Sea Hurricane **154**
Hawker Typhoon **155**
Hawker Tempest **161**
Hawker Tornado **165**
Hawker Sea Fury **166**
Miles M.3B Falcon Six **167**
Miles M.11A Whitney Straight **167**
Miles M.14 Magister **168**
Miles M.16 Mentor **169**
Miles M.17 Monarch **169**
Miles M.20 **170**
Miles M.25 Martinet **171**
Miles M.28 **172**
Miles M.33 Monitor **173**
Miles M.35 **174**
Miles M.38 Messenger **174**
Miles M.39B **175**

Miles Master(M.9,M.19,M.24 and M.27)**176**
Percival Proctor **178**
Percival Q.6 Petrel **179**
Saro A.27 London **180**
Saro S.36 Lerwick **181**
Short S.19 Singapore III **182**
Short S.25 Sunderland **183**
Short S.45 Seaford **187**
Short S.26 'G' Class **188**
Short S.29 Stirling **189**
Supermarine Stranraer **193**
Supermarine Walrus **194**
Supermarine Sea Otter **196**
Supermarine Spitfire **197**
Supermarine Seafire **210**
Supermarine Spiteful/Seafang **212**
Vickers Vildebeest **213**
Vickers Vincent **214**
Vickers Valentia **215**
Vickers Wellesley **216**
Vickers Wellington **217**
Vickers Warwick **222**
Vickers Windsor **224**
Westland Wapiti **225**
Westland Wallace **226**
Westland Lysander **227**
Westland Whirlwind **230**
Westland Welkin **235**
Index **236**

Airspeed AS.5 Courier

History and notes

Airspeed Ltd was formed in March 1931, and its first design to be built in a significant number was the AS.5 Courier, designed by one of the founder directors, A. Hessell Tiltman. It originated from a proposal which Tiltman made in 1931, but with the new company very short of capital, it was not until September 1932 that construction of the prototype began.

Of conventional low-wing monoplane layout, and of mixed construction, the Courier introduced what was then a most advanced feature: retractable tailwheel type landing gear. There were, of course, the usual 'prophets of doom', who could see no worthwhile advantage to be gained by the introduction of such a complex piece of new-fangled equipment. Tiltman proceeded with his plans without comment, and was able to demonstrate in due course an improvement of some 20 mph (32 km/h) in cruising speed with the main landing gear units retracted. Powered by an uncowled 240-hp (179-kW) Armstrong Siddeley Lynx IVC radial engine, the prototype was flown for the first time on 11 April 1933. Subsequently, the engine was enclosed in a neat Townend ring cowling, and versions for 'English' use were designated AS.5A. The alternative 'Colonial' version had a 305-hp (227-kW) Armstrong Siddeley Cheetah V radial engine and was designated AS.5B.

In February 1934 the RAF acquired one of these five/six-seat AS.5As for use as a communications aircraft, returning it to Airspeed in 1935 for the incorporation of drag and high-lift devices for, once airborne, the Courier was reluctant to return to mother earth. These consisted of Handley Page slotted flaps installed at the trailing-edges of the outer wing panels; split flaps at the trailing-edge of the centre-section, beneath the fuselage; and the introduction of aileron droop. Used appropriately, these devices could be used either to increase lift or drag.

Production of Couriers totalled 16 aircraft, and of these 10 were to serve with the RAF for communications and transport during World War II. These comprised the original example procured for the RAF (D4047), plus nine aircraft impressed from civil sources. Only one survived to be returned to civil service on 18 January 1946.

Specification

Type: five/six-seat light transport aircraft
Powerplant (AS.5B): one 305-hp (227-kW) Armstrong Siddeley Cheetah V radial piston engine
Performance: maximum speed 165 mph (266 km/h) at sea level; cruising speed 145 mph (233 km/h) at 1,000 ft (305 m); service ceiling 17,000 ft (5180 m); range 640 miles (1030 km)
Weights: empty 2,328 lb (1056 kg); maximum take-off 4,000 lb (1814 kg)
Dimensions: span 47 ft 0 in (14.33 m); length 28 ft 6 in (8.69 m); wing area 250 sq ft (23.23 m²)
Armament: none
Operator: RAF

G-ADAX was an Airspeed Courier of the Portsmouth Southsea & Isle of Wight Aviation company until impressed in 1940 for personnel ferrying with the Air Transport Auxiliary until struck off charge in May 1941.

Airspeed AS.6 Envoy

History and notes

The design of this Airspeed aircraft, which became designated AS.6 Envoy, began in late 1933 as a larger, twin-engined development of the AS.5 Courier. The prototype was flown for the first time on 26 June 1934 and for a British civil aircraft of that era was subsequently produced 'extensively', with 50 being built, this total including the prototype.

With standard accommodation for a pilot and eight passengers the Envoy, like the earlier Courier, was of conventional all-wood construction, with all control surfaces fabric-covered. Retractable tailwheel type landing gear and a variable-incidence tailplane were features of the design which, in the period 1934-9 when these aircraft were being produced, was to appear in three versions. The initial Series I (17 examples built) was without trailing-edge flaps; the Series II (13) introduced split flaps which extended from aileron to wing root on the trailing-edge of each wing, and also from wing root to wing root beneath the centre-section; and the Series III (19) was generally similar, but had a number of detail improvements.

The most unstandard feature of the Envoys was their powerplant, and these included the AS.6 with 200-hp (149-kW) Wolseley AR.9; the AS.6A with 240-hp (179-kW) Armstrong Siddeley Lynx IVC; the AS.6D with 350-hp (261-kW) Wright R-760-E2 Whirlwind 7; the AS.6E with 340-hp (254-kW) Walter Castor II; the AS.6G with 250-hp (186-kW) Wolseley Scorpio I; the AS.6H with 225-hp (168-kW) Wolseley Aries III; and the AS.6J and AS.6JM/C with 350-hp (261-kW) Armstrong Siddeley Cheetah IX.

Envoys were to fly in many different skies, being supplied to China, Czechoslovakia, France, India and Japan. For military service they were used by the RAF, Royal Navy and South African Air Force, and a number were used in the Spanish Civil War. The first Envoy Series II to be supplied to the RAF was of historical significance as this aircraft, initially G-AEXX and later L7270, was the founder member of the King's (now Queen's) Flight. The RAF also acquired two Envoys for communications service in India, and five for home service in a similar role, and at least one of these was used throughout World War II by the Fleet Air Arm. In addition, three impressed Envoys served with the RAF during the war. South Africa acquired seven Envoys in 1936: three of these for use by the SAAF each had an armament comprising a forward firing machine-gun and a dorsal gun turret. The four civil Envoys which made up the total, and which were for operation by South African Airways, were capable of quick conversion for use in a military role.

Specification

Type: seven-seat light transport aircraft
Powerplant (AS.6J): two 350-hp (261-kW) Armstrong Siddeley Cheetah IX radial piston engines
Performance: maximum speed 210 mph (338 km/h) at 7,300 ft (2225 m); cruising speed 180 mph (290 km/h) at 10,000 ft (3050 m); service ceiling 22,500 ft (6860 m); range 650 miles (1046 km)
Weights: empty 4,057 lb (1840 kg); maximum take-off 6,300 lb (2858 kg)
Dimensions: span 52 ft 4 in (15.95 m); length 34 ft 6 in (10.52 m); height 9 ft 6 in (2.90 m); wing area 339 sq ft (31.49 m²)
Armament: generally none, but see text
Operators: RAF, Royal Navy, SAAF

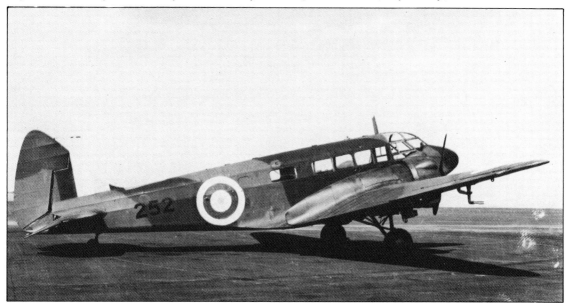

The Airspeed Envoy saw only limited military use, including three Convertible Envoy IIIs for the South African Air Force, one of which is illustrated. Conversion from military to civil use took 32 hours.

Airspeed AS.10 Oxford

History and notes

Established in 1931, Airspeed had little prospect of obtaining a significant military contract in its early years. However, in 1936 the company was given the opportunity of submitting a proposal to meet Air Ministry Specification T.23/36, which called for a twin-engined trainer. Airspeed's design for this was based on the successful AS.6 Envoy, of which about 24 were already in civil use and earning a reputation for reliability which, possibly, may have helped the Air Ministry's decision to order an initial quantity of 136 AS.10s.

The prototype AS.10, by then bearing the name Oxford, made its first flight on 19 June 1937, and token deliveries began in November of that year, with four of the first six going to the RAF's Central Flying School, the other two to No.11 Flying Training School. Very similar in overall proportions and configuration to the AS.6 Envoy, it shared also its wooden construction, tailwheel type retractable landing gear and basic airframe. The variations came in powerplant, internal layout and, in the Oxford I, provision of an Armstrong Whitworth gun turret with one machine-gun for the training of air gunners.

The Oxford was to be built in large numbers and used extensively for the Commonwealth Air Training Scheme when World War II began, and the considerable thought which Airspeed had put into its internal layout undoubtedly had a bearing on the demand for this aircraft. Normal accommodation was for a crew of three at any one time, but in addition to seats for a pilot/pupil and co-pilot/instructor, there were positions for the training of an air-gunner, bomb-

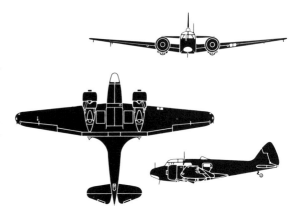

Airspeed Oxford

aimer, camera operator, navigator, and radio operator. Dual controls were standard, making the Oxford suitable for use as a twin-engined trainer; with the dual-control set removed from the co-pilot's position a bomb aimer could take up a prone position and drop smoke practice bombs which were carried in the centre-section well; or the seat could be slid back and a chart table, hinged to the fuselage side, erected for use by a trainee navigator; an aft facing seat behind the co-pilot position was available for a radio operator; and, in the Oxford I, a turret was provided for an air gunner's training. A hood was also available so that the Oxford could be used for instrument training.

Powerplants varied according to mark. The Mk I, a general-purpose, bombing and gunnery trainer, and the Mk II pilot, radio operator and navigator trainer

Air-to-air firing practice: the dorsal gunner of an Airspeed Oxford I advanced trainer fires on the drogue towed by the yellow/black-striped Fairey Battle TT.I target-tug.

Airspeed AS.10 Oxford

Three Airspeed Oxford IIs formate above the clouds. The Mk II was generally similar to the Mk I apart from having no dorsal turret as the type was intended more specifically for pilot rather than aircrew training.

were both powered by two 375-hp (280-kW) Armstrong Siddeley Cheetah X radial engines, with fixed-pitch propellers. The Mk V, equipped for the same role as the Mk II, had two 450-hp (336-kW) Pratt & Whitney R-985-AN6 radial engines, driving constant-speed propellers. The Oxford Mk III, of which only a single example was built, had two 425-hp (317-kW) Cheetah XV radials and Rotol constant-speed propellers; the Mk IV was a projected trainer version of the Mk III, but none was built. One example of a Mk II aircraft was fitted experimentally with two 250-hp (186-kW) de Havilland Gipsy Queen inline engines. Odd variants included an early Oxford I equipped with special McLaren landing gear, the main units of which could be offset to cater for a reasonable degree of cross-wind at both take-off and landing, and one with a tail unit which included twin endplate fins and rudders, especially installed for a series of spin recovery tests.

As mentioned above, the outbreak of World War II created an enormous demand for these trainers, not only for use by the RAF, but by those nations which were involved in the Commonwealth Air Training Scheme. These included Australia (nearly 400 Oxfords), Canada (200), New Zealand (300), Rhodesia (10), and South Africa (700). Examples went also to the Free French air force and, under reverse Lend-Lease, a number were used by USAAF units in Europe. In addition to their use for training purposes, a number were equipped to serve as air ambulances, for radar calibration, and for communications. Many served with anti-aircraft co-operation squadrons, these including Nos. 285, 286, 289, 290, 567, 577, 598, 631, 667 and 691.

The Fleet Air Arm also had one training unit, No. 758 Instrument Flying Squadron, equipped with Oxfords from June 1942.

The demand for Oxfords was beyond Airspeed's productive capacity, the company building a total of 4,411 at Portsmouth, Hants and 550 at Christchurch, Hants. Other construction was by de Havilland at Hatfield (1,515), Percival Aircraft at Luton (1,360), and Standard Motors at Coventry (750), to give a grand total of 8,586. Airspeed built its last example in July 1945, and the Oxford remained in service with the RAF at No. 10 Advanced Flying Training School, Pershore, until 1954. Many were supplied after the war to the Dutch air force.

Specification

Type: two-seat general-purpose trainer
Powerplant (Mk V): two 450-hp (336-kW) Pratt & Whitney R-985-AN6 Wasp Junior radial piston engines
Performance: maximum speed 202 mph (325 km/h) at 4,100 ft (1250 m); service ceiling 21,000 ft (6400 m); range 700 miles (1127 km)
Weights: empty 5,670 lb (2572 kg); maximum take-off 8,000 lb (3629 kg)
Dimensions: span 53 ft 4 in (16.26 m); length 34 ft 6 in (10.52 m); height 11 ft 1 in (3.38 m); wing area 348 sq ft (32.33 m²)
Armament (Oxford I): one 0.303-in (7.7-mm) machine-gun in dorsal turret
Operators: FFAF, Portugal, RAAF, RAF, RCAF, RN, RNZAF, Rhodesia, SAAF, USAAF

Airspeed AS.30 Queen Wasp

History and notes

Air Ministry Specification Q.32/35 called for a higher-speed and more effectively controlled pilotless target aircraft than the de Havilland Queen Bee, which was a variant of the Tiger Moth. The Queen Bee had first entered service in 1935-6, but its maximum speed of little over 100 mph (161 km/h) was considered to be far from representative of contemporary service aircraft.

Under the designation AS.30, Airspeed submitted a design proposal to meet this requirement, and two prototypes were ordered in May 1936. One of these was to have wheeled landing gear, for evaluation by the RAF; the other was to be equipped as a floatplane, so that it could be tested by the Royal Navy for air-firing practice at sea.

A clean looking single-bay biplane with tapered wings, the AS.30 had only a single I-section streamline interplane strut on each side and a minimum of bracing wires. Full-span single-slotted flaps occupied the entire trailing-edge of the upper wing. The lower wing carried slotted ailerons, which were interconnected with the flaps so as to droop when they were lowered. Construction was all-wood, with fabric-covered control surfaces. The wheeled landing gear had cantilever main units which were well faired and provided with wheel speed fairings. The float landing gear, though of necessity well braced, appeared to be far more elegant. The enclosed cabin was equipped with a single seat for a pilot, so that the AS.30 could be flown independently of its radio control system.

Named Queen Wasp, the landplane and floatplane prototypes flew for the first time on 11 June 1937 and 19 October 1937 respectively. Testing began shortly after these dates, and the Royal Navy version was successfully catapulted from HMS *Pegasus* in November. As in the case of the single-engine Courier, however, low speed control and handling characteristics

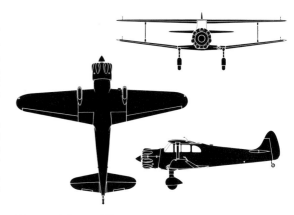

Airspeed Queen Wasp

were considered to be poor, and this probably accounts for the fact that only three more examples were completed and delivered to the RAF.

Specification

Type: pilotless target aircraft
Powerplant: one 350-hp (261-kW) Armstrong Siddeley Cheetah IX radial piston engine
Performance: maximum speed (landplane) 172 mph (277 km/h) at 8,000 ft (2440 m); cruising speed (landplane) 151 mph (243 km/h) at 10,000 ft (3050 m); service ceiling 20,000 ft (6100 m)
Weights: maximum take-off (landplane) 3,500 lb (1588 kg), (seaplane) 3,800 lb (1724 kg)
Dimensions: span 31 ft 0 in (9.45 m); length (landplane) 24 ft 4 in (7.42 m), (seaplane) 29 ft 1 in (8.86 m); height (landplane) 10 ft 1 in (3.07 m), (seaplane) 13 ft 0 in (3.96 m)
Armament: none
Operators: RAF, RN

The Airspeed Queen Wasp was designed for operation on wheel or float landing gear as a radio-controlled gunnery target, though the second prototype shown here has a test crew of two in the cockpit.

Airspeed AS.45 Cambridge

The Airspeed Cambridge, of which only two prototypes were built, was designed as an advanced trainer offering the crew a high degree of safety in the event of a crash. The type was excessively heavy, however.

History and notes

Designed to satisfy Air Ministry Specification T.34/39 for an advanced trainer, Airspeed's AS.45 design was conventional in appearance and in the same general mould as the Miles Master, being of low-wing monoplane layout, having retractable tailwheel type landing gear, and being powered by a radial air-cooled engine. Following Air Ministry approval of the design, which was given the provisional name Cambridge, two prototypes were ordered, the first of these making a successful maiden flight on 19 February 1941.

Construction was fairly typical of that era, with wings and tail unit of wood with plywood skins, except for control surfaces which were fabric covered. The trailing-edge of each wing was shared almost equally by ailerons and flaps. The fuselage was of steel tube, and a hefty overturn structure was integral with this to provide instructor and pupil with some protection in the event of an accident. Four doors were provided, two on each side, so that exit in emergency could be made on either side. The main units of the Dowty landing gear retracted inwards, the wheels lying flush in the undersurface of the wing centre-section. Instructor and trainee were seated in tandem beneath an extensively glazed canopy. Powerplant comprised a 730-hp (544-kW) Bristol Mercury VIII radial engine.

Flight testing of these two prototypes was to show that low-speed flight characteristics were poor, and speed was below that which had been estimated. Both of the aircraft were handed over to the RAF in July 1942, following a decision not to proceed with production. This may well have been because performance of the prototypes was disappointing, but the official reason given at the time was that design of the Cambridge had been initiated to fill an anticipated shortage of advanced trainers which had not materialised, due to an adequate supply of Masters and, via Lend-Lease, the excellent North American Harvard.

There seems little doubt that Airspeed could have remedied the shortcomings of the AS.45, but the answer may well be that with the reasonable supplies of advanced trainers in service, it was far more important to the RAF for Airspeed to concentrate on production of the Horsa and Oxford.

Specification

Type: two-seat advanced trainer
Powerplant: one 730-hp (544-kW) Bristol Mercury VIII radial piston engine
Performance: maximum speed 237 mph (381 km/h) at 16,000 ft (4875 m); service ceiling 24,800 ft (7560 m); range 680 miles (1094 km)
Weights: no data available
Dimensions: span 42 ft 0 in (12.80 m); length 36 ft 1 in (11.00 m); height 11 ft 6 in (3.51 m); wing area 290 sq ft (26.94 m²)
Armament: none
Operator: RAF, for evaluation only

Airspeed AS.51/AS.58 Horsa

History and notes

Early deployment by Germany of paratroops, and of gliders carrying airborne troops or supplies, had been seen to be tactically advantageous. It was considered essential in Britain that its armed forces should be similarly equipped and the United States, at a later date, came to the same decision.

In December 1940 Airspeed received Air Ministry Specification X.26/40, which called for a troop-carrying glider, and this was to have almost double the capacity of the Waco CG-4A Hadrian which was designed and developed in America for the US Army during 1941. Following acceptance of Airspeed's design proposal, the Air Ministry ordered seven prototypes. Two of these when fabricated were assembled at Fairey's works, these being the flight test examples. The remaining five were assembled at Airspeed's factory at Portsmouth, and these were for use by the British Army to carry out trials in the loading and unloading of typical equipment that they would be expected to carry.

By comparison with the design for a contemporary fighter or bomber aircraft, one would expect that of Airspeed's AS.51 to be simple. This would have been true if it had not been an essential requirement that the glider must be composed of a number of easily assembled units, instead of being built conventionally

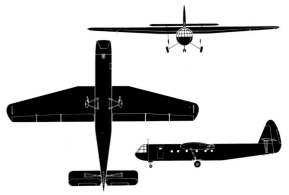

Airspeed Horsa II

on a production line. Thus, it consisted of 30 separate assemblies built mainly by woodworking subcontractors, such as furniture manufacturers. These were subsequently assembled and test flown at RAF Maintenance Units, with some 3,000 of these gliders being constructed in this way. Only about 700 of all the AS.51s that were built were manufactured, assembled and test flown in one place, and these originated from Airspeed at their Christchurch, Hants, factory. Produced simultaneously with the AS.51, which became designated Horsa I, was the AS.58 with a hinged nose

An aerial illustration of a Horsa I shows the tow-attachment points of this trooping version at the junction of the main landing gear legs and spar. The Mk II's attachment point was on the nosewheel leg.

Airspeed AS.51/AS.58 Horsa

The Airspeed Horsa was the main British assault glider of the war, in two versions: the Mk I troop version for 25 men, and the Mk II freight version with a hinged nose, double nosewheels and revised tow system.

for the direct loading of vehicles and guns, and this was designated Horsa II.

Almost entirely of wood construction, the cantilever high-set wing was built in three sections, had ailerons, split trailing-edge flaps, and underwing dive brakes. The fuselage was also in three sections, and provided accommodation for two pilots and a maximum of 25 troops. Landing gear was of the fixed tricycle type, and there was provision to jettison the main units for landing on very rough areas, when the nosewheel and sprung landing skid on the underfuselage centreline had to suffice. The AS.58 had twin nosewheels.

The first prototype, towed by an Armstrong Whitworth Whitley, was flown from Fairey's Great West Aerodrome on 12 September 1941, and soon after this date the Horsa began to enter service with the RAF, towed for operational purposes by powered aircraft of RAF Transport Command. They were used to carry men and equipment of the Air Landing Brigades of the 1st and 6th Airborne Divisions, piloted mainly by men of the British Army's Glider Pilot Regiment but also, as and when necessary, by RAF pilots.

The first significant operational use of the Horsa was on 10 July 1943 when 27 survivors of 30 air-towed from Britain to North Africa were deployed during the invasion of Sicily. Horsas subsequently played an important part in the Normandy invasion of June 1944, operated by the RAF and the USAAF, in the invasion

of southern France in August 1944, at Arnhem in September 1944, and during the Rhine crossing in March 1945.

It is impossible to quote accurate production figures for the Horsa. The totals agreed by several researchers, however, cannot be too far out, and are as near as possible to the true number. These comprise 470 Mk I and 225 Mk IIs by Airspeed, plus the original seven prototypes; 300 Mk Is and 65 Mk IIs by the Austin Motor Company; and 1,461 Mk Is and 1,271 Mk IIs by subcontractors in the woodworking industry, the majority produced by the furniture manufacturer Harris Lebus. This amounts to a grand total of 3,799.

Specification
Type: troop and cargo combat glider
Powerplant: none
Performance: maximum towing speed 150 mph (241 km/h); normal gliding speed 100 mph (161 km/h)
Weights: empty 8,370 lb (3797 kg); maximum take-off (Horsa I) 15,500 lb (7031 kg), (Horsa II) 15,750 lb (7144 kg)
Dimensions: span 88 ft 0 in (26.82 m); length (Horsa I) 67 ft 0 in (20.42 m), (Horsa II) 67 ft 11 in (20.70 m); height (Horsa I) 19 ft 6 in (5.94 m), (Horsa II) 20 ft 4 in (6.20 m); wing area 1,104 sq ft (102.56 m²)
Armament: none
Operators: RAF, USAAF

Armstrong Whitworth A.W.38 Whitley

Groundcrew work at an apparently leisurely pace on an Armstrong Whitworth Whitley V of No. 78 Squadron. The Mk V was the major production variant of this early-war mainstay of Bomber Command.

History and notes

Designed to Air Ministry Specification B.3/34, which was circulated in July 1934, the Armstrong Whitworth A.W.38 Whitley was the most extensively built of the company's designs, production reaching a total of 1,814 aircraft. It also marked a departure from Armstrong Whitworth's traditional steel-tube construction, the Whitley's fuselage being a light alloy monocoque structure.

Production was authorised while the aircraft was still in the design stage, an order for 80 aircraft being placed in August 1935. Alan Campbell-Orde flew the first prototype at Whitley Abbey on 17 March 1936, the machine's two Armstrong Siddeley Tiger X engines turning the then-new three-blade, variable-pitch de Havilland propellers. A second prototype built to Specification B.21/35 had the more powerful Tiger XI engines and was flown by Charles Turner Hughes on 24 February 1937.

Trials at the Aircraft and Armament Experimental Establishment at Martlesham Heath were undertaken in the autumn of 1936, and the first production Whitley Mk Is were delivered early in 1937, including the second aircraft which was flown to RAF Dishforth on 9 March for No. 10 Squadron. Thirty-four Mk Is were built before the Mk II was introduced. This mark had Tiger VIII engines with two-speed superchargers, the first fitted to an RAF aircraft; 46 Whitley Mk IIs completed the initial order for 80.

Mk I and Mk II Whitleys had Armstrong Whitworth manually-operated nose and tail turrets, each with a 0.303-in (7.7-mm) Vickers machine-gun, but in the Mk III the nose turret was replaced by a power-operated Nash and Thompson turret, and a retractable ventral

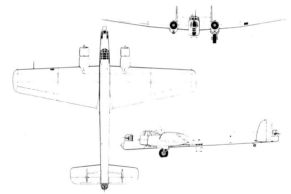

Armstrong Whitworth Whitley III (dashed line: retractable ventral turret)

turret with two 0.303-in Brownings was added. The 80 Whitley IIIs also had modified bomb bays to accommodate larger bombs.

By far the most numerous of the Whitley variants were those with Rolls-Royce engines. A Whitley I was fitted with Merlin IIs and test-flown at Hucknall on 11 February 1938, although engine failure prematurely concluded the second flight. The programme was quickly resumed, however, and during April and May the aircraft carried out trials at Martlesham Heath.

Merlin IVs of 1,030 hp (768 kW) were installed in production Whitley IVs, the first of which flew on 5 April 1939. Other changes incorporated in this version included a power-operated Nash and Thompson tail turret with four 0.303-in Browning guns, a transparent panel was added in the lower nose to improve the view for the bomb-aimer, and two additional wing tanks

Armstrong Whitworth A.W.38 Whitley

Armstrong Whitworth Whitley V of
No. 77 Squadron, RAF, in 1940

17

Armstrong Whitworth A.W.38 Whitley

The Armstrong Whitworth Whitley V was similar to the Whitley IV apart from a very slight lengthening of the rear fuselage to provide the tail gunner with a better field of fire for his four 0.303-in (7.7-mm) guns.

were fitted to bring total capacity to 705 Imperial gallons (3205 litres). Production totalled 33, together with seven Mk IVAs which had 1,145-hp (854-kW) Merlin X engines.

The same engines were retained for the Whitley V, which incorporated a number of improvements. The most noticeable of these were modified fins with straight leading-edges and an extension of 1 ft 3 in (0.38 m) to the rear fuselage to provide a wider field of fire for the rear gunner. Rubber de-icer boots were fitted to the wing leading-edges, and fuel capacity was increased to 837 Imperial gallons (3805 litres), or 969 Imperial gallons (4405 litres) if extra tanks were

The Armstrong Whitworth Whitley V (an aircraft of No. 78 Squadron is shown) was the most widely built Whitley variant, and was the basis of the Whitley GR. VII radar-equipped maritime-reconnaissance model.

carried in the bomb bay. Production totalled 1,466 aircraft.

The Whitley VI was a projected version with Pratt & Whitney engines, studied as an insurance against short supply of Merlins. It was not built, however, and the ultimate production Whitley was the Mk VII which was essentially a Mk V with auxiliary fuel tanks in the bomb bay and in the rear fuselage to bring the total capacity to 1,100 Imperial gallons (5001 litres), increasing the range to 2,300 miles (3701 km) for maritime patrol duties. Externally the Mk VIIs could be distinguished by the dorsal radar aerials of the ASV Mk II air-to-surface radar. Production reached 146, and some Mk Vs were converted to the later standard.

As noted above, No.10 Squadron at RAF Dishforth was the first to equip with the Whitley, which replaced the Handley Page Heyford in March 1937. Nos.51 and 58 Squadrons at RAF Leconfield soon followed and, during the night of 3 September 1939, 10 Whitley IIIs from these two squadrons flew a leaflet raid over Bremen, Hamburg and the Ruhr. Just under a month later, during the night of 1 October, No. 10 Squadron flew a similar mission over Berlin. The first bombs were dropped on Berlin during the night of 25 August 1940, the attacking squadrons including Nos. 51 and 78 with Whitleys. To mark the entry of the Italians into the war, 36 Whitleys drawn from Nos. 10, 51, 58, 77 and 102 Squadrons were tasked to raid Genoa and Turin during the night of 11 June 1940, although only 13 actually reached their targets, weather and engine troubles taking their toll.

Armstrong Whitworth A.W.38 Whitley

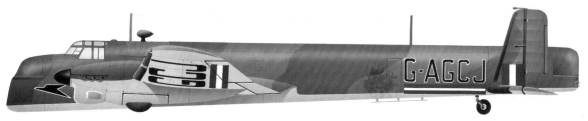

Armstrong Whitworth Whitley V of BOAC in 1942

Armstrong Whitworth Whitley II modified for use by the Central Landing School, Manchester (UK) in 1940

Armstrong Whitworth Whitley III of No. 10 Operational Training Unit, RAF, Abingdon (UK) in 1939

Armstrong Whitworth Whitley V trials aircraft with glider-towing yoke at rear of fuselage in 1943

Armstrong Whitworth Whitley VII of No. 502 Squadron, RAF Coastal Command, in 1942

Armstrong Whitworth Whitley V of No. 78 Squadron, RAF, in late 1939

Armstrong Whitworth A.W.38 Whitley

Armstrong Whitworth Whitley I (without nose turret) of No. 78 Squadron, RAF, Dishforth (UK) in 1937

Armstrong Whitworth Whitley I of No. 10 Squadron, RAF, Dishforth (UK) in 1937

Armstrong Whitworth Whitley IV in 1938

The Whitley was retired from Bomber Command in April 1942, the last operation being flown against Ostend during the night of 29 April, although some aircraft from operational training units were flown in the '1,000 Bomber' raid on Cologne on the night of 30 May 1942.

Coastal Command's association with the Whitley began in September 1939 when No. 58 Squadron was transferred to Boscombe Down to operate anti-submarine patrols over the English Channel. This lasted until February 1940, when the unit returned to Bomber Command, but during 1942 it took up patrol duties once again, flying over the Western Approaches from St Eval and Stornoway. Other units similarly occupied at that time included Nos. 51 and 77 Squadrons, the latter operating in the Bay of Biscay area.

Mk V Whitleys replaced the Avro Ansons of No. 502 Squadron at RAF Aldergrove in the autumn of 1940 and a second Coastal Command Whitley unit, No. 612 Squadron, formed in May 1941. The Mk Vs were replaced by the ASV Mk II-equipped Whitley VII, and an aircraft of No. 502 Squadron sank the type's first German submarine when it attacked *U-205* in the Bay of Biscay on 30 November 1941.

Whitleys were also used at No. 1 Parachute Training School at Ringway, Manchester, and were adapted for use as glider tugs, becoming attached to No. 21 Glider Conversion Unit at Brize Norton for the training of tug

pilots. The paratroop raid on the German radar site at Bruneval used Whitleys of No. 51 Squadron, and the aircraft of 'special duty' units at RAF Tempsford (Nos. 138 and 161 Squadrons) flew numerous sorties, dropping agents into occupied territory and supplying Resistance groups with arms and equipment. Fifteen Whitley Vs were handed over to BOAC in May 1942 and, stripped of armament, but with additional fuel tanks in the bomb bays, flew regularly from Gibraltar to Malta carrying supplies for the beleaguered island.

Specification

Type: five-seat long-range night-bomber
Powerplant (Mk V): two 1,145-hp (854-kW) Rolls-Royce Merlin X inline piston engines
Performance: maximum speed 230 mph (370 km/h) at 16,400 ft (5000 m); cruising speed 210 mph (338 km/h) at 15,000 ft (4570 m); service ceiling 26,000 ft (7925 m); range 1,500 miles (2414 km)
Weights: empty 19,350 lb (8777 kg); maximum take-off 33,500 lb (15 195 kg)
Dimensions: span 84 ft 0 in (25.60 m); length 70 ft 6 in (21.49 m²); height 15 ft 0 in (4.57 m); wing area 1,137 sq ft (105.63 m²)
Armament: four 0.303-in (7.7-mm) machine-guns in powered tail turret and one similar gun in nose turret, plus up to 7,000 lb (3175 kg) of bombs
Operator: RAF

Armstrong Whitworth A.W.41 Albemarle

Armstrong Whitworth Albemarle V of No. 297 Squadron, RAF, in July 1943

History and notes

The Albemarle originated as a Bristol Aeroplane Company design to meet Air Ministry Specification P.9/38 for a twin-engined bomber, being allocated the company identification Type 155. With a change in the official specification, however, design responsibility was transferred to Armstrong Whitworth, under a team led by John Lloyd who was set the difficult task of taking over another company's creation and adapting it to meet Specification B.18/38 for a reconnaissance bomber. This duly became identified as the Armstrong Whitworth A.W.41, given the name Albemarle, which in detail and construction was very different from the original Bristol concept.

Designed for mixed composite steel and wood construction, the prototype flew in 1939, but was destroyed in a crash before the flight of the second prototype on 20 March 1940. The Albemarle's form of structure enabled wide use of sub-contracting, even to small companies outside the aircraft industry (one source mentions almost 1,000 sub-contractors), and an additional bonus came from conservation of light alloy and other strategic materials; the tricycle landing gear was of Lockheed design.

The first 42 aircraft were built as bombers, although not used as such, and there was considerable delay in establishing production lines. The first three production Albemarles left the factory in December 1941, by which time the decision had been made to adapt the aircraft as a glider tug and airborne forces transport.

Deliveries to the RAF began in January 1943 when No. 295 Squadron received its first aircraft; the type was blooded with Nos. 296 and 297 Squadrons, part of No. 38 Wing operating from North Africa, in the invasion of Sicily in July 1943. On D-Day (6 June 1944) six No. 295 Squadron Albemarles, operating from Harwell, served as pathfinders for the 6th Airborne Division, dropping paratroops over Normandy.

In the glider tug role, four squadrons of Albemarles were used to tow Airspeed Horsas to France in support of ground operations, while in September 1944 two of No. 38 Group's squadrons participated in the ill-fated Arnhem operation, towing gliders carrying troops of the 1st Airborne Division.

Production of the Albemarle, apart from the prototypes, was undertaken by A.W. Hawksley Ltd, part of the Hawker Siddeley Group; production came to an end in December 1944 when 600 Albemarles had been built. Original orders had covered 1,080.

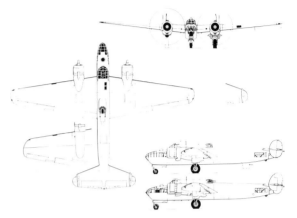

Armstrong Whitworth Albemarle (top side view: 1st prototype with ventral turret and smaller vertical tail surfaces, as in scrap view above; scrap view on left: outer wing planform of 1st prototype)

Deliveries to the RAF consisted of 359 transport versions (78 Mk I, 99 Mk II, 49 Mk V and 133 Mk VI) and 197 glider tugs (80 Mk I and 117 Mk VI). Additional to these were the original 42 bombers which were subsequently converted to transports. Ten Albemarles were delivered to the Russian air force from RAF stocks and were used as transports.

All Albemarles used the 1,590-hp (1186-kW) Bristol Hercules XI engine, apart from a single Mk IV prototype with Wright Double Cyclones, and differences in the marks were primarily in equipment. The original bomber versions were fitted with a four-gun Boulton Paul dorsal turret.

Specification

Type: four-seat transport and glider tug
Powerplant: two 1,590-hp (1186-kW) Bristol Hercules XI radial piston engines
Performance (glider tug): maximum speed 265 mph (426 km/h) at 10,500 ft (3200 m); cruising speed 170 mph (274 km/h); service ceiling 18,000 ft (5485 m); range 1,300 miles (2092 km)
Weight: maximum take-off 22,600 lb (10 251 kg)
Dimensions: span 77 ft 0 in (23.47 m); length 59 ft 11 in (18.26 m); height 15 ft 7 in (4.75 m); wing area 803.5 sq ft (74.65 m²)
Armament (glider tug and transport): twin 0.303-in (7.7-mm) Vickers 'K' machine-guns in dorsal position
Operators: RAF, Soviet Air Force

Avro 621 Tutor/Sea Tutor

History and notes

In the early 1930s it became necessary to replace the Avro 504N as the RAF's basic trainer and the logical choice as its successor was the Avro 621.

Designed by Roy Chadwick in 1929, the Tutor employed welded steel-tube construction with fabric-covered surfaces. The civil registered prototype, powered by a 155-hp (116-kW) Armstrong Siddeley Mongoose IIIA radial engine, went to the Aircraft and Armament Experimental Establishment, Martlesham Heath, for comparative trials in December 1929, making its first public appearance in the New Types Park at the RAF Display, Hendon, on 28 June 1930.

Following its service trials against other aircraft, the Tutor was selected by the RAF in 1930 and a trial batch of 21 was ordered to Specification 3/30, retaining the five-cylinder Mongoose engine. Virtually all the following production aircraft had the 240-hp (179-kW) Armstrong Siddeley Lynx IV engine under a narrow chord Townend ring cowling, differing from the Mongoose-powered aircraft which had uncowled engines.

A number of civil 621s were built, plus others for foreign air forces, including three for the Irish Air Corps, seven for the Royal Canadian Air Force, two for the South African Air Force, 30 for the Greek air force, three for the Danish navy and five for the Kwangsi (Chinese) air force.

The biggest production orders came from the RAF, which had received 394 aircraft from the total of 795 built by the time Tutor production ceased in May 1936. The majority were built to Specification 18/31 but 14 twin-float seaplane versions, known as Sea Tutors, were delivered against Specification 26/34. These were delivered between 1934 and 1936 for waterborne trials at Felixstowe and for use by the Seaplane Training School at Calshot. Sea Tutors had been withdrawn from service by April 1938.

Standard RAF Tutor deliveries began with a batch for the Central Flying School in 1933, and these were followed by deliveries to the RAF College, Cranwell, No. 5 Flying Training School, Sealand, and No. 3 FTS, Grantham. As the Tutors moved in to the flying training schools to replace Avro 504Ns they became standard equipment; a number were also delivered to the university air squadrons and to station flights of the Auxiliary Air Force.

The Tutor's excellent handling qualities made it an ideal aircraft for aerobatic displays and the CFS Tutors first appeared in this role at the RAF Display, Hendon, on 26 June 1933, with the upper surfaces of both wings painted in a red and white 'sunburst' pattern.

A licence was granted to permit Avro 621 production in South Africa, and 57 were built in that country. Additionally, three were built in Denmark. A navigation trainer variant built for the RAF was named Prefect. With the impending re-equipment of RAF fighter squadrons in the late 1930s with the new Supermarine Spitfire and Hawker Hurricane, the RAF favoured monoplane trainers and the Tutors were phased out, to be replaced in the elementary training role by Miles Magisters.

Specification

Type: two-seat elementary trainer
Powerplant (Tutor): one 240-hp (179-kW) Armstrong Siddeley Lynx IVC radial piston engine
Performance: maximum speed 122 mph (196 km/h); cruising speed 105 mph (169 km/h) at 1,000 ft (305 m); service ceiling 16,200 ft (4940 m); range 250 miles (402 km)
Weights: empty 1844 lb (836 kg); maximum take-off 2,458 lb (1115 kg)
Dimensions: span 34 ft 0 in (10.36 m); length 26 ft 6 in (8.08 m); height 9 ft 7 in (2.92 m); wing area 301 sq ft (27.96 m²)
Armament: none
Operators: Danish Navy, Greek Air Force, Irish Air Corps, Kwangsi Air Force, RAF, RCAF, SAAF

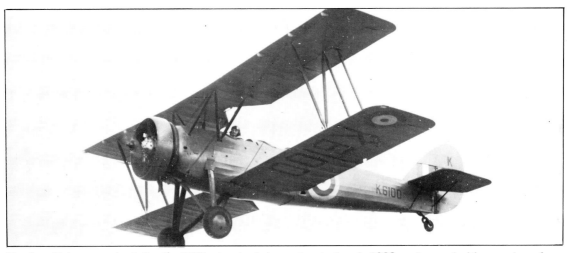

The Avro Tutor was adopted as the RAF's standard elementary trainer in 1932, and served with a number of Flying Training Schools and university air squadrons until superseded in the late 1930s by the Magister.

Avro 626/Prefect

Avro 626 of the Royal New Zealand Air Force

History and notes

Following the success of the Avro 621 Tutor, the manufacturers produced a redesign of the basic airframe in 1930 specifically for foreign air forces.

The new model, the Type 626, was un-named at the time, and featured special conversion kits enabling it to be used for a wide variety of training roles. These included, in addition to the basic *ab initio* role, blind-flying, bombing, gunnery, navigation, night flying, photographic, seaplane, and wireless instruction. It was basically a two-seater, but had provision for a gunner's position behind the aft cockpit.

A South American demonstration tour was undertaken in 1931, when the Type 626 was flown both in landplane and seaplane configuration; in the course of the tour Captain Norman Macmillan, the demonstration pilot, made the first all-British crossing of the Andes. An immediate result of the tour was the purchase of the demonstrator and 14 additional aircraft by the Argentine air force.

The Type 626 entered production with an impressive order book and by 1939, when construction ceased, 178 had been built to military orders as follows: Argentina 14, Belgium 12, Brazil 15, Canada 12, Chile 20, China 9, Egypt 27, Eire 4, Estonia 4, Greece 21, Lithuania 4, New Zealand 3, Portugal 26, and UK 7.

Following delivery of the 26 aircraft for Portugal, the government aircraft factory OGMA built some further Type 626s under licence. The RAF and RNZAF aircraft were known as Prefects, the latter being delivered in July 1935 and the RAF machines between January and July of that year. These were specialised navigation trainers to replace the Andover School of Air Navigation's Mongoose-engined Avro 621 Tutors.

Avro 626s were delivered either with the 240-hp (179-kW) Armstrong Siddeley Lynx IVC or the slightly more powerful 260-hp (194-kW) Armstrong Siddeley Cheetah V.

At least three 626s survived World War II to fly under civil markings.

Specification

Type: two/three-seat multi-purpose trainer
Powerplant: one 240-hp (179-kW) Armstrong Siddeley Lynx IVC radial piston engine
Performance: maximum speed 112 mph (180 km/h); cruising speed 95 mph (153 km/h); service ceiling 14,800 ft (4510 m); range about 220 miles (354 km)
Weights: empty 1,765 lb (801 kg); maximum take-off 2,750 lb (1247 kg)
Dimensions: span 34 ft 0 in (10.36 m); length 26 ft 6 in (8.08 m); height 9 ft 7 in (2.92 m); wing area 300 sq ft (27.87 m²)
Armament: none
Operators: Argentina, Belgium, Brazil, Chile, China, Egypt, Eire, Estonia, Greece, Lithuania, Portugal, RAF, RCAF, RNZAF

The Avro Prefect was the RAF's version of the Avro 626, and seven were ordered to meet the requirements of Specification 32/34, being delivered between January and July 1935. Shown here is the first of the seven, which later became an instructional airframe with the serial number 1594M. In service use the Prefects replaced Mongoose-Tutors at the Air Navigation School, Andover, during 1935.

Avro 652A Anson

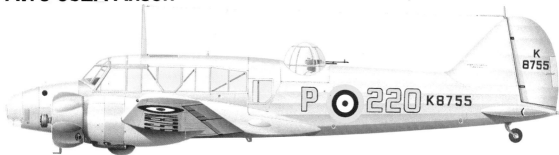

An Avro Anson I of No. 220 Squadron, RAF Coastal Command, in the overall silver prewar finish

Early-war markings and camouflage on an Avro Anson I of No. 206 Squadron, RAF Coastal Command

History and notes

The Avro Anson enjoyed one of the longest production runs of any British aircraft, this status being maintained from 1934 until 15 May 1952 when the last Anson T.21 completed its acceptance trials. Its origin lay in an Imperial Airways specification, sent to A.V.Roe in April 1933, which required that the resulting aircraft should be capable of transporting four passengers over 420-mile (676-km) sectors at a cruising speed in excess of 130 mph (209 km/h). Other requirements were that the stalling speed should not exceed 60 mph (97 km/h) and that the machine should be capable of maintaining 2,000 ft (610 m) on one engine.

In August 1933, a design team headed by Roy Chadwick produced a study, bearing the Avro type number 652, for a low-wing monoplane with retractable landing gear, to be powered by two Armstrong Siddeley Cheetah V engines, and with a design gross weight of 6,500 lb (2948 kg). A change in the Imperial Airways specification to enable the aircraft to fly the Karachi-Bombay-Colombo night mail service resulted in modifications which raised the gross weight to 7,650 lb (3470 kg).

An order for two Avro 652s was placed in April 1934, and the first flew on 7 January 1935. Type certification was awarded in March, and these two aircraft were delivered to Imperial Airways at Croydon on 11 March, to remain in service until sold to Air Service Training Ltd in 1938 for use as navigation trainers.

On 7 May 1934 the Director of Contracts at the Air Ministry notified A.V.Roe of a requirement for twin-engined landplanes for use as coastal reconnaissance aircraft, and requested information as to the possibility of adapting existing designs. A new design study, based on the Imperial Airways machine, was designated Type 652A. This was completed within the

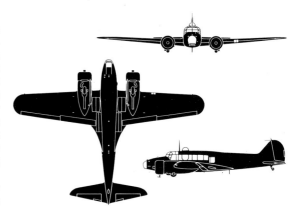

Avro Anson X

month and selected for prototype development, together with the militarised de Havilland 89.

The resulting Air Ministry contract called for delivery in March 1935, giving the company less than six months to complete detail design and prototype construction for the military version of an aircraft which had not then flown in civil form. External changes included rectangular rather than the round windows on the 652, and the addition of an Armstrong Whitworth dorsal turret with a single Lewis gun.

The prototype was flown on 24 March 1935 and delivered to Martlesham Heath for official trials in the following month. After minor modifications to tailplane and elevators, the machine was transferred to the Coastal Defence Development Unit at Gosport for a competitive fly-off with the D.H.89M. A fleet exercise provided a practical test of the capabilities of the contenders and the superior range and endurance of the Avro 652A enabled it to win the competition.

Avro 652A Anson

Specification 18/35 was written to cover production aircraft, designated Anson GR. Mk I, and the first was flown on 31 December 1935. On 6 March 1936 No. 48 Squadron at Manston became the first operational RAF Anson unit; it also proved to be the last to use the type in front-line service, converting to the Lockheed Hudson in January 1942. Twenty-one Coastal Command squadrons used Ansons in general reconnaissance, and search and rescue roles.

The Anson I was armed with a fixed forward-firing Vickers gun in the nose, mounted on the port side, and the Armstrong Whitworth dorsal turret with its single Lewis gun. A bomb aimer's position was provided in the nose and bomb load comprised two 100-lb (45-kg) bombs carried in the wing centre-section and eight 20-lb (9-kg) bombs under the wings. No. 500 Squadron at Detling fitted its aircraft with a swivel mounting for a 0.303-in (7.7-mm) Vickers 'G' gun on each side of the main cabin and, later in the war, to improve the Anson's effectiveness against E-boats, a 20-mm cannon was installed in the commanding officer's Anson, firing downward through a hole in the floor between the wing spars. On 1 June 1940 one of the squadron's Ansons was attacked by three Messerschmitt Bf 109s, one being shot down by the pilot using the nose gun, while another was despatched by the turret gunner.

Further RAF orders followed, together with export contracts which included aircraft for Australia, Egypt, Eire, Estonia, Finland and Greece, and almost 1,000 had been manufactured by the outbreak of war in September 1939. Some of these were training aircraft, and it was in this role that the Anson was to make its greatest contribution to the war effort. Although A.V.Roe had proposed a trainer version as early as November 1936, there was some delay before the first Anson Trainers, with dual controls and trailing-edge flaps, made their appearance. They were to serve in various forms with Operational Training Units, Pilots Advanced Flying Units, Schools of Air Navigation and Army Co-operation, Air Observer Schools and Air Gunnery Schools, the last using Ansons with Bristol B1 Mk VI power-operated turrets. Total Mk I production totalled 6,742, of which 3,935 were built at Woodford and the balance at Yeadon.

On 18 December 1939 the British Commonwealth Air Training Plan was instituted, and the Anson was selected as one of the standard training aircraft.The production contract was placed in Britain, engineless airframes being shipped to Canada from Woodford, to be fitted on arrival with either Jacobs L-6MB or Wright Whirlwind R-975-E3 radial engines. The former were designated Mk III and the latter Mk IV; Mk IIIs were later modified to incorporate Dowty hydraulically-actuated flaps and landing gear. Those British airframes which had turrets when delivered retained them, although most Ansons used in Canada did not have this equipment.

As the situation in Britain deteriorated, and after 223 airframes had been delivered, production was initiated in Canada, with Federal Aircraft Ltd set up to co-ordinate a multi-company manufacturing programme. The first version produced entirely in Canada was the Anson Mk II, with Jacobs engines, a moulded plywood nose, and hydraulically-actuated flaps and landing gear. The first of them was flown on 21 August 1941, and production totalled 1,832, 50 of which were supplied to the US Army Air Force as crew trainers under the designation AT-20.

The use of moulded plywood in the Mk II led to adoption of this material for the entire fuselage, in which the familiar 'glasshouse' or square window gave way to circular portholes. With standard Mk II components fitted to this new fuselage, the aircraft became the Anson V, powered by 450-hp (336-kW) Pratt & Whitney R-985-AN-12B engines, and accommodating five trainee crew members instead of three as in earlier versions. Mk V navigation trainers were built to the number of 1,050, and a single example of a gunnery training version, with a Bristol B1 Mk VI dorsal turret, was produced in 1943. The designations Mk VII, VIII and IX were allocated for Canadian versions which were not built.

Subsequent marks were developed and manufactured in Britain, commencing with the Anson X, a Mk I with a strengthened cabin floor for freight/passenger use, and which saw service with the Air Transport Auxiliary as a communications aircraft for ferry pilots. It retained the 350-hp (261-kW) Cheetah IX engines of the later Mk Is and the manually-operated landing gear, but the fluted cowlings were replaced by smooth ones, as used on the two Avro 652s. Gross weight was increased to 9,450 lb (4286 kg), and 103 of this version were built at Yeadon.

The raising of the roofline, to provide more headroom in the cabin for passenger operations, led to the introduction of the Mks XI and XII, which had hydraulically-operated flaps and landing gear, and three large square windows on each side of the fuselage. The Anson XI was powered by 395-hp (295-kW) Cheetahs XIXs, driving fixed-pitch Fairey-Reed metal propellers, and the Mk XII by 420-hp (313-kW) Cheetah XVs with variable-pitch Rotol propellers. Later Mk XIIs were designated Series 2, to denote the provision of an all-metal wing in place of the standard wooden assembly. Ambulance versions of both marks were produced, first flights having taken place on 30 July and 27 October 1944 respectively. Yeadon manufactured 91 Mk XIs and 254 Mk XIIs.

The Ansons XIII and XIV were to have been gunnery trainers, with Cheetah XI or XIX, and Cheetah XV engines respectively, but these, like the Mks XV and XVI which were to have been navigation and bombing trainers, were not produced. The Mk XVII designation was not allocated. Early in 1945, with the end of the war in sight, the company produced a Mk XI airframe with five oval windows on each side of the fuselage and a furnished interior, meeting the requirements of the Brabazon Committee's civil transport Specification 19, and acquiring the designation Avro 19. It was operated over British internal routes, at that

Avro 652A Anson

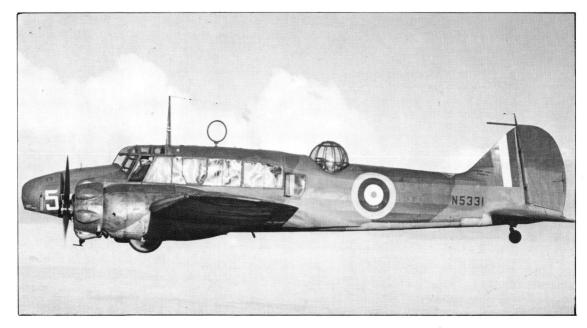

Some 11,000 Avro Ansons were built for general reconnaissance and training duties between 1935 and 1952. Illustrated is an Anson I, notable for the 'helmets' over the Cheetah engine's cylinders and the dorsal turret.

time administered by the Associated Airways Joint Committee, and then put into production as a civil feederliner. Among early customers was Railway Air Services, with a fleet of 14 aircraft, which were flown on routes from Croydon to the north of England, the Isle of Man and Dublin until replaced by Douglas Dakotas, when the company was nationalised and absorbed into British European Airways.

The same aircraft in RAF service became the Anson C.19, and 264 of these were built between 1945 and 1947. Twenty were converted Mk XIIs, and 158 were Series 2 aircraft with metal wings and tailplanes. The production line at Woodford was reopened, producing three Series 1s and 167 Series 2s, while 137 Series 1s and 18 Series 2s were built at Yeadon. Developed from the Avro 19 were 12 specially equipped Ansons for police patrol, communications and aerial survey duties and this version, designated Mk 18, had been ordered by the Royal Afghan Air Force. In addition 13 Anson 18Cs with Cheetah 15 engines were ordered by the Indian government for civil aircrew training, and all 25 of these aircraft were built at Woodford.

The Anson T.20 was developed from the Anson 19 Series 2 to Specification T.24/46, for service as a bombing and navigation trainer in Southern Rhodesia. This was fitted with a transparent nose for the bomb aimer and with racks for 16 practice bombs under the fuselage and wings. The prototype flew on 5 August 1947 and a further 59 production T.20s were manufactured at Woodford. Specification T.25/46 covered the Anson T.21 navigation trainer, which lacked the transparent nose and bomb racks of the T.20, but was otherwise similar. Following the maiden flight of the prototype on 6 February 1948, the Yeadon factory built

252 T.21s for Flying Training Command, the last finally closing the production line in May 1952. The T.21 was not the last production variant, however, that distinction falling to the T.22 which was developed to Specification T.26/46. Fifty-four of these radio trainers were built, the prototype having made its first flight on 21 June 1948.

The Anson's long service career, spanning 22 years, ended officially on 28 June 1968 when six aircraft of the Southern Communications Squadron carried out a formation fly-past at their Bovington, Hampshire, base.

Specification

Type: three/five-seat conversion, navigation, bombing, gunnery and radio trainer, or 8/11-seat communications aircraft

Powerplant (Mk I): two 350-hp (261-kW) Armstrong-Siddeley Cheetah IX radial piston engines

Performance: maximum speed 188 mph (303 km/h) at 7,000 ft (2135 m); cruising speed 158 mph (254 km/h); service ceiling 19,000 ft (5790 m); range 790 miles (1271 km)

Weight: empty 5,375 lb (2438 kg); maximum take-off 8,000 lb (3629 kg)

Dimensions: span 56 ft 5 in (17.20 m); length 42 ft 3 in (12.88 m); height 13 ft 1 in (3.99 m); wing area 410 sq ft (38.09 m²)

Armament: one 0.303-in (7.7-mm) fixed forward-firing machine-gun and one 0.303-in gun in dorsal turret, plus up to 360 lb (163 kg) of bombs

Operators: Australia, Belgium, Egypt, Eire, Estonia, Finland, Netherlands, RAF, RN, SAAF, USAAF

Avro 679 Manchester

Avro Manchester I of No. 207 Squadron, RAF, Waddington (UK) in summer 1941

History and notes

Seldom has the marriage between a new airframe and new engines been satisfactory, and the Avro 679 Manchester was no exception. Designed to Specification P.13/36 as a twin-engined medium bomber with the new Rolls-Royce Vulture 24-cylinder engine, the Manchester would have been in competition with the Handley Page H.P.56. Plans for this latter were abandoned in 1937, however, leaving a clear field for the Avro design, while Handley Page concentrated its efforts on the four-engined Halifax, itself to become a rival to the Lancaster when the latter eventually replaced the Manchester.

The first of two Manchester prototypes flew on 25 July 1939, to be followed by the second on 26 May 1940. A production contract had been placed for 200 aircraft to meet another Air Ministry Specification, 19/37, on 1 July 1937, and this was later increased to 400.

Following flight trials the wing span was increased by 10 feet (3.05 m) and a central fin was added to supplement the small twin fins and rudders. Later, after a number of Manchesters had been delivered as Mk Is, the central fin was deleted and the twin fins increased in area; in this form it became the Mk IA. The prototype and first two production aircraft were delivered to the Aircraft and Armament Experimental Establishment, Boscombe Down, for tests while the second prototype went to the Royal Aircraft Establishment, Farnborough.

The first squadron delivery was to No. 207, which re-formed at Waddington on 1 November 1940, and six Manchesters of the 18 on squadron strength carried out their first operational flight, to Brest, on the night of 24/25 February 1941.

As deliveries built up, so squadrons became equipped with the new bomber, and others to receive Manchesters included Nos. 49, 50, 57, 61, 83, 97, 106, 408 and 420, while No. 144 Squadron of Coastal Command received enough aircraft to form one flight.

The Manchester proved to be a failure mainly because of the unreliability of the Vulture engines, and the inability of these powerplants to deliver their designed power; there were also a number of airframe defects and it was with great relief that squadrons began to relinquish their Manchesters from mid-1942 as Lancasters began to replace them.

The last Bomber Command Manchester operation took place on 25/26 June 1942 against Bremen, and in

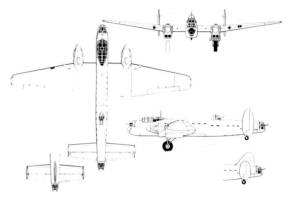

Avro Manchester 1A (scrap views: tail unit of Manchester I)

the final tally it was found that the type had flown 1,269 sorties, dropping 1,826 tons (1855 tonnes) of HE plus incendiaries. Some 202 aircraft were built, of which about 40 per cent were lost on operations and 25 per cent were written off in crashes.

However, on the credit side, the Manchester paved the way for the Lancaster, and without the earlier aircraft one must conjecture whether or not the RAF's finest bomber would have seen the light of day. One Victoria Cross was awarded to a member of a Manchester crew. Flg. Off. L. T. Manser, a pilot of No. 50 Squadron, for his actions on 30 May 1942.

Specification

Type: seven-seat medium bomber
Powerplant: two 1,760-hp (1312-kW) Rolls-Royce Vulture inline piston engines
Performances: maximum speed 265 mph (426 km/h) at 17,000 ft (5180 m); cruising speed 185 mph (298 km/h) at 15,000 ft (4570 m); service ceiling 19,200 ft (5850 m); range 1,630 miles (2623 km) with 8,100-lb (3674-kg) bomb load
Weights: empty 29,432 lb (13 350 kg); maximum take-off 56,000 lb (25 401 kg)
Dimensions: span 90 ft 1 in (27.46 m); length 69 ft 4 in (21.13 m); height 19 ft 6 in (5.94 m); wing area 1,131 sq ft (105.63 m²)
Armament: eight 0.303-in (7.7-mm) machine-guns (two each in nose and dorsal turrets, and four in tail turret), plus up to 10,350 lb (4695 kg) of bombs
Operator: RAF

Avro 683 Lancaster

History and notes

No one would dispute the statement that the Avro 683 Lancaster was the finest British heavy bomber of World War II; few would even argue against the premise that it was the finest heavy bomber serving on either side during the conflict, and it is therefore strange to recall that it had its genesis in the unsuccessful twin-engined Manchester.

However, it is not entirely true to say that the Lancaster was virtually a four-engined Manchester; a four-engined installation in the basic airframe had been proposed before Manchester deliveries to the RAF began. But the prototype Lancaster was, in fact, a converted Manchester airframe with an enlarged wing centre section and four 1,145-hp (854-kW) Rolls-Royce Merlin Xs. This prototype initially retained the Manchester's triple tail assembly, but was later modified to the twin fin and rudder assembly which became standard on production Lancasters.

The prototype flew on 9 January 1941 and later that month went to the Aircraft and Armament Experimental Establishment, Boscombe Down, to begin intensive flying trials. The second prototype, with some modifications and Merlin XX engines, flew on 13 May 1941, while by September of that year the first prototype had been delivered to No. 44 Squadron at Waddington for crew training and evaluation.

The new bomber was an immediate success, and large production orders were placed. Such was the speed of development in wartime that the first production Lancaster was flown in October 1941, a number of partially completed Manchester airframes being converted on the line to emerge as Lancaster Is (from 1942 redesignated Lancaster B.Is).

Avro's first contract was for 1,070 Lancasters, but others soon followed, and when it became obvious that the parent company's Chadderton and Yeadon production facilities would be unable to cope with the demand, other companies took on the task of building complete aircraft. They included Armstrong Whitworth at Coventry, Austin Morris at Birmingham, Metropolitan Vickers at Manchester and Vickers Armstrong at Chester and Castle Bromwich. Additionally, a large number of sub-contractors were involved in various parts of the country.

Lancasters soon began to replace Manchesters, and such was the impetus of production that a shortage of Merlin engines was threatened. This was countered by licence-production by Packard in the USA of the Merlin not only for Lancasters but for other types. An additional insurance was effected in another way, the use of 1,735-hp (1294-kW) Bristol Hercules VI or XVI radial engines.

In this form, as the Lancaster II, a prototype was flown on 26 November 1941 and results were sufficiently encouraging to warrant this version going into production by Armstrong Whitworth at Coventry. Delays were caused by the Ministry of Aircraft Production's insistence on maintaining construction of Whitley bombers, but in May 1942 the changeover to

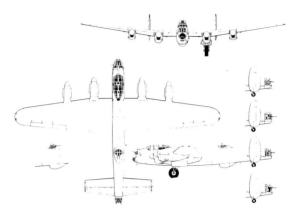

Avro Lancaster B.III (scrap views: turret variants)

Lancaster B.II production began, only to be halted for four months as a result of air-raid damage.

The first two Hercules-powered Lancasters were completed in September 1942 and went to the Aircraft and Armament Experimental Establishment, where they were later joined by the third. Other Mk IIs from this first production batch were delivered to No. 61 Squadron at Syerston, Nottingham, the service trials unit for this version and a former Lancaster I squadron.

Early use of the Lancaster B.II by No. 61 Squadron was plagued with minor problems, but during its six months of operations the squadron did not lose a single Mk II and in February 1943 was able to hand over the full complement of nine aircraft to No. 115 Squadron at East Wretham, a Wellington unit in No. 3 Group.

Gradually Lancaster B.IIs began to re-equip other squadrons, but the Mk II never achieved the success of the Merlin-engined Lancaster: it could not attain so high an altitude, was slightly slower, and had a bomb load 4,000 lb (1814 kg) less than the other marks. Production ceased after 301 had been built, and the Armstrong Whitworth factory changed over to Lancaster B.Is. It has been said that the phasing out of the Lancaster B.II was in order to effect standardisation, for the Handley Page Halifax B.III with Hercules engines was able to offer equal if not better possibilities, and with Lancaster Is, Short Stirlings and Halifaxes all in service, variations in spares requirements needed to be cut as much as possible.

The final Lancaster B.II operation was flown by No. 514 Squadron on 23 September 1944, but a few continued in service for a short while into the postwar era, mainly as test-beds, until the last survivor was scrapped in 1950. Although overshadowed by its Merlin-engined contemporaries, the Lancaster II did not disgrace itself and achieved on average more than 150 flying hours per aircraft.

Meanwhile, the Merlin Lancasters were going from strength to strength. The prototype's engines gave way to 1,280-hp (954-kW) Merlin XXs and XXIIs, or 1,620-hp (1208-kW) Merlin XXIVs in production aircraft. Early thoughts of fitting a ventral turret were soon discarded, and the Lancaster B.I had three

Avro 683 Lancaster

Avro Lancaster I of No. 207 Squadron, RAF,
in spring/summer 1942

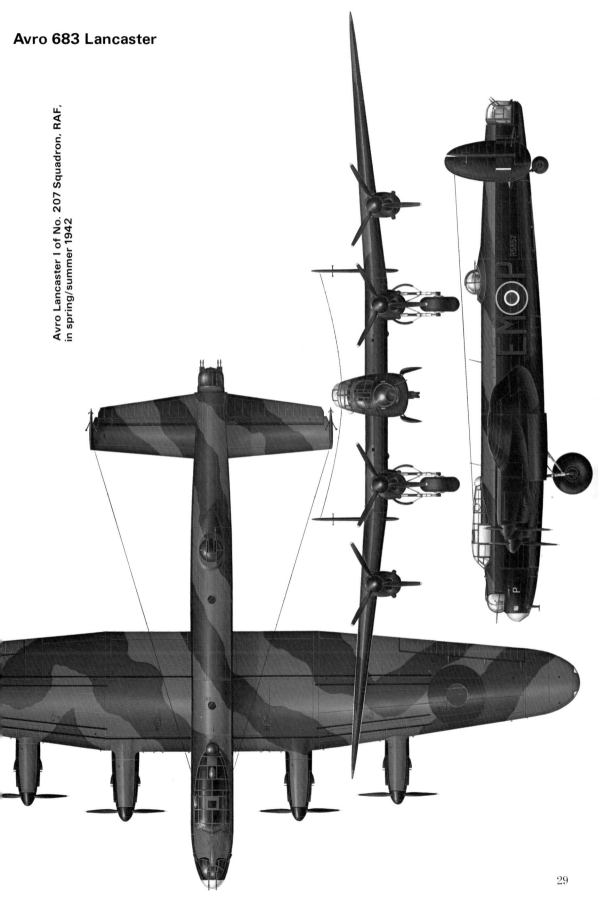

Avro 683 Lancaster

A fine aerial study of an Avro Lancaster (Mk I or III) of No. 50 Squadron, which operated Lancasters from 1942 to 1945 from its base at Skellingthorpe as part of No. 5 Group, Bomber Command.

Frazer-Nash hydraulically operated turrets with eight 0.303-in (7.7-mm) Browning machine-guns: two each in the nose and mid-upper dorsal positions and four in the tail turret. The bomb-bay, designed originally to carry 4,000 lb (1814 kg) of bombs, was enlarged progressively to carry bigger and bigger bombs: up to 8,000 and 12,000 lb (3629 and 5443 kg) and eventually to the enormous 22,000-lb (9979-kg) 'Grand Slam', the heaviest bomb carried by any aircraft in World War II.

Production of the Lancaster was a comparatively simple affair considering its size. It had been designed for ease of construction and this undoubtedly contributed to the high rate of production. Lancasters were built to the total of 7,377 all marks.

As mentioned earlier, No. 44 Squadron was the first to receive a Lancaster when the prototype arrived for trials and this squadron was also the first to be fully equipped with Lancasters, notching up another 'first' when it used the type operationally on 3 March 1942 to lay mines in the Heligoland Bight.

The Lancaster's existence was not revealed to the public until 17 August of that year, when 12 aircraft from Nos. 44 and 97 Squadrons carried out an unescorted daylight raid on Augsburg. Flown at low level, the raid inflicted considerable damage on a factory producing U-boat diesel engines, but the cost was high, seven aircraft being lost. Squadron Leaders Nettleton and Sherwood each received the Victoria Cross, the latter posthumously, for leading the operation which perhaps confirmed to the Air Staff that unescorted daylight raids by heavy bombers were not a practicable proposition, and it was to be more than two years before the US Army Air Force was to resume such attacks.

As Packard-built Merlins became available, so the Lancaster B.III appeared with these engines, although the B.I remained in production alongside the Packard-engined B.III. Externally the B.III was distinguishable by an enlarged bomb aimer's 'bubble' in the nose but

there were few other differences other than in minor equipment changes.

To swell the UK production lines, Victory Aircraft in Canada was chosen in 1942 to build Lancasters, and these were known as B.Xs. Powered by Packard-built Merlins, the Canadian Lancasters were delivered by air across the Atlantic and had their armament fitted on arrival in the UK. The first B.X was handed over on 6 August 1943, and 430 were built before production was completed.

Mention must be made of the Lancaster B.VI, production of which was proposed using Merlins, either 85s or 87s, of 1,635 hp (1219 kW). Nine airframes were converted by Rolls-Royce for comparative tests. No. 635 Squadron used several operationally on pathfinder work with nose and dorsal turrets removed, and fitted with an improved H_2S radar bombing aid and early electronic countermeasures equipment, but although performance was superior to the earlier marks no production aircraft were built.

It would be true to say that development of the Lancaster went hand-in-hand with development of bombs. The early Lancasters carried their bomb loads in normal flush-fitting bomb bays, but as bombs got larger it became necessary, in order to be able to close the bomb doors, to make the bays deeper so that they protruded slightly below the fuselage line. Eventually, with other developments, the bomb doors were omitted altogether for certain specialist types of bomb.

In this connection the most drastic changes suffered by the Lancaster were made to enable Dr Barnes Wallis's 'bouncing bombs' to be carried to the Ruhr by No. 617 Squadron in its attacks on the Mohne, Eder and Sorpe dams, probably the best known raid made by either side in the European theatre during World War II. For this operation, the Lancaster B.IIIs had their bomb doors and front turrets removed and spotlights fitted beneath the wings arranged in such a way that the beams merged at exactly 60 feet (18.3 m) below the

Avro 683 Lancaster

Avro Lancaster I of No. 514 Squadron, RAF, in 1944

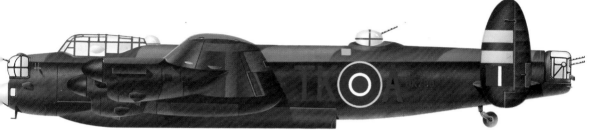

Avro Lancaster I of No. 149 Squadron, RAF, in spring 1945

Avro Lancaster I of No. 463 Squadron, Royal Australian Air Force, Skellingthorpe (UK) in winter/spring 1945

Avro Lancaster I (Special) of No. 617 Squadron, RAF, Waddington (UK) in spring 1945

Avro Lancaster I of No. 83 Squadron, RAF, in 1942

Avro 683 Lancaster

Avro Lancaster production in full swing. Note the hinged inner leading-edge panels to allow access to the aircraft's 'plumbing', the open bomb-bay doors, the bomb-aimer's position, and the twin-gun nose turret.

aircraft—the altitude from which the bombs had to be dropped if they were to be effective. Nineteen Lancasters took part in the attack on the night of 17 May 1943, the attackers breaching the Mohne and Eder dams for the loss of eight aircraft.

The German battleship *Tirpitz* was attacked on several occasions by Lancasters until, on 12 November 1944, a combined force from Nos. 9 and 617 Squadrons found the battleship in Tromso Fjord, Norway, and sank her with a 12,000-lb (5443-kg) 'Tallboy' bomb, also designed by Barnes Wallis. The ultimate in conventional high explosive bombs was reached with the 22,000-lb (9979-kg) 'Grand Slam', a weapon designed to penetrate concrete and explode some way beneath the surface, so creating an earthquake effect. No. 617 Squadron first used the 'Grand Slam' operationally against the Bielefeld Viaduct on 14 March 1945, causing considerable destruction amongst its spans.

Final production version of the Lancaster was the B.VII, which had an American Martin dorsal turret with two 0.50-in (12.7-mm) guns in place of the normal Frazer-Nash turret; the new turret was also located further forward.

In spite of the other variants built from time to time, the Lancaster B.I (B.1 from 1945) remained in production throughout the war, and the last was delivered by Armstrong Whitworth on 2 February 1946. Production had encompassed 2 Mk I prototypes, 3,425 Mk Is, 301 Mk IIs, 3,039 Mk IIIs, 180 Mk VIIs and 430 Mk Xs, a total of 7,377. These were built by Avro (3,673), Armstrong Whitworth (1,329), Austin Motors (330), Metropolitan Vickers (1,080), Vickers-Armstrong (535) and Victory Aircraft (430). Some conversions between different mark numbers took place.

Statistics show that at least 59 Bomber Command squadrons operated Lancasters, which flew more than 156,000 sorties and dropped, in addition to 608,612 tons (618380 tonnes) of high explosive bombs, more than 51 million incendiaries.

As the war in Europe was drawing to its close, plans were being made to modify Lancasters for operation in the Far East as part of Bomber Command's contribution to 'Tiger Force', but Japan surrendered before this could take place.

A number of Lancasters were used to bring home prisoners of war from Europe, and various aircraft were modified for test flying in the UK and other European countries. Some were supplied to the French navy and others were converted for temporary use as civil transports, with faired in nose and tail areas, under the name Lancastrian. The Avro York transport used Lancaster wings and engines, plus a central fin in addition to the twin endplate fins.

A few Lancasters still survive, notably one airworthy example with the RAF Battle of Britain Memorial Flight.

Specification

Type: seven-seat heavy bomber
Powerplant (Mk I): four 1,640-hp (1223-kW) Rolls-Royce Merlin XXIV inline piston engines
Performance: maximum speed 287 mph (462 km/h) at 11,500 ft (3505 m); cruising speed 210 mph (338 km/h) at 20,000 ft (6100 m); service ceiling 24,500 ft (7470 m); range 2,530 miles (4072 km) with 7,000-lb (3175-kg) bomb load
Weights: empty 36,900 lb (16 738 kg); maximum take-off 70,000 lb (31 751 kg)
Dimensions: span 102 ft 0 in (31.09 m); length 69 ft 6 in (21.18 m); height 20 ft 0 in (6.10 m); wing area 1,297 sq ft (120.49 m²)
Armament: eight 0.303-in (7.7-mm) machine-guns, (two each in nose and dorsal turrets, and four in tail turret), plus bomb load comprising one 22,000-lb (9979-kg) bomb or up to 14,000 lb (6350 kg) of smaller bombs
Operators: RAAF, RAF, RCAF

Avro 685 York

Avro York C. I in 1944

History and notes

One of the wartime agreements concluded between Britain and the United States allocated to the Americans responsibility for building all transport aircraft for Allied use, enabling the British industry to concentrate on fighters and bombers. Despite this, at Avro's Chadderton factory in February 1942, designer Roy Chadwick and his team completed the drawings for a four-engined long-range transport. This united the wings, tail assembly, engines and landing gear of the Lancaster with a new square-section fuselage.

Shortly before the prototype flew at Ringway, Manchester, on 5 July 1942, an official order was placed for four aircraft, the first two to have Rolls-Royce Merlin XXs and the others Bristol Hercules VIs. All four were in fact ultimately flown with the former engines, the sole Hercules-powered aircraft being the prototype which was re-engined with Hercules XVIs late in 1943 to become the York II. To compensate for the additional side area forward of the centre of gravity, a central third fin was added from the third aircraft, which, named *Ascalon*, was delivered to No. 24 Squadron at RAF Northolt in March 1943. Equipped as a flying conference room, principally for the use of Prime Minister Winston Churchill, it carried him to Algiers in May and, just a few days later, His Majesty King George VI used it for his visit to troops in North Africa.

Production built up slowly, first at Ringway but transferred to Yeadon in October 1945, and the first two aircraft were delivered to No. 24 Squadron for VIP duties. Other VIP-configured Yorks included those allocated for official duties to Louis Mountbatten, Field Marshal Smuts and the Duke of Gloucester. Five early aircraft were delivered to BOAC for the operation of a UK-Morocco-Cairo service from April 1944 and a further 25 were delivered from August 1945 for joint operation with Transport Command.

During 1945 No. 511 Squadron at Lyneham became the first to receive a full complement of Yorks; 10 squadrons were eventually to fly the aircraft in RAF service, and seven of these squadrons were equipped in time to take part in the Berlin Airlift from 1 July 1948. Production ceased with the delivery of the 257th York to RAF Honington on 29 April 1948. This total comprised four prototypes, 208 for the Royal Air

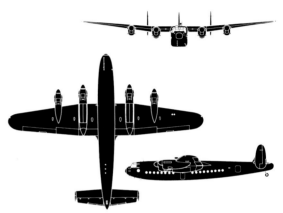

Avro York C. I

Force, 25 for BOAC, 12 for British South American Airways Corporation, five for FAMA of Argentina and two for Skyways Ltd; one York was built in Canada by Victory Aircraft.

Yorks were produced in three variants: all-passenger, all-freight and mixed passenger/freight. When superseded by Handley Page Hastings Ltd. transports in RAF Transport Command service, Yorks continued in their accustomed roles when operated by civilian firms with government contracts for troop-carrying. The last RAF York was *Ascalon II*, which remained in service with the Far East Air Force Communications Squadron at Changi until 1957.

Specification

Type: long-range passenger and cargo transport
Powerplant: four 1,280-hp (954-kW) Rolls-Royce Merlin XX inline piston engines
Performance: maximum speed 298 mph (480 km/h) at 21,000 ft (6400 m); cruising speed 210 mph (338 km/h); service ceiling 23,000 ft (7010 m); range 2,700 miles (4345 km)
Weight: empty 42,040 lb (19 069 kg); maximum take-off 68,597 lb (31 115 kg)
Dimensions: span 102 ft 0 in (31.09 m); length 78 ft 6 6 in (23.93 m); height 17 ft 10 in (5.44 m); wing area 1,297 sq ft (120.49 m²)
Armament: none
Operator: RAF

Avro 694 Lincoln

Avro Lincoln B.II of No. 57 Squadron, RAF, in August 1945

History and notes

Although the Avro Lancaster was still the spearhead of Bomber Command's offensive power in 1943, the Air Ministry drew up specification B14/43 to cover its replacement. Known originally as the Lancaster IV, Avro's new design was for a long-range high-altitude development of the earlier aircraft, to be powered by Rolls-Royce Merlin 85 engines.

A number of Lancaster components were used, but the extent of the changes was such that the machine became identified as the Type 694 Lincoln. A new wing of increased span and higher aspect ratio was fitted to a longer fuselage, heavier armament was to be carried and, as gross weight rose, a stronger landing gear was required. The unarmed first prototype was flown by Captain H.A.Brown at Ringway, Manchester, on 9 June 1944 and four days later was delivered to Boscombe Down for service trials. A Martin dorsal turret was later added, although this was to be replaced by a Bristol turret in the other prototypes and production Lincolns. The second prototype was flown on 13 November 1944 and plans were made to produce a total of 2,254 aircraft by Avro at Chadderton and Yeadon, by Metropolitan Vickers at Trafford Park, and by Armstrong Whitworth's factories at Baginton and Bitteswell. In fact, British production totalled three prototypes, 72 Mk Is and 465 Mk IIs; the last of the 168 Avro-built Lincolns was delivered in the spring of 1946 and the last of 299 from Armstrong Whitworth's line on 5 April 1951. In 1947, 30 Mk IIs were supplied to the Argentine air force. One Mk XV was completed by Victory Aircraft in Canada and the Government Aircraft Factory in Australia produced 43 Mk 30s and 30 Mk 30As. In 1951 20 Australian aircraft were fitted with a 6 ft 6 in (1.98 m) nose extension to house two radar operators and their equipment, with the designation Mk 31.

The major user, however, was the Royal Air Force and production Lincoln B.Is were delivered from February 1945. By VE-Day about 50 had been test-flown and delivered to maintenance units or to specialist organisations such as the Telecommunications Flying Unit at Defford, the Aircraft Torpedo Development Unit at Gosport, to Rolls-Royce at Hucknall for engine trials and, of course, to Boscombe Down. The Bomber Development Unit at Feltwell received its first Lincolns on 21 May 1945 and the first RAF squadron, No. 57 at East Kirby, received an initial

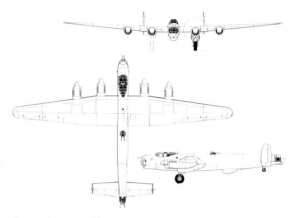

Avro Lincoln B.II

allocation of three Lincoln B.IIs for its Lincoln Trials Flight in August 1945. The B.II was powered by Merlin 66 or 68 engines and was fitted with the Bristol B17 dorsal turret, Boulton Paul 'D' rear turret, and Mk IIIG H_2S radar. The surrender of the Japanese and the disbandment of the 'Tiger Force' destined for the Pacific, coupled with delays in getting the Lincoln into service, meant that the type was not used operationally during World War II, although it was to see the RAF into the jet era, operating in Malaya and Kenya until it was replaced by the Canberra. The last was withdrawn in 1963.

Specification

Type: seven-seat long-range bomber
Powerplant (B.I): four 1,750-hp (1305-kW) Rolls-Royce Merlin 85 inline piston engines
Performance: maximum speed 295 mph (475 km/h) at 15,000 ft (4750 m); cruising speed 215 mph (346 km/h) at 20,000 ft (6100 m); service ceiling 30,500 ft (9295 m); range 1,470 miles (2366 km) with maximum bomb-load
Weights: empty 43,400 lb (19 686 kg); maximum take-off 75,000 lb (34 019 kg)
Dimensions: span 120 ft 0 in (36.58 m); length 78 ft 3½ in (23.86 m); height 17 ft 3½ in (5.27 m); wing area 1,421 sq ft (132.01 m²)
Armament: two 0.50-in (12.7-mm) machine-guns in each of nose, dorsal and tail turrets, plus up to 14,000 lb (6350 kg) of bombs
Operators: RAAF, RAF

Blackburn B-6 Shark

History and notes

Coming at the end of a distinguished line of Blackburn torpedo biplanes which had served with the Fleet Air Arm, the Shark upheld the high reputations of its predecessors, the Dart, Ripon and Baffin.

Begun as a private venture to meet Specification S.15/33, the aircraft was based on the company's M.1/30A prototype, first flown on 24 February 1933. The Shark prototype, known as the B-6, flew on 24 August 1933 at Brough and was flown to the Aircraft and Armament Experimental Establishment, Martlesham Heath, for testing on 26 November 1933. Deck landing trials aboard HMS *Courageous* early the following year were successful and a contract for 16 aircraft was placed for the Fleet Air Arm in August 1934.

The prototype was fitted with twin floats and flown at Brough the following April, and successful sea trials took place from Felixstowe. Further contracts followed, and during the three-year production run Blackburn delivered 238 Sharks to the Fleet Air Arm, with which the Shark served in both seaplane and landplane configurations. Sharks from the first production batch went to No. 820 Squadron at Gosport early in 1935, replacing the squadron's Fairey Seals aboard HMS *Courageous*.

Shark Is, like the prototype, used the 700-hp (522-kW) Armstrong Siddeley Tiger IV engine, but the last aircraft in the first production batch was used for development flying with the uprated Tiger VI developing 760 hp (567 kW), 100 hours being flown by relays of pilots in just over seven days. This engine was used in the Shark II, production of which began in 1936, and an alternative engine was available for the next production variant, the Shark III, in the form of the 800-hp (597-kW) Bristol Pegasus III engine. Ninety-five Shark IIIs were delivered between April 1937 and the end of the year.

As Sharks were replaced by the Fairey Swordfish, they were relegated to second-line duties and a number were converted for target towing in various parts of the country.

Six Shark IIA floatplanes were purchased by the Portuguese navy and delivered in March 1936; powered by 700-hp (522-kW) Armstrong Siddeley Tiger VIC engines, they served for several years on coastal defence duties.

The only other overseas customer for the Shark was Canada, and seven Shark IIs were bought for the Royal Canadian Air Force in 1936. Such was their success that Boeing Aircraft of Canada, a subsidiary of the American company, secured an agreement for licence production at Vancouver and 17 Shark IIIs were built following delivery of two pattern aircraft from Blackburn. The Canadian Shark IIIs were fitted with the 840-hp (626-kW) Bristol Pegasus IX engine and served until 1944, when they were withdrawn. Five were transferred in June of that year to the British Air Observers School at Trinidad, where they served faithfully if without distinction.

Produced as a torpedo-spotting-reconnaissance biplane, the Blackburn Shark had by 1939 been relegated to target-towing. It was used operationally in the evacuation of Dunkirk and of the Channel Islands in 1940.

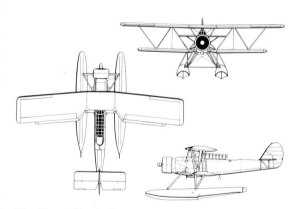

Blackburn Shark III

Specification

Type: two/three-seat torpedo/reconnaissance biplane

Powerplant (Mk II): one 760-hp (567-kW) Armstrong Siddeley Tiger VI radial piston engine

Performance (torpedo landplane): maximum speed 150 mph (241 km/h) at sea level; cruising speed 118 mph (190 km/h); service ceiling 16,000 ft (4875 m); range 625 miles (1006 km)

Weights: empty 4,039 lb (1832 kg); maximum take-off 8,050 lb (3651 kg)

Dimensions: span 46 ft 0 in (14.02 m); length 35 ft 3 in (10.74 m); height 12 ft 1 in (3.68 m); wing area 489 sq ft (45.43 m²)

Armament: one fixed forward-firing 0.303-in (7.7-mm) machine-gun and one 0.303-in (7.7-mm) gun on flexible mount in rear cockpit, plus one 1,500-lb (680-kg) torpedo or equivalent weight in bombs

Operators: Portuguese Navy, RCAF, RN

Blackburn B-24 Skua

History and notes

Designed to Specification O.27/34, the all-metal Blackburn B-24 Skua broke away from the Royal Navy's long tradition of biplanes with fabric covering: it was Britain's first naval dive-bomber and the country's first deck-landing aircraft to have flaps, retractable landing gear and a variable-pitch propeller.

The Skua competed with designs from Avro, Boulton Paul, Hawker and Vickers for the naval contract, and two prototypes were ordered in April 1935, the first of which flew at Brough on 9 February 1937, powered by an 840-hp (626-kW) Bristol Mercury IX.

After appearing in the New Types Park at the RAF Display, Hendon, on 26 June 1937 and the SBAC Display at Hatfield two days later, the prototype was sent to the Aircraft and Armament Experimental Establishment, Martlesham Heath, for the customary handling trials. Favourable reports were given on the Skua's handling qualities, and it subsequently carried out gunnery trials at Martlesham and, later, ditching experiments at Gosport.

Orders for 190 Skuas had been placed six months before the flight of the prototype and some sub-contract work was awarded to speed up production. Because all Mercury engines were required for Bristol Blenheims, production Skuas were given the 890-hp (664-kW) Bristol Perseus XII sleeve-valve engine, in which form they became Mk IIs.

The first production aircraft flew at Brough on 28 August 1938 and few modifications to the basic design were required apart from fitting upturned wingtips and a modified tailwheel oleo to cure juddering. The entire production run of 190 aircraft was delivered between October 1938 and March 1940, no mean feat at that period, although the programme was about a year behind schedule.

The first Fleet Air Arm squadrons to receive Skuas late in 1938 were Nos. 800 and 803, for service on HMS *Ark Royal* where they replaced Hawker Nimrods and Ospreys. No. 801 Squadron aboard HMS *Furious* was also re-equipped and Skuas also joined No. 806 Squad-

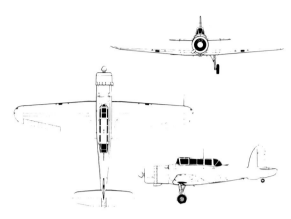

Blackburn Skua II

ron, then at Eastleigh, before the outbreak of war.

As a fighter, the Skua was already obsolete, but it made its mark in the dive-bombing role early in the war when 16 aircraft from Nos. 800 and 803 Squadrons, flying from Hatston in the Orkneys, sank the German cruiser *Königsberg* in Bergen harbour at dawn on 10 April 1940. Although at the very limits of their range, all but one Skua returned from this long night flight. The squadrons suffered a severe setback 11 days later, however, losing most of their Skuas during an attack on Narvik.

Skuas from No. 801 Squadron flying from Detling covered the Dunkirk evacuation, but the type was withdrawn from operational service in 1941 when Nos. 800 and 806 Squadrons re-equipped with Fairey Fulmars, while Nos. 801 and 803 received Hawker Sea Hurricanes.

The remaining Skuas ended their days comparatively peacefully as target tugs and on general training duties.

The burnt-out remains of one Skua, recovered from a Norwegian lake, are preserved at the Fleet Air Arm Museum, Yeovilton.

Specification

Type: two-seat naval fighter/dive-bomber
Powerplant (Mk II): one 890-hp (664-kW) Bristol Perseus XII radial piston engine
Performance: maximum speed 225 mph (362 km/h) at 6,500 ft (1980 m); cruising speed 165 mph (266 km/h) at 15,000 ft (4570 m); service ceiling 20,200 ft (6160 m); range 760 miles (1223 km)
Weights: empty 5,490 lb (2490 kg); maximum take-off 8,228 lb (3732 kg)
Dimensions: span 46 ft 2 in (14.07 m); length 35 ft 7 in (10.85 m); height 12 ft 6 in (3.81 m); wing area 312 sq ft (28.98 m²)
Armament: four 0.303-in (7.7-mm) forward-firing machine-guns in wings and one Lewis gun on flexible mount in rear cockpit, plus one 500-lb (227-kg) bomb beneath fuselage and eight 30-lb (14-kg) practice bombs on underwing racks
Operator: RN

The Fleet Air Arm's first operational monoplane, the Blackburn Skua suffered the operational limitations of trying to combine in one airframe the divergent functions of a fighter and a dive-bomber.

Blackburn B-25 Roc

Another misguided attempt to produce a turret fighter, this time for naval use, the Blackburn Roc was soon seen to have severe tactical shortcomings and to possess wholly inadequate combat performance.

History and notes

Developed from the Skua dive-bomber, the Blackburn B-25 Roc was the first Fleet Air Arm aircraft to have a power-driven gun turret. The idea was that four guns would be brought to bear in broadside attacks on enemy bombers, but with a maximum speed of less than 200 mph (322 km/h) it is doubtful if the Roc could have caught an enemy bomber and the idea was dropped.

Orders for 136 Roes to Specification O.15/37 were received on 28 April 1937 and, because of Blackburn's involvement with the Skua programme, production was undertaken by Boulton Paul at Wolverhampton, the first aircraft flying on 23 December 1938. Following trials at Brough, the Roc went to the Aircraft and Armament Experimental Establishment, Martlesham Heath, in March 1939, and was joined there by the next two aircraft so that simultaneous handling and armament trials could be undertaken. As expected, the heavy turret penalised the Roc by comparison with the Skua, but the former could still be held steady in a steep dive with the use of dive brakes. An enlarged propeller was fitted, and various other means of improving performance were tried, without much success.

Four Rocs were flown as seaplanes, fitted with Blackburn Shark floats, and these reduced the already low speed by another 30 mph (48 km/h), stability was rather poor and low altitude turns had to be avoided.

After familiarization with several Fleet Air Arm units, the first four Rocs to go into service were delivered to No. 806 Squadron at Eastleigh in February 1940 to serve alongside eight Skuas. Six Rocs went to join No. 801 Squadron's Skuas at Hatston, Orkney, four months later. No. 2 Anti-Aircraft Co-operation Unit at Gosport received 16 Rocs to replace its Blackburn Sharks and supplement its Skuas in June 1940, but perhaps the most unusual role for the Roc fell to four which had been damaged in a Junkers Ju 87 raid on Gosport and were used as machine-gun posts with

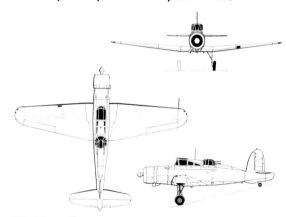

Blackburn Roc

their turrets permanently manned.

Other Rocs were dispersed to various locations in the UK and even to Bermuda and the type gradually faded away until the last two aircraft were withdrawn from service in August 1943 for lack of spares after an undistinguished career.

Specification

Type: two-seat naval fighter/target tug
Powerplant: one 905-hp (675-kW) Bristol Perseus XII radial piston engine
Performance (landplane): maximum speed 223 mph (359 km/h) at 10,000 ft (3050 m); cruising speed 135 mph (217 km/h); service ceiling 18,000 ft (5485 m); range 810 miles (1304 km)
Weights: empty 6,124 lb (2778 kg); maximum take-off 7,950 lb (3606 kg)
Dimensions: span 46 ft 0 in (14.02 m); length 35 ft 7 in (10.85 m); height 12 ft 1 in (3.68 m); wing area 310 sq ft (28.80 m²)
Armament: four 0.303-in (7.7-mm) machine-guns in electrically actuated Boulton Paul turret
Operators: RAF, RN

Blackburn B-26 Botha

History and notes

When the Air Ministry issued Specification M.15/35 for a three-seat twin-engine reconnaissance bomber with ability to carry a torpedo, it attracted submissions by Blackburn and Bristol. Both envisaged 850-hp (634-kW) Bristol Perseus engines, but a change in the requirement increased the crew to four, leading to the new Specification 10/36, and both types were ordered respectively as the Botha and Beaufort.

Because of the greater weight of the revised designs the Beaufort was given 1,130-hp (843-kW) Bristol Taurus radials, but these were in short supply and Blackburn was accordingly committed to using 880-hp (656-kW) Bristol Perseus X engines in the initial production version of the Botha.

Orders for 442 were received in 1936, and the first production aircraft flew at Brough on 28 December 1938. Trials at the Experimental Establishment, Martlesham Heath, resulted in an increase in tailplane area and fitting of a horn balanced elevator to provide better elevator control. Tests at the Torpedo Development Unit at Gosport began late in 1939 and production lines were established at Brough and Dumbarton. The first Botha to be delivered to the RAF was the third aircraft off the Dumbarton line which arrived at No. 5 Maintenance Unit, Kemble, on 12 December 1939.

A number of unexplained fatal accidents occurred in the first half of 1940 and the Botha came in for considerable criticism in view of its shortcomings and the fact that it was underpowered. Bristol managed to squeeze a little more power out of the Perseus engine, the Mk XA producing 930-hp (694-kW), and some other improvements were incorporated.

The fact that the Botha was underpowered and unfit for operational duties gave the Air Staff the idea that it could be relegated to training units where, not surprisingly, it continued to suffer fatal accidents. Probably the most appropriate, and certainly the safest Botha deliveries, came in late 1942 when some time-expired airframes went to RAF Schools of Technical Training. A few Bothas were fitted with winch gear and used by

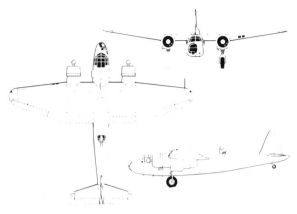

Blackburn Botha I

the Target Towing Unit at Abbotsinch as T.T.Is.

A total of 580 Bothas was built, 380 at Brough and 200 at Dumbarton, and the type was finally withdrawn from service in September 1944.

Specification

Type: four-seat reconnaissance/torpedo-bomber/trainer

Powerplant: two 930-hp (694-kW) Bristol Perseus XA radial piston engines

Performance: maximum speed 249 mph (401 km/h) at 5,500 ft (1675 m); cruising speed 212 mph (341 km/h) at 15,000 ft (4570 m); service ceiling 17,500 ft (5335 m); range 1,270 miles (2044 km)

Weights: empty 11,830 lb (5366 kg); maximum take-off 18,450 lb (8369 kg)

Dimensions: span 59 ft 0 in (17.98 m); length 51 ft 1½ in (15.58 m); height 14 ft 7½ in (4.46 m); wing area 518 sq ft (48.12 m²)

Armament: one fixed forward-firing 0.303-in (7.7-mm) machine-gun and two 0.303-in (7.7-mm) guns in dorsal turret, plus an internal torpedo, bombs or depth charges up to 2,000 lb (907 kg) in weight

Operator: RAF

Desperately underpowered as an operational torpedo-bomber, the Blackburn Botha was quickly retired to a short and undistinguished career as a reconnaissance, gunnery and radio trainer until the end of 1943.

Blackburn B-37 Firebrand

Conversion of the Blackburn Firebrand I naval interceptor into the Firebrand II torpedo-fighter (illustrated) was effected by the widening of the centre section by 18 in (0.46 m) and the addition of a rack.

History and notes

The origins of the Blackburn B-37 Firebrand lay in Naval Staff Requirement N.9/39, issued in December 1939 and inviting submissions for a four-gun single-seat fleet fighter. In January 1941 three prototypes were ordered to Specification N.11/40, and the first of these was rolled out just a year later, making its first flight on 27 February 1942 in the hands of Flt Lt Arthur Thompson. The second, armed with two 20-mm Hispano cannon in each wing and with racks for two 500-lb (227-kg) bombs, was flown on 15 July and the third on 15 September. All three were powered by the 2,305-hp (1719-kW) Napier Sabre III engine, as were nine production Firebrand F.Is.

The second prototype undertook deck landing trials aboard HMS *Illustrious* in February 1943, operating from Macrahanish in Kintyre, and following an accident it was rebuilt as the prototype Firebrand TF.II, the centre-section of the wing being widened by 1 ft 6 in (0.46 m) to allow a 1,850-lb (839-kg) torpedo to be carried between the wheel bays. The first flight took place on 31 March 1943 and 12 production machines were completed. No. 708 Squadron at RNAS Lee-on-Solent flew TF.IIs as a trials unit, the only squadron to receive Firebrands during World War II.

Allocation of Sabre engine production for installation in the Hawker Typhoon led to the substitution of the 2,400-hp (1790-kW) Bristol Centaurus VII in the Firebrand TF.III. The prototype was flown on 21 December 1943, followed by a second prototype and 27 production machines. These suffered some directional instability on take-off, the fault being remedied by the fitting of a fin and rudder of increased area to the TF.4, which also had wing dive-brakes and a two-position torpedo carrier. The first of 102 Firebrand TF.4s flew on 17 May 1945 and the type entered service with No. 813 Squadron, re-formed at RNAS Ford, on 1 September 1945.

The final production variants were the TF.5 and TF.5A, the latter having powered ailerons in addition

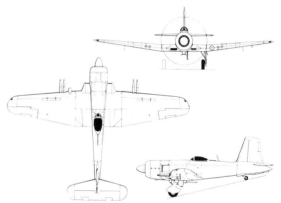

Blackburn Firebrand TF.4

to the horn-balanced rudder and elevators and the longer span aileron tabs common to all Mk 5s. Sixty-eight were manufactured and saw service with Nos. 813 and 827 Squadrons, both of which were later to re-equip with the Westland Wyvern.

Specification

Type: single-seat carrier-based torpedo-strike fighter
Powerplant (TF.5): one 2,520-hp (1879-kW) Bristol Centaurus IX radial piston engine
Performance: maximum speed 340 mph (547 km/h) at 13,000 ft (3960 m); cruising speed 256 mph (412 km/h); service ceiling 28,500 ft (8685 m); range 740 miles (1191 km)
Dimensions: span 51 ft 3½ in (15.63 m); length 38 ft 9 in (11.81 m); height 13 ft 3 in (4.04 m); wing area 383 sq ft (35.58 m²)
Weights: empty 11,385 lb (5368 kg); maximum take-off 17,500 lb (7938 kg)
Armament: four 20-mm cannon in wings, plus one 1,850-lb (839-kg) torpedo, or two 1,000-lb (454-kg) bombs, or rocket projectiles
Operator: RN

Boulton Paul Defiant

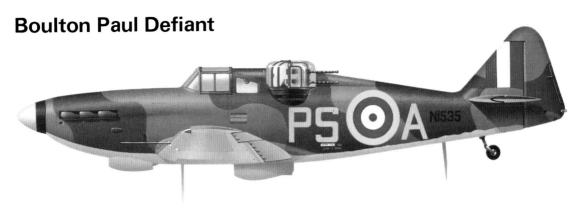

Boulton Paul Defiant I of Sqn Ldr P.A. Hunter, CO of No. 264 Squadron, RAF, Kirton-in-Lindsey (UK) in mid-1940

History and notes

Fighters were fighters not just for the reason that they were the fastest and most manoeuvrable of aeroplanes, but because they carried offensive weapons to attack and destroy other aircraft. This had been a slowly developing process, originating with such weapons as the revolvers which had first been used in anger by pilots or observers of reconnaissance aircraft that took to the skies over the Western Front during World War I. From that point development was rapid, leading first to rifles and then to a variety of machine-guns. By the end of that war twin machine-guns, firing forward and provided with synchronising gear to 'time' the moment of fire of each cartridge, so that the bullet passed between the revolving propeller blades, was considered to be the best form of armament for a fighter aircraft.

There was to be little change until the 1930s and the introduction of monoplane fighters. This factor, coupled with the greater reliability of machine-gun mechanisms, made it possible to dispense with the synchronising gear, and to mount the guns in the wing to fire forward, well clear of the propeller disc. So far as the UK was concerned, the ultimate appeared to have been reached with the Hawker Hurricane, which first entered service with the RAF in December 1937. This 40-ft (12.19-m) span fighter carried eight machine-guns, and

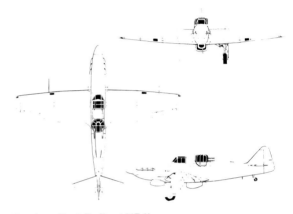

Boulton Paul Defiant NF.II

it can be appreciated that with these eight guns harmonised to concentrate their fire at an optimum aiming point the Hurricane represented a formidable weapon. It was not long, of course, before the fighter aircraft of other nations became similarly equipped, and the tactical advantage held initially by the Hurricane and Supermarine Spitfire was of comparatively short duration.

A new tactical concept, first conceived in 1935, proposed the use in fighters of a power-operated multi-

Compared with the Defiant I, the Boulton Paul Defiant II had an additional 150 hp (112 kW) of power plus a revised and more capacious fuel system. The example illustrated was operated by No. 151 Squadron.

Boulton Paul Defiant

Boulton Paul Defiant II of No. 151 Squadron, RAF, in 1941

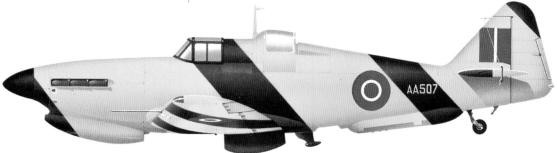

Boulton Paul Defiant TT.I of an RAF fighter OTU, Middle East in 1945

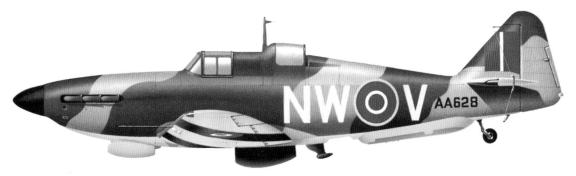

Boulton Paul Defiant TT.I of No. 286 Squadron, RAF, Exeter (UK) in 1944

gun turret. This appeared to have more than one advantage: firstly, it relieved the fighter pilot of the dual task of flying the aircraft and concentrating on finding, holding and hitting a target; secondly, the weapons could be used offensively, or defensively, over a far greater field of fire than that possible for a fixed battery. The use of a power-operated turret was not entirely new, however, for a Hawker Demon biplane had been so equipped in 1934, but for a very different reason. This resulted in the fact that the high performance of this two-seat fighter made it almost impossible for the observer/gunner in the aft cockpit to sight and fire the single Lewis gun with sufficient accuracy. A total of 59 Demons was manufactured for Hawker by Boulton Paul Aircraft under sub-contract, and each had a Frazer-Nash hydraulically operated turret installed; in addition many Demons of Hawker

manufacture were modified retrospectively.

Thus, when the Air Ministry issued Specification F.9/35, calling for a two-seat fighter with a power-operated gun turret, both Boulton Paul and Hawker made submissions. The Hawker Hotspur prototype was not, however, to compete against the two which were ordered from Boulton Paul, primarily because the Hawker factories had no productive capacity available, and consequently the Hotspur prototype was abandoned.

Named Defiant, the first of Boulton Paul's prototypes made its initial flight on 11 August 1937. It was a low-wing cantilever monoplane of all-metal construction, provided with retractable tailwheel type landing gear, and powered by a 1,030-hp (768-kW) Rolls-Royce Merlin I inline engine: the second prototype had a Merlin II engine. Both, of course, had the large and

Boulton Paul Defiant

Tactically successful in its first encounters because of its novel armament, the Boulton Paul Defiant turret fighter was soon revealed as a day fighter deathtrap, and relegated to night-fighting and target-towing.

heavy four-gun turret mounted within the fuselage aft of the pilot's cockpit. Its weight, and the high degree of drag imposed by the protruding section of the turret, no matter how cleverly faired in, was to impose limits on speed and manoeuvrability.

The first production Defiant F. Mk I day fighter was flown on 30 July 1939, and deliveries to No. 264 Squadron began in December of that year. It was this squadron which first deployed the type operationally, on 12 May 1940 over the beaches of Dunkirk, achieving complete tactical surprise. Fighters making conventional attack on the tail of the Defiants were met with an unprecedented burst of fire from the four machine-guns: on one day they claimed 38 enemy aircraft destroyed, and a total of 65 by the end of May. It was, however, only brief air superiority, for it did not take long for Luftwaffe fighter pilots to discover that they could attack head-on, or against the belly of the Defiant, with complete immunity. The days of these fighters were numbered, and they were withdrawn from daylight operations in August 1940.

It was instead decided to use the Defiant in a night fighter role, and the comparatively new and highly secret AI radar was installed in many of the Mk I aircraft, comprising either AI Mk IV or Mk VI, aircraft so fitted being designated NF.Mk IA. With this equipment they were to prove a valuable addition to Britain's night defences in the winter of 1940-1, and during this period they were to record more 'kills' per interception than any other contemporary night fighter.

In an attempt to improve the performance of the Defiant, two Mk Is served for conversion as prototypes of a new Mk II version. Apart from the installation of a

more powerful Merlin XX engine, fuel capacity was increased, a rudder of greater area was provided, and there were modifications to the engine cooling and fuel systems. First flown on 20 June 1940, the Defiant Mk II was built to the number of 210 examples, of which many were later converted as TT. Mk I target tugs. In addition 150 Mk Is were converted to TT. Mk IIIs, and 140 new production TT. Mk Is were built to bring total construction, including prototypes, to 1,065 when production ended in 1943.

At the peak of its deployment as a night fighter, Defiants equipped 13 RAF squadrons. They were used subsequently at home, and in the Middle and Far East, as target-tugs, and in addition about 50 Mk Is were modified for use in air/sea rescue role, serving with Nos. 275, 276, 277, 280 and 281 Squadrons.

Specification

Type: two-seat night fighter

Powerplant (Mk II): one 1,280-hp (954-kW) Rolls-Royce Merlin XX inline piston engine

Performance: maximum speed 313 mph (504 km/h) at 19,000 ft (5790 m); cruising speed 260 mph (418 km/h); service ceiling 30,350 ft (9250 m); range 465 miles (748 km)

Weights: empty 6,282 lb (2849 kg); maximum take-off 8,424 lb (3821 kg)

Dimensions: span 39 ft 4 in (11.99 m); length 35 ft 4 in (10.77 m); height 11 ft 4 in (3.45 m); wing area 250 sq ft (23.23m²)

Armament: four 0.303-in (7.7-mm) machine guns in power-operated dorsal turret

Operator: RAF

Bristol Type 105 Bulldog

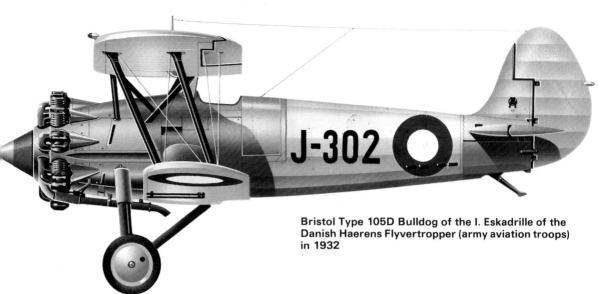

Bristol Type 105D Bulldog of the I. Eskadrille of the Danish Haerens Flyvertropper (army aviation troops) in 1932

History and notes

With a need to re-equip the RAF's fighter squadrons, to enable them to cope with bomber aircraft with performance in the category of that of the Fairey Fox, the Air Ministry drew up Specification F.9/26. This called for a single-seat day/night fighter, to be powered by a radial air-cooled engine, and armed with two Vickers machine-guns. A number of competing types resulted, with Bristol's Type 105 Bulldog winning narrowly from the Hawker Hawfinch.

Bristol's Bulldog Mk I prototype flew for the first time on 17 May 1927, and was modified subsequently with large span wings for an attempt on the altitude and climb-to-height records. The Mk I had been superseded for test purposes by a lengthened fuselage Mk II prototype, and it was the production version of this aircraft which entered service with the RAF's No. 3 Squadron at Upavon, Wiltshire, in June 1929. This was an unequal-span single-bay biplane, the basic structure of the airframe being all-metal with fabric covering. The tail unit incorporated a variable-incidence tailplane, and the tailskid landing gear had through-axle main units with rubber-in-compression shock-absorption. Powerplant of this version comprised one Bristol Jupiter VII radial engine. Equipment included oxygen and a short wave radio transmitter and receiver. The Bulldog was used widely in RAF service, a total of 312 of all versions equipping no fewer than 10 squadrons and remaining in use until 1937. In addition to the Bulldogs which served with the RAF, many were exported for the armed forces of Australia, Denmark, Estonia, Finland, Latvia, Siam, and Sweden.

Specification

Type: single-seat day/night fighter
Powerplant (Mk II): one 440-hp (328-kW) Bristol Jupiter VII radial piston engine

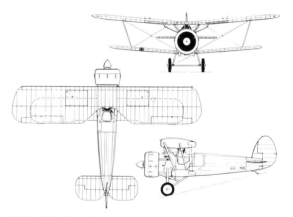

Bristol Bulldog IVA

Performance: maximum level speed 174 mph (280 km/h) at 10,000 ft (3050 m); service ceiling 27,000 ft (8230 m)
Weights: empty 2,200 lb (998 kg); maximum take-off 3,490 lb (1583 kg)
Dimensions: span 33 ft 11 in (10.34 m); length 25 ft 0 in (7.62 m); height 9 ft 10 in (3.00 m); wing area 306.6 sq ft (28.47 m²)
Armament: two fixed forward-firing synchronised Vickers machine-guns, and four 20 lb bombs on underwing racks

Variants:

Bulldog IIA Major production version, generally similar to Mk II, but with a 490-hp (365-kW) Bristol Jupiter VIIF engine, strengthened structure for operation at a higher gross weight, and wider main landing gear. Later Mk IIAs had the tailskid replaced by a tailwheel, and brakes incorporated in the main wheels.

43

Bristol Type 105 Bulldog

A Bristol Bulldog IVA biplane fighter of the Finnish air force, which acquired 17 of the type in 1935. They were the last Bulldogs built, and the only examples of the type to be flown in combat, during 1940-1.

Bulldog IIIA Designation of two interim aircraft with the 560-hp (418-kW) Bristol Mercury IVS.2 engine.
Bulldog IVA Final fighter production version with strengthened ailerons, and powered by the 640-hp (477-kW) Bristol Mercury VIS.2 engine.
Bulldog TM Training version (TM : training machine)

with a special removable rear fuselage incorporating a second cockpit, dual controls as standard, and no armament. The training rear fuselage could be replaced by a standard rear fuselage, and there was provision for the installation of machine-guns so that the TM could be converted to serve as a fighter.

Bristol Bulldog IIA of the Västeras Flygkar (F1), Royal Swedish air force in 1935

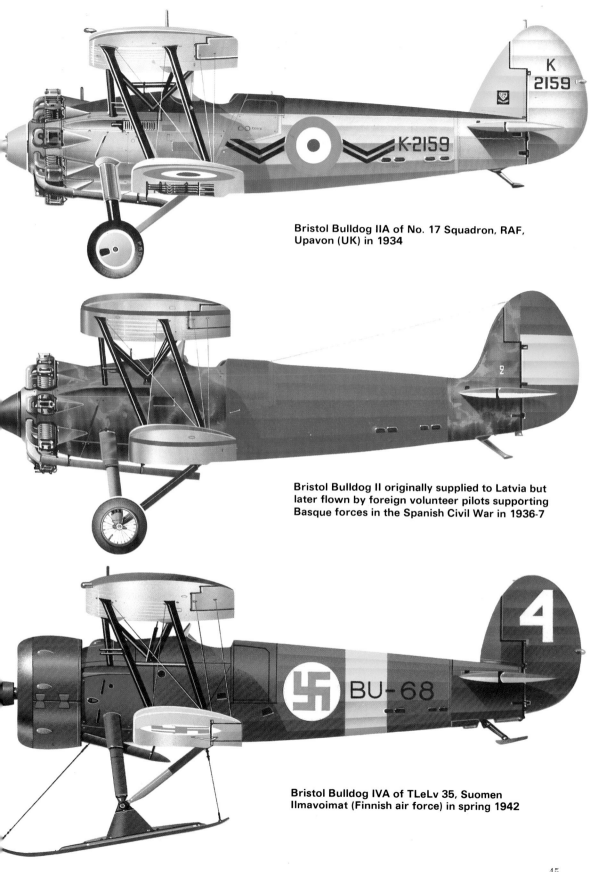

Bristol Bulldog IIA of No. 17 Squadron, RAF,
Upavon (UK) in 1934

Bristol Bulldog II originally supplied to Latvia but
later flown by foreign volunteer pilots supporting
Basque forces in the Spanish Civil War in 1936-7

Bristol Bulldog IVA of TLeLv 35, Suomen
Ilmavoimat (Finnish air force) in spring 1942

Bristol Type 130 Bombay

Bristol Bombay of No. 216 Squadron, RAF, Middle East in 1940

History and notes

Designed to Air Ministry Specification C.26/31 as a replacement for the Vickers Valentia serving in the Middle East and India, the Bristol Type 130 Bombay was intended as a troop or cargo carrier. But it had also to be capable of self-defence and to double as a long-range bomber — one might almost say Britain's answer to the Junkers Ju 52/3m. A contract was awarded for one prototype in March 1933 and this made its first flight from Filton on 23 June 1935 flown by Cyril Uwins. It was at that time the largest aircraft built at Filton. Military trials at the Aircraft and Armament Experimental Establishment, Martlesham Heath, were undertaken by Flt Lt 'Bill' Pegg, later to join the company and become its chief test pilot. Development testing resulted in various improvements being made, including the installation of more powerful engines: Bristol Pegasus XXIIs of 1,010 hp (753 kW) in place of the original 750-hp (559-kW) Pegasus IIIs.

A production contract for one batch of 50 was awarded to meet the revised Specification 47/36, but with Filton's production lines geared to the Bristol Blenheim it was decided to undertake Bombay production in Belfast, by Short Brothers & Harland at a new government-owned factory.

The first production Bombay flew in March 1939, and the initial squadron to receive the type was No. 216 in Egypt the following September. Other deliveries followed to Nos. 117, 267 and 271 Squadrons, and Bombays fulfilled their dual transport and bomber roles during the Libyan campaign of 1940. Although few in numbers, the Bombays were very active, and among their achievements was the evacuation of the Greek royal family from Crete to Egypt. A few UK-based aircraft ferried supplies across the English Channel before the collapse of France in 1940.

Bombays were eventually replaced by more modern types in the transport role as the bomber/transport concept became outdated, and the type passed quietly out of service in the mid-1940s, having achieved all and more than its designer had intended but receiving little of the limelight.

Specification

Type: bomber-transport with a crew of 3 and up to 24 troops
Powerplant: two 1,010-hp (753-kW) Bristol Pegasus XXII radial piston engines
Performance: maximum speed 192 mph (309 km/h) at 6,500 ft (1980 m); cruising speed 160 mph (257 km/h) at 10,000 ft (3050 m); service ceiling 25,000 ft (7620 m); range 880 miles (1416 km) or 2,230 miles (3589 km) with fuselage tanks
Weights: empty 13,800 lb (6260 kg); maximum take-off 20,000 lb (9072 kg)
Dimensions: span 95 ft 9 in (29.18 m); length 69 ft 3 in (21.11 m); height 19 ft 11 in (6.07 m); wing area 1,340 sq ft (124.49 m²)
Armament: two 0.303-in (7.7-mm) Vickers 'K' machine-guns (one each in nose and tail turrets), plus up to 2,000 lb (907 kg) of bombs.
Operator: RAF

Intended for use by Middle Eastern squadrons of the RAF, the Bristol Bombay successfully met the need to operate as a transport (24 troops) and as a bomber (up to 2,000 lb/907 kg of bombs) with underfuselage racks.

Bristol Types 142M, 149 & 160 Blenheim

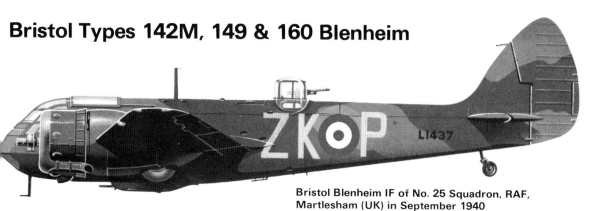

Bristol Blenheim IF of No. 25 Squadron, RAF, Martlesham (UK) in September 1940

History and notes

Great Britain's *Daily Mail* newspaper had championed the cause of aviation from the very beginning of powered flight, with Lord Northcliffe ever ready to remind his readers that the world was on the threshold of a new era of scientific and technical progress that would affect the lives of all its citizens. It was he who, in 1906, engaged one Harry Harper to become the world's first aviation journalist and, between them, the idea of the famous *Daily Mail* prizes for progress in aviation was born. The first of those prizes went to A.V.Roe in 1907, his elastic-powered biplane proving an easy winner of the Model Aeroplane Competition held at London's Alexandra Palace. A whole series of 'encouragement' prizes followed, highlighting such powered aircraft flights as the first 'all-British', the first London-to-Manchester, the first Channel crossing, the first Circuit of Britain, and the first non-stop Atlantic crossing.

Such a background will help to explain to the uninitiated why in 1934 Lord Rothermere, who was then proprietor of the *Daily Mail*, should have expressed a desire to obtain for his personal use a fast and spacious private aeroplane, for this aviation-minded organisation had then appreciated the potential of what is today called the business or corporate aircraft. Lord Rothermere envisaged his requirements as a fast aircraft that would accommodate a crew of two and six

Bristol Blenheim I

passengers, and it just so happened that the Bristol Aeroplane Company had already drawn up the outline of a light transport in this category.

The brain-child of that doyen of Bristol's designers, Frank Barnwell, the new aeroplane had been designed originally to be powered by two 500-hp (373-kW) Bristol Aquila I engines which were then under development. Lord Rothermere's interest in a high-speed transport resulted in Barnwell's proposal to mount a couple of 650-hp (485-kW) Bristol Mercury VIS engines in his embryo airframe and this was to

In this illustration of a Bristol Blenheim IF of No. 54 OTU it is impossible to see the ventral gunpack, carrying four 0.303-in (7.7-mm) machine-guns, by which the Blenheim bomber was turned into a night-fighter.

Bristol Types 142M, 149 and 160 Blenheim

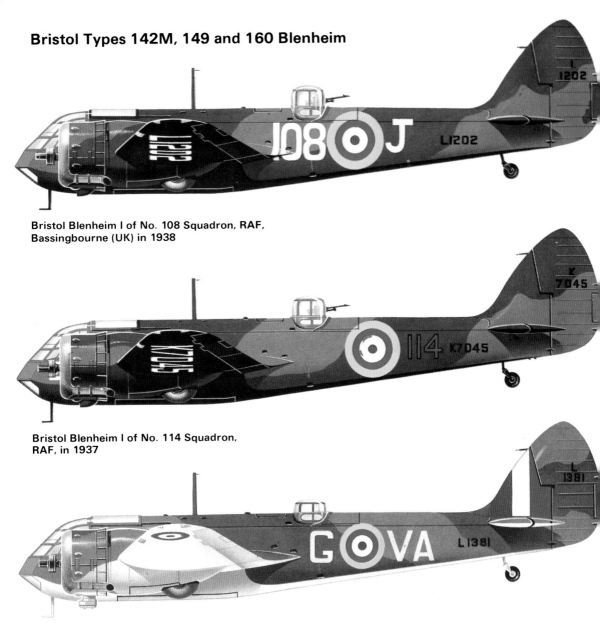

Bristol Blenheim I of No. 108 Squadron, RAF,
Bassingbourne (UK) in 1938

Bristol Blenheim I of No. 114 Squadron,
RAF, in 1937

Bristol Blenheim I of No. 113 Squadron, RAF,
Larissa (Greece) in 1941

result in the Bristol Type 142. First flown at Filton on 12 April 1935, it was to spark off a hubbub of comment and excitement when during its initial trials it was found to be some 30 mph (48 km/h) faster than the prototype of Britain's most-recently procured fighter. Named *Britain First*, it was presented to the nation by Lord Rothermere after the Air Ministry had requested that they might retain it for a period of testing to evaluate its potential as a light bomber. This, then was the sire of the Bristol Blenheim which was to prove an important interim weapon at the beginning of World War II.

Aware of Air Ministry interest in the Type 142, Bristol busied themselves with homework to evolve a

military version (Type 142M) of this aircraft, and in the summer of 1935 the Air Ministry decided to accept the company's proposal, placing a first order for 150 aircraft to Specification 28/35 in September. The new aircraft was very similar to the Type 142, but there had of course been some changes to make it suitable for the military role, primarily to accommodate a bomb aimer's station, a bomb bay and a dorsal gun turret. Little time was lost by either the Bristol company or the Air Ministry, for following the first flight of the prototype, on 25 June 1936, initial deliveries to RAF squadrons began in March 1937, and in July 1937 the Air Ministry placed a follow-on order for 434 additional Blenheim Is, as the type had by then been named.

Bristol Types 142M, 149 and 160 Blenheim

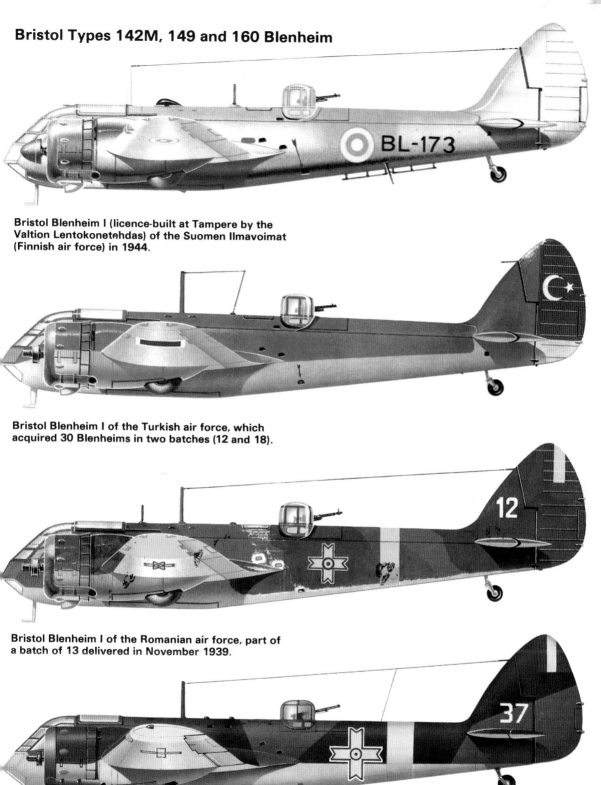

Bristol Blenheim I (licence-built at Tampere by the Valtion Lentokonetehdas) of the Suomen Ilmavoimat (Finnish air force) in 1944.

Bristol Blenheim I of the Turkish air force, which acquired 30 Blenheims in two batches (12 and 18).

Bristol Blenheim I of the Romanian air force, part of a batch of 13 delivered in November 1939.

Bristol Blenheim I of the Romanian air force, in service against Russia from July 1941 onwards.

Bristol Types 142M, 149 and 160 Blenheim

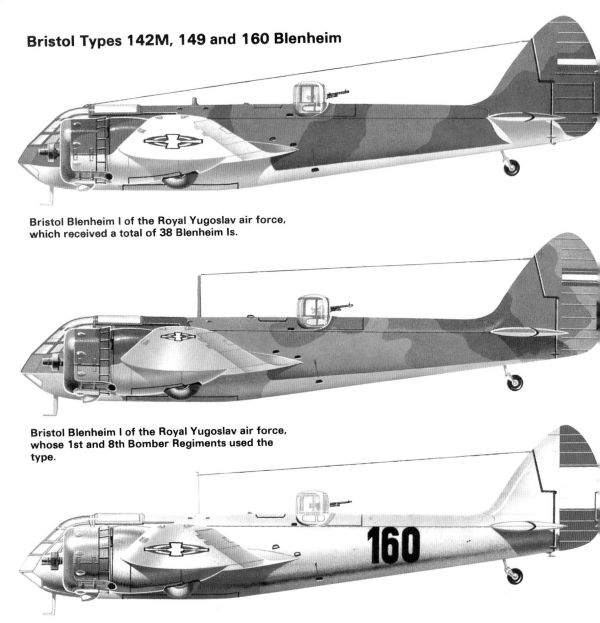

Bristol Blenheim I of the Royal Yugoslav air force, which received a total of 38 Blenheim Is.

Bristol Blenheim I of the Royal Yugoslav air force, whose 1st and 8th Bomber Regiments used the type.

Bristol Blenheim I of the Royal Yugoslav air force, which had 22 British- and 16 Yugoslav-built aircraft.

Of all-metal construction, except for fabric-covered control surfaces, the Blenheim I was a cantilever mid-wing monoplane, with the wing having Frise mass-balanced ailerons and split trailing-edge flaps. The fuselage nose extended only slightly forward of the engines, and both fuselage and tail unit were conventional light alloy structures. Landing gear was of the retractable tailwheel type. The tailwheel of the prototype had retracted, operated by cables linked to the main landing gear but, wisely, this feature was not carried forward into the production aircraft. The powerplant comprised two 840-hp (626-kW) Bristol Mercury VIII engines, mounted in nacelles on the wing leading-edge, and driving three-blade variable-pitch propellers. Accommodation was provided for a pilot, navigator/bomb-aimer, and air gunner/radio operator. A bomb bay in the wing centre-section could contain a maximum 1,000 lb (454 kg) of bombs, and standard armament comprised a 0.303-in (7.7-mm) machine-gun in the port wing, plus a Vickers 'K' gun in the dorsal turret.

The first RAF squadron to receive Blenheim Is was No. 114, then based at RAF Wyton, and it was this unit which first demonstrated the new type officially to the public at the RAF's final Hendon Display in the summer of 1937. The Blenheims were to arouse excited comment with their high speed and modern appearance, being launched on their career in an aura of emotion

Bristol Types 142M, 149 and 160 Blenheim

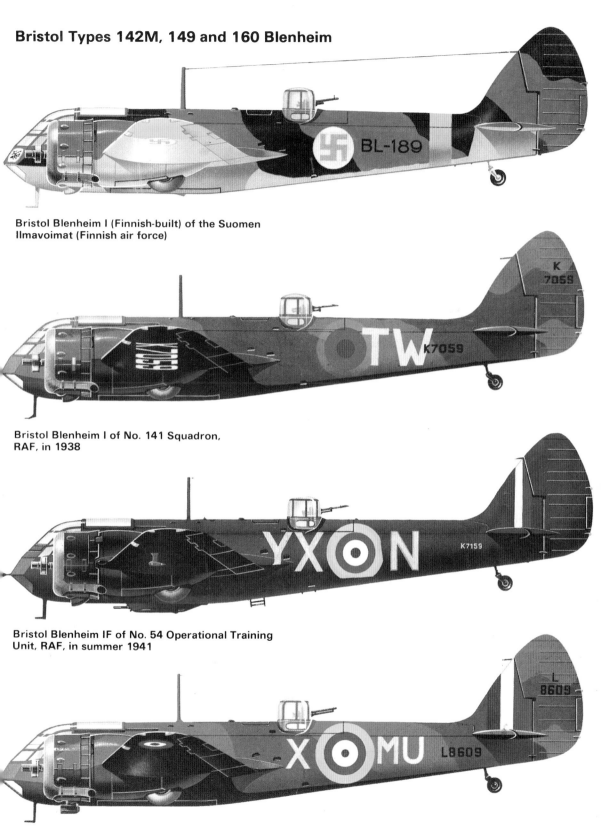

Bristol Blenheim I (Finnish-built) of the Suomen
Ilmavoimat (Finnish air force)

Bristol Blenheim I of No. 141 Squadron,
RAF, in 1938

Bristol Blenheim IF of No. 54 Operational Training
Unit, RAF, in summer 1941

Bristol Blenheim I of No. 60 Squadron, RAF,
Far East in 1941

Bristol Types 142M, 149 and 160 Blenheim

The crew of a Bristol Blenheim IV light bomber board their aircraft, distinguishable from the preceding Mk I by its longer nose with a peculiarly scalloped upper surface and by its more powerful Mercury XVs.

created by the belief that, in an unsettled Europe, the RAF was armed with the world's most formidable bomber aircraft. Production contracts soared, necessitating the establishment of new construction lines by A.V. Roe at Chadderton and Rootes Securities at Speke, both these factories being in Lancashire. Between them the three lines built a total of 1,552 Blenheim Is which, at their peak, equipped no fewer than 26 RAF squadrons at home and overseas, the Blenheim's first overseas deployments being with No. 30 Squadron in Iraq and No. 11 Squadron in India, in January and July 1938 respectively.

However, by the outbreak of World War II few Blenheim Is remained in service with home-based bomber squadrons, having been superseded in the bombing role by the Blenheim IV, which incorporated the lessons learned from the experience which squadrons had gained in operating the Mk I. But their usefulness was by no means ended, many continuing to serve as conversion trainers and, initially, as crew trainers in OTUs. More valuable by far were some 200 which were converted to serve as night fighters, pioneering the newly conceived technique of AI (Airborne Interception) radar, carrying AI Mk III or Mk IV. The single forward-firing machine-gun was totally inadequate for this role, of course, and a special underfuselage pack to house four 0.303-in (7.7-mm) machine-guns was produced. So equipped, Blenheim IFs scored the first AI success against an enemy aircraft on the night of 2-3 July 1940.

Export versions of the Blenheim I were sold before the war to Finland, Turkey and Yugoslavia, and were also built under licence by these first two nations. In addition, a small number had been supplied to Romania as a diplomatic bribe in 1939, but this proved to be unsuccessful. The result, of course, was that Blenheim Is fought for and against the Allies.

When, in August 1935, the Air Ministry had initiated Specification G.24/35 to find a successor to the Avro Anson for use in a coastal reconnaissance/light bomber role, Bristol had proposed its Type 149. Very similar to the Blenheim I, this was based on the use of Bristol Aquila engines to confer long range with the existing fuel capacity, but proved unacceptable to the Air Ministry. Subsequently renewed interest was shown in the Type 149 for use in a general-reconnaissance role, and a prototype was built, by conversion of an early Blenheim I, this retaining the Mercury VIII engines and being provided with increased fuel capacity. The fuselage nose was lengthened to provide additional accommodation for the navigator/observer and his equipment, and this was to be finalised as that which graced the Blenheim IV.

The Air Ministry then had misgivings about the Type 149, fearing that its introduction and manufacture would interfere with the production or urgently needed Blenheims. Instead, the Type 149 was adopted by the Royal Canadian Air Force for production in Canada as the Bolingbroke I, the Bristol prototype being shipped to Canada to help in the establishment of a production line by Fairchild Aircraft at Longueuil, Quebec. The first Bolingbroke Is had Mercury VIII engines, but after 18 of these had been built production changed to the definitive Canadian version, the Bolingbroke IV

Bristol Types 142M, 149 and 160 Blenheim

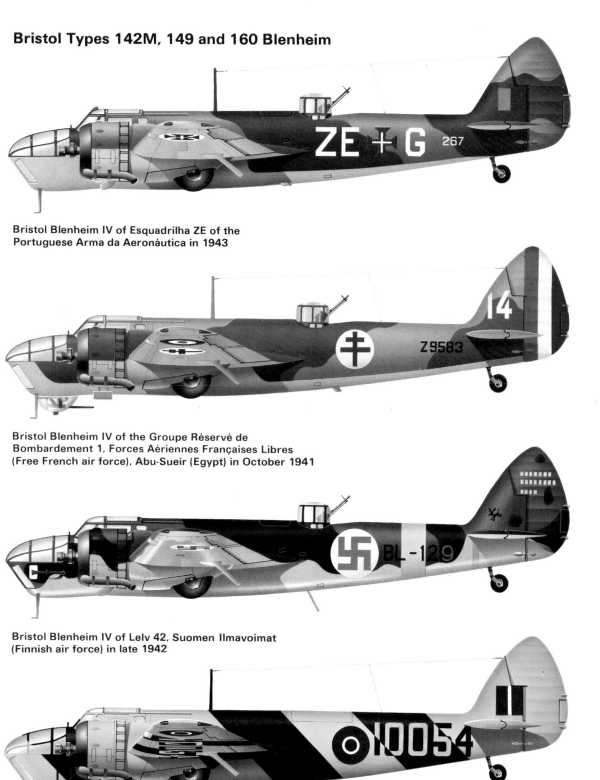

Bristol Blenheim IV of Esquadrilha ZE of the
Portuguese Arma da Aeronáutica in 1943

Bristol Blenheim IV of the Groupe Réservé de
Bombardement 1, Forces Aériennes Françaises Libres
(Free French air force), Abu-Sueir (Egypt) in October 1941

Bristol Blenheim IV of Lelv 42, Suomen Ilmavoimat
(Finnish air force) in late 1942

Bristol Bolingbroke IV target-tug of the Bombing
and Gunnery Schools, No. 1 Training Command,
Royal Canadian Air Force in 1944

Bristol Types 142M, 149 and 160 Blenheim

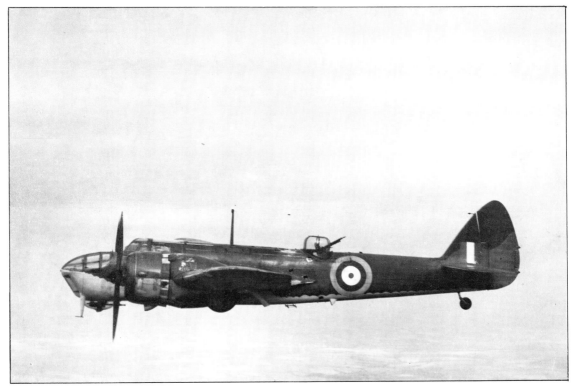

The Bristol Blenheim was a key part of the UK's air expansion scheme of the 1930s, and though obsolescent by 1939 it played a useful part until 1943. Illustrated is a Blenheim IV with a gun in the undernose blister.

with Mercury XV engines, and equipment from Canadian and US manufacturers. Later variants included a small number of Bolingbroke IV Ws with 1,200-hp (895-kW) Pratt & Whitney R-1830 Twin Wasp engines, and a number of Bolingbroke IV T multipurpose trainers.

Having blown hot and then cold over the Type 149, there was a sudden renewal of interest, primarily as an interim measure until the Type 152 torpedo-bomber, derived from the Blenheim, should become available. The decision was taken, therefore, to introduce the longer nose and stepped windscreen of the Bolingbroke, and to make provision for longer range by the introduction of increased wing fuel capacity. The Bristol designation Type 149 was retained for this changed configuration, the new RAF designation being Blenheim IV. This change took place quietly on the production lines towards the end of 1938, although the first 68 Blenheim IVs were built without the 'long-range wing'. The powerplant comprised two more powerful Mercury XV engines, and these allowed gross weight to be increased eventually by 16 per cent.

No. 90 Squadron was the initial unit to be equipped with Blenheim IVs in March 1938, the first of more than 70 squadrons to operate these aircraft, and consisting of units from Army Co-operation, Bomber, Coastal, Far East Bomber, Fighter and Middle East Commands, both at home and overseas. Inevitably, such extensive use brought changes in armament and equipment, but especially the former, for the armament of the first Blenheim IVs was unchanged from the initial two-gun armament of the Mk I. As finalised the number became five, the single forward-firing gun in the wing being retained, a new dorsal turret carrying two guns being adopted, and a completely new remotely-controlled Frazer-Nash mounting being added beneath the nose to hold two aft-firing machine-guns. Protective armour was also increased, but while it was not possible to enlarge the capacity of the bomb bay, provision was made for an additional 320 lb (145 kg) of bombs to be carried externally, under the inner wings, for short-range missions.

With so many squadrons operating the type it was inevitable that Blenheims should notch up many wartime 'firsts' for the RAF. These included the first reconnaissance over German territory, made on 3 September 1939, by a Blenheim IV of No. 139 Squadron; and the type was the first to drop bombs on German targets, on 4 September 1939, when 10 aircraft from Nos. 107 and 110 Squadrons made an attack on the German fleet in the Schillig Roads, off Wilhelmshaven. From the beginning of the war, until replaced in home squadrons of Bomber Command by Douglas Bostons and de Havilland Mosquitoes in 1942, Blenheim IVs were used extensively in the European theatre. Although vulnerable to fighter attack, they were frequently used for unescorted daylight operations and undoubtedly the skill of their crews and the aircraft's

Bristol Types 142M, 149 and 160 Blenheim

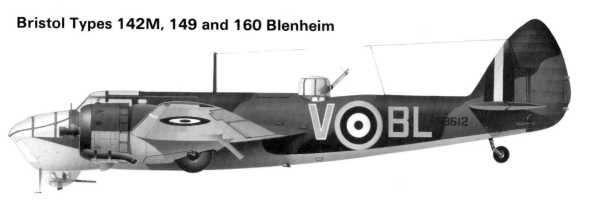

Bristol Blenheim IV of No. 40 Squadron, RAF, Wyton
(UK) in July 1940

Bristol Blenheim IV of No. 84 Squadron, RAF, Aqir
(Palestine) in April 1941

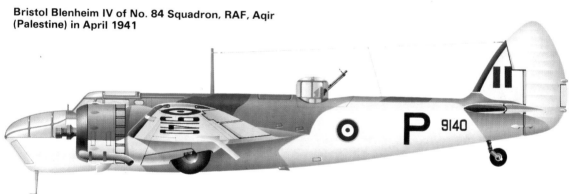

Bristol Bolingbroke IV of No. 115 (BR) Squadron,
Royal Canadian Air Force, Patricia Bay BC (Canada)
in August 1943

Bristol Blenheim IV of No. 55 Squadron, RAF, Fuka
(Egypt) in early 1942

Bristol Types 142M, 149 and 160 Blenheim

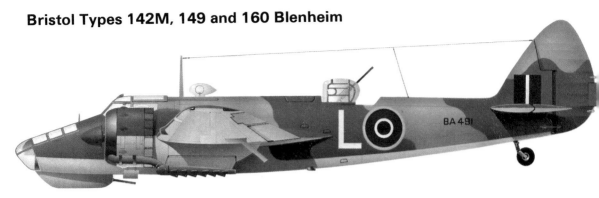

Bristol Blenheim V of RAF unit in Western Desert

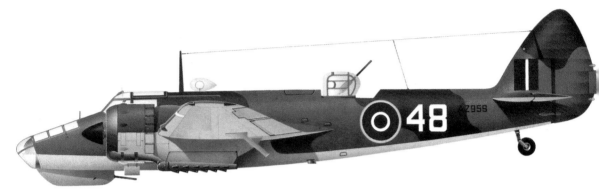

Bristol Blenheim V of No. 12 (P) AFU, Grantham (UK) in 1944

ability to absorb a great deal of punishment were the primary reasons for their survival, for high speed and heavy firepower was certainly not their forte. In the overseas squadrons Blenheims continued to serve long after their usefulness had ended in Europe, and except in Singapore, where they were no match for the Japanese fighters, they proved a valuable weapon. A total of 1,930 had been built when production ended, and in addition to serving with the RAF had been used by the French Free and South African air forces, and supplied in small numbers to Finland, Greece and Turkey.

Last of the direct developments of the Blenheim design was Bristol's Type 160, known briefly as the Bisley, which was to enter service in the summer of 1942 as the Blenheim V. Envisaged originally as a low-altitude close-support bomber, it was in fact to be built for deployment as a high-altitude bomber, powered by Mercury XV or XXV engines. Except for a changed nose, some alterations in detail and updated equipment, these aircraft were basically the same as their predecessors. Some 940 were built, all produced by Rootes at their Speke and Stoke-on-Trent factories, and the first unit to receive Blenheim Vs was No. 18 Squadron. The type was to equip six squadrons in the Middle East and four in the Far East, where they were used without distinction. This resulted from an increase in gross weight of over 17 per cent which, without the introduction of more powerful engines,

had brought about a serious fall of performance. It was only when the Blenheim Vs were deployed in the Italian campaign, contending with the advanced fighters in service with the Luftwaffe, that losses rose to quite unacceptable proportions, and the Blenheim Vs were withdrawn from service.

Specification

Type: three-seat light bomber/fighter
Powerplant (Blenheim IV): two 905-hp (675-kW) Bristol Mercury XV radial piston engines
Performance: maximum speed 266 mph (428 km/h) at 11,800 ft (3595 m); cruising speed 198 mph (319 km/h); service ceiling 27,260 ft (8310 m); maximum range 1,460 miles (2350 km)
Weights: empty 9,790 lb (4441 kg); maximum take-off 14,400 lb (6532 kg)
Dimensions: span 56 ft 4 in (17.17 m); length 42 ft 7 in (12.98 m); height 9 ft 10 in (3.00 m); wing area 469 sq ft (43.57 m²)
Armament: five 0.303-in (7.7-mm) machine-guns (one forward-firing in port wing, two in power-operated dorsal turret, and two remotely controlled in mounting beneath nose and firing aft), plus up to 1,000 lb (434 kg) of bombs internally and 320 lb (145 kg) of bombs externally
Operators: Croatia, FFAF, Finland, Greece, Portugal, RAAF, RAF, RCAF, RNZAF, Romania, SAAF, Turkey, Yugoslavia

Bristol Type 152 Beaufort

Bristol Beaufort torpedo-bombers of No. 217 Squadron, RAF Coastal Command. The squadron became operational in Malta during June 1942, adding greatly to the problems of Axis shipping.

History and notes

In 1935 the Air Ministry had issued two specifications, M.15/35 and G.24/35, which detailed requirements for a torpedo-bomber and a general reconnaissance/ bomber respectively. The latter was required to replace the Avro Anson in service for this role and, as mentioned in the Bristol Blenheim entry, was to be met by the Bristol Type 149 which was built in Canada as the Bolingbroke. To meet the first requirement, for a torpedo-bomber, Bristol began by considering an adaptation of the Blenheim, identifying its design as the Type 150. This proposal, which was concerned primarily with a change in fuselage design to provide accommodation for a torpedo and the installation of more powerful engines, was submitted to the Air Ministry in November 1935.

After sending off these details of the Type 150, the Bristol design team came to the conclusion that it would be possible to meet both of the Air Ministry's specifications by a single aircraft evolved from the Blenheim, and immediately prepared a new design outline, the Type 152. By comparison with the Blenheim IV, the new design was increased slightly in length to allow for the carriage of a torpedo in a semi-exposed position, provided a navigation station, and seated pilot and navigator side-by-side; behind them were radio and camera positions which would be manned by a gunner/camera/radio operator. The Type 152 was more attractive to the Air Ministry, but it was

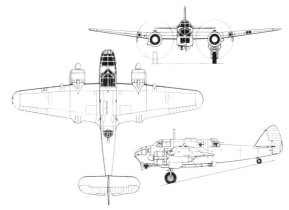

Bristol Beaufort I

considered that a crew of four was essential, and the accommodation was redesigned to this end. The resulting high roof line, which continued unbroken to the dorsal turret, became a distinguishing feature of this new aircraft, built to Air Ministry Specification 10/36, and subsequently named Beaufort.

Detail design was initiated immediately, but early analysis and estimates showed that the intended powerplant of two Bristol Perseus engines would provide insufficient power to cater for the increase of almost 25 per cent in gross weight without a serious loss of performance. Instead, the newly developed

A typically Mediterranean setting for this Bristol Beaufort torpedo-bomber, seen under maintenance in its dispersal pen on the island fortress of Malta, where the type was flown by Nos 39 and 217 Squadrons.

Bristol Type 152 Beaufort

twin-row Taurus sleeve-valve engine was selected for the Beaufort, the only concern being whether it would be cleared for production in time to coincide with the construction of the new airframe. The initial contract, for 78 aircraft, was placed in August 1936, but the first prototype did not fly until just over two years later, on 15 October 1938. There had been a number of reasons for this long period of labour, one being overheating problems with the powerplant, and another the need to disperse the Blenheim production line to shadow factories before the Beaufort could be built.

Test flying of the prototype revealed a number of shortcomings, leading to the provision of doors to enclose the main landing gear units when retracted, repositioning of the engine exhausts, and an increase to two machine-guns in the dorsal turret. These and other items, added to continuing teething problems with the new engine, delayed the entry into service of the Beaufort Is, these first equipping No. 22 Squadron of Coastal Command in January 1940. It was this unit which, on the night of 15-16 April 1940, began the Beaufort's operational career by laying mines in enemy coastal waters, but in the following month all in-service aircraft were grounded until engine modifications could be carried out.

Earlier, the Australian government had shown interest in the Beaufort, and following the visit of a British Air Mission in early 1939, it was decided that railway and industrial workshops could be adapted to produce these aircraft, resulting in the establishment of two assembly plants (at Fishermen's Bend, Melbourne, and at Mascot, Sydney) with the production backing of railways workshops at Chullora, Islington and Newport. Twenty sets of airframe parts and the eighth production aircraft as a working sample were shipped out, but at an early stage the Australians decided they did not want the Taurus powerplant. Accordingly, they had obtained a licence from Pratt & Whitney to build the Twin Wasp, and these were to power all Australian-built Beauforts, which eventually totalled 700.

Australian production began in 1940, the first Australian Beaufort V making its initial flight in May 1941. Apart from the change in engines, these were generally similar to their British counterparts except for an increase in fin area to improve stability with the powerful Twin Wasp engine. In fact, engine and propeller changes accounted for most of the different variants produced by the Australian factories. These included the Beaufort V (50) and Beaufort VA (30), both with licence-built Twin Wasp S3C4-G engines; Beaufort VI (60 with Curtiss propellers) and Beaufort VII (40 with Hamilton propellers), all 100 being powered by imported S1C3-G Twin Wasps due to insufficient licence production; and the Beaufort VIII with licence-built S3C4-Gs. This last mark was the definitive production version, of which 520 were built, and had additional fuel tankage, Loran navigation system and variations in armament, with production ending in August 1944. Some 46 of the last production batch were subsequently converted to serve as unarmed transports; designated Beaufort IX, this variant had the dorsal turret removed and the resulting aperture faired in. The powerplant rating of all the Australian versions was 1,200 hp (895 kW). The Beaufort was used extensively by the Royal Australian Air Force in the Pacific theatre, serving from the summer of 1942 until the end of World War II.

The early trials of the Australian Beaufort V with Twin Wasp engines induced the Air Ministry to specify this powerplant for the next contract, and a prototype with these American engines was flown in November 1940. The first production Beaufort II flew in September 1941, and by comparison with the Beaufort I revealed much improved take-off performance. However, because of a shortage of Twin Wasps in the UK, only 164 production Mk IIs were built before Mk Is with improved Taurus XII engines were reintroduced on the line. In addition to the powerplant change, this version had structural strengthening, a changed gun turret, and ASV radar with Yagi aerials. When production of this version ended in 1944, well over 1,200 Beauforts had been built in Britain.

The final two Beaufort designations, Mk III and Mk IV, related respectively to a version with Rolls-Royce Merlin XX engines of which none were built, and a version with two 1,250-hp (932-kW) Taurus XX engines of which only a prototype was built.

Beauforts were the standard torpedo-bomber in service with Coastal Command during 1940-3, equipping Nos. 22, 42, 86, 217, 415 and 489 Squadrons in home waters, and Nos. 39, 47 and 217 in the Middle East. They were to acquit themselves well until superseded by the Beaufighter, involved in many of the early and bloody attacks against the German battle-cruisers *Gneisenau* and *Scharnhorst*, and the heavy cruiser *Prinz Eugen*, three vessels which often seemed to be invincible, at least to aircraft carrying conventional weapons.

Specifications

Type: four-seat torpedo-bomber
Powerplant (Beaufort I): two 1,130-hp (843-kW) Bristol Taurus VI, XII, or XVI radial piston engines
Performance: maximum speed 260 mph (418 km/h) at 6,000 ft (1830 m); cruising speed 200 mph (322 km/h); service ceiling 16,500 ft (5030 m); normal range 1,035 miles (1666 km)
Weights: empty 13,107 lb (5945 kg); maximum take-off 21,230 lb (9630 kg)
Dimensions: span 57 ft 10 in (17.63 m); length 44 ft 7 in (13.59 m); height 12 ft 5 in (3.78 m); wing area 503 sq ft (46.73 m²)
Armament: four 0.303-in (7.7-mm) machine-guns (two each in nose and dorsal turrets) and (in some aircraft) three additional 0.303-in (7.7-mm) guns (one in blister beneath the nose and two in beam positions), plus up to 1,500 lb 1680 kg) of bombs or mines, or one 1,605-lb (728-kg) torpedo
Operators: RAAF, RAF, RCAF, RN, Turkey

Bristol Type 156 Beaufighter

Bristol Beaufighter IC (retrofitted with a dihedral tailplane) of No. 30 Operational Training Unit, RAF, in 1942

Bristol Beaufighter IF of No. 25 Squadron, RAF, in summer 1940

History and notes

Many of the younger men who had survived the worst that World War I could do, only to be confronted with another major war 20 years later, were convinced of, and never ceased to express, their strongly held opinion that Britain always 'muddled through'. History proves the comment to be true, whether emanating from them or their great-grandfathers: but 'muddling through' is perhaps unkind, and that term really highlights the undoubted flair for improvisation which untold generations of Britons have possessed in abundance.

Bristol's Type 156 design, subsequently to become known as the Beaufighter, is a typical example of this technique, and was born by an improvisation forced upon the Bristol design staff headed by Roy Fedden and Leslie Frise. This had come in the wake of the Munich crisis of 1938 which, by the sacrifice of Czechoslovakia, had bought a little time in which the British and French sought to prop up their fragile defences. Both nations had air forces which, in the main, were comprised of geriatric aircraft, but the UK had initiated an expansion programme and its first fruits, such as the Hawker Hurricane, were then beginning to ripen.

The RAF was, however, still desperately short of modern fighters and, in particular, of heavily armed aircraft suitable for deployment in the long-range escort or night fighter roles. Bristol had then virtually completed design of the Beaufort torpedo-bomber, developed from the Blenheim, the prototype Beaufort I flying first on 15 October 1938. The suggested improvisation, to produce a long-range fighter in the shortest possible time, hinged upon use of the wings, tail unit and landing gear of the Beaufort, powered by two of

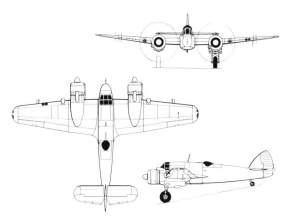

Bristol Beaufighter IF

the company's Hercules sleeve-valve radial piston engines: this required, in effect, only a new fuselage to unite these assemblies. It was possible for a draft proposal to be knocked together within a few days and this, submitted to the Air Ministry in October 1938, resulted in an order for four prototypes. Within just over eight months from initiation of detail design in November the first prototype was in the air, making its maiden flight on 17 July 1939, which just goes to prove what inspired improvisation can do.

A mid-wing cantilever monoplane of all-metal construction, except for fabric-covered control surfaces, the Type 156 Beaufighter had wings incorporating wide-span split flaps. The fuselage and tail unit were conventional structures, and landing gear was of the retractable tailwheel type. The powerplant consisted of two Hercules radial engines, and the first two proto-

Bristol Type 156 Beaufighter

The pugnacious appearance of the Bristol Beaufighter heavy fighter was more than equalled by the type's punch. This example is moving along an improvised taxi-way on the island of Malta.

types each had de Havilland three-blade propellers of 13 ft 0 in (3.96 m) diameter. The first prototype had two Hercules I-SM engines, the second two Hercules I-M, and the third and fourth prototypes flew initially with 1,300-hp (969-kW) Hercules IIs.

Factory and service testing revealed few airframe problems, although action was taken to incorporate a number of improvements considered to be desirable for future use. The area of concern centred upon the engines, for while the first prototype had been able to demonstrate its estimated speed of 335 mph (539 km/h) at 16,800 ft (5120 m), the second prototype was some 7½ per cent below this figure. What was even more disconcerting was the fact that the aircraft were then being flown without operational equipment, and it was realised by the company that introduction of the planned 1,400-hp (1044-kW) Hercules III would provide little, if any, improvement. The only alternative engine available at short notice was the 1,500-hp (1119-kW) Hercules XI, an uprated version of the III which used 100-octane fuel, and it was decided to use these engines for the initial production versions.

The other vital factor to be settled, before the Beaufighter went into service, was the selection of suitable armament. This, of course, was to vary somewhat according to the basic role in which a particular version was intended to operate. The Beaufighter IF was visualised as a night fighter as soon as it was appreciated that there was ample room within its fuselage to accommodate the then bulky AI radar, and this dictated a concentration of heavy fire to destroy or immediately disable an enemy aircraft after AI contact had brought the night fighter to optimum range. Standard armament of the IF was four 20-mm cannon in the fuselage nose, plus four 0.303-in (7.7-mm) machine-guns in the starboard wing and two more in the port wing, although early production aircraft off the Filton line had only the four cannon. Radar comprised AI Mk IV installed in the fuselage nose, and this was to

become the standard equipment for Fighter Command Beaufighters.

Contracts for the Beaufighter having reached large proportions long before any of the type entered service, three production lines had been established. These were at the Bristol works at Filton, in a new Bristol factory at Weston-super-Mare, Somerset, and at the Fairey factory at Stockport in Lancashire. The first production Beaufighter IF completed on this last production line made its initial flight on 7 February 1941; the first from Weston-super-Mare on 20 February 1941, but long before that, on 27 July 1940, the first Beaufighters were handed over to the RAF.

Nos. 25 and 29 Squadrons each received their first example of the Beaufighter on 2 September 1940; by 17 September No. 29 Squadron was fully operational with the type, followed by No. 25 on 10 October, and Nos. 219, 600 and 640 Squadrons were close behind. It was this last squadron which was to record the first Beaufighter victory with the AI Mk IV radar, on 19 November 1940, when a Junkers Ju 88 was mortally damaged over Oxfordshire and crashed before it could cross the English Channel. Unfortunately for the RAF, interception by AI Mk IV alone was inadequate, and it was not until the introduction of Ground Controlled Interception (GCI) in January 1941, which was able to put the night fighter within AI contact range of its adversary, that the Beaufighter IF was able to justify its promise.

An alternative employment for the Beaufighter IF arose even while the initial night fighter squadrons were being equipped in the autumn of 1940, for there was an urgent need for long-range day fighters to operate around the Mediterranean and in the Western Desert. To meet this demand about 80 Beaufighter IFs were provided with desert equipment and their range extended by the temporary expedient of installing a 50-Imperial gallon (227-litre) fuel tank on the fuselage floor. At a later date additional tankage was

Bristol Type 156 Beaufighter

A Bristol Beaufighter IF of No. 604 Squadron, which was one of four squadrons to receive this radar-equipped night-fighter in September 1940. Notable in this three-view illustration are the black finish of this early night-fighter, the aerials of the AI Mk IV radar (projecting from the nose and from the outer leading edges of each wing) and the armament of four cannon in the lower nose and six machine-guns (two in the port and four in the starboard wing).

Looking less than immaculate, a Bristol Beaufighter I of a Desert Air Force squadron undergoes engine tests before an operational sortie from its North African airfield. Note the sealing of the gun ports with pieces of fabric to prevent the ingress of foreign matter and to improve streamlining until the guns were fired.

Bristol Type 156 Beaufighter

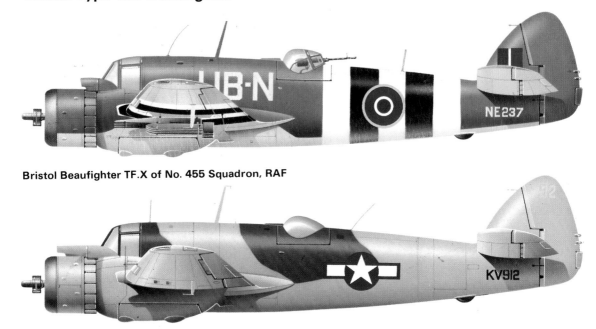

Bristol Beaufighter TF.X of No. 455 Squadron, RAF

Bristol Beaufighter VIF of the US 1st Tactical Air Command, Middle East in 1942-3

provided in the wing outer panels, but this necessitated deletion of the wing guns.

The provision of special Coastal Command radio, plus navigation facilities, distinguished the initial Beaufighter ICs (Coastal) which began to enter service with No. 143 Squadron in the spring of 1941. The aircraft of this mark proved a valuable weapon from the outset, becoming gradually more important as their capability was expanded.

A heavy demand for Hercules engines, which also were used to power the Short Stirling bomber, made it prudent to experiment with an alternative engine installation so that, in the event of a temporary or long-term interruption in the supply of these powerplants, Beaufighter production would not be penalised. Accordingly, two of three airframes supplied to Rolls-Royce at Hucknall were provided with 1,075-hp (802-kW) Merlin X inline engines, and these when test flown were found to give slightly improved performance but brought about a change in the aircraft's centre of gravity. This manifested itself in some directional instability, leading to a variety of tail-end modifications: a tailplane of increased chord, a lengthened dorsal fin, twin fins and rudders, and a tailplane with 12° dihedral. It was this last remedy which provided the solution, and it was adopted both retrospectively and on all subsequent production aircraft. Merlin-engined Beaufighters were designated Mk II, and the first production Beaufighter IIF with 1,280-hp (954-kW) Merlin XX engines made its initial flight on 22 March 1941. The Beaufighter IIF was, in fact, the only Merlin-engined version to be built, and the type served primarily as a home-defence night fighter, but was used also by Nos. 721, 723, 775, 779 and 789 Squadrons of the Fleet Air Arm.

The only other variant to fly among the early marks was a Beaufighter V, armed with only two forward-firing 20-mm cannon, and the wing guns replaced by a Boulton Paul four-gun turret, mounted in the fuselage just aft of the pilot. This, however, was found to erode performance so drastically that development of the project was abandoned.

Fortunately for both Bristol and the RAF, the feared shortage of Hercules engines did not materialise. On the contrary, production began to rise, and the more powerful Hercules VI, which had a rating of 1,670 hp (1245 kW) at 7,500 ft (2285 m), became available for installation in Beaufighters. Following tests of three aircraft provided with this powerplant, the Hercules VI or XVI was accepted as standard. Airframes so powered became designated Beaufighter VI, supplanting both Is and IIs on the production lines towards the end of 1941, and the first Mk VIs began to enter service with Coastal and Fighter Command squadrons at the beginning of 1942.

These more powerful engines were to make possible a far wider variation in equipment and weapons, expanding the variety of roles which this superb aircraft was able to undertake. Wing guns could be replaced by a 50-Imperial gallon (227-litre) tank (starboard) and a 24-Imperial gallon (109-litre) tank (port) to confer longer range; two 250-lb (113-kg) bombs could be carried beneath the wings; eight 90-lb (41-kg) rocket projectiles could be carried in place of wing guns; and following experiments carried out in May 1942, it was made possible for the Beaufighter to carry and launch an American- or British-made standard marine torpedo. An initial batch of 16 Beaufighter VICs were similarly converted to equip No. 254 Squadron, and the

Bristol Type 156 Beaufighter

Bristol Beaufighter TF.X of the Aviação Maritima (Portuguese naval air arm) in 1946

Bristol Beaufighter X reduced to Mk VI standard for service with the Aviación Militar Domenicana (Dominican air force) in 1948

resulting 'Torbeaus', as they were unofficially nick-named, carried out a first successful operation against enemy shipping in early April 1943. This combination of Beaufighter and torpedo was to represent a most formidable weapon in the air-sea war.

Beaufighter VIFs were the first of the type to serve in the Burma-India theatre, used initially by No. 176 Squadron in the defence of Calcutta. Beaufighters of this mark was also used by four squadrons of the USAAF's 1st Tactical Air Command during operations in the Mediterranean theatre. Beaufighter VICs which equipped Coastal Command were supplemented by an anti-shipping strike version designated TF. Mk X. These were powered by a modified version of the Hercules VI engine, designed to give peak output at low levels, and were also the first to standarise on AI Mk VIII radar mounted in a so-called 'thimble-nose', as this combination had been found to be particularly suitable for ASV use, as may be judged by the fact that Beaufighter TF. Mk Xs of Nos. 236 and 254 squadrons were to locate and destroy five German U-boats in the short space of 48 hours during March 1945. Other versions to serve with Coastal Command included 60 torpedo-carrying Mk VICs with Hercules XVI engines and eight underwing rockets in lieu of wing guns. These were designated Beaufighter VI (ITF), for Interim Torpedo Fighter, and were employed to swell the ranks pending delivery of the TF. Mk Xs. These 60 were, in fact, subsequently converted to Mk X configuration. Final British production version was the Beaufighter XIC for Coastal Command, this being generally similar to the Mk X but without the ability to carry a torpedo, and the 163 of this version brought total British construction to over 5,500 aircraft.

Of these more than 50 had been supplied to Australia during 1941-2, and this country was to build under licence during 1944-5 a total of 364 aircraft, generally similar to the TF. Mk X, under the designation Beaufighter Mk 21. It was the Australian Beaufighters which, blasting Japanese naval and merchant ships without pity, were to earn for this superb aeroplane the picturesque if grim name 'Whispering Death'. After the war, many of the RAF's Beaufighters were converted to serve as target tugs, under the designation Beaufighter TT. 10, and the last example was withdrawn from service in 1960.

Specification

Type: two-seat night/long-range/anti-shipping strike fighter

Powerplant (TF. Mk X): two 1,770-hp (1320-kW) Bristol Hercules XVIII radial piston engines

Performance: maximum speed 303 mph (488 km/h) at 1,300 ft (395 m); maximum cruising speed 249 mph (401 km/h) at 5,000 ft (1525 m); service ceiling 15,000 ft (4570 m); range 1,470 miles (2366 km)

Weights: empty 15,600 lb (7076 kg); maximum take-of 25,200 lb (11 431 kg)

Dimensions: span 57 ft 10 in (17.63 m); length 41 ft 8 in (12.70 m); height 15 ft 10 in (4.83 m); wing area 503 sq ft (46.73 m²)

Armament: four forward-firing 20-mm cannon, six forward-firing 0.303-in (7.7-mm) machine-guns, and one 0.303-in (7.7-mm) Vickers 'K' gun in dorsal position, plus one torpedo, and two 250-lb (113-kg) bombs or eight 90-lb (41-kg) rocket projectiles

Operators: Italy, RAAF, RAF, RCAF, RN, RNZAF, SAAF, USAAF

Bristol Type 163 Buckingham

Intended as a replacement for the Blenheim, the Bristol Buckingham was rendered superfluous as a bomber by the success of the Mosquito. Some were completed as bombers (illustrated), but later became transports.

History and notes

When design of a Bristol Blenheim replacement was begun, the Bristol team had no means of knowing that their new tactical day bomber, the Type 163 Buckingham, was to be rendered obsolete before it had even flown by the superlative performance of a private venture wooden bomber, the de Havilland Mosquito, which could carry the same 4,000-lb (1814-kg) bomb load at a speed 50 mph (80 km/h) faster with a crew of two instead of four, although admittedly for a lesser distance.

Bristol's earlier project to Specification B.2/41, itself replacing a previous Bristol Beaufighter bomber scheme, was revised as a result of official delays in finalising requirements, but was further delayed by teething troubles with the new Bristol Centaurus engines, and it was not until 4 February 1943 that the prototype Buckingham flew, without armament. The second, armed, prototype followed shortly afterwards and was followed by two more, all with Centaurus IV engines with high-altitude rating, although production aircraft were to have medium-altitude Centaurus VIIs or XIs.

Minor control modifications were made before the first production Buckingham flew on 12 February 1944, but changes were made to the tail surfaces after 10 had been completed to improve stability, particularly in single-engine performance.

Although outclassed by the Mosquito in European operations, it was felt that the Buckingham's superior range would prove a great asset against the Japanese. But by the time production aircraft were being delivered the end of the Far East war was in sight and the original order was cut from 400 to 119, plus the four prototypes.

With the end of their potential usefulness as bombers, it was decided to convert the Buckinghams to fast courier transports; the last batch of 65 on the line were completed as C.1s, and it was intended that the earlier B.1s would be retrospectively modified to the same standard. In this configuration (with extra tankage, seats for four passengers and a crew of three), the Buckingham had a range of 3,000 miles (4828 km) and was used on services to Malta and Egypt, although it was uneconomical with such a small passenger

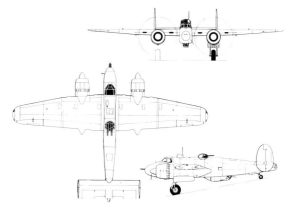

Bristol Buckingham B.1

capacity. Two were adapted to accommodate seven passengers, but the modification proved too expensive and was not taken further.

Although the 54 bomber versions were returned to Filton for conversion most were stored and eventually scrapped with very low hours, the last surviving Buckingham being used as a ground test rig until 1950.

Specification

Type: four-seat tactical day bomber/seven-seat courier transport
Powerplant (B.1): two 2,520-hp (1879-kW) Bristol Centaurus VII or XI radial piston engines
Performance: maximum speed 330 mph (531 km/h) at 12,000 ft (3660 m); cruising speed 285 mph (459 km/h); service ceiling 25,000 ft (7620 m); range 3,180 miles (5118 km)
Weights: empty 24,042 lb (10 905 kg); maximum take-off 38,050 lb (17 259 kg)
Dimensions: span 71 ft 10 in (21.89 m); length 46 ft 10 in (14.27 m); height 17 ft 6 in (5.33 m); wing area 708 sq ft (65.77 m²)
Armament: 10 0.303-in (7.7-mm) machine-guns (four each in fixed forward position and dorsal turret, and two in ventral cupola, plus up to 4,000 lb (1814 kg) of bombs
Operator: RAF

Bristol Type 164 Brigand

Designed as a torpedo-bomber in 1942, the Bristol Brigand was eventually used from 1946 as a light ground-attack bomber. The torpedo is visible under the fuselage of this aircraft, one of the four prototypes.

History and notes

Following the success of the Beaufighter as a torpedo-bomber the Air Ministry issued Specification H.7/42 for a Coastal Command Beaufighter replacement and Bristol submitted its Type 164, later to become the Brigand. Four prototypes were ordered in April 1943, the first flying on 4 December the following year, and production began using some jigs from the Buckingham.

The first 11 Brigand torpedo-bombers were delivered in 1946 to Nos. 36 and 42 Squadrons and the Air/Sea Weapons Development Unit, Coastal Command, but by this time the requirement for coastal strike aircraft had ceased and the Brigands eventually returned to Filton for conversion to fill a new RAF requirement: a light bomber for use in Burma and Malaya.

The Brigand B.1 had armour plating, a redesigned cockpit and a one-piece transparent canopy which could be jettisoned in emergency. Provision for the rear-firing gun was deleted, but the four 20-mm nose cannon remained in modified blast tubes.

Sixteen unarmed meteorological reconnaissance Brigands were delivered under the designation Met.3 to No. 1301 Flight in Ceylon, and by the time production ended in the spring of 1949 a total of 147 Brigands had been built, including the four prototypes. Two B.1s went to the Pakistan air force for evaluation in 1948; one crashed and the other returned, after major overhaul, to the RAF, where it received a new serial number, and another new B.1 was built as an RAF replacement for the crashed aircraft.

Nine new radar trainer versions designated T.4 were delivered to No. 228 Operational Conversion Unit at Leeming in 1950 and were used to train airborne interception (AI) radar operators for a year, the unit reforming at Colerne as No. 238 OCU in June 1952. In 1955 the Brigand T.5 made its appearance, differing in the AI installation, and this mark was a conversion from B.1s and T.4s.

The Brigand was phased out of service at No. 238 OCU, which had moved to North Luffenham, in March

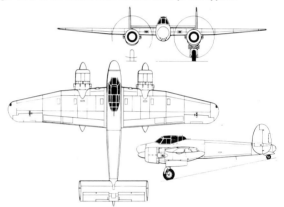

Bristol Brigand TF.1

1958 when the unit was disbanded; 600 radar navigators had been trained on the T.4s and 5s, and the Brigand was the RAF's last piston-engined attack aircraft, being replaced in this role by the English Electric Canberra.

Specification

Type: three-seat ground-attack bomber/radar trainer
Powerplant (B.1): two 2,470-hp (1842-kW) Bristol Centaurus 57 radial piston engines
Performance: maximum speed 358 mph (576 km/h) at 16,000 ft (4875 m); cruising speed 311 mph (501 km/h); service ceiling 26,000 ft (7925 m); range 2,800 miles (4506 km) with drop tanks
Weights: empty 25,598 lb (11 611 kg); maximum take-off 39,000 lb (17 690 kg)
Dimensions: span 72 ft 4 in (22.05 m); length 46 ft 5 in (14.15 m); height 17 ft 6 in (5.33 m); wing area 718 sq ft (66.70 m²)
Armament: four fixed 20-mm nose cannon, plus underwing racks for rockets or up to 2,000 lb (907 kg) of bombs
Operator: RAF

Bristol Type 166 Buckmaster

Derived from the Buckingham bomber, the Bristol Buckmaster was the RAF's most powerful advanced trainer of World War II, offering pupils easy access to the intricacies of high speeds and high wing loadings.

History and notes

Derived from the Model 163 Buckingham as an advanced trainer, the Bristol Type 166 Buckmaster had considerable commonality with its predecessor, and in fact the last 110 Buckinghams were converted to Buckmasters by installation of dual controls and other modifications to meet specification T.13/43.

The prototype flew from Filton on 27 October 1944, and a second followed later, both being conversions from partly completed Buckinghams.

One hundred and fifty additional sets of Buckingham components had already been manufactured when the contract was cut back and these were used for the Buckmasters, the first of 110 production aircraft being completed in 1945 and the last the following year.

Although several Buckmasters served with No. 8 Squadron at Aden on communications duties, most were delivered to Operational Conversion Units to train Brigand pilots, and the Buckmaster had the distinction of being one of the most powerful and fastest trainers to serve with the RAF when it was introduced. Blind flying instruction and instrument training could be undertaken, and the normal crew complement was pilot, instructor and air signaller.

The last Training Command Buckmasters served with No. 238 OCU at Colerne into the mid-1950s, while one or two were used on experimental work at Filton.

One of these, probably the last survivor, was relegated to RAF Halton where it served as an instructional airframe until broken up for scrap metal in 1958.

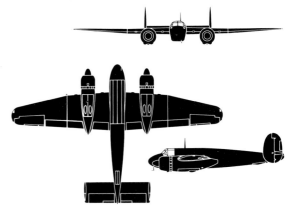

Bristol Buckmaster T.1

Specification

Type: three-seat advanced trainer

Powerplant: two 2,520-hp (1879-kW) Bristol Centaurus VII radial piston engines

Performance: maximum speed 352 mph (566 km/h) at 12,000 ft (3660 m); service ceiling 30,000 ft (9145 m); range 2,000 miles (3219 km)

Weights: empty 23,000 lb (10 433 kg); maximum take-off 33,700 lb (15 286 kg)

Dimensions: span 71 ft 10 in (21.89 m); length 46 ft 5 in (14.15 m); height 17 ft 6 in (5.33 m); wing area 708 sq ft (65.77 m²)

Armament: none

Operator: RAF

British Taylorcraft Auster Series

History and Notes

In 1936 the Taylorcraft Aviation Company was formed in the USA to design and manufacture lightplanes for private use. Most successful of the pre-war aircraft to emanate from this company were designated Models B, C, and D, and in November 1938 Taylorcraft Aeroplanes (England) Ltd was established at Thurmaston, Leicestershire, to build these aircraft under licence.

Six American-built Model As were imported into Britain, followed by one Model B, and these were typical of the aircraft to be built by the new company at Thurmaston. Of braced high-wing monoplane configuration, with a fabric-covered wing of composite wood and metal construction, the aircraft featured a fuselage and tail unit both of welded steel tube with fabric covering. Accommodation within the enclosed cabin was for two persons, seated side by side, and landing gear was of basic non-retractable tailwheel type, with main unit shock-absorption by rubber bungee. Powerplant of the imported Model As consisted of one 40-hp (30-kW) Continental A-40 flat-four engine, and the Model B differed by having a 50-hp (37-kW) A-50 engine from the same manufacturer.

The British-built equivalent to the Model A was designated originally Model C, but this was soon to become redesignated Plus C, reflecting the improved performance resulting from installation of a 55-hp (41-kW) Lycoming O-145-A2 engine. Including the prototype (G-AFNW), 23 Plus Cs were built. With a 90-hp (67-kW) Cirrus Minor 1 engine, the designation changed to Plus D, and nine civil aircraft were completed as such before the outbreak of World War II.

Of the 32 British-built aircraft mentioned above, 20 of the Plus Cs and four of the Plus Ds were impressed for service with the RAF. The Plus Cs, re-engined with the Cirrus Minor for RAF use, became redesignated Plus C.2. Most of these aircraft were used by No.651 Squadron for evaluation of their suitability for deployment in AOP and communications roles. This led to an initial order for 100 generally similar aircraft for military use under the designation Auster I.

Other than provision of split trailing-edge flaps to improve short-field performance, Austers were to change little throughout the war. During this time more than 1,600 were built for service use under the designations Auster I, III, IV and V, the Auster I entering service with No.654 Squadron in August 1942. Only two Auster IIs, with 130-hp (97-kW) Lycoming O-290 engines, were built because of a shortage of the American powerplant. This led to the Auster III, basically identical to the Auster I, but with a 130-hp (97-kW) Gipsy Major I engine. The 470 Auster IIIs were followed by 254 Auster IVs, which reverted to the Lycoming engine, and introduced a slightly larger cabin to provide space for a third seat. Major production version was the Auster V, of which approximately 800 were built, and this differed from the Auster IV by introducing blind-flying instrumentation.

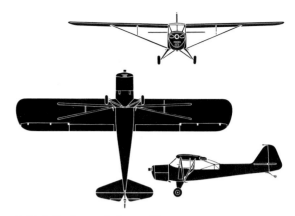

British Taylorcraft Auster V

At the height of their utilisation, Austers equipped Nos.652, 653, 657, 658, 659, 660, 661, 662, 664 and 665 Squadrons of the 2nd Tactical Air Force, and Nos.651, 654, 655, 656, 663, 666, 671, 672, and 673 Squadrons of the Desert Air Force. They were used also in small numbers by associated Canadian and Dutch squadrons. Their initial deployment in an operational role was during the invasion of Algeria, and they were to prove an indispensible tool in the Sicilian and Italian campaigns. Just three weeks after D-Day, these unarmed lightplanes were in the forefront of the action as the Allied armies advanced into France.

Specification

Type: light liaison/observation aircraft
Powerplant (Auster V): one 130-hp (97-kW) Lycoming O-290-3 flat-four piston engine
Performance: maximum speed 130 mph (209 km/h) at sea level; cruising speed 112 mph (180 km/h); normal range 250 miles (402 km)
Weights: empty 1,100 lb (499 kg); maximum take-off 1,850 lb (839 kg)
Dimensions: span 36 ft 0 in (10.97 m); length 22 ft 5 in (6.83 m); height 8 ft 0 in (2.44 m); wing area 167.0 sq ft (15.51 m²)
Armament: none
Operators: Netherlands Air Force, RAF, and RCAF

Unglamorous and unglamorised, artillery observation aircraft nevertheless played a decisive part in the war. The main British types were the five British Taylorcraft Auster marks, of which the Mk IV is shown.

de Havilland D.H.82 Tiger Moth

de Havilland D.H.82A Tiger Moth II of an RAF Elementary or Reserve Flying Training School

History and notes

The success of the de Havilland Moth as a civil trainer led, inevitably, to the development of a military version. Known as the D.H.60T Moth Trainer, this was supplied to a number of overseas air forces, including those of Brazil, China, Egypt, Iraq, and Sweden, though not to the Royal Air Force which was already using the D.H.60G Gipsy Moth for training and communications. Compared with the earlier civil machine, the D.H.60T was strengthened to allow it to operate at a higher all-up weight, and could carry four 20-lb (9-kg) practice bombs under the fuselage. It could also be fitted with a camera gun, or reconnaissance cameras, and was therefore suitable for various training roles.

To aid escape from the front cockpit in emergency, the rear flying wires were angled forward to the front wing root fitting, and the cockpit doors were deepened. The centre section struts still surrounded the front cockpit, however, and in the new trainer which was developed to Specification 15/31, these were moved forward to provide improved egress. To lessen the effect of centre of gravity changes caused by this staggering of the wings, the mainplanes were given 19 inches (0.48 m) of sweepback at the tips. The 120-hp (89-kW) Gipsy III inverted inline engine was installed, the sloping line of the engine cowling providing improved visibility from the cockpit.

Eight preproduction aircraft were built, still designated D.H.60T, but bearing the name Tiger Moth. These were followed by a machine with increased lower wing dihedral and sweepback and this, redesignated D.H.82, was first flown at Stag Lane on 26 October 1931. An order for 35 was placed to Specification T.23/31, and first deliveries were made to No. 3 Flying Training School at Grantham in November 1931. Others went to the Central Flying School in May 1932, and a team of five CFS pilots displayed their skill and the inverted flying capability of this new trainer at the 1932 Hendon display. Similar machines were supplied to the air forces of Brazil, Denmark, Persia, Portugal and Sweden and two, with twin floats supplied by Short Brothers, were built to specification T.6/33 for RAF evaluation at Rochester and Felixstowe.

De Havilland then developed an improved version,

de Havilland D.H.82 Tiger Moth

with a 130-hp (97-kW) Gipsy Major engine, and plywood rear fuselage decking in place of the fabric covering of the initial production aircraft. This was designated D.H.82A and named Tiger Moth II by the RAF, which ordered 50 to Specification T.26/33. They were fitted with hoods which could be positioned over the rear cockpit for instrument flying instruction, and were delivered to Kenley between November 1934 and January 1935. Others were supplied to the Bristol Aeroplane Company, the de Havilland School of Flying, Brooklands Aviation Ltd, Phillips and Powis School of Flying, Reid and Sigrist Ltd, Airwork Ltd and Scottish Aviation Ltd for the Elementary and Reserve Flying Schools which these companies operated under the RAF expansion scheme.

Prewar licence manufacture of the Tiger Moth included aircraft built in Norway, Portugal and Sweden, and by de Havilland Aircraft of Canada, whose prewar output included 227 D.H.82As. The company was later to build 1,520 of a winterised version, designated D.H.82C, which had a 145-hp (108-kW) Gipsy Major engine with a revised, easy-access cowling, sliding cockpit canopies, cockpit heating, Bendix wheel brakes, and a tailwheel in place of the standard skid. Skis or floats could also be fitted if required, and some were powered by a Menasco Pirate engine when Gipsy Majors were in short supply. A batch of 200 D.H.82Cs

de Havilland D.H.82 Tiger Moth

The de Havilland Tiger Moth was widely used by the RAF as an elementary trainer. It is here seen with its single pilot in the rear seat, to preserve the aircraft's centre of gravity.

was ordered by the US Army Air Force, with the designation PT-24, although they were diverted for use by the Royal Canadian Air Force.

The outbreak of war saw civil machines impressed for RAF communications and training duties, and larger orders were placed. A further 795 were built at Hatfield, before the factory was turned over to de Havilland Mosquito production, and the Tiger Moth line was re-established at the Cowley works of Morris Motors Ltd, where some 3,500 were to be manufactured. De Havilland Aircraft of New Zealand built a further 345, and in Australia de Havilland Aircraft Pty produced a total of 1,085.

On 17 September 1939, just two weeks after war had been declared, 'A' Flight of the British Expeditionary Force Communications Squadron (later No. 81 Squadron) was despatched to France. Throughout the winter and the following spring, the unit's Tiger Moths operated in northern France, providing valuable communications facilities until the Dunkirk evacuation, when surviving aircraft were flown back to Britain.

Preparations were also made for the Tiger Moth to be used in an offensive role, to combat the threatened German invasion. Racks designed to carry eight 20-lb (9-kg) bombs were fitted under the rear cockpit or, more suitably, beneath the wings. Although some 1,500 sets of racks were made and distributed to the flying schools, none were used operationally. Rather earlier, in December 1939, six coastal patrol squadrons were formed, five of them equipped with Tiger Moths. However futile this may seem, it was considered that despite an inability to attack, the sound of any engine might deter a U-boat commander from running on the surface or at periscope depth, and thus reduce his capacity to attack shipping.

In the Far East a small number of Tiger Moths were converted for use as ambulance aircraft with No. 224 Group Communications Squadron, the necessary modification being effected at Comilla, East Bengal in late 1944. The luggage locker lid was enlarged and a hinged lid cut into the rear fuselage decking, providing a compartment some 6 ft (1.83 m) long, which could accommodate one casualty. Flying in and out of small strips, they performed valuable service until replaced by Stinson Sentinels.

It was in a wartime trainer role, however, that the Tiger Moth made its greatest contribution. The type equipped no fewer than 28 Elementary Flying Training Schools in Britain, 25 in Canada (plus four Wireless Schools), 12 in Australia, four in Rhodesia (plus a Flying Instructors' School), seven in South Africa, and two in India.

Specification

Type: two-seat elementary trainer and communications aircraft

Powerplant (D.H.82A): one 130-hp (97-kW) de Havilland Gipsy Major inline piston engine

Performance: maximum speed 109 mph (175 km/h) at 1,000 ft (305 m); cruising speed 93 mph (150 km/h); service ceiling 13,600 ft (4145 m); range 302 miles (486 km)

Weights: empty 1,115 lb (506 kg); maximum take-off 1,770 lb (803 kg)

Dimensions: span 29 ft 4 in (8.94 m); length 23 ft 11 in (7.29 m); height 8 ft 9½ in (2.68 m); wing area 239 sq ft (22.20 m²)

Armament: none normally, but see text

Operators: Burma, Denmark, Indian Air Force, RAAF, RAF, RCAF, RN, RNZAF, SAAF

de Havilland D.H.89 Dominie

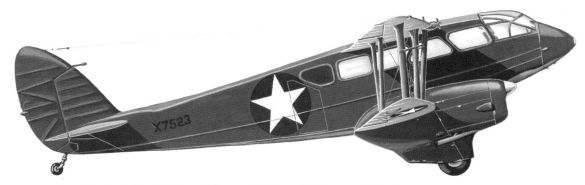

de Havilland D.H.89A Dominie II used by the US Army Air Force in the UK

History and notes

Designed in the light of experience gained in the production and operation of the de Havilland D.H.84 Dragon and D.H.86 Express light transports, the prototype D.H.89 Dragon Six, powered by two 200-hp (149-kW) de Havilland Gipsy Six engines, was flown at Stag Lane by Hubert Broad on 17 April 1934. Production aircraft, which were named Dragon Rapide, were delivered from July 1934, the first customers including Hillman's Airways Ltd, Railway Air Services and Olley Air Service Ltd. From March 1937 small trailing-edge flaps were fitted to the lower wings, outboard of the engine nacelles, and the type was redesignated D.H.89A.

A militarised version, designated D.H.89M, was developed to meet Air Ministry Specification G.18/35, which called for a general reconnaissance aircraft for service with Coastal Command. A forward-firing gun was fitted in the nose, to the right of the pilot's seat, and a gun mounting ring was installed in the roof, aft of the cabin door. Although the competition was won by the Avro 652A Anson, armed Rapides were supplied to the Spanish government in 1936, for operation in Morocco.

Although the D.H.89M did not gain a production contract, the Dragon Rapide was selected as a communications aircraft, a single example having been purchased for the use of the Air Council and operated by No. 24 Squadron at Hendon; two more were delivered in November 1938. Civil Rapides were used to supply British forces in France in the spring and early summer of 1940, and many were impressed for communications duties, particularly with the Air Transport Auxiliary.

In 1939, three D.H.89s had been acquired as wireless trainers, to Air Ministry Specification T.29/38, followed by a further 14 for use by No. 2 Electrical and Wireless School. The first two D.H.89As, also for No. 2 E & WS, were delivered in September 1939. The trainer version was identified by the direction-finding loop in the cabin roof, later being designated Dominie Mk I, the communications version becoming the Dominie Mk II.

Of 728 Rapides built before production ended in July

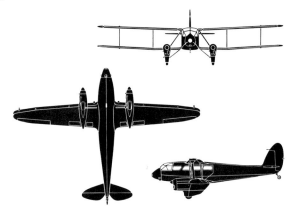

de Havilland D.H.89A Dragon Rapide

1946, 521 were to British military contracts, mostly as D.H.89Bs. Some 186 were built at Hatfield before pressure of work on other aircraft resulted in the transfer of production to Brush Coachworks Ltd at Loughborough, Leicestershire. The military D.H.89 figure includes 65 aircraft used by the Royal Navy, between 1940 and 1958, when the last was retired; some were impressed civil machines, some supplied new, and others transferred from the RAF.

Specification

Type: five/six-seat radio or navigation trainer, and eight/ten-seat communications aircraft
Powerplant: two 200-hp (149-kW) de Havilland Gipsy Queen inline piston engines
Performance: maximum speed 157 mph (253 km/h) at 1,000 ft (305 m); cruising speed 132 mph (212 km/h); service ceiling 16,700 ft (5090 m); range 570 miles (917 km)
Weights: empty 3,230 lb (1465 kg); maximum take-off 5,500 lb (2945 kg)
Dimensions: span 48 ft 0 in (14.63 m); length 34 ft 6 in (10.52 m); height 10 ft 3 in (3.12 m); wing area 340 sq ft (31.59 m²)
Armament: none
Operators: RAF, RN, USAAF

de Havilland D.H.91 Albatross

The de Havilland Albatross was built in limited numbers as a mailplane and airliner before World War II, and during the war the two prototype mailplanes were impressed for service with the RAF's No. 271 Squadron.

History and notes

Forty years after its first flight, there were still few aircraft which could match the de Havilland D.H.91 Albatross for sheer beauty of line, but the war effectively put a stop to its development.

Originating in Air Ministry Specification 36/35 for two transatlantic mailplanes, the prototype flew at Hatfield on 20 May 1937, a combination of a brand-new wooden aeroplane (foreshadowing this construction in the de Havilland Mosquito) and new engines (de Havilland Gipsy Twelves).

Modifications were made to the tail assembly and, following breakage of the second prototype's rear fuselage when landing during overload trials, the fuselage was strengthened.

Seven D.H.91s were built, the first two being used by Imperial Airways in long-range mail flight experiments while the other five were passenger versions which differed in details, and in having more windows.

When war broke out the seven aircraft operated from Bristol/Whitchurch to Lisbon and Shannon.

In September 1940 the two mailplanes were transferred to No. 271 Squadron operating between Prestwick and Reykjavik, but both were damaged beyond repair in landing accidents within 18 months.

Of the five passenger versions, one was destroyed in a forced landing in October 1940, two months later another was destroyed in an air raid, and in July 1943 a third crashed at Shannon. With the consequent lack of spares the two survivors were broken up in the autumn of 1944.

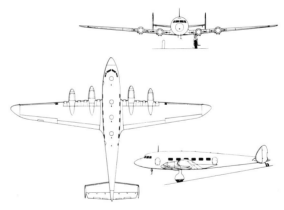

de Havilland D.H.91 Albatross

Specification

Type: 22-passenger commercial transport aircraft
Powerplant: four 525-hp (391-kW) de Havilland Gipsy Twelve inline piston engines
Performance: maximum speed 225 mph (362 km/h); cruising speed 210 mph (338 km/h); service ceiling 17,900 ft (5455 m); range 1,040 miles (1674 km)
Weights: empty 21,230 lb (9630 kg); maximum take-off 29,500 lb l(13 381 kg)
Dimensions: span 105 ft 0 in (32.00 m); length 71 ft 6 in (21.79 m); height 22 ft 3 in (6.78 m); wing area 1,078 sq ft (100.15 m²)
Armament: none
Operator: RAF

de Havilland D.H.95 Flamingo

The Flamingo was unusual for a prewar de Havilland aircraft in being of all-metal construction. Some 12 civil Flamingo airliners were built, plus three for the King's Flight. The civil models were impressed

History and notes

The ability to fly two new airliner prototypes of such completely different design within 19 months from the same factory was a remarkable achievement, the all-metal de Havilland D.H.95 Flamingo following the wooden Albatross on 23 December 1938. Like the Albatross, however, the Flamingo's promise was stifled by the war.

Its initial performance trials attracted the attention of military and civil customers alike, and the Air Ministry evaluated the prototype as a military transport in March 1939.

Proving flights from Heston and Eastleigh to the Channel Islands in May 1939 were carried out by Guernsey and Jersey Airways Ltd, but the outbreak of war put a stop to these operations and the two Flamingos ordered by the airline were delivered, along with the prototype, to No. 24 Squadron at Hendon for use as VIP transports.

Of the remaining 13 Flamingoes completed, 10 were built to civil standards and three went to the RAF. The first two of these were delivered to the King's Flight at Benson on 7 September 1940, to be joined by a third later, for possible emergency evacuation of the Royal family.

A contract for 30 aircraft to military specifications under the name Hertfordshire was placed, but cancelled after the first had been delivered and tested at Boscombe Down. The only visible difference in the single Hertfordshire was the substitution of portholes for windows.

Seven Flamingoes were operated by BOAC in the Near East on a number of routes radiating from Cairo and including Asmara, Aden, Addis Ababa, Adana, Jeddah and Lydda. Of these aircraft, two were lost in 1943 in separate crashes at Asmara, one crashed at Adana in 1942 and the other four were brought back to the UK, being scrapped at Redhill in 1950.

A single Flamingo, the 11th aircraft, was impressed

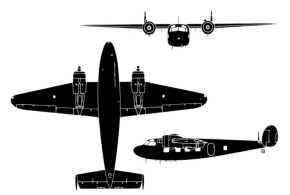

de Havilland D.H.95 Flamingo

by the Admiralty in 1940 and based with the Fleet Air Arm's No. 782 Squadron at Donibristle, whence it served the Orkneys, Shetlands and Northern Ireland. It was joined in 1945 by an ex-RAF Flamingo.

The former aircraft was the last survivor of the breed; after demobilisation in 1945 it flew for a while in its original civil marks but was eventually scrapped in May 1954 at Redhill.

Specification

Type: 17-passenger transport aircraft
Powerplant: two 930-hp (694-kW) Bristol Perseus XVI radial piston engines
Performance: maximum speed 243 mph (391 km/h); cruising speed 204 mph (328 km/h); service ceiling 20,900 ft (6370 m); range 1,345 miles (2165 km)
Weights: empty 11,325 lb (5137 kg); maximum take-off 18,000 lb (8165 kg)
Dimensions: span 70 ft 0 in (21.34 m); length 51 ft 7 in (15.72 m); height 15 ft 3 in (4.65 m); wing area 651 sq ft (60.48 m²)
Armament: none
Operators: RAF, RN

de Havilland D.H.98 Mosquito

de Havilland Mosquito B.IV Series 2 of No. 105 Squadron, RAF, Horsham St Faith and Marham (UK) in 1943

de Havilland Mosquito B.XVI of No. 571 Squadron, RAF, Oakington (UK) in 1944-5

History and notes

It was something of a salutary experience at a low-ebb period of World War II to find, within a very short space of time, the disappearance of all the ageing, 260 mph (418 km/h) Bristol Blenheim Is and IVs from one of the RAF's No. 2 Group OTUs, and their replacement by the de Havilland Mosquito. It seemed that at long last the days of 'muddling along' with obsolescent aeroplanes had come to an end, and that here was a new-generation aircraft which would enable the RAF to play an even more vital role in the defeat of the Axis powers.

That it had Rolls-Royce inline engines instead of Bristol radials, and was of wood instead of metal construction, was a trifle shattering, for the unit's airframe and engine mechanics and fitters were almost entirely of wartime vintage with no background of suitable experience. But they, like the aircrew who were to train on and fly these 'wooden wonders', were to rise quickly to the challenge of these very exciting aeroplanes, bringing to life a new standard of efficiency and a new spirit born of pride.

It was, indeed, an aeroplane to be proud of, planned as a private venture by the de Havilland company in the autumn of 1938, and intended for use as an unarmed bomber, or reconnaissance, aircraft that would fly so fast and high that defensive armament would be superfluous. The powerplant was to comprise two Rolls-Royce Merlins, and to save strategic materials all-wood construction had been chosen. Although

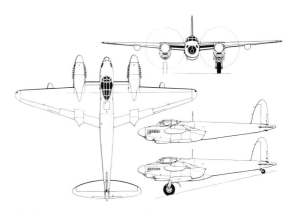

de Havilland Mosquito B.XVI (top side view: Mosquito B.IX)

this may not now, with the benefit of hindsight, seem a very advanced aircraft, it was certainly far too much for the Air Ministry of that day to swallow, and de Havilland's proposal was neatly filed in the 'pending' tray.

It was not until World War II had started that the cobwebs were dusted off de Havilland's proposal, and it was decided that in the event of the German U-boats hindering imports to the extent that light alloy came into short supply, an all-wood aircraft might be a useful ace up the sleeve. Even then, the committal to proceed was only to the extent of authorising detail design, so expenses were then still very much in the 'petty cash'

de Havilland D.H.98 Mosquito

A line-up of de Havilland Mosquito B.IV bombers of No. 139 Squadron. The nacelles, extending aft of the wing to improve streamlining, are worthy of note, as are the shrouded exhausts for nocturnal raids.

stage. De Havilland's design team began work at the end of December 1939, resulting in an order for 50 aircraft against Air Ministry Specification B.1/40 on 1 March 1940. Even then the way ahead was not clear, for in the post-Dunkirk frenzy of concentration to build up stocks of standard in-production aircraft, de Havilland's new bomber was temporarily postponed.

In due course the programme was re-instated, and eventually, on 25 November 1940, the prototype Mosquito, as the type had been named, flew for the first time, in the form of the Mk I. There was little doubt from factory testing that this new bomber was capable of development into an outstanding aircraft, comfortably exceeding the performance margins of the specification. When demonstrated to military and government officials shortly afterwards, these sceptical gentlemen were to discover that the new bomber had the manoeuvrability of a fighter, a dashing high speed that was not far short of 400 mph (644 km/h), and were staggered to see it performing smooth climbing rolls on the power of one engine, the propeller of the second engine 'feathered' to prevent windmilling and to cut drag to a minimum.

Official trials followed immediately, beginning on 19 February 1941 and leading to the initiation of priority production by July of that year. Three prototypes had been built, and the last of these to fly, on 10 June, 1941, was of a photo-reconnaissance version. The promised combination of high speed and high altitude had made the Mosquito a natural selection for such a role, and it

was the first of these exciting new aircraft to enter operational service. The initial sortie, a daylight reconnaissance over Brest, La Pallice and Bordeaux, was made on 20 September 1941, and immediately confirmed the concept of high speed and no armament as being correct, for during this initial deployment the lone Mosquito, a PR. Mk I, was able easily to outpace three Messerschmitt Bf 109s which attempted to intercept.

Next into service was the bomber version, the first being designated B.Mk IV. Deliveries to the RAF's No. 2 Group began in November 1941, the Mosquitoes going first to No. 105 Squadron, then based at Swanton Morley, Norfolk. The winter months were spent in familiarisation and working up, for the Mosquito was a very different aeroplane from the Blenheim which it had replaced. This pioneering squadron had not only to learn how to handle a very much faster and more manoeuvrable aircraft, but also how best to deploy it in attacks against the enemy. At that time there must have been some doubt among the crews that were to fly these aircraft of just how this 'plywood' bomber would withstand the enemy's defences.

These aircrew, like the men and women who were to maintain the aircraft on the ground, soon discovered that the Mosquito had an enormous capacity to absorb punishment and, furthermore, its structure was easy to repair. By no means did it consist only of plywood, but the strength and flexibility of this material was exploited to the full in its construction. The cantilever

de Havilland D.H.98 Mosquito

de Havilland Mosquito PR.IX of No. 105 Squadron, RAF, Marham (UK) in late 1943/early 1944

de Havilland Mosquito NF.II of No. 23 Squadron, RAF, in 1942

wing, mounted in a mid-position, was a one-piece assembly, with plywood used for the spar webs and all skins. Those of the upper surface were double thickness, with stringers bonded between them, and fabric covered the structure overall. Tail unit structure was similar, but the fuselage was entirely different. This consisted of a plywood-balsa-plywood sandwich, built up onto spruce formers, and was constructed in two halves which were completely equipped individually with their appropriate control, pipe and wiring runs before the two halves were united.

Retractable tailwheel type landing gear was unusual in that shock absorption dispensed with costly-to-build oleo-pneumatic struts, substituting rubber-in-compression springing. All versions had accommodation for a crew of two, seated side-by-side. The powerplant of the early examples were mainly 1,280-hp (954-kW) Rolls-Royce Merlin 21, or 1,390-hp (1037-kW) Merlin 23 engines, these driving three-blade constant-speed and fully-feathering propellers.

No. 2 Group began its operations against enemy targets on 31 May 1942, when four of No. 105 Squadron's Mosquitoes made a follow-up attack on Cologne during the aftermath of the '1,000-bomber' raid on the same target during the previous night. Not surprisingly, the air defences were very active, but caused no embarrassment to the Mosquitoes, which had little difficulty in avoiding the defending fighters. The second of No. 2 Group's squadrons, No. 139, was formed at Marham, Norfolk, in October 1942, and these

two squadrons were to cause a great deal of heartache for the Germans as they ranged far and wide. Even before that date, No. 105 Squadron had hit the headlines with a daring low-level attack on the Gestapo headquarters in Oslo.

The ability to make these high-speed precision attacks resulted from the long spell of working up which had taken place at Swanton Morley between November 1941 and May 1942. During this period many tactical approaches to the most effective deployment of the aircraft had been tried out, leading to the simultaneous use of two formations. One, attacking from about 2,000 ft (610 m), was adequate to keep the enemy sufficiently occupied for the second to streak in virtually unseen at low level. They were also to cause considerable annoyance to two of Germany's VIPs when, on 31 January 1943, No. 105 Squadron became the first Mosquito unit to attack Berlin, successfully accomplishing the task of scattering a parade which was to be addressed by Hermann Goering, head of the Luftwaffe. His oft-repeated boast that no enemy aircraft would fly unscathed over Berlin must then have been seen to be a lot of hot air. When, in the afternoon of the same day, No. 139 Squadron gave precisely the same treatment to a parade to be brain-washed by Dr Goebbels, it was probably true to say that No. 2 Group's activities were becoming extremely embarrassing. They were to get far worse before the end of May 1943, when all the group's Mosquitoes were switched from daylight to night operations.

de Havilland D.H.98 Mosquito

As noted above, the first of the three Mosquito prototypes was a bomber version, and the last intended for photo-reconnaissance. The second, first flown on 15 May 1941, was equipped as a night fighter, fitted at first with AI Mk IV radar and a nose armament of four 20-mm cannon and four 0.303-in (7.7-mm) machine-guns. Designated Mosquito NF. Mk II, the type began to enter service first with No. 157 Squadron, which made its first operational sortie on the night of 27/28 April 1942. NF. Mk IIs equipped No. 23 Squadron shortly afterwards, and this was the first unit to operate the type in the Mediterranean theatre when based at Luqa, Malta, from December 1942. These were deployed not only as night fighters, but also in a day or night intruder role, making the first night intruder sortie on 30/31 December 1942. The missing gap in the versions detailed so far is the T.Mk III, a dual-control trainer used for conversion to the type, of which 343 were constructed.

The success story of the Mosquito is too extensive to receive other than very superficial coverage in a book of this nature, but a list of versions and variants will give some appreciation of the very extensive role which this aircraft played throughout the remainder of World War II, enhancing very much the RAF's contribution to victory. The four basic aircraft already mentioned are not included in this list.

B.Mk V: Prototype only, a development of the B.Mk IV with underwing hardpoints to carry two 50-Imperial gallon (227-litre) underwing tanks, or two 500-lb (227-kg) bombs; it was used as the basis of the Canadian-built B.Mk VII (see below).

B.Mk IX: Developed high-altitude version of the B.Mk IV, powered by two 1,680-hp (1253-kW) Rolls-Royce Merlin 72 engines with two-speed two-stage superchargers. The mark had the so-called 'Standard Wing', introduced on the B.Mk V prototype, so that this version had a maximum bomb-load of 3,000 lb (1361 kg) with the addition of the underwing bombs. Alternatively, the bomb bay and underwing hardpoints could all be used to carry extra fuel. All were converted in 1944 to carry one 4,000-lb (1814-kg) 'block-buster' bomb, this requiring the provision of a special 'bulged' bomb bay.

B.Mk XVI: A development of the B.Mk IX, with Merlin 72 or 76 (starboard) and Merlin 73 or 77 (port) engines, the latter driving a supercharger to pressurise the cabin. All were converted in 1944 to accommodate a 4,000-lb (1814-kg) bomb internally, and could carry also two wing-mounted 50-Imperial gallon (227-litre) drop tanks or, alternatively, four 500-lb (227-kg) bombs internally plus two 100-Imperial gallon (454-litre) drop tanks. This was the definitive British-built production version, of which some 1,200 were built.

B.Mk 35: Development of the B.Mk XVI with Merlin 113/114 engines, 122 built by Airspeed, last one in the summer of 1946. Served with Nos. 109 and 139 Squadrons after the war until replaced by Canberras in 1952-3.

FB.Mk VI: Developed from the Mk II fighter prototype, retaining its armament, and powered by Merlin 21, 23 or 1,620-hp (1208-kW) Merlin 25 engines. It was provided with the Standard Wing, and could carry up to 2,000 lb (907 kg) of bombs in internal bomb bay; provision was made in 1944 to carry four rocket projectiles on launchers beneath each wing. The version was extensively built by de Havilland (1,218), Airspeed (300) and Standard Motors (1,200). Many rocket-equipped FB.Mk VIs were used by RAF Coastal Command.

FB.Mk XVIII: Development of the FB.Mk VI, with Merlin 25 engines, of which 25 were built for Coastal Command. The fuselage was modified to accept the 57-mm Molins anti-tank gun in lieu of the four 20-mm cannon, and extensive armour protection was provided for crew and engines. The Standard Wing could carry two 500-lb (227-kg) bombs, or eight rocket projectiles, or two 50-Imperial gallon (227-litre), or two 100-Imperial gallon (454-litre) drop tanks. The mark was used primarily for attacks on enemy U-boats and shipping.

NF.Mk XII: A conversion of 97 NF.Mk IIs, with Merlin 21 or 23 engines, four nose-mounted 20-mm cannon, and the new AI Mk VIII centimetric radar. The four nose-mounted 0.303-in (7.7-mm) guns were deleted.

NF.Mk XIII: New-production (270 built) counterpart of NF.Mk XII, with increased wing fuel tankage.

NF.Mk XV: Special high-altitude version of which only five were procured to combat Junkers Ju 86P high-altitude reconnaissance aircraft. They were converted from B.Mk IV bombers, and provided with extended wingtips, AI Mk VIII radar, and armament supplemented by an underfuselage pack of four 0.303-in (7.7-mm) machine-guns. Weight-saving was effected by reduced fuel tankage and armour.

NF.Mk XVII: 100 converted from NF.Mk XIIIs, and equipped with AI Mk X or American SCR720 radar.

NF.Mk XIX: Developed NF.Mk XIIIs with Merlin 25 engines, increased gross weight, and able to accept AI Mk VIII, AI Mk X or SCR 720 radar.

NF.Mk 30: A high-altitude version of the NF.Mk XIX, with 1,290-hp (962-kW) Merlin 72 or 1,250-hp (932-kW) Merlin 76 engines, AI Mk X, and early ECM-type equipment.

NF.Mk 36: Postwar development of the NF.Mk 30, primary change being the installation of 1,710-hp (1275-kW) Merlin 113/114 engines.

NF.Mk 38: Final fighter version built in Britain, a modification of the NF.Mk 36 with AI Mk IX radar.

PR.Mk IV: 32 converted from B.Mk IVs, with provision for up to four cameras in place of bomb load.

PR.Mk VIII: Five new-construction photographic reconnaissance aircraft, generally similar to the B.Mk IV, but powered by 1,290-hp (962-kW) Merlin 61 supercharged engines for high-altitude sorties.

PR.Mk IX: Photographic reconnaissance variant of B.Mk IX (90 built).

de Havilland D.H.98 Mosquito

de Havilland Mosquito B.IV Series 2 of No. 105 Squadron, RAF, Marham (UK) in late 1942/early 1943

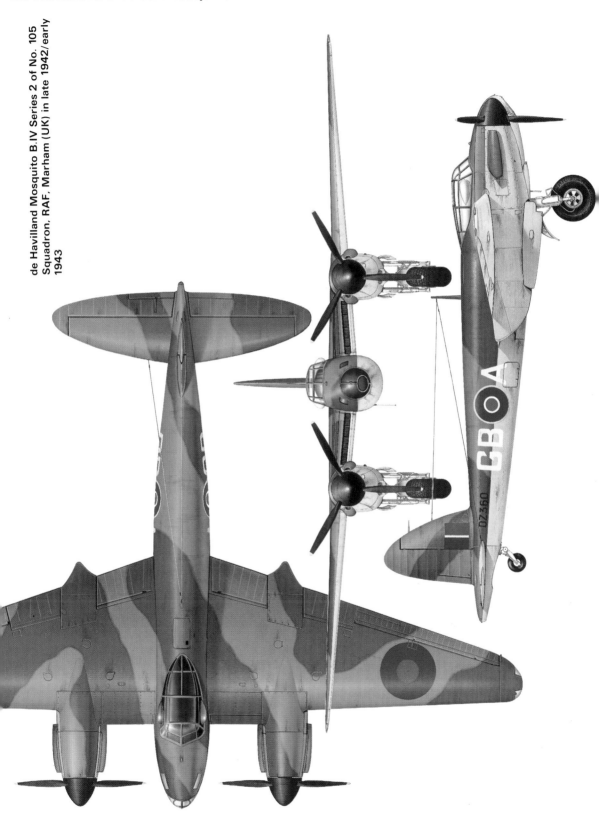

Clean lines, low structure weight and high power all contributed to the operational success of the de Havilland Mosquito, here seen in the form of B.IVs of No. 139 Squadron, which operated Mosquitoes from June 1942 until June 1953.

de Havilland D.H.98 Mosquito

The de Havilland Mosquito had beautifully clean lines, as exemplified by this night-fighter example of No. 23 Squadron seen just over the coast of Malta. The Mosquito was also remarkably versatile.

PR.Mk XVI: Photographic reconnaissance variant of B.Mk XVI, and first pressurised PR version; introduced small astrodome on starboard upper surface of cockpit canopy (432 built).

PR.Mk 32: Five converted from PR.Mk XVIs and provided with extended wingtips and Merlin 113 engines; used for high-altitude reconnaissance sorties.

PR.Mk 34: Very long-range reconnaissance version which had been intended for use in South-East Asia: it carried two 200-Imperial gallon (909-litre) drop tanks beneath each wing which, together with additional tanks in the 'bulged' bomb bay, could provide range of up to 3,500 miles (5633 km). The powerplant comprised Merlin 76 or 113 engines. It was the main photographic reconnaissance type to serve in RAF after the war.

In addition to Mosquitoes built in Britain, it had been planned in July 1941 that the type would also be built by the de Havilland plant in Canada. Nine months later, negotiations were completed for their construction by the de Havilland offshoot in Australia. Details of the variants built in those countries are as follows:

Australia:

FB.Mk 40: First Australian-built version, generally similar to British FB.Mk VI, but powered by 1,418-hp (1057-kW) Packard Merlin 31 engines. The first example made its maiden flight on 23 July 1943 (178 built).

T.Mk 43: Two-seat trainer version of above, also with Packard Merlin engines.

Canada:

B.Mk VII: Canadian-built version of the B.Mk V prototype, powered by two 1,418-hp (1057-kW) Packard Merlin 31 engines (25 built).

B.Mk XX: As above, but with US or Canadian equipment. A total of 145 was built, of which 40 were converted for photo-reconnaissance duties with the USAAF under the designation F-8.

B.Mk 25: Successor to the B.Mk XX, powered by 1,620-hp (1208-kW) Packard Merlin 225 engines (400 built).

FB.Mk 21: As British FB.Mk VI, but with Packard Merlin 31/33 engines (3 built).

FB.Mk 26: Development of the British FB.Mk VI, but with Packard Merlin 225 engines (338 built).

T.Mk 22: Dual-control trainer, similar to FB.Mk 21 (few built).

T.Mk 27: Development of the T.Mk 22 with Packard Merlin 225 engines.

Many examples of the Mosquito continued to provide valuable service in the RAF in the immediate postwar years. Photographic reconnaissance Mosquitoes saw considerable service in the Middle and Far East, and No. 81 Squadron in Malaya was the last unit to use the Mosquito operationally, in late 1955. The bomber versions were displaced by English Electric Canberras in 1952-3, some then being used in a training role, with others converted for photo-reconnaissance or target tug duties. Some in this latter role remained in service until 1961.

When the production lines around the world came to a halt 7,781 examples of the Mosquito had been built.

Specification

Type: two-seat bomber, fighter-bomber, night fighter and photographic reconnaissance aircraft

Powerplant (FB.Mk VI): two 1,620-hp (1208-kW) Rolls-Royce Merlin 25 inline piston engines

Performance: maximum speed 362 mph (583 km/h) at 5,500 ft (1675 m); maximum cruising speed 325 mph (523 km/h) at 15,000 ft (4570 m); service ceiling 33,000 ft (10 060 m); range with internal bomb load 1,650 miles (2655 km)

Weights: empty 14,300 lb (6486 kg); maximum take-off 22,300 lb (10 115 kg)

Dimensions: span 54 ft 2 in (16.51 m); length 40 ft 10¾ in (12.47 m); height 15 ft 3 in (4.65 m); wing area 454 sq ft (42.18 m²)

Armament: four 20-mm cannon and four 0.303-in (7.7-mm) machine-guns in nose, plus 2,000 lb (907 kg) of bombs, or 1,000 lb (454 kg) of bombs and eight rocket projectiles

Operators: RAAF, RAF, RCAF, RNZAF, SAAF, USAAF

de Havilland D.H. 103 Hornet

The beautiful lines of the de Havilland Hornet reveal the aircraft to be a blend of the basic design of the Mosquito with a slimmer fuselage. Armament was the standard four 20-mm cannon plus rockets or bombs.

History and notes

The ultimate in twin piston-engined fighter design, the de Havilland Hornet started life as the D.H.103 private venture design for a long-range fighter to combat Japanese aircraft in the Pacific. Using new, low-frontal Merlin engines in very sleek nacelles, the design was eventually approved by the Ministry of Aircraft Production and Specification F.12/43 was written round it.

The prototype Hornet flew on 28 July 1944 and a second prototype followed with provision for two 200-Imperial gallon (909-litre) drop tanks and pylons for 1,000 lb (454 kg) of bombs beneath the wings.

A first batch of 60 was ordered, initial deliveries to the RAF beginning in 1945, but the first squadron deliveries were to No. 64 Squadron at Horsham St Faith in March 1946, replacing North American P-51 Mustangs. No. 19 Squadron at Church Fenton followed and other squadrons to use the Hornet included Nos. 41 and 65 in the UK and Nos. 33, 45 and 80 in the Far East.

The first 60 Hornets were F.1s, while the next 132 were F.3s, which featured a dorsal fin fillet and an increase in internal tankage from 360 to 540 Imperial gallons (1637 to 2455 litres). The last batch of 12 Hornets for the RAF, bringing the total to 204, were FR.4s, a fighter-reconnaissance version with an F.52 vertical camera.

The Royal Navy maintained a weather eye on the Hornet as a possibility for carrier use in the Far East, and in 1946 three F.1s were converted by the Heston Aircraft Company. These were given folding wings, an arrester hook, catapult pick-up points and naval radar mountings. Long-stroke landing gear units were fitted. The first of these aircraft was flown on 19 April 1945 and the third, when flown, carried out deck landing trials aboard HMS *Ocean*.

Results were satisfactory, and a production order was placed against specification N.5/44. A total of 77 single-seat Sea Hornet F.Mk 20s was built, plus 78 of a

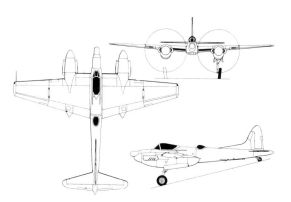

de Havilland Sea Hornet NF.21

two-seat night fighter version designated NF.Mk 21, all production and delivery of these aircraft being made after the end of World War II.

Specification

Type: single-seat long-range fighter/fighter-bomber
Powerplant (F.3): two 2,030-hp (1514-kW) Rolls-Royce Merlin 133/134 inline piston engines
Performance: maximum speed 472 mph (760 km/h) at 22,000 ft (6705 m); service ceiling 37,500 ft (11 430 m); range 1,500 miles (2414 km) with two 100-Imperial gallon (455-litre) drop tanks
Weights: empty 12,880 lb (5842 kg); maximum take-off 20,900 lb (9480 kg)
Dimensions: span 45 ft 0 in (13.72 m); length 36 ft 8 in (11.18 m); height 14 ft 2 in (4.32 m); wing area 361 sq ft (33.54 m²)
Armament: four 20-mm cannon in nose, plus underwing racks for eight 60-lb (27-kg) rockets or up to 2,000 lb (907 kg) of bombs
Operators: RAF, RN

Fairey Fox

History and notes

Inspired by the 450-hp (336-kW) Curtiss D-12 12-cylinder engine used in the USA's Curtiss CR-3 Navy Racer in the 1923 Schneider Trophy contest, Richard Fairey raised the money to buy a D-12 engine and the right to manufacture it in Britain, together with its Curtiss-Reed metal propeller, high efficiency airfoil sections, and wing-surface radiators. The engine manufacturing licence was not taken up but about 50 D-12s were imported for development and installation in Fairey Foxes.

Flown on 3 January 1925 from Hendon, the Fox prototype was promising; although a number of inadequacies had to be cured, the aircraft's top speed of 158 mph (254 km/h) was around 40 mph (64 km/h) faster than the current Fairey Fawn day bomber, but the fact that it had an American engine caused some problems in getting British military orders. However, an initial contract for 18 to Specification 21/25 was placed, the aircraft going to No. 12 Squadron at Andover in December 1925, replacing Fawns. Later another nine Foxes were ordered, and eventually, as the Rolls-Royce F.XIIA engine (later named Kestrel) became available, the Foxes were retrospectively re-engined and given the designation Fox IA. The first of these flew on 29 August 1927 with the first Rolls-Royce F.XI engine, while the first fully developed F.XIIA engine flew in a Fox in December 1928.

A further development, the Fox IIM, flew at Northolt on 25 October 1929; this was of metal construction with fabric covering, and powered by a Rolls-Royce F.XIB (later Kestrel IB) of 480 hp (358 kW). This was offered to the RAF, but the Hawker Hart had already been ordered to fill the day bomber role. Consequently, the Fox IIM was offered for sale abroad and accepted by Belgium. Twelve were ordered in January 1931, the first three aircraft being delivered to Brussels/Evère airfield on 10 January 1932.

A new factory was built at Gosselies, near Charleroi, for the company's Belgian associate, Avions Fairey. This had been established to build the Fairey Fox under licence, and the first Belgian-assembled Fox flew on 21 April 1933. The company's official records

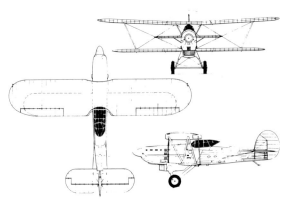

Fairey Fox VII

show 177 Fox derivatives as being produced up to 1939, these comprising 11 different versions with such engines as the Kestrel IIS, Kestrel V and Hispano-Suiza 12Y, plus one Serval-engined example completed as a dual-control trainer. The Mks IIIC and VIC had enclosed cockpits, and a single-seat fighter developed from the Mk VI was the Mk VII Mono-Fox, known unofficially as the Kangourou because of its large pouch-like ventral radiator.

The most significant of the Belgian-built Foxes was the Mk VI, powered by an 860-hp (641-kW) Hispano-Suiza engine, and with a cockpit canopy and landing gear fairings, all of which helped to raise maximum speed to over 220 mph (354 km/h), giving a take-off run of only 180 ft (55 m) and an ability to reach 20,000 ft (6100 m) in only 8½ minutes. The Belgian air force received 94 Foxes, these being armed with two forward-firing machine-guns, one on each side of the fuselage, and it was these aircraft that were deployed against the invading German forces from 10 May 1940. During the 18 days of Belgium's courageous but futile defence of its territory, the obsolete Foxes were continually in action.

Some further Foxes were built in Britain, including six floatplanes for Peru, but the exact numbers are not known. The few Foxes acquired by the RAF remained in service until replaced by Hawker Harts in 1931.

Specification

Type: two-seat day bomber
Powerplant (Mk I): one 480-hp (358-kW) Curtiss D-12 inline piston engine
Performance: maximum speed 156 mph (251 km/h) at sea level; service ceiling 17,000 ft (5180 m); range 650 miles (1046 km)
Weights: empty 2,609 lb (1183 kg); maximum take-off 4,117 lb (1867 kg)
Dimensions: span 38 ft 0 in (11.58 m); length 31 ft 2 in (9.50 m); height 10 ft 8 in (3.25 m); wing area 324 sq ft (30.10 m²)
Armament: one machine-gun firing forward and one gun in rear cockpit, plus up to 460 lb (209 kg) of bombs
Operators: Belgian Air Force, Peru, RAF

The Fairey Fox was built in a bewildering number of variants in the UK and in Belgium between 1925 and the mid-1930s. Seen here is a Fox VI reconnaissance fighter, of which some 85 were built in Belgium.

Fairey Seafox

History and notes

One of the less glamorous but necessary tasks performed by Fleet Air Arm aircraft was the fleet spotting and reconnaissance undertaken by aircraft catapulted from capital ships.

Specification S.11/32 for such an aircraft attracted a tender from Fairey for a biplane floatplane with a crew of two. The design was unusual in that the pilot sat in an open cockpit while the observer/gunner was in an enclosed rear cockpit, an arrangement designed to facilitate catapult launches and the subsequent recovery of the aircraft from the sea by crane. Construction was mixed, the fuselage being a metal monocoque, while the wings were fabric-covered. Fairey's bid was accepted, and a contract for 49 aircraft to be named Seafox was awarded in January 1936, with a follow-on contract for a further 15 in September the same year.

As originally designed the Seafox was to have had a 500-hp (373-kW) Bristol Aquila radial engine, but for some obscure reason the Napier Rapier 16-cylinder 'H' air-cooled engine of only 395 hp (295 kW) was chosen, and the Seafox was consequently underpowered throughout its life. The first prototype flew at Hamble on 27 May 1936, while the second, with wheel landing gear, followed on 5 November 1936. The latter was later converted to floatplane configuration.

Production Seafoxes began to come off the line in 1937, the first flying on 23 April. Meanwhile the prototypes were being tested at the Marine Aircraft Experimental Establishment at Felixstowe, and at the Royal Aircraft Establishment at Farnborough. Felixstowe's report, not issued until the aircraft had been in service for some months, commented favourably on the handling aspects but was critical of the engine cooling and high landing speed: about 58 mph (93 km/h) instead of the 46 mph (74 km/h) which had been specified. On take-off at high weights the lack of power was particularly noticeable, and the Seafox showed a marked reluctance to get up 'on the step', particularly in calm water.

Catapult tests at the RAE with one of the prototypes in March 1937 were followed by trials on board HMS *Neptune* off Gibraltar, and as production aircraft became available, they were formed into catapult flights. Those equipped with Seafoxes were Nos. 702, 713, 714, 716 and 718, and in January 1940 these flights were pooled to form No. 700 Squadron. The type also served with Nos. 753 and 754 Squadrons in the training role. At the outbreak of World War II, Seafoxes equipped a number of cruisers, sharing this task with Walrus amphibians and Swordfish floatplanes, and it was not long before they were in action against the German pocket battleship *Admiral Graf Spee* during the action in the River Plate in December 1939. Pursued by the British cruisers HMS *Achilles*, *Ajax* and *Exeter,* the battleship had severely damaged the British ships and the two Walrus amphibians aboard *Exeter* had been put out of action. One of the two Seafoxes from HMS *Ajax* was catapulted and spotted

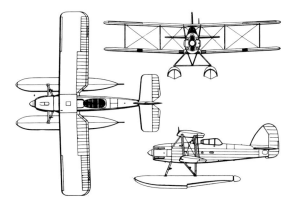

Fairey Seafox

Fairey Seafox floatplane prototype, built to meet the requirements of Specification 11/32. The aircraft was eventually relegated to instructional status, with the serial number 1463M.

for the guns—the first such occasion in World War II, and winning for its pilot, Lt E.D.G. Lewin, the DSC, the first Fleet Air Arm decoration of the war.

Seafox production had ended in 1938, but the type continued in front-line service until about 1942, when it was replaced on ships' catapults by the Vought-Sikorsky Kingfisher. Even then, a few Seafoxes lingered on in the training role until July 1943.

Specification

Type: two-seat spotter reconnaissance seaplane
Powerplant: one 395-hp (295-kW) Napier Rapier VI inline piston engine
Performance: maximum speed 124 mph (200 km/h) at 5,860 ft (1785 m); cruising speed 106 mph (171 km/h); service ceiling 11,000 ft (3350 m); range 440 miles (708 km)
Weights: empty 3,805 lb (1726 kg); maximum take-off 5,420 lb (2458 kg)
Dimensions: span 40 ft 0 in (12.19 m); length 35 ft 5½ in (10.81 m); height 12 ft 1 in (3.68 m); wing area 434 sq ft (40.32 m²)
Armament: one rear-firing 0.303-in (7.7-mm) machine-gun
Operator: RN

Fairey Gordon

History and notes

When the time came to replace the ubiquitous Fairey IIIF, it was decided that the best replacement was in fact another IIIF, and the prototype Gordon was a conversion from a IIIF Mk IVM fitted with an Armstrong Siddeley Panther IIA radial engine of 525 hp (391 kW) in place of the IIIF's 570-hp (425-kW) Napier Lion. While this may sound an odd decision, the lower-powered Gordon was some 400 lb (181 kg) lighter when loaded and had a superior performance, particularly at take-off. Other changes were made in electrical, fuel and oil systems and in the mounting of the forward-firing machine-gun.

Ordered to Specification 18/30 for a two-seat day bomber and general-purpose aircraft, the Gordon first flew on 3 March 1931 and 178 were built for the RAF before production ended in 1934.

First RAF production deliveries were in April 1931 to No. 40 Squadron at Upper Heyford, while the first overseas squadron to be equipped was No. 6 in the Middle East, a former Bristol Fighter unit. Aircraft from Nos. 35 and 207 Squadrons formed part of the RAF reinforcement of the Middle East during the Abyssinian crisis of 1935.

Gordons were still serving with first-line squadrons at home and overseas in 1938 while others were in service on target towing duties at the outbreak of World War II. The last surviving example was probably K2743 which was reported to be still on charge as late as September 1941.

Contemporary with the Gordon was the Fleet Air Arm's Fairey Seal which was, to all intents and purposes, a naval version operated on wheels or floats.

Specification

Type: two-seat day bomber/general-purpose aircraft
Powerplant: one 525-hp (391-kW) Armstrong Siddeley Panther IIA radial piston engine
Performance: maximum speed 145 mph (233 km/h) at 3,000 ft (915 m); cruising speed 110 mph (177 km/h); service ceiling 22,000 ft (6705 m); range 600 miles (966 km)
Weights: empty 3,500 lb (1588 kg); maximum take-off 5,906 lb (2679 kg)
Dimensions: span 45 ft 9 in (13.94 m); length 36 ft 9 in (11.20 m); height 14 ft 2 in (4.32 m); wing area 438 sq ft (40.69 m²)
Armament: one forward-firing 0.303-in (7.7-mm) machine-gun and one aft-firing 0.303-in (7.7-mm) gun
Operators: Brazil, China, RAF

Fairey Swordfish

History and notes

Having arrived at a stage of World War II when a biplane, other than the odd small-span Avro Tutor or de Havilland Tiger Moth, was a very rare sight indeed, the appearance of a large and noisy biplane in the circuit created more than average interest. By some curious means it was treated with the dignity and precedent accorded to a sailing ship at sea, swinging into finals ahead of the Gloster Meteors and de Havilland Mosquitoes then operating on the unit. It was a breath of air from a far earlier and more gracious age, catching the eye of innumerable men and women around the airfield who would have given you nothing for a squadron of Spitfires, and yet who watched its every move as it taxied slowly towards the watch office.

Despite appearances, this beautifully ugly aeroplane was no anachronism, for the Fairey Swordfish, as it was named, had then still a vital role to play in World War II, a role for which it was so well engineered that it fought in the battle against the Axis from the very first moment of that conflict until victory for the Allies in Europe had been assured. In so doing, the Swordfish outlived and outfought aircraft which had been designed to replace it in service, and during this period created a record of machine achievement in association with human courage that makes pages of the Fleet Air Arm's history a veritable saga.

Approaching obsolescence in 1939, the Swordfish had originated from Fairey's private-venture T.S.R.I biplane of 1933. When this was destroyed in an

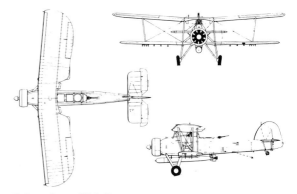

Fairey Swordfish II

accident during September of that year, its progress had been sufficiently worthwhile to warrant further development. When, therefore, the Air Ministry issued its Specification S.15/33 which called for a carrier-based torpedo-spotter-reconnaissance aircraft, Fairey submitted its layout for the improved T.S.R.II on which the design office had been working. This was to become the prototype of the Swordfish (K 4190), first flown on 17 April 1934.

It differed from the T.S.R.I. by having a changed upper wing, slightly swept, to compensate for a fuselage which had been lengthened to improve the stability problems that had led to the loss of the T.S.R.I. Other changes brought the inclusion of an additional wing bay, and modification of the tail unit. Subjected to intensive testing, both in landplane and

Fairey Swordfish

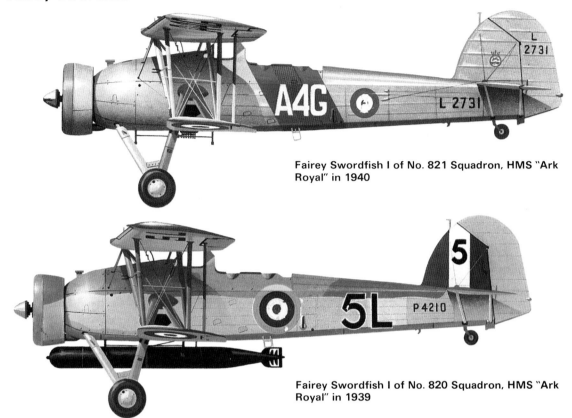

Fairey Swordfish I of No. 821 Squadron, HMS "Ark Royal" in 1940

Fairey Swordfish I of No. 820 Squadron, HMS "Ark Royal" in 1939

alternative floatplane form, the type was ordered into production in April 1935 with a first contract for 86 aircraft, to be named Swordfish.

The initial Swordfish Mk I, built to Air Ministry Specification S.38/34, was powered by a 690-hp (515-kW) Bristol Pegasus IIIM radial engine, driving a three-blade fixed-pitch metal propeller. The two-bay biplane wings were of all-metal construction, fabric covered, with ailerons on both upper and lower wings, the biplane configuration and its structural integrity maintained by robust interplane struts, flying and landing wires. For shipboard stowage the wings could be folded about rear spar hinges.

The tail unit was entirely conventional, with a strut-braced tailplane, and fin and rudder of metal construction with fabric covering. The fuselage, with two open cockpits to accommodate the pilot forward, and crew of one or two aft, was also of metal construction, but covered by a combination of light alloy panels forward and fabric aft. Landing gear was of the fixed tailwheel type, with the individual main units each having an oleo shock-absorber. These were easily exchanged for an alternative float landing gear, consisting of two single-step light alloy floats, each provided with a small rudder to simplify directional control on the surface of the water.

Armament comprised one synchronised forward-firing 0.303-in (7.7-mm) Vickers machine-gun, one Vickers 'K' gun or Lewis gun in the aft cockpit, and

mountings to carry one 18-in (0.46-m) 1,610-lb (730-kg) torpedo beneath the fuselage. Alternative weapon loads of the Mk I included one 1,500-lb (680-kg) mine, or two 500-lb (227-kg) bombs beneath the fuselage plus two 250-lb (113-kg) bombs on underwing racks, or one 500-lb (227-kg) bomb beneath the fuselage and one 500-lb (227-kg) bomb beneath each wing.

Swordfish Is began to enter service with the FAA in July 1936, equipping first No. 825 Squadron as a replacement for the Fairey Seals which had first been allocated to squadrons some three years earlier. Next to go, before the end of 1936, were the Blackburn Baffins which had seen but little service with Nos. 811 and 812 Squadrons before their replacement, and also the Seals of No. 823 Squadron. When, in 1938, the Blackburn Sharks of Nos. 810, 820 and 821 Squadrons were superseded (although they had seen even less service than the Seals), the FAA's torpedo-bomber squadrons had become equipped exclusively by the Swordfish.

At the beginning of World War II the FAA had 13 squadrons operational with the Swordfish, 12 of these squadrons at sea aboard the carriers HMS *Ark Royal*, *Courageous*, *Eagle*, *Furious* and *Glorious*, but the 'phoney' start to the war meant that these aircraft had virtually no fighting until the beginning of the Norwegian campaign in 1940. This, of course, was beneficial rather than detrimental to the Swordfish cause, giving all squadrons ample time in which to work up to a state

Fairey Swordfish

Looking decidedly war-weary, a Fairey Swordfish patrols over water infested with U-boats. Note the rear two crew members scanning the sea below to the left and right of their open, and therefore draughty, cockpit.

of perfection. It was to prove of immense value when on 11 April torpedo-carrying Swordfish went into action for the first time from the carrier *Furious*. Two days later a catapulted Swordfish from HMS *Warspite* sank submarine *U-64*, the first U-boat sinking of the war to be credited to the FAA.

Fairey's production commitments were such that the growing contracts for Swordfish were becoming a little embarrassing, so continued construction was left in the capable hands of Blackburn Aircraft at Brough, Yorkshire, a company which had been concerned primarily with the design and manufacture of naval aircraft from its earliest days. Only a single example was built by Blackburn in 1940, but in the following year 415 were produced.

Before 1940 had ended, however, Swordfish had become involved in a different type of operation, under the guidance of RAF's Coastal Command. This involved them in mine-laying operations and bombing attacks on the German-occupied Channel ports, carrying a crew of two and with auxiliary fuel tanks mounted in the rear cockpit. These tanks were essential to provide the necessary range, but could hardly be described as ideal additions to the gunner/observer's cockpit in a shooting war.

Also in 1940 came the supreme triumph of the Swordfish, the memorable attack on the Italian fleet at anchor in Taranto harbour, made after reconnaissance

sorties had shown that six battleships, plus attendant cruisers and destroyers, were sheltering there. The attack, made by 21 Swordfish on the night of 11 November 1940, was launched in two waves, with an hour interval between them. All of the aircraft had long-range tanks in the rear cockpit, limiting crew to two in each aircraft, and of the total four carried flares for target illumination, six had bombs, and 11 were armed with torpedoes. The first flares were dropped at 23.00, the aircraft of the initial wave going in through a protective umbrella of barrage balloons, a task so difficult that there was little time to consider the intense barrage of light and heavy fire being thrown at them. In spite of the conditions targets were being hit left and right, and only one Swordfish was lost. The second wave also lost one of its number, but was also able to launch a concerted attack. Although initial debriefing suggested the entire operation to be a success, it needed reconnaissance confirmation to clarify the picture. When it came, the following day, it was realised that the Italian navy had been dealt a shattering blow: three battleships were damaged severely, two of them under water; a cruiser and two destroyers had been hit; and two auxiliary vessels had been sunk.

In the short space of one hour the balance of naval power in the Mediterranean had been irrevocably changed, confirming the belief of prophets such as the

Fairey Swordfish

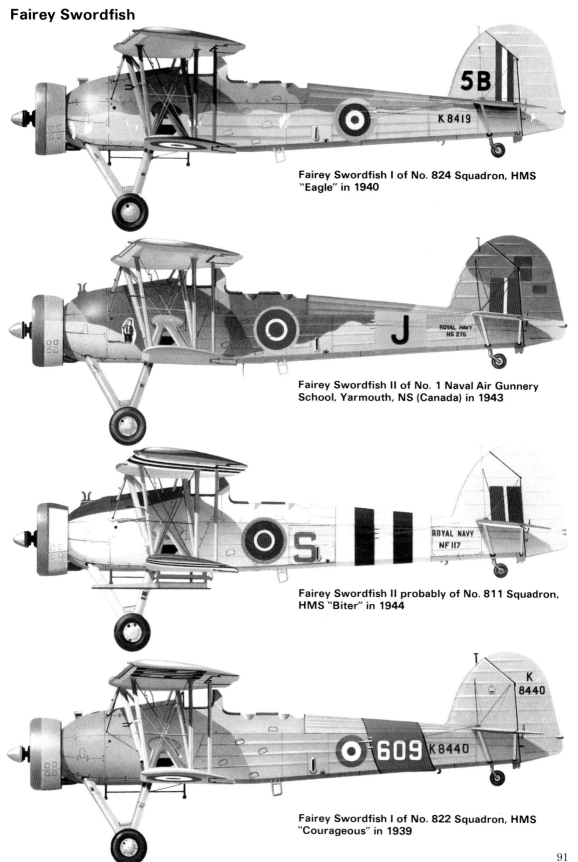

Fairey Swordfish I of No. 824 Squadron, HMS "Eagle" in 1940

Fairey Swordfish II of No. 1 Naval Air Gunnery School, Yarmouth, NS (Canada) in 1943

Fairey Swordfish II probably of No. 811 Squadron, HMS "Biter" in 1944

Fairey Swordfish I of No. 822 Squadron, HMS "Courageous" in 1939

Fairey Swordfish

One of the truly classic aircraft of World War II, the Fairey Swordfish in 1939 seemed obsolete but continued in service as an effective and versatile weapon. Illustrated is a rocket-armed Swordfish II

USA's 'Billy' Mitchell, by demonstrating the potential of a force of 'obsolescent' aeroplanes to eliminate a naval fleet without any assistance from surface vessels. Those involved in this victorious achievement had come from Nos. 813, 815, 819 and 824 Squadrons, all embarked on HMS *Illustrious* for this operation.

The last of the great torpedo attacks made by these aircraft came in 1942, when a futile attempt was made to prevent the German battle-cruisers *Gneisenau* and *Scharnhorst*, accompanied by the heavy cruiser *Prinz Eugen*, from making good their escape eastwards through the English Channel. Almost as a last resort, six Swordfish of No. 825 Squadron, led by Lieutenant Commander Esmonde, were detailed to make a torpedo attack, but as they approached the battleships with their escorting destroyers and umbrella of fighters overhead, it was clear to the crews that their task was hopeless. Despite such odds, however, Esmonde led his men into the attack. Immediately they were met by a concentrated hail of anti-aircraft fire, and attacked from all angles by the defending fighters. Not a single Swordfish survived, and it was a miracle that five of the 18 crew members were rescued. All were subsequently decorated and the gallant leader, Esmonde, was posthumously awarded the Victoria Cross, the first to be given to a member of the FAA.

This experience gave confirmation, if any were needed, of the fact that it was no longer a practical proposition to deploy the Swordfish on torpedo attacks. Such operations called for a long, accurate approach if the weapon was to be successfully launched; but such an approach also provided the enemy with an excellent opportunity of destroying its attacker. This led to the redeployment of the Swordfish in an anti-submarine warfare (ASW) role, using as its weapons against these underwater vessels conventional depth charges and, for on-surface attack, the newly-developed rocket projectiles.

This led to development of the Swordfish Mk II, which entered service in 1943, and differed from the earlier version by having the lower wing strengthened and metal skinned so that it could carry and launch rocket projectiles. Early production Mk IIs retained the Pegasus IIIM engine, but later examples had the more powerful Pegasus XXX. The Swordfish Mk II was followed in the same year by what was to prove the final production version, the Swordfish Mk III, which mounted a radome carrying a scanner for its ASV (Air-to-Surface Vessel) Mk X radar between the landing gear main units; in other respects it was generally similar to the Mk II. There were, in addition to the three main production versions, a few examples converted from Mk IIs and provided with an enclosed cabin for operation in the much colder Canadian waters, these aircraft having the designation Swordfish Mk IV.

Fairey Swordfish

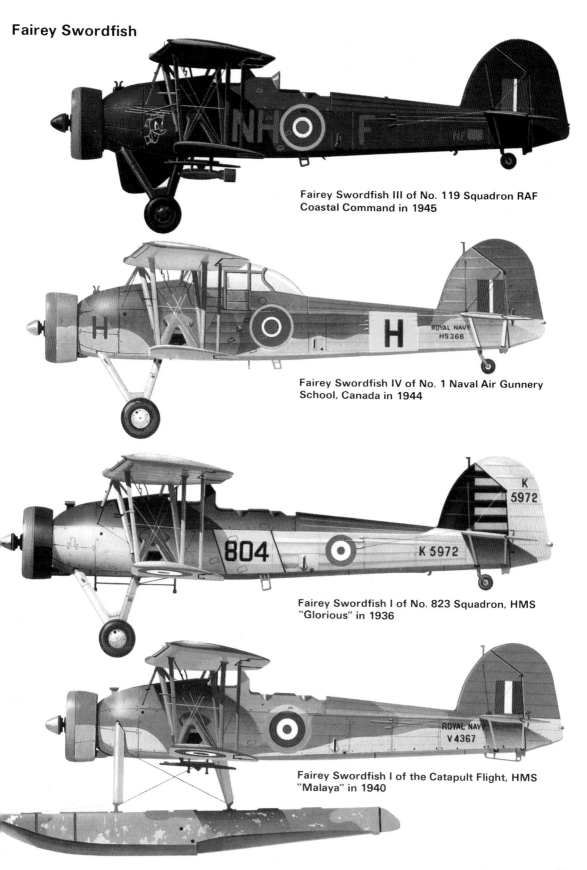

Fairey Swordfish III of No. 119 Squadron RAF
Coastal Command in 1945

Fairey Swordfish IV of No. 1 Naval Air Gunnery
School, Canada in 1944

Fairey Swordfish I of No. 823 Squadron, HMS
"Glorious" in 1936

Fairey Swordfish I of the Catapult Flight, HMS
"Malaya" in 1940

Fairey Swordfish

The Fairey Swordfish was a highly versatile aircraft, and seen here is the launch of a Swordfish I on floats. The apparatus under the fuselage is the rack for the aircraft's torpedo armament.

These changes were to bring new life to the old warrior which, at the peak of its deployment, equipped no fewer than 26 squadrons. Even at the beginning of 1945 no less than nine first-line squadrons were still operating their Swordfish successfully. The advent of the rocket projectile into the armoury of the Fleet Air Arm had been the responsibility of the Swordfish, which carried out suitability trials before the weapon was accepted as standard. With rockets and mines, these aircraft were to achieve unbelievable success in ASW operations, a highlight coming in September 1944 when Swordfish aboard the escort carrier HMS *Vindex*, then employed in escorting a convoy to north Russia, sank four U-boats in a single voyage.

Production ended in 1944, after Fairey had built 692 and Blackburn 1,699, for a grand total of 2,391. On 21 May 1945 No. 836 Squadron, the last first-line Swordfish squadron, was officially disbanded. Even then the Royal Navy was reluctant to lose such a doughty warrior, and odd examples were to remain in use for several years.

In a remarkable career this valiant biplane had achieved a record that will remain indelibly endorsed in the history of air warfare, and especially that of the FAA. In five years of hard-fought war it had served as a torpedo-bomber for the British fleet, as a shore-based minelayer, for convoy protection from escort carriers, as a night-flying flare-dropper, as a rocket-armed anti-shipping and ASW aircraft, as well as for training and general utility duties.

General utility was undoubtedly the task of the Swordfish which began this entry, for after visiting the watch office, a neatly attired naval officer unstrapped his bicycle from the torpedo hitches beneath the fuselage, and cycled off towards the main gate!

Specification
Type: two/three-seat torpedo-bomber/reconnaissance biplane
Powerplant (Mk II): one 750-hp (559-kW) Bristol Pegasus XXX radial piston engine
Performance (torpedo-bomber): maximum speed (landplane) 138 mph (222 km/h), (seaplane) 128 mph (206 km/h) at 5,000 ft (1525 m); cruising speed (landplane) 120 mph (193 km/h); service ceiling (landplane) 10,700 ft (3260 m); maximum range (landplane) 1,030 miles (1658 km)
Weights: empty (landplane) 4,700 lb (2132 kg), (seaplane) 5,300 lb (2404 kg); maximum take-off (landplane) 7,510 lb (3406 kg), (seaplane) 8,110 lb (3679 kg)
Dimensions: span 45 ft 6 in (13.87 m); length (landplane) 35 ft 8 in (10.87 m), (seaplane) 40 ft 6 in (12.34 in); height (landplane) 12 ft 4 in (3.76 m), (seaplane) 14 ft 7 in (4.44 m); wing area 607 sq ft (56.39 m²)
Armament: one forward-firing synchronised 0.303-in (7.7-mm) machine-gun in forward fuselage and one 0.303-in (7.7-mm) Lewis gun on Fairey high-speed mounting in aft cockpit, plus a torpedo of 1,610 lb (730 kg), or depth charges, mines or bombs up to 1,500 lb (680 kg), or up to eight rocket projectiles on underwing racks
Operators: RAF, RCAF, RN

Fairey Swordfish

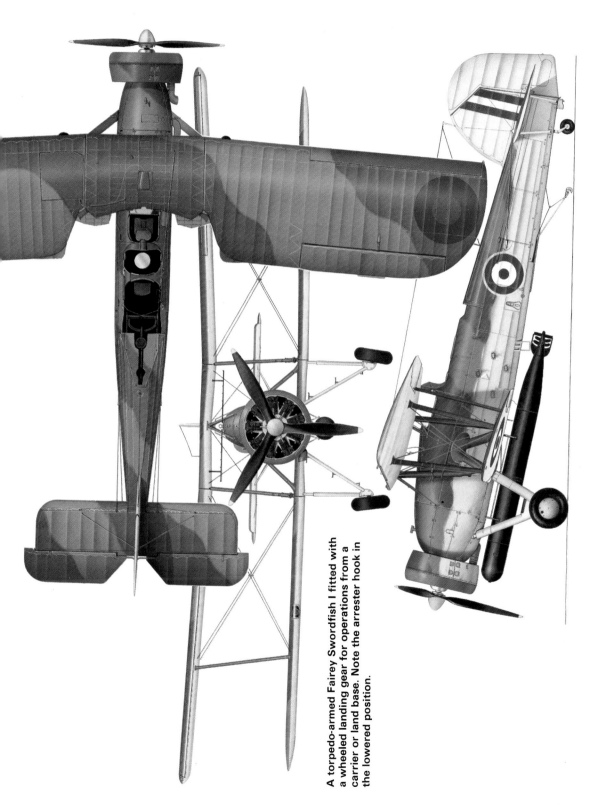

A torpedo-armed Fairey Swordfish I fitted with a wheeled landing gear for operations from a carrier or land base. Note the arrester hook in the lowered position.

Fairey Battle

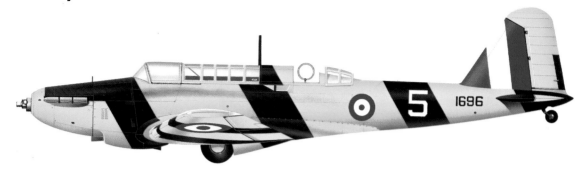

Fairey Battle T of No. 8 Service Training Flying School, Moncton (Canada) in mid-1943

History and notes

When the Fairey Battle prototype flew on 10 March 1936, it represented a significant step-up in performance over the Hawker Hart which it was designed to replace. However, when World War II began only three years later the type was already obsolete and the RAF was to learn, like the Luftwaffe with the Junkers Ju 87 Stuka, that it could only operate safely where air supremacy had been achieved.

Designed by Marcel Lobelle, the prototype Fairey Day Bomber, as it was then known, originated as the company's submission to Specification P.27/32 for a two-seat single-engined monoplane bomber capable of carrying 1,000 lb (454 kg) of bombs for 1,000 miles (1609 km) at 200 mph (322 km/h). This performance was to be bettered by Fairey's aircraft, which was competing against design proposals from Armstrong Whitworth, Bristol and Hawker, but only the first's A.W.29 joined Fairey's prototype in receiving orders. Fairey's contender won the competition, but a first production contract for 155 aircraft, to the revised Specification P.23/35, had been placed in 1935 even before the prototype had flown. The Battle had accommodation for a crew of three comprising pilot, bomb-aimer/observer, and radio operator/gunner. The first production aircraft was built, like the prototype, at Hayes and flew from the Great West Aerodrome (now part of Heathrow Airport), on 14 April 1937; it was used for performance trials during which it achieved 243 mph (391 km/h) at 16,200 ft (4940 m); the range of 1,050 miles (1690 m) was flown with maximum bomb load.

Despite its shortcomings as a first-line aircraft, the Fairey Battle I was admirably suited for use as an engine test-bed, here for the 1,280-hp (955-kW) Rolls-Royce Merlin XII with its chin radiator.

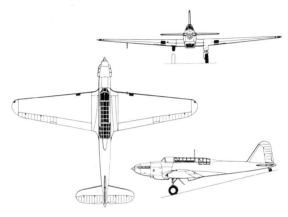

Fairey Battle

The second and subsequent production aircraft came from a production line established at a new purpose-built factory at Heaton Chapel, Stockport, and it was for the Battle that Rolls-Royce received its launching order for the famous 1,030-hp (768-kW) Merlin I engine, which powered the first 136 Fairey-built aircraft.

The aircraft's light alloy and stressed skin construction was a 'first' for Fairey, and the Battle proved to be extremely robust. In general it proved popular with the test pilots at the Aircraft and Armament Experimental Establishment at Martlesham Heath, and at the Royal Aircraft Establishment at Farnborough: it was said to be very easy to fly but the elevator was heavy on take-off; on the other hand the Royal Aircraft Establishment considered the elevator over-light at low speeds. Engine-off stall was described as 'innocuous', but the accommodation came in for some criticism: although the pilot's cockpit was considered to be roomy and comfortable with reasonable forward vision, it could sometimes become extremely hot. The rear gunner, behind the pilot, had his own problems: the screen intended to protect him from the slipstream was badly designed and it shape deflected a downdraught into his face, while the rear vision was described as 'poor'.

By the end of 1937, 85 Battles had been built by Fairey, and the first squadron to receive the new bomber in May 1937 was No. 63 at Upwood, Hunting-

Fairey Battle

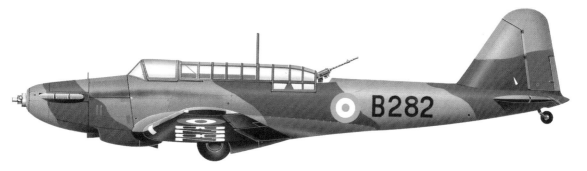

Fairey Battle I of 33 Mira Vomvardismou (33rd Bomber Squadron), Royal Hellenic Air Force, in October 1940

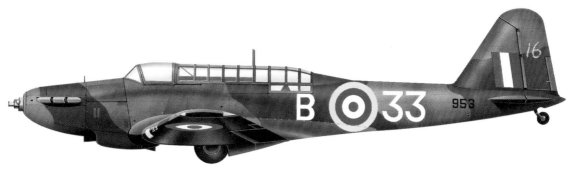

Fairey Battle I of No. 15 Squadron, SAAF, Algato (East Africa) in July 1941

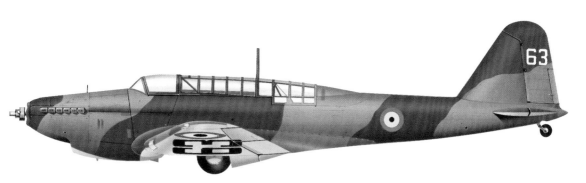

Fairey Battle I of 5e Escadrille, Groupe III, 3e Regiment of the Belgian Aéronautique Militaire, Evère-Bruxelles in May 1940

Fairey Battle I of No 106 Squadron, RAF, Abingdon (UK) in August 1938

Fairey Battle

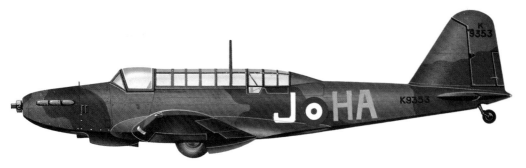

Fairey Battle of No. 218 Squadron, RAF, northern France in May 1940

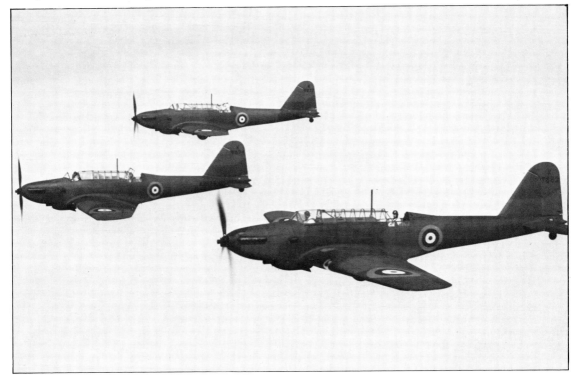

The Fairey Battle light bomber was a considerable improvement on the Hawker Harts and Hinds it superseded in the mid-1930s, but by 1939 was totally obsolete in terms of performance and armament.

donshire, where it replaced the Hawker Audax. Other squadrons which re-equipped that year were Nos. 52, 88, 105 and 226.

As new orders for Battles were placed, production sub-contracts were awarded to Austin Motors at Longbridge, Birmingham. Meantime, the last 19 Battles of the initial Fairey order for 155 were provided with Merlin II engines, and these were fitted also to the Austin-built aircraft. The first Battle from the Longbridge factory flew in July 1938, and 29 had been completed there by the end of the year. By March the following year Austin was producing more than 30 Battles a month, but even then the programme was running late. After 60 Austin-built Battles had been completed, the Merlin II engine was introduced on the production line.

By the outbreak of World War II more than 1,000 Battles had been delivered, and aircraft of No. 226 Squadron were the first to be sent to France as part of the Advanced Air Striking Force. It was here that the Battle's inability to defend itself against enemy fighters became obvious. On armed daylight reconnaissance missions the type occasionally tangled with Bf 109s, and although one of the latter was destroyed by a Battle's rear gunner in September 1940, the light bombers invariably suffered heavy casualties.

As the period of the so-called 'phoney war' came to an end, the Battle squadrons were thrown in on 10 May 1940 to try to stop the advancing German ground forces. Without fighter escort, and attacking from a height of only 250 ft (76 m) with delayed-action bombs the Battles came under heavy ground fire, losing 13 of

Fairey Battle

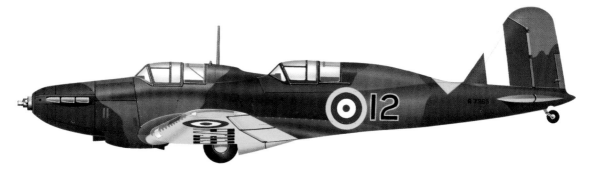

Fairey Battle T of RAF in September 1941

Fairey Battle T of No. 3 Bombing and Gunnery School, MacDonald (Canada) in 1943

the 32 aircraft sent on the mission, while all the others were damaged. The next day seven out of eight were lost, and on 12 May five Battles of No. 12 Squadron, flown by volunteer crews, attacked two vital road bridges over the Albert Canal. In the face of extremely heavy ground fire the attack was pressed home and one bridge seriously damaged, but at a cost of all five aircraft. The first RAF Victoria Crosses of World War II were awarded posthumously to Flying Officer D.E. Garland and his observer, Sergeant T. Gray, who led the formation.

Further heavy losses came on 14 May, when 35 out of 63 Battles failed to return from attacks against bridges and troop concentrations. These losses marked the end of the Battle's career as a day bomber, and although a few remained in front-line service until late 1940 the survivors were mostly diverted to other duties. The most important of these was for training, and 100 were built as dual-control trainers with separate cockpits, while 266 target-towing variants were also supplied.

The last production aircraft, Austin-built, was a target tug, and it was delivered on 2 September 1940. It brought total Battle production to 2,185 including the prototype, 1,156 being built by Fairey and 1,029 by Austin Motors.

Canada used a large number of Battles for training and target towing in the Commonwealth Air Training Plan, the first being supplied to the Royal Canadian Air Force at Camp Borden in August 1939. They were the vanguard of 739 of these aircraft, this total including seven airframes for instructional purposes. The Royal

Australian Air Force received four British-built Battles and assembled 360 in Australia, including 30 target tugs, while other export customers were Belgium (16), Turkey (29), South Africa (several) and Eire, where an RAF aircraft which landed at Waterford in 1941 was interned and later taken over by the Air Corps.

A number of Battles were used as test-beds for such engines as the Napier Dagger and Sabre; Bristol Hercules and Taurus; Rolls-Royce 'X' and Merlin XII; and Fairey Prince. Other Battles were used for experiments with various types of propellers.

Specification

Type: three-seat light bomber
Powerplant (Mk I): one 1,030-hp (768-kW) Rolls-Royce Merlin I inline piston engine
Performance: maximum speed 257 mph (414 km/h) at 20,000 ft (6100 m); cruising speed 210 mph (338 km/h); service ceiling 25,000 ft (7620 m); range 1,000 miles (1609 km) at 16,000 ft (4875 m) at 200 mph (322 km/h)
Weights: empty 6,647 lb (3015 kg); maximum take-off 10,792 lb (4895 kg)
Dimensions: span 54 ft 0 in (16.46 m); length 42 ft 4 in (12.90 m); height 15 ft 6 in (4.72 m); wing area 422 sq ft (39.20 m²)
Armament: one 0.303-in (7.7-mm) machine-gun in starboard wing and one Vickers 'K' gun in rear cockpit, plus bomb load of 1,000 lb (454 kg)
Operators: Belgian Air Force, Eire, Greek Air Force RAAF, RAF, RCAF, SAAF, Turkey

Fairey Albacore

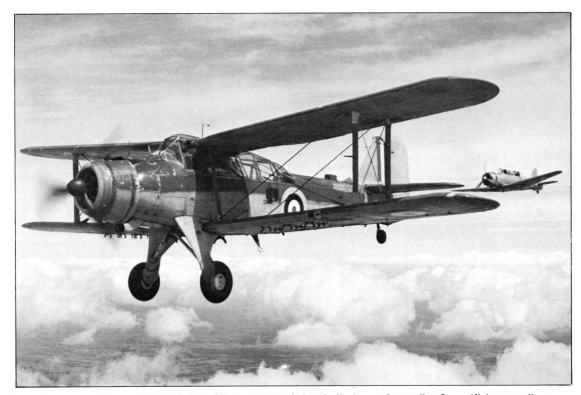

Escorted by a Blackburn Roc, a Fairey Albacore reveals its similarity to the earlier Swordfish, as well as its sturdier and cleaner lines. The Albacore's operational life spanned the years from 1940 to 1944 only.

History and notes

As a replacement for the antiquated Fairey Swordfish, the Fairey Albacore appeared to have everything going for it. Neat in appearance, and with an enclosed cabin providing such luxuries as heating, a windscreen wiper and automatic emergency dinghy ejection, the Albacore nevertheless failed to come up to expectations. Far from supplanting the Swordfish, it merely complemented the older biplane and, ironically, was outlived by the latter in service.

Designed to Specification S.41/36, the Albacore was ordered off the drawing board in May 1937, the Air Ministry placing a contract for two prototypes and 98 production aircraft. The first prototype flew on 12 December 1938 from Fairey's Great West Aerodrome (now part of London's Heathrow Airport), and production began in 1939. The prototype was tested on floats at Hamble in 1940, but the results did not justify further development along these lines.

Later in the same year the first production aircraft underwent tests at the Aircraft and Armament Experimental Establishment at Martlesham Heath, and it was this source that first reported all was not well with the Albacore. Elevators and ailerons were said to be very heavy, the stall with slots free was 'uncomfortable', the front cockpit was too hot in normal summer weather, and the rear cockpit was cold and draughty. There were a few things on the credit side, however: the Albacore was steady in a dive, with a smooth

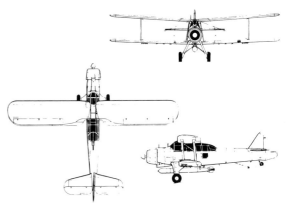

Fairey Albacore

recovery when carrying a torpedo, and the pilot's view was excellent. Despite this rather unpromising background, Albacores began to roll off the production line after a hold-up caused by engine development problems: the 1,065-hp (794-kW) Bristol Taurus II installed in early aircraft was replaced by the Taurus XII of 1,130 hp (843 kW).

No. 826 Squadron was formed at Ford, Sussex, specially to fly the Albacore, and received 12 aircraft on 15 March 1940. The squadron went into action on 31 May, attacking E-boats off Zeebrugge and road and rail targets at Westende, Belgium. The squadron

Fairey Albacore

Designed to replace the Swordfish, the Fairey Albacore had improvements such as additional power, flaps and enclosed accommodation. In the event, however, the Albacore was outlasted by its evergreen predecessor.

moved to Bircham Newton, Norfolk the following month, operating under the direction of Coastal Command until November, making night attacks, laying mines and bombing shipping. Three more Albacore squadrons formed before the end of 1940: No. 829 at Lee-on-Solent, No. 828 at Ford and No. 827 at Yeovilton, the last moving to Stornoway for anti-submarine patrols.

Albacores finally went to sea when Nos. 826 and 829 Squadrons joined HMS *Formidable* on 26 November 1940, for convoy escort duty to Cape Town. Aircraft from these squadrons took part in the Battle of Cape Matapan in March 1941, pressing home their torpedo attacks in the true Swordfish tradition against the Italian battleship *Vittorio Veneto*, the first occasion on which they had used torpedoes in action.

By mid-1942 some 15 Fleet Air Arm squadrons were equipped with Albacores, operating from the Arctic Circle on Russian convoys, to the Western Desert, the Mediterranean and the Indian Ocean, and in November of that year Albacores of Nos. 817, 820, 822 and 832 Squadrons were in action during the Allied invasion of North Africa, flying anti-submarine patrols and bombing enemy coastal guns. Albacores had reached their zenith in 1942, and the next year Fairey Barracudas began to replace them in all squadrons except No. 832, which was to be equipped with Grumman Avengers. The last two squadrons to give up their Albacores were Nos. 820 and 841 in November 1943, aircraft from

the latter squadron being passed to No. 415 Squadron, Royal Canadian Air Force, at Manston for use in English Channel operations on D-Day.

Total Albacore production between 1939 and 1943 amounted to 800 including two prototypes, all built at Fairey's Hayes factory and test-flown at what became Heathrow Airport.

Specification

Type: three-seat torpedo bomber
Powerplant: one 1,130-hp (843-kW) Bristol Taurus XII radial piston engine
Performance: maximum speed 161 mph (259 km/h) at 4,500 ft (1370 m); cruising speed 116 mph (187 km/h) at 6,000 ft (1830 m); service ceiling 20,700 ft (6310 m); range 930 miles (1497 km) with 1,600-lb (726-kg) weapons load
Weights: empty 7,250 lb (3289 kg); maximum take-off 10,460 lb (4745 kg)
Dimensions: span 50 ft 0 in (15.24 m); length 39 ft 10 in (12.14 m); height 14 ft 2 in (4.32 m); wing area 623 sq ft (57.88 m²)
Armament: one forward-firing 0.303-in (7.7-mm) machine-gun in starboard wing and twin 0.303-in (7.7-mm) Vickers 'K' guns in rear cockpit, plus one 1,610-lb (730-kg) torpedo beneath the fuselage, or six 250-lb (113-kg) or four 500-lb (227-kg) bombs beneath the wings
Operators: RCAF, RN

Fairey Fulmar

History and notes

The Fleet Air Arm desperately needed a new aircraft to replace its antiquated biplanes, but the philosophy of the period dictated that if the Royal Navy was to get a high-performance fighter, a crew of two was desirable to cope with the growing sophistication of navigational aids. Inevitably the extra size and weight imposed a performance penalty, but until the arrival of the Hawker Sea Hurricane and Supermarine Seafire, the Fairey Fulmar was the best aircraft available.

Two prototypes of a light bomber to Specification P.4/34 had been flown, the first on 13 January 1937, and from them emerged, with comparatively few modifications, the Fulmar to specification O.8/38. The P.4/34 was smaller and lighter than the contemporary Fairey Battle, certainly better looking, and was stressed for dive-bombing. The second prototype was used as the flying mock-up of a fleet fighter, with certain changes to meet naval requirements and the O.8/38 specification. An early stipulation that the Fulmar should be capable of operating with floats was dropped.

Within seven weeks of receiving the detailed specification, on 16 March 1938, Fairey confirmed to the Admiralty that a modified version of the P.4/34 would meet the requirements, and an initial order was placed for 127 aircraft to be known as the Fulmar. This was increased to 250 at the time of the Munich crisis in September 1938, but Fairey warned that production could not begin until their new factory at Heaton Chapel, Stockport, was completed.

While the P.4/34 had been powered by the 1,030-hp (768-kW) Rolls-Royce Merlin II, the initial production Fulmar I was to have the 1,080-hp (805-kW) Merlin VIII, although in fact the first aircraft flew at Ringway on 4 January 1940 with a modified Merlin III. The first with the Merlin VIII engine flew on 6 April 1940 and following the usual pattern was submitted to the Aircraft and Armament Experimental Establishment at Boscombe Down for testing and then to HMS *Illustrious* for carrier trials. The pilots found the Fulmar viceless, manoeuvrable and pleasant to fly, although when fully equipped its longitudinal stability was said to be marginal. Not surprisingly, its performance in speed, rate of climb and ceiling came in for some criticism, but it should be remembered that when the original concept was evolved it was considered that as a carrier-based aircraft the Fulmar was unlikely to be pitted against land-based fighters of superior performance. Certainly it had the same eight-gun armament of the contemporary Hurricane and Spitfire, carried twice as much ammunition as the land-based fighters, and had an endurance of five hours (also double that of contemporary land-based fighters). In these circumstances the Fulmar, with the extra weight of its second crew member and wing-folding mechanism, could be considered to have a reasonable performance, and in any case was superior to the types it replaced, including the Blackburn Roc.

Once production began it proceeded apace, and in

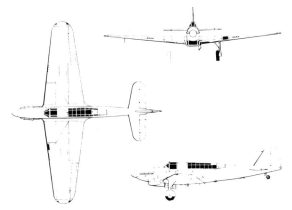

Fairey Fulmar II

the first three months 6, 12 and 20 Fulmars were built respectively, while by the fourth month (August 1940) the monthly rate of 25, agreed as the maximum, had been achieved; by the end of the year 159 Fulmars had been delivered.

The first squadron to receive Fulmars was No. 808 at Worthy Down in June 1940, embarking later in HMS *Ark Royal*. No. 806 Squadron at Eastleigh received 12 Fulmars in July to replace its Blackburn Skuas and Rocs, and the remaining squadron to get the new aircraft that year was No. 807, which formed at Worthy Down in September. As production increased so squadrons were formed or re-equipped: five in 1941 and six in 1942, but by 1943 the Fulmar was starting to be replaced by the Seafire. The last of 602 Fulmars built was delivered to the Fleet Air Arm in February 1943. Of this total, the first 250 were Mk Is, while subsequent aircraft were to Mk II standard. These had a 1,300-hp (969-kW) Merlin 30 engine, a new propeller, tropical equipment and various other changes. A useful weight reduction of 350 lb (159 kg) had been achieved, and although the Mk II was only a little faster than the Mk I it had a much better rate of climb, enabling it to reach 15,000 ft (4570 m) in 12 minutes against 15 minutes for the earlier version.

Tests with a night fighter model of the Fulmar were begun in 1941, following a series of night attacks on the Mediterranean Fleet by Italian air force torpedo-bombers. Installation of Air Interception (AI) radar Mark VI was carried out on a Fulmar II at Lee-on-Solent, but the poor results led to a modified AI Mk IV being substituted. Extra drag and other problems held up the issue to front-line squadrons until February 1944, but this version was used from June 1942 to train night fighter crews in preparation for the Fairey Firefly.

Around 100 Fulmar IIs were converted to night fighters, in more or less equal numbers for operational and training purposes. The arrival of a new lightweight high-frequency wireless telegraphy set, in early 1942, enabled the Fulmars to operate effectively as long-range reconnaissance aircraft over the Indian Ocean.

Throughout its career the Fulmar, like most types,

Fairey Fulmar

Like other naval fighters, the Fairey Fulmar was hindered by its size and two crew, but nevertheless introduced to naval service eight-gun armament and modern flying characteristics. A Mk II is shown.

was subject to modifications to improve its fighting efficiency. Ammunition capacity was increased from 750 to 1,000 rounds per gun (three times that of the Hurricane) and tests of 0.50-in (12.7-mm) machine-guns in place of the standard 0.303-in (7.7-mm) weapons gave good results, but shortage of the former resulted in only a few of the final production aircraft being fitted with the larger-calibre weapons.

Perhaps the Fulmar's weakest point was its lack of rear-firing armament; in some cases the crew improvised with such weapons as the Thompson sub-machine gun or a Verey pistol, but it has been said that the most unusual weapon was a bundle of lavatory paper. Held together by an elastic band this, when thrown into the slipsteam, scattered in all directions causing the pursuers to break away in confusion.

The Fulmar figured briefly in the early stages of experiments to prove the feasibility of catapulting fighters from armed merchant ships. Intended to provide some protection for convoys, such an operation was invariably a one-way trip, as there was nowhere to land back on board. After combat the pilot had to bale-out and hope to be picked up by one of the convoy. On 11 January 1941 a Fulmar of No. 807 Squadron was launched in this way from HMS *Pegasus*, but for future operations Hurricanes were used.

After serving in all theatres, the Fulmar ignominiously ended its first-line operational career on 8 February 1945, when a Mk II of No. 813 Squadron missed the arrester wire when landing back on HMS *Campania*, and was written-off in the subsequent argument with the safety barrier.

As the Firefly began to enter service in 1945, so the Fulmars were withdrawn until the only remaining example, by coincidence the first one built, ended its days with Fairey as a communications aircraft. Later, for a short time, it flew in its original colours before being grounded, and is now preserved in the Fleet Air Arm Museum at RNAS Yeovilton.

Specification

Type: two-seat carrier-based fighter
Powerplant (Mk I): one 1,080-hp (805-kW) Rolls-Royce Merlin VIII inline piston engine
Performance: maximum speed 247 mph (398 km/h) at 9,000 ft (2745 m); service ceiling 21,500 ft (6555 m); patrol endurance 4 hours with reserves
Weights: empty 8,720 lb (3955 kg); maximum take-off 10,700 lb (4853 kg)
Dimensions: span 46 ft 4½ in (14.14 m); length 40 ft 2 in (12.24 m); height 14 ft 0 in (4.27 m); wing area 342 sq ft (31.77 m²)
Armament: eight 0.303-in (7.7-mm) machine-guns in wings
Operator: RN

Fairey Barracuda

History and notes

Aircrew converting from antiquated Fairey Swordfish and Albacore biplanes to the Fairey Barracuda must have thought their new mount an extremely complicated machine. It was at least more streamlined than its predecessors, although with landing gear down and a full radar array its appearance was distinctly odd.

The Barracuda originated with Specification S.24/37 to which six companies (Bristol, Blackburn, Fairey, Hawker, Vickers and Westland) tendered, and an order for two prototypes to be built at Hayes was placed with Fairey in July 1938. The original engine selected was the 1,200-hp (895-kW) Rolls-Royce 24-cylinder 'X' engine, but when the makers stopped work on the new engine in favour of Merlins, Peregrines and Vultures, the decision was taken to use the 1,300-hp (969-kW) Merlin 30 in the Barracuda Mk I.

The first prototype flew on 7 December 1940, and differed from later aircraft in having an Albacore-type tail unit with low-set tailplane on top of the fuselage, but flight testing showed that the Fairey-Youngman flaps at negative angle created an air wake which caused tail buffeting, loss of elevator effectiveness and vibration at high speeds. The result was a redesigned tail in which the tailplane was strut-braced high up on a taller, narrower fin.

Large flaps were provided to give additional wing area when set in the neutral position, and for take-off these were lowered 20° to increase lift. In the landing configuration they were lowered to provide maximum drag, while for diving attacks they adopted a negative angle of 30°. Prototype testing soon confirmed the vast performance increase of the Barracuda over its biplane ancestors: speeds of 269 mph (433 km/h) were reached in level flight at 9,000 ft (2745 m) in 'clean' configuration, and this was lowered by about 20 mph (32 km/h) when an underslung torpedo was carried. In this condition, the Barracuda prototype could climb at 1,100 ft (335 m) per minute

Priority construction of fighters and bombers inevitably slowed work on the prototype, until the Admiralty intervened with the Ministry of Aircraft Production and managed to get full production of aircraft for the Royal Navy reinstated.

The second prototype flew with the new tail unit on 29 June 1941, and in the meantime the first prototype, on loan to No. 778 Squadron, had carried out deck-landing trials aboard HMS *Victorious* on 18/19 May 1941, following which it was returned to Fairey for the new tail to be fitted. Handling trials at the Aircraft and Armament Experimental Establishment at Boscombe Down commenced in October that year, but some unserviceability and modifications delayed their completion until February 1942.

It was at this point that a problem arose which was to remain with the Barracuda for the rest of its career—it was overweight. Strengthening of the airframe and addition of equipment not included in the original specification played havoc with the take-off and climb performance. The result was that after the

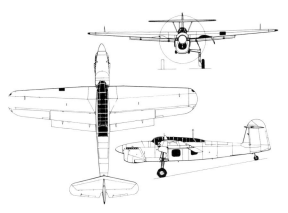

Fairey Barracuda II

first 30 production aircraft had been built, subsequent aircraft, known as Mk IIs, had the 1,640-hp (1223-kW) Merlin 32 engine installed, this providing an increase of some 30 per cent in rated output over the earlier powerplant. No changes were made to the airframe of the Mk II, but a four-blade propeller was substituted for the three-blade version of the Mk I.

The Mk II, ordered in quantity, was the main production version and other companies were selected to build the type, these companies including Blackburn, Boulton Paul and Westland. By November 1941, 1,050 Barracudas had been ordered, but Westland were to build only five Mk Is and 13 Mk IIs before the remainder of its order (for another 232) was cancelled to allow the company to build Supermarine Seafires.

Barracudas built by Blackburn and by Boulton Paul began to enter service in spring 1943, and although additional orders were placed, some of these were cancelled with the end of the war in Europe. In all, 1,688 Mk IIs were built, plus 30 Mk Is and two prototypes.

The Barracuda Mk III was evolved to take a new ASV radar installation, with a blister radome beneath the rear fuselage. The prototype, converted from a Boulton Paul-built Mk II, flew first in 1943. Following orders placed that year, production of this version began in early 1944, alongside Mk IIs, and 852 Mk IIIs were manufactured by Boulton Paul and Fairey.

The final production variant was the Barracuda V (the Mk IV being an unbuilt project), and this differed considerably in appearance although the basic structure was unchanged. The shortfall on power of the Merlins available in 1941 made the designers consider alternatives, and the decision was taken to use a Rolls-Royce Griffon. Initial development was slow and the first Griffon-powered aircraft, converted from a Fairey-built Mk II, did not fly until 16 November 1944.

In its production form, the Barracuda V had a longer, squarer wing than earlier versions, enlarged fin area to counteract the greater torque of the 2,030-hp (1514-kW) Griffon 37, and increased fuel capacity. However, this development had come too late, and of the 140 Mk Vs ordered only 30 were delivered before the end of

Fairey Barracuda

A Fairey Barracuda II torpedo-bomber of the Fleet Air Arm runs up its Merlin engine before take-off. The outward-facing 'TV aerial' above the port wing is part of the ASV Mk IIN radar system.

the war brought cancellation of the outstanding balance.

The Barracuda's operational service life began when No. 827 Squadron received 12 Mk IIs on being re-formed at Stretton, Cheshire, on 10 January 1943. Its companion squadron, No. 810, was re-equipped the following month and by January 1944 there were 12 Barracuda squadrons, first into action being No. 810 from HMS *Illustrious* in September 1943.

Barracudas made their mark when 42 aircraft dive-bombed the German battleship *Tirpitz* on 3 April 1944, inflicting heavy damage, and further attacks were made on the same target during the next four months.

The Barracuda squadrons of HMS *Illustrious*, Nos. 810 and 847, introduced the type to the Pacific theatre in April 1944, supporting US Navy dive-bombers in an attack on Japanese installations in Sumatra. Barracudas flew from small escort carriers on anti-submarine patrols in European operations, using rocket-assisted take-off gear from the short decks. Most squadrons were disbanded soon after VJ-Day, or re-equipped with other aircraft, and after some shuffling within squadrons the last Barracudas in front-line service were replaced in 1953 by Grumman Avengers.

The Mk Vs never entered front-line service, being used by Nos. 705, 744 and 753 Squadrons for training until 1950.

Specification

Type: three-seat torpedo- and dive-bomber
Powerplant (Mk II): one 1,640-hp (1223-kW) Rolls-Royce Merlin 32 inline piston engine
Performance (without torpedo): maximum speed 240 mph (386 km/h) at 1,750 ft (535 m); cruising speed 205 mph (330 km/h) at 5,000 ft (1525 m); service ceiling 16,600 ft (5060 m); range 1,150 miles (1851 km) without bombs
Weights: empty 10,818 lb (4907 kg); maximum take-off 14,250 lb (6464 kg)
Dimensions: span 49 ft 2 in (14.99 m); length 39 ft 9 in (12.12 m); height 12 ft 3 in (3.73 m); wing area 414 sq ft (38.46 m²)
Armament: two 0.303-in (7.7-mm) machine-guns, plus one 1,620-lb (735-kg) torpedo, or up to 1,600 lb (726 kg) of bombs, or six 250-lb (113-kg) depth charges, or 1,640 lb (744 kg) of mines
Operator: RN

Fairey Firefly

Designed as a powerful carrierborne reconnaissance fighter, the Fairey Firefly entered service in its Mk I form (illustrated) in 1943. Despite its power and armament, it was hampered by its size and two crew.

History and notes

Designed to Admiralty Specification N.5/40, which defined a requirement for a two-seat reconnaissance fighter, the Fairey Firefly represented a considerable advance on the earlier Fairey Fulmar, both in speed and firepower. A design team headed by H.E.Chaplin completed the submission in September 1939, and an order for 200 aircraft was placed on 12 June 1940. The first of four development aircraft was flown from Fairey's Great West Aerodrome on 22 December 1941, the pilot being Christopher Staniland, who also flew the second aircraft on 4 June 1942. The third machine was flown on 26 August, joining the test programme some six weeks after the crash of the second, and some minor changes resulted. These included a mass-balanced rudder and metal-skinned ailerons. Carrier trials were carried out aboard HMS *Illustrious* at the end of 1942.

The first aircraft from the Hayes production line was delivered in March 1943, powered by the 1,730-hp (1290-kW) Griffon IIB engine, although later machines had the 1,990-hp (1484-kW) Griffon XII. Other changes introduced during the Firefly F.I production run included a deeper windscreen, fairings for the four 20-mm cannon mounted in the wings, and deletion of the two-man dinghy stowed in the rear fuselage, in favour of individual K-type dinghies for pilot and observer. A total of 459 Firefly F.Is was built, 327 by Fairey at Hayes and 132 under sub-contract by General Aircraft Ltd at Hanworth. The addition of ASH radar in a pod beneath the engine identified the Firefly FR.I, of which 236 were built. A number of F.Is were modified to FR.I standard, but designated F.IA.

Fairey developed a night fighter version, designated NF.II, which had an 18-inch (0.46 m) fuselage extension behind the engine firewall. This was necessary to adjust the centre of gravity, compensating for the weight of the AI Mk 10 radar equipment in the rear cockpit. When it was found that this equipment could

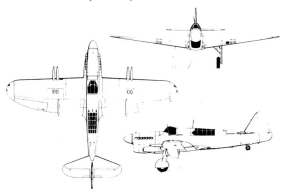

Fairey Firefly F.1

be carried in a pod under the engine, as could the ASH radar in the FR.I, the planned 328-aircraft programme was cancelled in favour of modifications to FR.Is on the production line, these emerging as NF.Is, of which 140 were built. The 37 NF.IIs were converted back to Mk I standard. Postwar conversions of the Mk I included the unarmed dual-control T.1 pilot trainer, with a raised rear cockpit, which appeared in production form in September 1947; the T.2 operational trainer, with two 20-mm cannon, first flown on 19 August 1949; and the T.3 observer trainer of 1951, which retained the flush rear cockpit and was equipped for training in anti-submarine operations. A few target tug Firefly TF.Is were also converted.

Although 100 were ordered, the Griffon 61-engined Firefly III was built only as a prototype in 1944, and development work was concentrated on the Mk IV which was powered by a 2,100-hp (1566-kW) Griffon 74 engine with a four-blade propeller. The wingtips were clipped, a dorsal fillet added to the fin, and new outer wing nacelles could both carry fuel, or an ASH radar scanner to port and fuel to starboard. Some 160 Mk 4s were built, the first FR.4 being delivered in July 1946

Fairey Firefly

Compared with earlier Fairey Firefly models, the FR.4 had a considerably more powerful Griffon engine, revised wing and fin shapes, and two underwing housings (fuel to starboard and a radar scanner to port).

and the last in February 1948. Some were converted later to TT.4 standard, with an ML Type G winch under the centre-section.

Externally the Mks 5 and 6 were similar to the Mk 4, the first aircraft of each variant flying on 12 December 1947 and 23 March 1949 respectively. Some 352 Firefly 5s were built in three versions designated FR.5, NF.5 and AS.5, the last equipped with American sonobuoys and other equipment which distinguished it from the British-equipped AS.6, of which version 133 were manufactured. A few dual-control T.5 trainers were converted from AS.5s in Australia, as were some TT.5s and TT.6s, while a Mk 5 later delivered to the Royal Canadian Navy was the first Firefly with power-folding wings.

Despite the handling problems experienced with the beard radiator of the sole Mk III, this feature was reintroduced in the Griffon 59-powered AS.7, necessitating the fitting of an enlarged rudder with a horn balance and longer rudder servo tab. The leading-edge radiators were deleted, of course, and the full span wing reintroduced. The rear cockpit accommodated two radar operators under a large, bulged canopy, and although the AS.7 was without offensive armament and intended to operate only in the search role, few were completed as anti-submarine aircraft, the majority being observer trainer T.7s. The first production AS.7 flew on 16 October 1951 and the last T.7 was built in December 1953. Mk 7 production totalled 110 at Hayes and 41 at Heaton Chapel, the latter factory being responsible for the conversion of 34 pilotless target Firefly U.8s from T.7s and 40 similar U.9s from Mk 4 and Mk 5 aircraft. These were used for missile development, and by the Royal Navy as targets for its Firestreak-armed fighters and Seaslug-carrying ships.

Fireflies entered service with No. 1770 Squadron at Yeovilton on 1 October 1943 and, embarked on HMS *Indefatigable*, were active in operations against the German battleship *Tirpitz* in Norway in July 1944. The carrier was then transferred to the East Indies Fleet and on 2 January 1945 Lt D. Levitt of No. 1770 Squadron scored the type's first victory when he shot down a Nakajima Ki-43 'Oscar'. This occurred during softening-up operations in preparation for attacks later that month on Japanese oil refineries in Sumatra, during which rocket-firing Fireflies joined bomb-carrying Grumman Avengers.

In June 1945 Fireflies of No. 1771 Squadron, operating from HMS *Implacable*, took part in attacks in the Carolinas, while in July No. 1772's aircraft, from HMS *Indefatigable*, were flying strikes against shipping and ground targets in the Japanese home islands. After war broke out in Korea, in 1950, Firefly 5s operated from Australian and British light fleet carriers, the squadrons comprising No. 810 aboard HMS *Theseus*, Nos. 812 and 820 aboard HMS *Glory*, No. 817 aboard HMAS *Sydney*, No. 825 aboard HMS *Ocean* and No. 827 aboard HMS *Triumph*. In 1954, No. 825 Squadron, embarked in HMS *Warrior*, was in action in the ground-attack role in Malaya.

Specification

Type: two-seat carrier-based fleet reconnaissance fighter/fighter-bomber
Powerplant (F.I): one 1,730-hp (1290-kW) Rolls-Royce Griffon IIB inline piston engine
Performance: maximum speed 316 mph (509 km/h) at 14,000 ft (4265 m); service ceiling 28,000 ft (8535 m); range 1,300 miles (2092 km)
Weights: empty 9,750 lb (4423 kg); maximum take-off 14,020 lb (6359 kg)
Dimensions: span 44 ft 6 in (13.56 m); length 37 ft 7¼ in (11.46 m); height 13 ft 7 in (4.14 m); wing area 328 sq ft (30.47 m²)
Armament: four 20-mm cannon in wings, plus provision for eight 60-lb (27-kg) rocket projectiles or two 1,000-lb (454-kg) bombs beneath the wings
Operator: RN

General Aircraft G.A.L.48 Hotspur

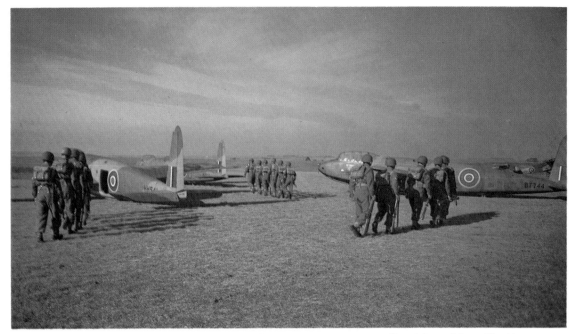

Men of a parachute regiment troop out to their General Aircraft Hotspur II training gliders. The Hotspur II differed from the Mk I supposed assault version in having reduced-span wings and dual controls.

History and notes

Designed to meet the requirement of Air Ministry Specification 10/40 for an assault glider, the General Aircraft G.A.L.48 design was launched into production with an initial order for 400. These, designated Hotspur Mk I, were of all-wood construction and with plywood skins. The mid-set cantilever monoplane wing had wide-span split trailing-edge flaps, and fuselage and tail unit were quite conventional structures. Landing gear comprised two main units, with twin wheels mounted on a rubber-in-compression shock strut, a tail skid, and a long central skid on rubber blocks for rough terrain landing when the main units had been jettisoned. Accommodation included a nose compartment with tandem seating, and small cabins fore and aft of the wing to seat six combat troops.

Testing of the Mk I was to show that its design performance of a full-load glide of 100 miles (161 km) from a 20,000-ft (6100-m) point of release could not be achieved and, as a result, none were used operationally. They were, however, to become the standard trainer of the Glider Pilot Regiment, and subsequently more than 1,000 were built, mostly by furniture manufacturer Harris Lebus of Tottenham, London, to equip Nos. 1, 2, 3, 4 and 5 GTS (Glider Training Schools). The later Mk II gliders all had their wing span reduced 16 ft 0 in (4.88 m) by comparison with that of the Mk I, and the Mk II was distinguished by the introduction of dual controls, and in having flaps and ailerons modified. Final production version was the Mk III, which introduced complete duplication of flying controls and instruments for the pupil pilot, and which had also an externally-braced tail unit.

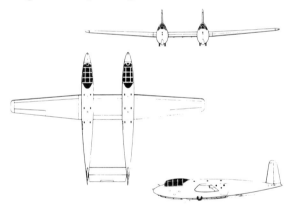

General Aircraft Twin Hotspur

Specification

Type: eight-seat training glider
Powerplant: none
Performance: maximum towing speed 130 mph (209 km/h); maximum gliding speed 90 mph (145 km/h); landing speed 56 mph (90 km/h); maximum gliding range following launch at 20,000 ft (6100 m) 83 miles (134 km)
Weights: empty 1,661 lb (753 kg); maximum take-off 3,598 lb (1632 kg)
Dimensions: span (Mk I) 61 ft 10¾ in (18.87 m), (Mk II) 45 ft 10¾ in (13.99 m); length 39 ft 3½ in (11.98 m); height 10 ft 10 in (3.30 m); wing area 272 sq ft (25.27 m²)
Armament: none
Operators: British Army, RAF

General Aircraft G.A.L.49 Hamilcar

History and notes

Their success with the Hotspur encouraged General Aircraft to compete for Air Ministry Specification X.27/40, covering the design and construction of a large tank- or vehicle-carrying glider. This resulted in a contract for the design and manufacture of two prototypes of the G.A.L.49, the first making its maiden flight on 27 March 1942, and leading to the production of an additional 410 examples under the designation Hamilcar I.

These aircraft were all-wood structures, except for the control surfaces which had wooden framing and fabric covers. Configuration was that of a high-wing cantilever monoplane, with pneumatically actuated single-slotted trailing-edge flaps and slotted ailerons. The configuration was chosen, of course, to ensure that the wing centre-section structure in no way interfered with the loading of tanks or vehicles through the swing-nose of the fuselage. For the same reason, the crew of two was accommodated in a flight compartment high on the fuselage and directly above the wing leading-edge. Access to this compartment was gained via a ladder mounted within the fuselage, through a hatch in its upper surface, and along a walkway provided on top of the wing centre-section. The tail unit was conventional, and the tailwheel type landing gear had main units comprising side Vees hinged to the fuselage and tied by long oleo-pneumatic shock-absorbers. These could be deflated to bring the fuselage nose down for the loading or unloading of tanks or vehicles. Large under-fuselage ash skids, mounted on rubber blocks, were provided for emergency landing in rough terrain after the main landing gear units had been jettisoned.

Largest and heaviest of the transport gliders used by the Allies during World War II, it was also the first British glider to carry a tank into action, and was able to accommodate a 7-ton (7.1-tonne) Tetrarch tank or two Universal Carriers. It could, of course, carry any other cargo load up to a maximum of 17,600 lb (7983 kg), including a variety of Allied tracked and wheeled vehicles.

In 1944, to meet the requirements of Air Ministry Specification X.4/44, General Aircraft designed a powered version of the glider. This was generally similar to the Hamilcar I, except for the installation of two 965-hp (720-kW) Bristol Mercury 31 radial piston engines in nacelles on the wing leading-edges, plus the associated controls, instruments and fuel installation. One hundred of these were ordered as conversions from the Hamilcar I after a prototype, first flown in February 1945, had shown the conversion to be practical. Intended for deployment in the Pacific theatre, only 22 (including prototypes) had been completed before VJ-Day brought contract cancellation. None of these powered gliders, which had the designation Hamilcar X, were used operationally. Figures in parentheses, except for metric conversions, in the specification which follows apply to this Mk X version.

Specification

Type: tank-carrying or cargo glider (powered glider)
Powerplant: none (two 965-hp/720-kW Bristol Mercury 31 radial piston engines)
Performance: maximum towing speed 150 mph (241 km/h); (maximum speed 145 mph/233 km/h); stalling speed 65 mph (105 km/h); (normal range 705 miles/1135 km; maximum range with overload tanks 1,675 miles/2696 km)
Weights: empty 18,400 lb (8346 kg); maximum take-off 36,000 lb (16329 kg)
Dimensions: span 110 ft 0 in (33.53 m); length 68 ft 0 in (20.73 m); height 20 ft 3 in (6.17 m); wing area 1,657.5 sq ft (153.98 m²)
Armament: none
Operators: British Army, RAF

The cockpit enclosure of the large General Aircraft Hamilcar glider was located above the fuselage to allow an uninterrupted hold able to carry a light tank, or two Universal carriers, or a Bofors gun.

Gloster SS.19B Gauntlet

Gloster Gauntlet II of No. 17 Squadron, RAF, Kenley (UK) in late 1938

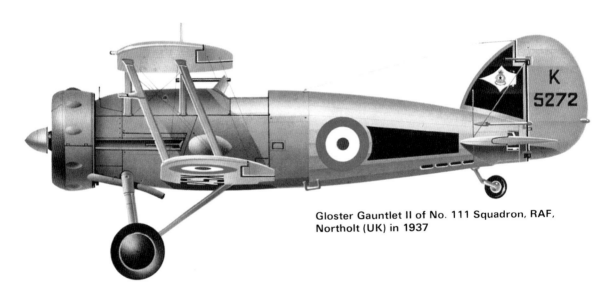

Gloster Gauntlet II of No. 111 Squadron, RAF, Northolt (UK) in 1937

History and notes

One of the two types that eventually replaced the Bristol Bulldog in RAF service, the Gloster Gauntlet I derived from the company's SS.18, SS.19, and SS.19B designs to meet the Air Ministry Specification 24/33 for a single-seat Bulldog replacement. It had equal-span biplane wings with ailerons on both, and wing, fuselage, and braced tail unit basic structure was of metal with fabric covering, except for metal panels on the forward fuselage. The tailwheel type fixed landing gear had oleo-pneumatic shock-struts and wheel brakes on the main units. Powerplant comprised a Bristol Mercury VIS.2 radial engine enclosed in a well fitting cowling. The Gauntlet provided outstanding performance, being considered at the time of its utilisation in RAF service as the world's leading day/night

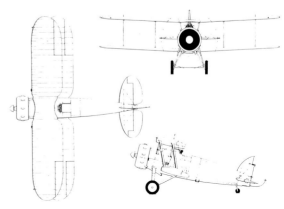

Gloster Gauntlet II

Gloster SS.19B Gauntlet

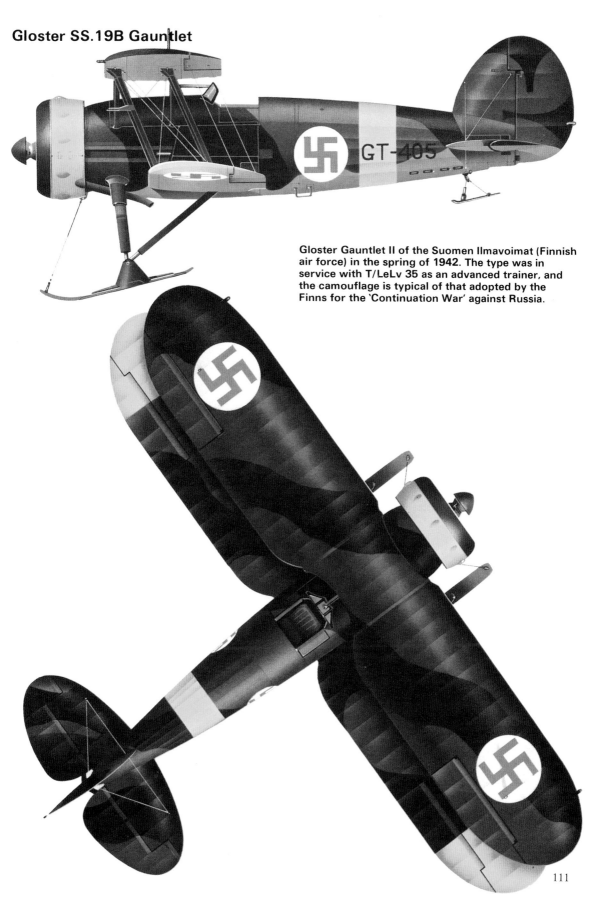

Gloster Gauntlet II of the Suomen Ilmavoimat (Finnish air force) in the spring of 1942. The type was in service with T/LeLv 35 as an advanced trainer, and the camouflage is typical of that adopted by the Finns for the 'Continuation War' against Russia.

Gloster SS.19B Gauntlet

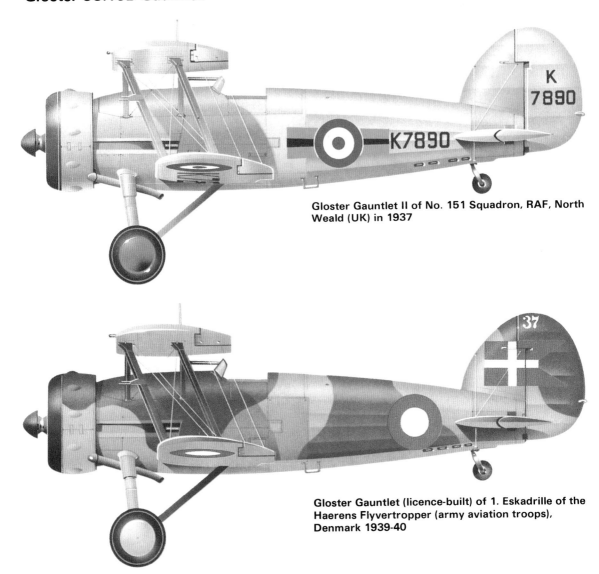

Gloster Gauntlet II of No. 151 Squadron, RAF, North Weald (UK) in 1937

Gloster Gauntlet (licence-built) of 1. Eskadrille of the Haerens Flyvertropper (army aviation troops), Denmark 1939-40

fighter. This resulted from the painstaking care that had been taken to ensure that drag was reduced to the absolute minimum for a biplane structure. Not only is the Gauntlet remembered as the last of the RAF's open cockpit biplane fighters, but the type had the distinction of being the world's first aircraft to carry out a radar-controlled interception of an aircraft in flight. This occurred in November 1937, when three Gauntlets of No. 32 Squadron were vectored on to a civil airliner over the Thames, under guidance from the experimental radar installation at Bawdsey Manor, Suffolk. A total of 228 Gauntlet I/IIs served with the RAF from 1935 to 1939; in 1937, when the Gauntlet was at the peak of its career, it equipped no fewer than 14 squadrons of Fighter Command.

In addition to service with the RAF, 17 were built under licence in Denmark, and ex-RAF machines were supplied to Finland (25), Rhodesia (3) and South Africa (4).

Specification

Type: single-seat day/night fighter
Powerplant: one 640-hp (477-kW) Bristol Mercury VIS.2 radial piston engine
Performance: maximum level speed 230 mph (370 km/h) at 15,800 ft (4815 m); service ceiling 33,500 ft (10210 m); range 460 miles (740 km)
Weights (Mk II): empty 2,700 lb (1256 kg); maximum take-off 3,970 lb (1801 kg)
Dimensions: span 32 ft 9½ in (9.99 m); length Mk I 26 ft 2 in (7.98 m), Mk II 26 ft 5 in (8.05 m); height 10 ft 3 in (3.12 m); wing area 315 sq ft (29.26 m²)
Armament: two fixed forward-firing synchronised Vickers machine-guns

Gloster SS.37 Gladiator

Gloster Gladiator I of No. 87 Squadron, RAF, Debden (UK) in 1937

History and notes

The inability of the British manufacturers to produce by the mid-1930s a Bristol Bulldog replacement, to the admittedly demanding Air Ministry Specification F.7/30, led to further orders for Gloster Gauntlets to equip additional squadrons proposed under the 1935 RAF expansion scheme. Although design studies for monoplane fighters were showing considerable promise, Gloster's designer H.P. Folland conducted a detailed examination of the Gauntlet design to define the extent to which performance might be improved. The wings were redesigned as single-bay units with strengthened main spars, and the landing gear was replaced by internally-sprung wheel assemblies mounted on cantilever struts. Both changes considerably reduced drag, promising a 10-15 mph (16-24 km/h) increase in maximum speed, and the 250 mph (402 km/h) target seemed attainable with an uprated Mercury engine then being developed by Bristol.

A prototype was built as a private venture, with the company designation SS.37, and flown in September by the company's chief test pilot, Flt Lt P.E.G. Sayer. With a Mercury IV engine installed a maximum speed of 236 mph (380 km/h) was recorded, and this was increased to 242 mph (389 km/h) after fitting a 645-hp (481-kW) Mercury VIS in November 1934. With the Gauntlet's two fuselage-mounted Vickers Mk III guns supplemented by two underwing Lewis guns, the SS.37 met another of the requirements of F.7/30, and it was flown to Martlesham Heath early in 1935 for official evaluation.

Gloster's design was submitted to the Air Ministry in June 1935 and Specification F.14/35 was written around it, accompanied by an order for 23 aircraft, the name Gladiator being announced on 1 July. The 840-hp (626-kW) Mercury IX was specified, and other changes included an enclosed cockpit, minor landing gear modifications, a revised tail unit, and the fitting of improved Vickers Mk V guns.

The first production batch of 23 Gladiator Is, de-livered in February and March 1937, carried Lewis guns under the wings, as did the first 37 of the second order, for 100 aircraft. All of this second batch were fitted with a universal armament mounting under each wing, capable of accepting any Vickers or Lewis gun or, indeed, the licence-built Colt-Browning which was installed in fuselage and wing positions in the majority of aircraft delivered in 1938. A third order, for 28 machines, brought the RAF's Gladiator I procurement to 231 aircraft, some of which were converted to Mk II standard.

The Royal Air Force later received 252 new Gladiator IIs, built to Specification F.36/37, with an 830-hp (619-kW) Mercury VIIIA engine fitted with automatic mixture control, electric starter and a Vokes air filter in the carburettor intake. Thirty-eight Gladiator IIs were fitted with arrester hooks and transferred to the Fleet Air Arm in December 1938, these being an interim replacement for Hawker Nimrods and Ospreys until the delivery of 60 fully navalised Sea Gladiators. These latter aircraft had an arrester hook, catapult points and a ventral dinghy stowage fairing. Gladiator production was to total 746, with orders from Belgium, China, Eire, Greece, Latvia, Lithuania, Norway and Sweden covering 147 Mk Is and 18 Mk IIs.

Gladiators were first issued in February 1937 to No. 72 Squadron at Church Fenton, and although most of the squadrons that received the type had been re-equipped with Hawker Hurricanes or Supermarine Spitfires by September 1939, some of their aircraft had been reissued to home-based auxiliary units, four of which were fully operational when war broke out. Two of them, Nos. 607 and 615 Squadrons, were posted to France in November 1939 as part of the Advanced Air Striking Force. No. 263 Squadron, together with No. 804 Squadron, Fleet Air Arm, participated in the Norwegian campaign and the handful of aircraft of Hal Far Fighter Flight, and of No. 261 Squadron, took part in the defence of Malta between April and June 1940. In the Middle East Gladiators saw service during the

Gloster Gladiator

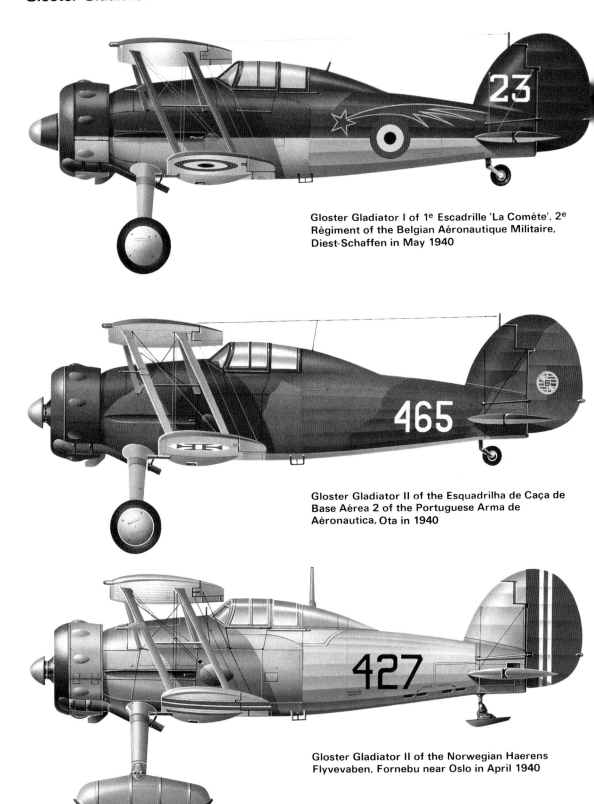

Gloster Gladiator I of 1e Escadrille 'La Comète', 2e Régiment of the Belgian Aéronautique Militaire, Diest-Schaffen in May 1940

Gloster Gladiator II of the Esquadrilha de Caça de Base Aérea 2 of the Portuguese Arma de Aéronautica, Ota in 1940

Gloster Gladiator II of the Norwegian Haerens Flyvevaben, Fornebu near Oslo in April 1940

Gloster Gladiator

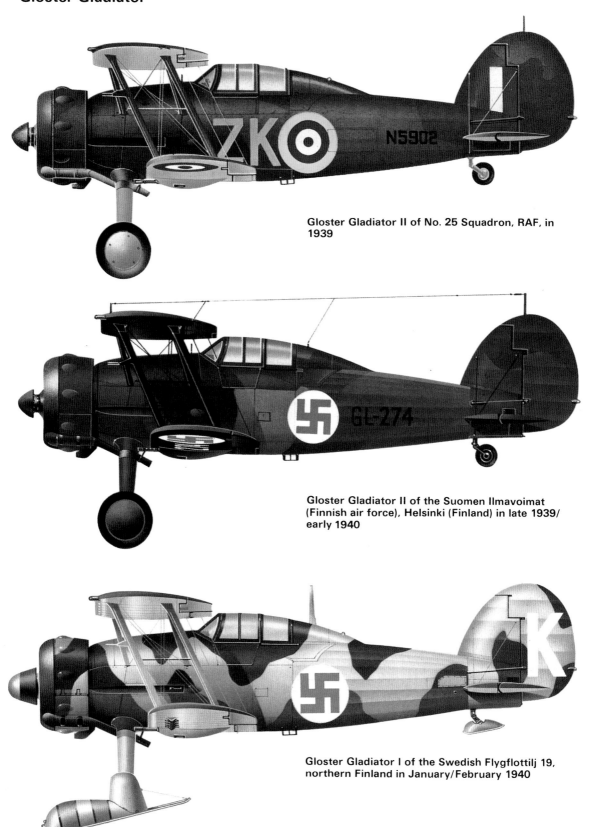

Gloster Gladiator II of No. 25 Squadron, RAF, in 1939

Gloster Gladiator II of the Suomen Ilmavoimat (Finnish air force), Helsinki (Finland) in late 1939/ early 1940

Gloster Gladiator I of the Swedish Flygflottilj 19, northern Finland in January/February 1940

Gloster Gladiator

Gloster Gladiator II of No. 615 Squadron, RAF,
Vitry-en-Artois (France) in May 1940

war with Nos. 6, 33, 80, 94, 112 and 127 Squadrons and
with No. 3 Squadron, Royal Australian Air Force. In
addition to No. 804 Squadron, Fleet Air Arm Sea
Gladiator units included Nos. 769, 801, 802, 805, 813 and
855 Squadrons. After withdrawal from first-line service, the Gladiator continued in RAF use for communications, liaison and meteorological reconnaissance
until 1944.

Specification

Type: single-seat biplane fighter
Powerplant (Mk II): one 830-hp (619-kW) Bristol
Mercury IX radial piston engine
Performance: maximum speed 257 mph (414 km/h)
at 14,600 ft (4450 m); service ceiling 33,500 ft

(10 210 m); range 440 miles (708 km)
Weights: empty 3,444 lb (1562 kg); maximum take-off
4,864 lb (2206 kg)
Dimensions: span 32 ft 3 in (9.83 m); length 27 ft 5 in
(8.36 m); height 11 ft 7 in (3.53 m); wing area 323 sq
ft (30.01 m²)
Armament: four forward-firing 0.303-in (7.7-mm)
machine-guns
Operators: Belgium, China, Egypt, Eire, Finland,
Greece, Latvia, Lithuania, Norway, RAAF, RAF,
Sweden.
Operators: Belgium, China, Egypt, Eire, Finland,
Greece, Latvia, Lithuania, Norway, RAAF, RAF,
Sweden.

The last of the RAF's biplane fighters, the Gloster Gladiator was a delight to fly, and introduced such
features as an enclosed cockpit and trailing-edge flaps. Production of the Gladiator totalled 746.

Gloster F.9/37

History and notes

From time to time misfortune, a change of policy, or just shortage of funds causes a good aircraft to be discarded. The Gloster F.9/37 was a case in point.

When the specification for a twin-engined single-seat fighter was issued in 1937, Gloster's chief designer, W.G. Carter, already had the basics on his drawing board. A series of specifications issued over the previous four years for two-seat turret fighters had either failed to produce any contenders or had been met, as in the case of F.9/35, where the Boulton Paul Defiant had been ordered.

In its original form to meet one of the earlier specifications, the F.9/37 was to have had a rear gun but this idea was abandoned. Some advanced thinking went into the Gloster submission, particularly with regard to ease of manufacture. Intended for dispersed production by semi-skilled labour, the structure broke down into small sub-assemblies. Nose and tail cones were detachable and the fuselage was built in two main sections, the forward of which contained the cockpit and two 20-mm cannon, while the rear two sub-assemblies carried the four 0.303-in (7.7-mm) machine-guns and the mainplane and tailplane attachment points.

Two prototypes were ordered and construction began in February 1938. The first to fly, on 3 April 1939, had two 1,050-hp (783-kW) Bristol Taurus radial engines, and in the subsequent flight test programme it proved to have a maximum speed of 360 mph (579 km/h), considerably in excess of any other twin-engine aircraft of the period. Pilots praised the handling qualities apart from a slight stability problem during climb with the engine cooling gills open.

Severe damage in a landing accident required the prototype to be rebuilt; immediately it had been rendered airworthy, it was returned to Boscombe Down, in April 1940. For some inexplicable reason, however, lower powered 900-hp (671-kW) Taurus engines had been installed, leading to a reduction in

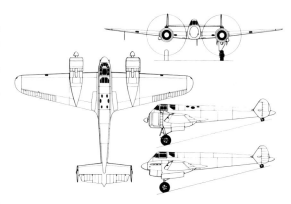

Gloster F.9/37 (bottom side view: 2nd prototype with Rolls-Royce Peregrine engines)

performance, although the aircraft was still capable of 332 mph (534 km/h).

A second prototype with 885-hp (660-kW) Rolls-Royce Peregrine inline engines flew on 22 February 1940; this had a speed of 330 mph (531 km/h). But in spite of their obvious good qualities, neither variant was ordered into production.

Specification

Type: single-seat fighter
Powerplant: two 1,050-hp (783-kW) Bristol Taurus T-S(a) radial piston engines
Performance: maximum speed 360 mph (579 km/h) at 15,000 ft (4570 m); service ceiling 30,000 ft (9145 m)
Weights: empty 8,828 lb (4004 kg); maximum take-off 11,615 lb (5268 kg)
Dimensions: span 50 ft 0½ in (15.25 m); length 37 ft 0½ in (11.29 m); height 11 ft 7 in (3.53 m); wing area 386 sq ft (35.86 m²)
Armament: two 20-mm nose cannon, and four 0.303-0.303-in (7.7-mm) machine-guns in fuselage
Operator: RAF (for evaluation only)

The Gloster F.9/37 was designed to meet a stringent requirement for a fast twin-engined fighter, and of the two prototypes one had Taurus radials (illustrated) and the other Peregrine inlines.

Gloster E.28/39

The UK's first turbojet-powered aircraft was the Gloster E.28/39. Though it had provision for armament, the E.28/39 was in reality an experimental type, albeit an important one.

History and notes

When Britain's first jet powered aircraft, the Gloster E.28/39, flew for the first time at Cranwell on 15 May 1941, there were few who could have foreseen the tremendous strides this form of propulsion would make within the next decade.

The W.1 gas turbine designed by Frank Whittle, and built by Power Jets Ltd under an Air Ministry contract awarded in March 1938, needed an airframe, and Specification E.28/39 was issued to Gloster on 3 February 1940. The wording of the specification indicated that the design was to be based on fighter requirements, and provision was to be made for the weight and space which would be occupied by four Browning 0.303-in (7.7-mm) machine-guns, although these would not be fitted in the test aircraft. Two prototypes were covered by the contract, and the aircraft were to have tricycle type landing-gear with a steerable nosewheel.

Within the short space of just over a year the first prototype was ready for taxying tests, which were undertaken at Gloster's Hucclecote airfield by the chief test pilot, P.E.G. Sayer, on 7 April 1941. The following day the aircraft made a few short hops, following which a new nose landing gear unit was fitted before the aircraft was dismantled and taken by road to Cranwell for flight trials, as it was felt that the longer runways there would be an advantage. In fact, the E.28/39 was airborne in about 1,800 ft (550 m) with a thrust of 860 lb (390 kg) from the Power Jets W.1 engine installed for initial flight tests.

The first flight, made on 15 May 1941, lasted for 17 minutes and was completely successful. A further 10 hours of flying was achieved in the following 13 days before the prototype was returned to the factory to await the new and more powerful 1,160-lb (526-kg) thrust W.1A engine. The new series of tests began on 4 February 1942 at Edgehill, Warwickshire but problems with the engine developed and the aircraft was slightly damaged. Pilots of the Royal Aircraft Establishment, Farnborough, also flew the aircraft and during one of these flights, on 30 July with the first prototype, then powered by a new Rover W.2B engine of 1,526-lb (692-kg) thrust, the ailerons jammed at 37,000 ft (11 275 m) putting the aircraft into an inverted spin: Sqdn Ldr Davie managed to bale out at 33,000 ft (10 060 m) but the E.28/39 was lost.

The second prototype had been re-engined with a Power Jets W.2/500 engine of 1,700-lb (771-kg) thrust and testing continued, concluding with some more flying at the RAE to obtain aerodynamic data. By this time an improved Power Jets W.2/500 had been fitted, giving 1,760-lb (798-kg) thrust. At the conclusion of its test programme, this aircraft was placed in the Science Museum, South Kensington, for permanent exhibition.

Specification

Type: single-seat turbojet-powered research aircraft
Powerplant: one 1,760-lb (798-kg) thrust Power Jets W.2/500 turbojet engine
Performance: maximum speed 466 mph (750 km/h) at 10,000 ft (3050 m); service ceiling 32,000 ft (9755 m)
Weights: empty 2,886 lb (1309 kg); maximum take-off 3,748 lb (1700 kg)
Dimensions: span 29 ft 0 in (8.84 m); length 25 ft 3¾ in (7.72 m); height 9 ft 3 in (2.82 m); wing area 146.5 sq ft (13.61 m²)
Armament: none
Operator: RAF (experimental use only)

Gloster G.41 Meteor

History and notes

The only Allied turbojet-powered aircraft to see action during World War II, the Gloster Meteor was designed by George Carter, whose preliminary study was given Air Ministry approval in November 1940 under Specification F.9/40. Its twin-engined layout was determined by the low thrust produced by the turbojet engines then available. On 7 February 1941 an order was placed for 12 prototypes, although only eight were actually built. The first of these was fitted with Rover W.2B engines, each of 1,000-lb (454-kg) thrust, and taxying trials were carried out at Newmarket Heath, commencing in July 1942. Delays in the production of flight-standard engines meant that the fifth airframe, with alternative de Havilland-developed Halford H.1 engines of 1,500-lb (680-kg) thrust was the first to fly, this event taking place at Cranwell on 5 March 1943.

Modified W.2B/23 engines then became available and were installed in the first and fourth prototypes, first flight dates being 12 June and 24 July respectively. On 13 November the third prototype made its maiden flight at Farnborough, powered by two Metrovick F.2 engines in underslung nacelles, and in the same month the second aircraft flew, initially with Power Jets W.2/500 turbojets. The sixth aircraft later became the prototype F.II, with two 2,700-lb (1225-kg) thrust de Havilland Goblin engines, and was flown on 24 July 1945. It had been preceded by the seventh, used for trials with a modified fin, rudder, and dive brakes, and

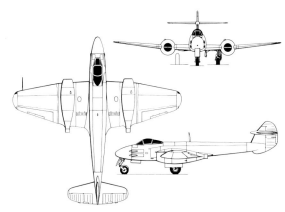

Gloster Meteor F.III

flown on 20 January 1944. The eighth, with Rolls-Royce W.2B/37 Derwent Is, was flown on 18 April 1944.

Twenty Gloster G.41A Meteor Mk Is comprised the first production batch, these being powered by W.2B/23C Wellands and incorporating minor airframe improvements, including a clear-view canopy. After a first flight on 12 January 1944 the first Mk I was delivered to the United States in February, in exchange for a Bell YP-59A Airacomet, the first American jet aircraft. Others were used for airframe and engine development, and the 18th later became the Trent-Meteor, the world's first turboprop-powered aircraft,

Production of the Gloster Meteor III totalled 280: the first 15 of these had Welland engines, but the rest had Derwent Is. The last of the batch also introduced lengthened nacelles typical of postwar developments.

Gloster G.41 Meteor

The Gloster Meteor I was really a development model, with a side-opening canopy and 1,700-lb (771-kg) thrust Rolls-Royce Welland Is, compared with the Mk III's rear-sliding hood and 2,000-lb (907-kg) Derwent Is.

which was flown on 20 September 1945. The Trent was basically a Derwent engine provided with reduction gearing and a drive shaft that turned a five-blade Rotol propeller of 7 ft 11 in (2.41 m) diameter, necessitating the introduction of longer-stroke landing gear to provide tip clearance. Each engine delivered 750 hp (559 kW) with a residual thrust of 1,000 lb (454 kW).

The first operational jet fighter squadron was No. 616, based at Culmhead, Somerset, which was equipped with Spitfire VIIs when its first two Meteor F.Is arrived on 12 July 1944. On 21 July the squadron moved to Manston, Kent, receiving more Meteors on 23 July to form a detached flight of seven. The first operational sorties were flown on 27 July, and on 4 August, near Tonbridge, Flying Officer Dean destroyed the first V-1 flying bomb to be claimed by a jet fighter, using the Meteor's wingtip to tip it over into a spin after the aircraft's four 20-mm cannon had jammed. On the same day, Flying Officer Roger shot down a second V-1 near Tenterden.

Conversion to Meteors was completed towards the end of August, and the autumn was spent preparing for operations on the continent. Between 10 and 17 October, however, four Meteors were detached to Debden, to take part in an exercise with the USAAF 2nd Bombardment Division and 65th Fighter Wing, to enable defensive tactics against the Luftwaffe's Messer-

schmitt Me 163 and Me 262 fighters to be devised. The first Meteor F.IIIs were delivered to Manston on 18 December, and on 17 January the squadron moved to Colerne, Wiltshire, where the remaining Mk Is were replaced. On 20 January 1945 one flight of No. 616's Meteors joined No. 84 Group, 2nd Tactical Air Force in Belgium, and in March No. 504 became the second Meteor F.III unit to operate on the other side of the English Channel.

The Meteor F.III, the second and last mark to see operational service during World War II, had increased fuel capacity and a sliding bubble canopy in place of the sideways-opening hood of the Mk I. Fifteen F.IIIs were completed with Welland engines and 265 with Derwents, some in lengthened engine nacelles. Derwents also powered the Meteor F.IV, later examples of which were modified by a 5 ft 10 in (1.78 m) reduction in wingspan. Of 657 built, 465 were supplied to the RAF, enabling Meteor F.IIIs to be passed to auxiliary units.

A 2 ft 6 in (0.76 m) fuselage extension, to accommodate a second cockpit in the Meteor F.IV airframe, was a feature of Gloster's private-venture Meteor Trainer, first flown on 19 March 1948. Unarmed and with dual controls, the aircraft was ordered for RAF use as the Meteor T.7, 712 of which were built, including aircraft for the Royal Navy and overseas air forces.

The most prolific variant, however, was the Meteor

Gloster G.41 Meteor

The Gloster Meteor was the Allies' only operational jet fighter of World War II, and the first unit to equip with the type was No. 616 Squadron, which received its first Meteor Is in July 1944.

F.8 which had a lengthened fuselage, a redesigned tail unit, an additional 95-Imperial gallon (432-litre) fuel tank, and a bubble cockpit canopy. Extra equipment included a gyro gunsight and a Martin Baker ejector seat. Derwent 8 turbojets of 3,600-lb (1633-kg) thrust were installed, to confer a top speed of almost 600 mph (966 km/h). The first of 1,183 Meteor F.8s was flown on 12 October 1948. For low-level tactical reconnaissance the Meteor FR.9 was developed from the F.8, carrying a camera nose and retaining the nose armament. The first of 126 examples was flown on 22 March 1950. They were followed by an unarmed high-altitude version, designated PR.10. These were hybrids, with the Mk 3 wing, Mk 4 tail unit, and FR.9 fuselage. The first of 58 made its initial flight on 29 March 1950.

Development of a night-fighter version to Specification F.24/28 was assigned to Armstrong Whitworth Aircraft in 1949. The T.7 cockpit section, with an extended forward fuselage to accommodate SCR 720 AI Mk 10 radar, was mated to an F.8 rear fuselage and tail unit, and a wing similar to that of the Mk I, but redesigned to house the four 20-mm cannon displaced from the nose. The definitive NF.11 prototype flew on 31 May 1950. A tropicalised version, the NF.13, was first flown on 23 December 1952 and used only by two Middle East squadrons. The NF.12, flown for the first time on 21 April 1953, had a higher limiting Mach

number than its predecessors, American-built APS 21 radar and fin leading-edge fairings. A revised clear-view canopy and some minor aerodynamic and equipment changes identified the final night-fighter variant, the NF.14.

Conversions included the U.15 and U.16 pilotless target aircraft, from Mk IV and Mk 8 airframes respectively. The U.21 was a similar Mk 8 conversion for use at the Woomera range in Australia. NF.11s equipped for target towing duties with the Royal Navy were designated TT.20. Meteors were phased out of service in the 1960s.

Specification
Type: single-seat day fighter
Powerplant (F.I): two, 1,700-lb (771-kg) thrust Rolls-Royce W.2B/23C Welland turbojets
Performance: maximum speed 415 mph (668 km/h) at 10,000 ft (3050 m); service ceiling 40,000 ft (12190 m)
Weights: empty 8,140 lb (3692 kg); maximum take-off 13,795 lb (6257 kg)
Dimensions: span 43 ft 0 in (13.11 m); length 41 ft 3 in (12.57 m); height 13 ft 0 in (3.96 m); wing area 374 sq ft (34.74 m²)
Armament: four 20-mm cannon
Operator: RAF

Handley Page H.P.52 Hampden

Handley Page Hampden I of No. 420 Squadron, RAF, in 1942

History and notes

In September 1932 the Air Ministry issued Specification B.9/32 for a twin-engine bomber for which both Handley Page and Vickers tendered. Each was awarded a contract and the resulting prototypes, the H.P.52 and the Vickers 271, flew within a week of one another, the former on 21 June 1936 and the 271, later known as the Wellington, on 15 June.

Considering that they shared the same specification, the two types could hardly have been more different, Handley Page going for an extremely slim 'pod and boom' fuselage, with three manually-operated gun positions, while Vickers adopted a portly fuselage with power-operated turrets and manual beam guns. In the event, the Wellington was to remain in service in the night bomber role for just over a year longer than its rival.

In spite of an antiquated appearance the Hampden, as it was subsequently named, had several remarkable characteristics. With the use of Handley Page leading-edge slots it was able to land at only 73 mph (117 km/h), while its maximum speed of 254 mph (409 km/h) was higher than either the Wellington or Whitley, and it could carry 4,000 lb (1814 kg) of bombs for 1,200 miles (1931 km), compared with the Wellington's 4,500 lb (2041 kg) load over the same distance.

Following an order for 180 Hampdens placed on 15 August 1936, to the new Specification B.30/36, the production prototype flew in 1937. Simultaneously with the first contract another was placed for 100 aircraft with Napier Dagger engines and responsibility for their manufacture, under the name Hereford, was given to Short Brothers and Harland in Belfast.

In May 1938 the first genuine production aircraft from the Handley Page line was flown at Radlett, and on 24 June the type was christened officially by the Viscountess Hampden.

Build up of the RAF was now in full swing and on 6 August 1938 other orders were placed: English Electric at Warton were contracted to build 75, and in Canada a British mission negotiated for 80 more to be constructed by a consortium named Canadian Associated Aircraft Ltd.

Following trials at the Aircraft and Armament Experimental Establishment, Martlesham Heath, and the Central Flying School at Upavon, deliveries to the RAF began in September 1938, with the first batch of Hampdens going to No. 49 Squadron at Scampton,

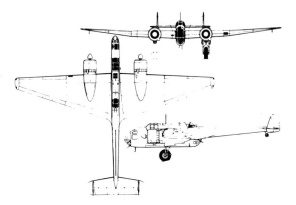

Handley Page Hampden I

Lincolnshire, replacing Hawker Hinds. No. 49 was part of No. 5 Group, which eventually was completely equipped with Hampdens; by the end of the year 36 were in service and when World War II broke out in September 1939 ten squadrons were using the type: Nos. 7 and 76 at Finningley; 44 and 50 at Waddington; 49 and 83 at Scampton; 61 and 144 at Hemswell; with Nos. 106 and 185 in reserve, the former in process of moving from Evanton to Cottesmore where No. 185 was already based.

Early operations in the daylight reconnaissance role were uneventful, but on 29 September the Hampden's shortcomings were vividly highlighted when five out of 11 aircraft in two formations were destroyed by German fighters when they were reconnoitring the Heligoland Bight area, within sight of the German coast. Not long after this it was decided to operate in future under cover of darkness, and some leaflet-dropping missions were carried out.

The sub-contracted Hampdens began to come off the production lines in 1940, the first English Electric aircraft flying on 22 February and the first Canadian Hampden in August.

By the winter of 1939-40, the Hampden had found its most useful role—as a minelayer. Aircraft from five squadrons sowed mines in German waters on the night of 13/14 April 1940, just after the German invasion of Norway, and by the end of the year No. 5 Group's Hampden squadrons had flown 1,209 minelaying sorties and delivered 703 mines, losing 21 aircraft in the operations—a loss rate of less than 1.8 per cent which was considered acceptable.

Handley Page H.P.42 Hampden

The Handley Page Hampden, seen here in the form of a Mk I, had an extremely narrow but deep fuselage of the pod-and-boom type, providing cramped accommodation for the crew of three.

The Norwegian campaign, however, once again showed the Hampden's 'Achilles heel': because of their inadequate defensive armament they suffered heavily at the hands of German fighters when used as day bombers.

Bomber Command's first Victoria Cross was awarded to Flt Lt R.A.B. Learoyd, a pilot of No. 49 Squadron, following an attack by five Hampdens on the Dortmund-Ems Canal on the night of 12 August 1940. Just over a month later a second VC was won, by an air gunner of No. 83 Squadron, Sgt John Hannah who, at 18 years of age, was the youngest RAF recipient of the award. Later that month Hampdens and Armstrong Whitworth Whitleys took part in the RAF's first raid on Berlin, and the Hampden continued to support the night bombing offensive until September 1942 when, on the night of 15/16, aircraft of the RCAF's No. 408 Squadron attacked Wilhelmshaven in the Hampden's final sorties with Bomber Command.

From April 1942, Hampdens had begun to transfer to Coastal Command for torpedo-bombing operations, a task for which experiments had been carried out at the Torpedo Development Unit, Gosport. The first two squadrons in this role were Nos. 144 and 455, the latter an RAAF unit, and detachments from both squadrons went to northern Russia for convoy protection operations. Thirty-two Hampdens from the two squadrons left Sumburgh in the Shetlands on 4 September 1942, but nine were lost in the crossing, including two which crashed in Norway and one which crashed on landing in Russia. The squadrons subsequently handed over their Hampdens to the Russians before leaving for the UK on 23 October.

No. 455 was the last operational unit with Hampdens, continuing to operate from Sumburgh, and sinking a U-boat on 4 April 1943, before re-equipping with Bristol Beaufighters at the end of the year.

And so the Hampden passed out of service. In spite of its inadequacies it had its good points: among them were pleasant handling characteristics and the excellent view which the pilot had. It was cramped, and crews could only change places with extreme difficulty, posing great problems in the case of airborne injuries. On a number of occasions Hampdens pursued and destroyed enemy aircraft of superior performance, such as the Messerschmitt Bf 110.

In all, 1,432 Hampdens were built, 502 of them by Handley Page, 770 by English Electric and 160 in Canada. A number of the 152 Herefords built by Short Brothers and Harland were subsequently converted to Hampdens.

Specification

Type: four-seat medium bomber
Powerplant: two 1,000-hp (746-kW) Bristol Pegasus XVII radial piston engines
Performance: maximum speed 254 mph (409 km/h) at 13,800 ft (4205 m); cruising speed 167 mph (269 km/h); service ceiling 19,000 ft (5790 m); range 1,885 miles (3034 km) with 2,000 lb (907 kg) of bombs
Weights: empty 11,780 lb (5343 kg); maximum take-off 18,756 lb (8508 kg)
Dimensions: span 69 ft 2 in (21.08 m); length 53 ft 7 in (16.33 m); height 14 ft 11 in (4.55 m); wing area 668 sq ft (62.06 m²)
Armament: two forward-firing 0.303-in (7.7-mm) machine-guns, twin 0.303-in (7.7-mm) guns in dorsal and ventral positions, plus up to 4,000 lb (1814 kg) of bombs
Operator: RAF

Handley Page H.P.52 Hereford

The Handley Page Hereford was identical to the more numerous Hampden apart from having Napier Dagger inlines in place of the Hampden's Bristol Pegasus radials. The Hereford was not used operationally.

History and notes

Like the Avro Manchester, the Handley Page H.P.52 Hereford was basically a good airframe with a bad engine. The prototype Hereford, a modified Hampden, was flown in June 1937 with two 955-hp (712-kW) Napier Dagger VIII H-type engines, and Short Brothers and Harland were contracted to build an initial batch of 100 aircraft, a number later increased to 152. The first of these production aircraft from the Belfast line flew on 17 May 1939.

Tests at the Aircraft and Armament Experimental Establishment, Martlesham Heath, showed the Hereford's performance to be almost the same as that of the Hampden, but there the similarity ended. The engines were unreliable, overheating on the ground and cooling too rapidly when airborne, while the very high pitched exhaust note proved uncomfortable for the crews.

One or two Herefords served alongside Hampdens in operational squadrons for a very short time, but were soon relegated to a training role, primarily with No. 16 Operational Training Unit (OTU) at Upper Heyford, Oxon, where first deliveries were made on 7 May 1940. Another Hereford unit was No. 14 OTU at Cottesmore, which had begun to operate the type as No. 185 Squadron; it was retitled No. 14 OTU in April 1940. One Hereford was used by the Torpedo Development Unit at Gosport, and at least 19 Herefords were subsequently re-engined and converted to Hampden standard.

Specification

Type: four-seat medium bomber

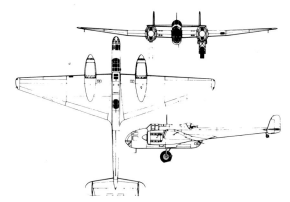

Handley Page Hereford

Powerplant: two 1,000-hp (746-kW) Napier Dagger VIII inline piston engines
Performance: maximum speed 265 mph (426 km/h) at 15,500 ft (4725 m); cruising speed 172 mph (277 km/h); service ceiling 19,000 ft (5790 m); range 1,200 miles (1931 km) with 4,000 lb (1814 kg) of bombs
Weights: empty 11,700 lb (5307 kg); maximum take-off 17,800 lb (8074 kg)
Dimensions: span 69 ft 2 in (21.08 m); length 53 ft 7 in (16.33 m); height 14 ft 11 in (4.55 m); wing area 668 sq ft (62.06 m²)
Armament: two forward-firing 0.303-in (7.7-mm) machine-guns, twin 0.303-in guns in dorsal and ventral positions, plus up to 4,000 lb (1814 kg) of bombs
Operator: RAF

Handley Page H.P.54 Harrow

Handley Page Harrow II of No. 214 Squadron, RAF, Feltwell (UK) in 1939

History and notes

Specification B.3/34 ushered in the era of the monoplane bomber for the Royal Air Force by asking, as it did, for modern twin-engine designs to replace the Handley Page Heyford and the lumbering Vickers Virginia.

Two companies were awarded contracts to the specification, one being Armstrong Whitworth who submitted the Whitley and the other Handley Page, whose H.P.54 was somewhat less original in concept, featuring a high wing and fixed landing gear. It should be acknowledged, however, that although the two designs were to the same basic specification the Handley Page H.P.54, later to be named Harrow, was intended initially as an interim bomber trainer and

later, when the more advanced bombers were in quantity production, as a transport aircraft. A hundred Harrows were ordered to a new specification, B.29/35, before the prototype flew on 10 October 1936. This new aircraft was based largely on the H.P.51 troop carrier, which had flown in May of the previous year.

Handley Page had initiated a new method of production for the Harrow, which enabled small parts to be manufactured by small firms under sub-contract, offering advantages both in construction and repair. The first 39 Harrows built were Mk Is with 850-hp (634-kW) Bristol Pegasus X engines, which conferred a top speed of 190 mph (306 km/h), but the following 61 aircraft were Mk IIs with Pegasus XX engines of 925 hp (690 kW) giving an extra 10 mph (16 km/h). Power-

When the Harrow was replaced in the bomber role by the Wellington, at least **12 aircraft were converted** into transports by the deletion of the turrets and bombing gear. In this guise they were known as **Sparrows.**

Handley Page H.P.54 Harrow

Although designed to a 1935 requirement for a troop transport, the Handley Page Harrow entered service in 1937 as a bomber with a standard defensive armament of four 0.303-in (7.7-mm) guns in three turrets.

operated gun turrets in the nose, tail and mid-upper positions were an advance over current service types; although the Mk Is did not have them when delivered, they were fitted later.

No. 214 Squadron at Feltwell was the first unit to receive Harrows, in January 1937, when the type began to replace Virginias, and by the end of that year four other squadrons had re-equipped with the new bomber: Nos. 37 (Feltwell), 75 (Driffield), 115 (Marham) and 215 (Driffield). No. 115 had been disbanded in 1919, and was re-formed in June 1937 to receive the Harrow, while No. 37 was also re-formed in April of that year from a nucleus of No. 214 Squadron.

Harrow production terminated with the 100th example in December 1937, but aircraft remained in service until the late stages of World War II.

A novel use of the Harrow was as an aerial minelayer when, in October 1940, No. 420 Flight was formed at Middle Wallop to carry out experiments under the code name 'Pandora'.

These aircraft carried 'Long Aerial Mines' (LAMs), which consisted of many small explosives charges suspended from parachutes with a 2,000-ft (610-m) length of piano wire trailing below. They were to be launched in the path of a bomber stream, and if one of these aircraft flew into the wires it was expected to release one or more of the charges, which then slid down the wires to explode on contacting the enemy bomber. Three months of trial proved the idea to be impractical, although four or five 'kills' were achieved, and No. 420 Flight re-formed as No. 93 Squadron, equipping with Vickers Wellingtons and Douglas Havocs.

No. 271 Squadron formed at Doncaster on 1 May 1940 to operate in the transport role, equipped with Harrows, Bristol Bombays and some impressed civil aircraft, and although most of the other types had been replaced by 1944 a flight of Harrows was retained. The squadron's headquarters moved to Down Ampney, Gloucestershire, in February 1944, when its Douglas Dakotas and Harrows supported the Allied forces in north-west Europe; two of the Harrows evacuated wounded from the Arnhem operation in September 1944.

Seven of the flight's Harrows were lost in the 1945 New Year's Day attack by the Luftwaffe on 2nd Tactical Air Force bases on the Continent, and the flight re-equipped with Dakotas in May 1945.

Specification

Type: four/five-seat bomber/20-seat transport
Powerplant: two 925-hp (690-kW) Bristol Pegasus XX radial piston engines.
Performance: maximum speed 200 mph (322 km/h) at 10,000 ft (3050 m); cruising speed 163 mph (262 km/h) at 15,000 ft (4570 m); service ceiling 22,800 ft (6950 m); range 1,250 miles (2012 km)
Weights: empty 13,600 lb (6169 kg); maximum take-off 23,000 lb (10 433 kg)
Dimensions: span 88 ft 5 in (26.95 m); length 82 ft 2 in (25.04 m); height 19 ft 5 in (5.92 m); wing area 1,090 sq ft (101.26 m²)
Armament: four 0.303-in (7.7-mm) machine-guns (one each in nose and dorsal turrets and two in tail turret) plus provision for 3,000 lb (1361 kg) of bombs
Operator: RAF

Handley Page H.P.57 Halifax

Handley Page Halifax B.III of No. 466 Squadron, Royal Australian Air Force, Driffield (UK) in 1944-5

History and notes

Second of the four-engined heavy bombers to enter service with the RAF, in November 1940, the Handley Page Halifax was one of the famous triad comprised of the Halifax, Avro Lancaster and Short Stirling which mounted Bomber Command's night-bombing offensive against Germany. In conjunction with the daylight attacks for which the USAAF had accepted responsibility, this round-the-clock battering of German targets was to reach its peak in 1944, causing almost unbelievable devastation. But although it entered service more than a year ahead of the Lancaster, the Halifax was always somewhat overshadowed in the bombing role by the achievement of the superb Lancaster. This was the result largely of the fact that the latter aircraft appeared to be capable of carrying ever-increasing bomb loads without serious degradation of its performance and handling capabilities, and in fact the Lancaster had flight and handling characteristics well above average. The Halifax, however, was to score over the Lancaster in its multi-role capability, for in addition to its deployment as a heavy night-bomber, it was equally at home when employed as an ambulance, freighter, glider tug, personnel transport, and maritime reconnaissance aircraft.

The origin of the Halifax stemmed back to an Air Ministry requirement of 1935 for a twin-engined bomber, to which Handley Page submitted a design identified as the H.P.55. This proved to be unsuccess-

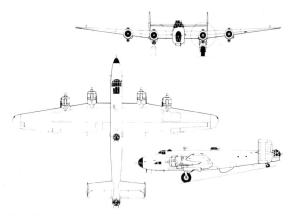

Handley Page Halifax B.VI

ful, Vickers being awarded a contract for what was to appear in mid-1942 as the Warwick. About a year later the Air Ministry issued a new specification, P.13/36, which called for a medium/heavy bomber to be powered by a 24-cylinder engine known as the Vulture which Rolls-Royce then had under development. Design proposals from Avro and Handley Page (H.P.56) were selected for prototype construction, that from Avro leading first to the Manchester which was to fly with the high-powered but under-developed Vulture engine. Presumably, Handley Page had an ear rather closer to the ground than Avro, for the company soon had grave

This Handley Page Halifax II of No. 78 Squadron has Merlin XX inlines, the fixed tailwheel of all early models, a twin-gun Boulton Paul dorsal turret, and no beam guns as fitted on Mk I Halifax bombers.

Handley Page H.P.57 Halifax

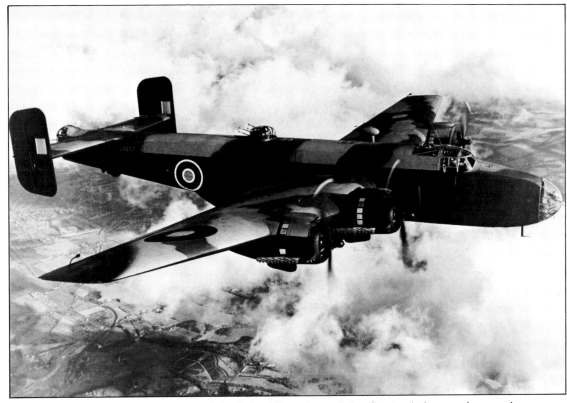

The Handley Page Halifax III introduced the Bristol Hercules radial and extended-span wings, and inherited from the Mk II Series IA the quadrilateral fins and long glazed nose without a turret.

doubts that the Vulture engine would emerge as a reliable production powerplant, and set about the task of redesigning the H.P.56 to take four Rolls-Royce Merlins instead. It was, of course, no easy task, but while the overall configuration was not greatly changed, the H.P.57 design which was submitted to the Air Ministry for approval was for a considerably larger and heavier aeroplane.

On 3 September 1937 Handley Page was awarded a contract for the manufacture of two prototypes of the H.P.57, with construction beginning in early 1938. When the first of these was nearing completion, it was realised that the company's airfield at Radlett, Hertfordshire, was too restricted for the first flight of such a large aircraft, and it was decided instead to use the nearest non-operational RAF airfield, which was at Bicester in Oxfordshire. Thus, final assembly was carried out in one of Bicester's hangars, and it was from there that the first flight was made on 25 October 1939.

As then flown the H.P.57 was a mid-wing cantilever monoplane of all-metal construction, the wing featuring automatic leading-edge slots, but these were to be deleted on production aircraft as the Air Ministry required that the wing leading-edges should be armoured and provided with barrage balloon cable cutters. Handley Page slotted trailing-edge flaps were fitted, and the large-span ailerons were fabric-covered. The tail unit comprised a large high-mounted tailplane

and rudder assembly with twin endplate fins and rudders. The fins of the prototype, and of production aircraft built until early 1943 were of triangular shape, the apex facing forward. The fuselage was a deep, slab-sided all-metal structure with considerable internal volume, and it was this feature which was to provide the later versions with a multi-role capability. Accommodation was provided for a crew of seven, including three gunners to man nose, beam and tail positions, but armament and turrets were not fitted for these early flights. Landing gear was of the retractable tailwheel type, and the powerplant comprised four Rolls-Royce Merlin engines. For its primary role, as a bomber, a variety of weapons could be carried in a 22-ft (6.71-m) long bomb bay in the lower fuselage, supplemented by two bomb compartments in the wing centre-section, one on each side of the fuselage.

An interesting feature of this design was its method of construction, each major unit breaking down into several assemblies. The wing, for example, comprised five sections, and the very considerable thought which had been given to this system of fabrication was to pay enormous dividends in subsequent large-scale production, and in the simplification of transport, maintenance and repair.

The second prototype made its first flight on 18 August 1940, followed just under two months later by the first production example, by then designated

Handley Page H.P.57 Halifax

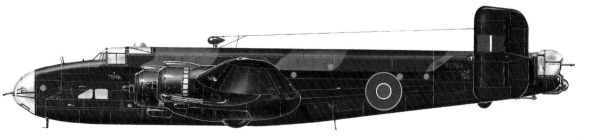

Handley Page Halifax A.IX of Nos. 47 and 113 Squadrons, RAF, in 1947

Halifax I, and this was powered by 1,280-hp (954-kW) Rolls-Royce Merlin X engines. Armament of these early production aircraft consisted of two and four 0.303-in (7.7-mm) machine-guns in nose and tail turrets respectively. Full designation of the first production version was Halifax B.Mk I Series I, and these began to equip the RAF's No. 35 Squadron during November 1940. It was this unit that, in early March 1941, was the first to use the Halifax operationally, in an attack on Le Havre, and a few days later the Halifax became the first of the RAF's four-engined bombers to make a night attack against a German target, when bombs were dropped on Hamburg. The Halifax was used for the first time in a daylight attack against Kiel on 30 June 1941, but it did not take long to discover that the aircraft's defensive armament was inadequate for daylight use, and by the end of 1941 the Halifaxes were used only by night in the bombing role.

This resulted in the provision of better armament for later versions, but there were two variants of the Mk I to appear before that: the B.Mk I Srs II was stressed for a higher gross weight, and the B.Mk I Srs III had standard fuel capacity increased by almost 18 per cent. Late production examples introduced Merlin XX engines, which, although having the same take-off rating as the Merlin X, provided 1,480 hp (1104 kW) at their optimum altitude.

Early deployment of the Halifax had confirmed that this new four-engined bomber had much to offer, but although contracts for large-scale construction very quickly exceeded the productive capacity of the Handley Page factories at Cricklewood and Radlett, prewar plans had been made for alternative sources of supply. The establishment of four new production lines was made easier by the unit method of construction which had been adopted for the Halifax, and the first of these sub-contract aircraft to fly, on 15 August 1941, came from the English Electric Company, which had earlier been involved in manufacture of Handley Page's Hampden medium bomber. The other three lines were those of Fairey at Stockport, Rootes Securities at Speke, and the London Aircraft Production Group. This last organisation was an interesting set-up, with rear fuselages being built by Chrysler Motors, forward fuselages and components by Duplex Bodies and Motors, inner wing sections by Express Motor and Body Works, outer wing sections by Park Royal Coachworks, and with the extensive works of

the London Passenger Transport Board responsible for the construction of many components and fittings, final erection, and testing at Leavesden.

The Halifax I was followed into service by the B.Mk II Srs I, which introduced a Boulton Paul twin-gun dorsal turret, and an increase of 15 per cent in standard fuel capacity; the powerplant, initially Merlin XXs, was later changed to the Merlin 22 of equal power output. These changes, plus others introduced after the prototypes had made their first flights, had resulted in a steady increase in gross weight. As there had been no surplus engine power from the outset, the result was that operational performance was being eroded by enhanced operational capability. This can be accepted during wartime conditions provided that the rate of attrition remains fairly constant. In the case of the Halifax II the dorsal turret represented 'the last straw', and steps were taken immediately to improve the performance of these aircraft.

The resulting B.Mk II Srs IA had a performance increase of some 10 per cent in both maximum and cruising speeds, which had been achieved by efforts to reduce both weight and drag. The nose turret was deleted, the nose acquiring a streamlined Perspex fairing; the dorsal turret was replaced by one which housed four instead of two guns, but which had a more shallow profile and created less drag; the aerial mast, fuel jettison pipes, and all possible equipment were deleted; new engine cooling radiators enabled the cross-sectional area of the engine nacelles to be reduced; the astrodome was of improved aerodynamic form; fuselage length increased by 1 ft 6 in (0.46 m); and the engines, initially Merlin 22s, were changed later to Merlins 24s which offered 1,620 hp (1208 kW) for take-off. News of these impending changes brought in-service adoption of those improvements which could most easily be introduced by squadron personnel. These included removal of the nose turret, dorsal turret and fuel jettison pipes, although only some aircraft had all of these modifications: the resulting Halifaxes were known as B.Mk II Srs I (Special). A later change introduced retrospectively to all aircraft then in service involved replacement of the triangular fins by larger units of rectangular shape. This came after extensive testing, following some inexplicable losses of fully loaded aircraft, had shown that it was possible for the Halifax to enter an inverted and uncontrollable spin.

Handley Page H.P.57 Halifax

HALIFAX I
MERLIN X
APRIL 1942.

Second of the RAF's four-engined heavy bombers to enter service, the Handley Page Halifax proved very versatile. In its Mk I version the Halifax was distinguishable by its Merlin X engines and triangular fins.

The last major production version was the Halifax B.Mk III, the first of the bombers to introduce Bristol Hercules VI or XVI radial engines, which offered 1,615 hp (1204 kW) for take-off. Wing span was also extended by 5 ft 4 in (1.63 m), the resulting increase of 25 sq ft (2.32 m²) in wing area improving the aircraft's operational ceiling. The first of the production Mk IIIs flew on 29 August 1943, and when this version entered squadron service in February 1944, it was found to have definite performance advantages.

Other bomber versions included the B.Mk V which, in Srs I (Special) and Srs IA variants, was virtually identical to the equivalent B.Mk IIs except for a change from Messier to Dowty landing gear. The B.Mk VI, with Hercules 100 engines which could develop 1,675 hp (1249 kW) for take-off and 1,800 hp (1342 kW) at 10,000 ft (3050 m), was virtually the last of the bombers, for the B.Mk VII was essentially the same, differing only in a reversion to Hercules XVI engines as the Hercules 100 was in short supply. Both the Mk VI and VII had a pressurised fuel system, plus small-particle filters over the engine intakes, as it had been envisaged that they would be used in the Pacific theatre after the war in Europe ended.

From their first introduction into operational service, Halifax bombers were in continuous use by Bomber Command, equipping at their peak usage no fewer than 34 squadrons in the European theatre, and four

more in the Middle East. Two flights were in early use in the Far East, and following VE-Day a number of squadrons operating with Halifax VIs flew their aircraft out for co-operation with the Allied forces fighting in the Pacific theatre. The Halifax was involved in the first Pathfinder operations in August 1942; was the first RAF aircraft to be equipped with the highly secret H_2S blind bombing radar equipment; was extensively involved in daylight attacks on German V-1 sites; and between 1941 and 1945 flew 75,532 sorties during which 227,610 tons (231 263 tonnes) of bombs were dropped on European targets.

The Halifax was also operated by nine squadrons of the RAF's Coastal Command for anti-submarine, meteorological and shipping patrols, the aircraft being converted from standard bombers and specially equipped, taking the designations GR.Mk II, Mk V, or Mk VI according to the bomber version from which they were derived. Similarly, RAF Transport Command acquired C.Mk III, Mk VI and Mk VII Halifaxes as casualty, freight and personnel transports. Little known in wartime was the work of Nos. 138 and 161 (Special Duties) Squadrons, which had the task of dropping special agents and/or supplies by parachute into enemy territory.

One other vital use of the Halifax was by the Airborne Forces, for under the designations A.Mk III, Mk V and Mk VII, equivalent bomber versions were

Handley Page H.P.57 Halifax

The chief distinguishing feature of the Halifax II Series I was its Boulton Paul Type C dorsal turret, a high-drag twin-gun installation later superseded by the low-drag four-gun Type A.

converted to serve for the deployment of paratroops or as glider tugs. The Halifax was, in fact, the only aircraft capable of towing the large General Aircraft Hamilcar glider, a capability first proven in February 1942. Soon after that date the Halifax tug made its operational debut when two Airspeed Horsas were hauled across the North Sea to attack the German heavy water plant in south Norway. They were subsequently to tow Horsas from Britain to North Africa in preparation for the invasion of Sicily, and were involved in this action as well as in airborne forces operations in Normandy, at Arnhem, and during the final crossing of the Rhine.

Although withdrawn from Bomber Command immediately after VJ-Day, the Halifax GR. Mk VI continued to serve with Coastal Command after the war, as did the A.Mk VII with transport squadrons at home and overseas. Postwar versions included the C.VIII which could accommodate an 8,000-lb (3629-kg) detachable cargo pannier beneath the fuselage, and the A.IX troop-carrier and supply-dropper for use by airborne forces. When production of these two versions ended, amounting to some 230 aircraft, a total of about 6,200 Halifaxes had been built, and examples remained in RAF service until late 1947.

Like several of the great wartime aircraft, this Handley Page masterpiece acquired the affectionately bestowed nickname of 'Halibag', an affection which most probably stemmed from its punishment-absorbing get-you-home durability. A typical example was one Halifax III which, in July 1944, was coaxed back to base after losing half of its tail assembly to accurately-placed German flak, and there must be many crews who still retain their own stirring, and grateful, memories of this bomber. Only one Halifax has been preserved for posterity.

Specification

Type: seven-seat long-range heavy bomber
Powerplant (B.Mk III): four 1,615-hp (1204-kW) Bristol Hercules XVI radial piston engines
Performance: maximum speed 282 mph (454 km/h) at 13,500 ft (4115 m); long-range cruising speed 215 mph (346 km/h) at 20,000 ft (6100 m); service ceiling 24,000 ft (7315 m); range with maximum bomb load 1,030 miles (1658 km)
Weights: empty 38,240 lb (17 345 kg); maximum take-off 65,000 lb (29 484 kg)
Dimensions: span 104 ft 2 in (31.75 m); length 70 ft 1 in (21.36 m); height 20 ft 9 in (6.32 m); wing area 1,275 sq ft (118.45 m²)
Armament: one 0.303-in (7.7-mm) machine-gun on flexible mount in nose and eight 0.303-in (7.7-mm) guns (four each in dorsal and tail turrets) plus up to 13,000 lb (5897 kg) of bombs
Operators: RAAF, RAF, RCAF

Hawker Hart

Hawker Hart of No. 57 Squadron, RAF, Upper Heyford (UK) in 1932-6

History and notes

The Hawker Hart day bomber, which first entered service with No. 33 Squadron of the RAF at East-church in January 1930, was originated to meet Air Ministry Specification 12/26. This called for design and development of a day bomber which was required to have an unprecedented maximum speed of 160 mph (257 km/h), a performance requirement that was comfortably exceeded thanks to a combination of excellent airframe design and the adoption of the Rolls-Royce F.XIB inline engine for the prototype, which was first flown in June 1928.

The Hart's introduction into service was to create immense problems for the Air Ministry, for not only was it very considerably faster than contemporary bombers, in some cases by as much as 50 mph (80 km/h), but could also show a clean pair of heels to any fighters then in service. Among the many uses for which Harts were adopted, one must mention their temporary deployment as fighters with No. 23 (Fighter) Squadron. In the annual air exercises of 1931, Hart bombers were able to make their attacks on selected targets with virtually complete immunity from interception by the defending fighters. Only when No. 23

The Hawker Hart light bomber's excellent handling characteristics and performance soon recommended that a Hart Trainer be developed, and this was characterised by two cockpits and long exhausts.

Hawker Hart

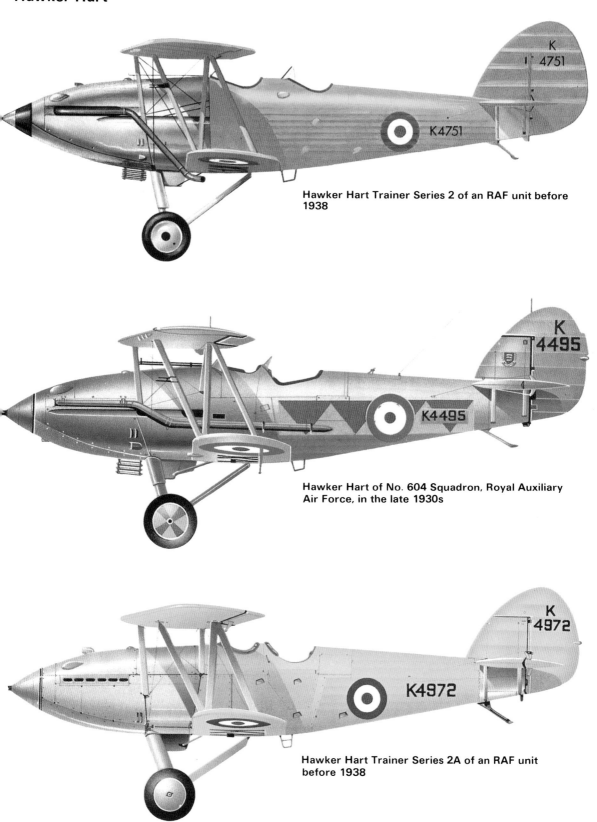

Hawker Hart Trainer Series 2 of an RAF unit before 1938

Hawker Hart of No. 604 Squadron, Royal Auxiliary Air Force, in the late 1930s

Hawker Hart Trainer Series 2A of an RAF unit before 1938

Hawker Hart

Squadron was brought into action was it possible to prevent them from gaining their target.

Such a state of affairs was, of course, to the ultimate benefit of the country and the RAF, for strenuous efforts were made to develop new fighter aircraft of much improved performance. The Hart, however, was a highly successful venture, for more aircraft of Hart design or origin were built in Britain during the 'between-wars' period than any other basic design. The Hart also proved to be adaptable for a variety of uses, including extensive employment by both Hawker and engine manufacturers to test engines or develop their installations. In addition, powerplants specified by export customers meant that Harts were to be seen with engines which included the Armstrong Siddeley Panther; Bristol Jupiter, Mercury, Pegasus and Perseus; Hispano-Suiza 12X; Lorraine Petrel; Napier Dagger; Rolls-Royce Kestrel (standard), Merlin and P.V.12. Total production, including 42 built under licence in Sweden, exceeded 1,000, an impressive total for an aircraft of the 1930s.

Hart bombers had been withdrawn from front-line service in the UK in 1938, but at the outbreak of war continued to be operational in the Middle East until gradually replaced by more modern types such as Bristol Blenheims. In service with the South African Air Force, Harts were deployed in a communication role until 1943.

Specification

Type: two-seat biplane day bomber
Powerplant: one 525-hp (391-kW) Rolls-Royce Kestrel IB, or 510-hp (380-kW) Kestrel X (DR) inline piston engine
Performance: maximum speed 184 mph (296 km/h) at 5,000 ft (1525 m); service ceiling 21,350 ft (6510 m); range 470 miles (756 km)
Weights: empty 2,530 lb (1148 kg); maximum take-off 4,554 lb (2066 kg)
Dimensions: span 37 ft 3 in (11.35 m); length 29 ft 4 in (8.94 m); height 10 ft 5 in (3.17 m); wing area 348 sq ft (32.33 m²)
Armament: one 0.303-in (7.7-mm) forward-firing machine-gun and one 0.303-in (7.7-mm) Lewis gun in aft cockpit, plus up to 520 lb (236 kg) of bombs
Operators: RAF, SAAF, Sweden

Hawker Osprey

History and notes

A contemporary of the Nimrod, the Hawker Osprey can best be described as a navalised version of the RAF's Hart day bomber. Its design originated to meet the requirements of Air Ministry Specification O.22/26, which called for what was virtually a new category of aeroplane for carrier service, a two-seat Fleet Spotter/Reconnaissance aircraft. The Osprey's close relationship to the Hart can be judged by the fact that the Hart prototype was converted to serve also as the Osprey prototype, being provided with folding wings for shipboard stowage, strengthened fuselage for catapult launching, and a specially designed mounting to make possible the rapid interchange of wheeled and float landing gear.

First flown in the summer of 1930, the Osprey prototype led to a revised Air Ministry Specification, 19/30, drawn up to cover production aircraft, the first of which appeared in the spring of 1932. These began to enter service, initially with Nos. 404 and 409 Flights, in November 1932. In mid-summer 1933 the Nimrod squadrons (Nos. 800, 801 and 802) were each supplied with three Ospreys to complement their numbers, and No. 803 Squadron was entirely equipped with the type. Early production Osprey Is were of conventional Hawker light alloy/steel construction, but from the closing months of 1932 the primary airframe structure was built of stainless steel to offset the corrosive effect which a maritime environment had on light alloy materials.

Osprey Is and IIs differed by having Mk I or Mk II floats respectively; the Osprey III, which was in production at the end of 1933, introduced a dinghy stowed in the starboard upper wing, an engine-driven generator, and a Fairey-Reed two-blade metal propeller. The final production variant, the Mk IV, of which 26 examples were built during 1935, was generally similar to the Mk III, except for provision of a Kestrel V engine which was slightly more powerful than the 630-hp (470-kW) Kestrel IIs that equipped all three earlier versions. The withdrawal of Ospreys from first-line service began in 1938, when they were issued to shore-based units where they served as advanced trainers, target tugs, or for communications until declared obsolete during 1940.

Specification

Type: two-seat spotter/reconnaissance aircraft
Powerplant (Mk IV): one 640-hp (477-kW) Rolls-Royce Kestrel V inline piston engine
Performance: maximum speed (landplane) 176 mph (283 km/h), (seaplane) 169 mph (272 km/h); cruising speed (landplane) 109 mph (175 km/h); service ceiling (landplane) 25,000 ft (7620 m), (seaplane) 22,000 ft (6705 m); endurance (landplane) 2 hours 15 minutes
Weights (landplane): empty 3,405 lb (1544 kg); maximum take-off 4,950 lb (2245 kg)
Dimensions: span 37 ft 0 in (11.28 m); length (landplane) 29 ft 4 in (8.94 m), (seaplane) 31 ft 9¾ in (9.70 m); height (landplane) 10 ft 5 in (3.17 m), (seaplane) 12 ft 5 in (3.78 m); wing area 339 sq ft (31.49 m²)
Armament: one 0.303-in (7.7-mm) forward-firing machine-gun and one 0.303-in (7.7-mm) Lewis gun on flexible mount in aft cockpit
Operator: RN

Hawker Demon

Hawker Demon of the Royal Australian Air Force in 1940

History and notes

Entry into service of the Hawker Hart in January 1930 brought another situation as embarrassing as that caused by the Fairey Fox in 1925. Once again, the RAF had acquired a bomber that could show a somewhat shattering clean pair of heels to any contemporary fighter. As before, it was necessary for the Air Ministry to take steps to redress this situation.

It seemed fairly logical to Hawkers to develop a fighter variant of the Hart, and two prototypes were prepared. Structurally similar to the Hart each prototype was given a Rolls-Royce Kestrel IIS supercharged engine, armed with two forward-firing Vickers machine-guns and a Lewis gun for the observer/gunner, and with the coaming of the rear cockpit modified to give him a maximum field of fire. Following service evaluation, a pre-production batch of six was ordered as Hart Fighters. These entered service with a flight of No.23 Squadron in May 1931, and the first production aircraft flew for the first time in February 1933. By then the Hart Fighter had been given the new name of Demon, and production was to total 305, including the prototype/pre-production aircraft and 64 for the Royal Australian Air Force.

Such was the pressure on Hawker's production capacity that the last 59 were sub-contracted to Boulton Paul. This company developed a hydraulically-actuated 'lobster back' shield to provide the gunner with some protection from the slipstream, and aircraft produced by Boulton Paul from late 1936 incorporated this feature as standard. When so equipped these aircraft were known as Turret Demons, and many Demons were retrospectively modified to this standard.

Demons remained in first-line service with the RAF until superseded by Bristol Blenheim IFs from late 1938, but a few were retained to serve as target tugs.

Specification

Type: two-seat interceptor fighter
Powerplant (original Demons): one 485-hp (362-kW) Rolls-Royce Kestrel IIS inline piston engine
Performance: maximum level speed 182 mph

Hawker Demon of No. 604 Squadron in 1938.

(293 km/h) at 13,000 ft (3960 m); service ceiling 27,500 ft (8380 m); endurance 2 hours 30 minutes
Weights (original Demons): empty 3,067 lb (1391 kg); maximum take-off 4,464 lb (2025 kg)
Dimensions: span 37 ft 3 in (11.35 m); length 29 ft 7 in (9.02 m); height 10 ft 5 in (3.17 m); wing area 348 sq ft (32.33 m²)
Armament: two fixed forward-firing synchronised Vickers machine-guns, one Lewis gun on flexible mounting in rear cockpit

Variants:

Turret Demon Version as described in text, but powered by one 584-hp (435-kW) Rolls-Royce Kestrel VDR (V de-rated) inline piston engine. Weight empty 3,336 lb (1513 kg); maximum take-off 4,668 lb (2117 kg).
Australian Demon Army co-operation fighter-bomber for service with the RAAF, generally similar to RAF Demons, but with Rolls-Royce Kestrel VDR engine, and provision for up to six Light Series bomb carriers beneath the wings. Weight empty 3,360 lb (1524 kg); maximum take-off 5,176 lb (2348 kg).
Australian Demon II Training version of the above, equipped with dual controls, of which ten were supplied.

Hawker Audax

From 1937 onwards, the Hawker Audax was fitted with the de-rated Kestrel X engine and used by training schools. The example illustrated served with No. 11 Flying Training School at Little Rissington.

History and notes

To meet Air Ministry Specification 7/31, which called for an army co-operation aircraft, Hawker was to propose yet another derivative of its Hart. Required to replace the Armstrong Whitworth Atlas, which had been the RAF's first army co-operation type when it entered service in October 1927, an early production Hart was used to evaluate the potential of this aircraft to meet the 7/31 requirement. It was, of course, eminently suitable for the task, and the first production Audax, as this new type was named, made its maiden flight on 29 December 1931.

These production aircraft, which first entered service with No. 4 Squadron in February 1932, differed little from the Hart except in equipment. The most valuable distinguishing feature for the amateur spotter was the long exhaust pipe which extended to mid-fuselage, just aft of the rear cockpit. This had been introduced to ensure that glare from the standard ejector exhausts, as fitted to the Hart, would not impair the pilot's view when flying close to the ground. The other external feature to serve as a recognition aid was the long message pick-up hook under the fuselage, which pivoted from the landing gear spreader bar.

Production for the RAF was to total 624 when construction ended in 1937, but examples had also been built for Iraq, Persia and the Straits Settlements. Because of the numbers involved, many of the RAF aircraft had been sub-contracted, with examples being manufactured by Bristol (141), Gloster (25), A. V. Roe (244), and Westland (43), the balance coming from Hawker's production.

The Audax was used to equip home-based army co-operation squadrons from the time it entered service in 1932 until it was replaced in 1937-8 and relegated to advanced training, communications, and glider tug duties. In these latter roles the Audax remained in home service well into the war years, and in the East African campaign No. 237 (Rhodesia) Squadron was operating during 1940 against the Italians in Eritrea and Somaliland. Others, based at Habbaniyah, were in action during the Iraqi revolt in May 1941.

Specification

Type: two-seat army co-operation aircraft
Powerplant: one 530-hp (395-kW) Rolls-Royce Kestrel IB inline piston engine
Performance: maximum speed 170 mph (274 km/h) at 2,400 ft (730 m); service ceiling 21,500 ft (6555 m); endurance 3 hours 30 minutes
Weights: empty 2,938 lb (1333 kg); maximum take-off 4,386 lb (1 989 kg)
Dimensions: span 37 ft 3 in (11.35 m); length 29 ft 7 in (9.02 m); height 10 ft 5 in (3.17 m); wing area 348 sq ft (32.33 m²)
Armament: one 0.303-in (7.7-mm) forward-firing machine-gun and one 0.303-in (7.7-mm) Lewis gun on flexible mount in rear cockpit, plus four 20-lb (9-kg) bombs or two 112-lb (51-kg) supply containers on underwing racks
Operators: Egypt, Iran, Iraq, RAAF, RAF, SAAF

Hawker Hartebeeste

History and notes

Developed from the Hart/Audax specially for service with the South African Air Force, only token numbers of the Hawker Hartebeeste were built in Britain to serve initially as construction examples to assist with licence-production in South Africa. The negotiations for a licence to build a version of the Audax had started in 1934, to meet a SAAF requirement for a ground support aircraft, and the Audax was generally agreed to most nearly satisfy this air force's need without an excess of modifications.

Four examples were built by Hawker, the first two being essentially the same as the RAF's Audax, except that the extended exhaust system was deleted and the Kestrel IB engine replaced by the 608-hp (453-kW) Kestrel VFP. These first two aircraft were flown initially in Britain, on 28 June 1935, before being despatched to South Africa in October 1935. The third and fourth examples were basically the same, differing only by having armour protection for the crew.

South African production was carried out at the Roberts Heights factory in Pretoria, the first examples being completed in the spring of 1937, and passing their acceptance tests successfully in July of that same year. Construction of production aircraft followed, 65 being built and supplied to two squadrons of the SAAF. A total of 53 of these remained in service at the outbreak of World War II and these were deployed in Kenya together with a number of ex-RAF Harts.

The Hartebeestes were to see considerable action against the Italians during operations on the Kenya-Ethiopia border in mid-1940, their most significant operation being an attack in strength carried out on 11 June 1940. Not long after this, however, the Hartebeestes were withdrawn from front-line service and relegated for use in training and communications roles, some remaining in service, surprisingly, as late as the postwar year of 1946.

Specification

Type: two-seat general-purpose/ground-support biplane
Powerplant: one 608-hp (453-kW) Rolls-Royce Kestrel VFP inline piston engine
Performance: maximum speed 176 mph (283 km/h) at 6,000 ft (1830 m); service ceiling 22,000 ft (6705 m); endurance 3 hours 10 minutes
Weights: empty 3,150 lb (1429 kg); maximum take-off 4,787 lb (2171 kg)
Dimensions: span 37 ft 3 in (11.35 m); length 29 ft 7 in (9.02 m); height 10 ft 5 in (3.17 m); wing area 348 sq ft (32.33 m²)
Armament: one 0.303-in (7.7-mm) forward-firing machine-gun and one 0.303-in (7.7-mm) Lewis gun on flexible mount in rear cockpit, plus underwing carriers for light bombs, smoke-laying equipment, supply canisters or water containers
Operator: SAAF

The Hawker Hartebeeste was in essence a tropicalised Audax for service with the South African Air Force (four squadrons). Used operationally in East Africa during 1940, the type was then turned into a trainer until 1946.

Hawker Hardy

The general-purpose variant of the Audax for Middle Eastern duties was the Hawker Hardy, the example illustrated serving with No. 6 Squadron in Palestine.

History and notes

Basically an adaptation of the Hart/Audax design, the Hawker Hardy was developed in response to Air Ministry Specification G.23/33, which called for an aircraft suitable as a replacement for the Westland Wapiti that was serving with the RAF's No. 30 Squadron on air policing duties in Iraq. The Hardy was fundamentally a Hart with special equipment, the prototype being a standard production Hart day bomber which was provided with a tropical radiator to enhance engine cooling and, like the Audax, had the extended engine exhaust system and message pick-up hook. To cater for a forced landing in the desert a tropical survival kit and water containers were added.

First flown in this form on 7 September 1934, the Hardy began RAF trials very shortly after this date. The Hardy then entered service with No. 30 Squadron at Mosul, Iraq, during 1935, and Gloster Aircraft was to build all 47 production machines under sub-contract. The Wapitis which the Hardy displaced had served long and faithfully, but the improved performance of the Hardy made it a valuable aircraft for the usually monotonous patrols over Iraq's desert areas.

In 1938, when No. 30 Squadron was re-equipped with Bristol Blenheims, the Hardies were transferred to No. 6 Squadron, where they were quickly involved in operations, providing close support for the British 16th Infantry Brigade during the trouble in Palestine.

Finally, all surviving Hardies in the Middle East were handed over to No. 237 (Rhodesian) Squadron, where they operated alongside the squadron's Hawker Audax aircraft. With this squadron they saw action at the beginning of World War II, deployed against the Italians in East Africa during 1940, and at least one aircraft is known to have survived as late as June 1941, used for communications duties.

Specification

Type: two-seat general-purpose biplane
Powerplant: one 530-hp (395-kW) Rolls-Royce Kestrel IB or 585-hp (436-kW) Kestrel X inline piston engine
Performance: maximum speed 161 mph (259 km/h) at sea level; service ceiling 17,000 ft (5180 m); endurance 3 hours
Weights: empty 3,196 lb (1450 kg); maximum take-off 5,005 lb (2270 kg)
Dimensions: span 37 ft 3 in (11.35 m); length 29 ft 7 in (9.02 m); height 10 ft 7 in (3.23 m); wing area 348 sq ft (32.33 m²)
Armament: one 0.303-in (7.7-mm) forward-firing machine-gun and one 0.303-in (7.7-mm) Lewis gun on flexible mount in rear cockpit, plus underwing racks and attachments for water containers, flares, or four 20-lb (9-kg) bombs
Operators: RAF, Rhodesia

Hawker Hind

History and notes

With the beginning of RAF expansion in 1934, the Air Ministry issued Specification G.7/34, which called for a light bomber that was required to serve as an interim replacement for the Hart bomber. This was considered a desirable course of action to bridge the gap until new-generation aircraft, such as the Bristol Blenheim and Fairey Battle, began to enter service.

Hawker's proposal to meet this requirement was a new derivative of the Hart, differing primarily by installation of the more powerful Kestrel V engine, but with changes which included modification of the aft cockpit to improve conditions, field of fire, and prone bombing position, and with a tailwheel replacing the Hart's tail skid.

Named Hind, the prototype of this new Hawker aircraft flew for the first time on 12 September 1934, and just under a year later, on 4 September 1935, the first production Hind was flown. First squadron to receive Hinds was No. 21, then at Bircham Newton, Norfolk, which was allocated sufficient to equip one flight, and at the same time one flight of Nos. 18 and 34 Squadrons were similarly equipped. Subsequent production aircraft were delivered to these squadrons until each was at full strength, after which Nos. 12 and 142 Squadrons were equipped. Such was the rate of production that by the spring of 1937 Bomber Command had received 338 Hinds, and a further 114 were in service with seven Auxiliary Air Force squadrons.

Like the Hart, the Hind was to attract considerable export interest, being built also for Afghanistan, Latvia, Persia, Portugal, Switzerland and Yugoslavia. As a result, Hinds were to operate with a variety of powerplants, including the Bristol Mercury VIII or IX, Gnome-Rhône Mistral K-9, and Rolls-Royce Kestrel VDR and XVI, in addition to the standard Kestrel V.

The peak utilisation of Hinds by the RAF came in 1937, when the Battles and Blenheims were entering service, and with a requirement for a bomber trainer for operation by the Volunteer Reserve FTS, it was decided to adapt the Hinds for this role. Changes included deletion of the rear cockpit gun mounting and modification of the aft cockpit to accommodate the instructor, with dual controls and full instrumentation, and the forward-firing gun was also deleted from most of these Hind trainers. In 1938, all were equipped with blind-flying hoods for instrument flight training.

Specification

Type: two-seat light bomber/trainer
Powerplant: one 640-hp (477-kW) Rolls-Royce Kestrel V inline piston engine
Performance: maximum speed 186 mph (299 km/h) at 16,400 ft (5000 m); service ceiling 26,400 ft (8045 m); range 430 miles (692 km)
Weights: empty 3,251 lb (1475 kg); maximum take-off 5,298 lb (2403 kg)
Dimensions: span 37 ft 3 in (11.35 m); length 29 ft 7 in (9.02 m); height 10 ft 7 in (3.23 m); wing area 348 sq ft (32.33 m²)
Armament: one 0.303-in (7.7-mm) forward-firing machine-gun and one 0.303-in (7.7-mm) Lewis gun on flexible mount aft, plus up to 500 lb (227 kg) of bombs on underwing racks
Operator: RAF

Developed from the Hart day bomber, the Hawker Hind light bomber differed from its predecessor in a number of detail refinements, but more importantly in having a fully supercharged Kestrel engine. Illustrated are Hinds of No. 40 Squadron.

Hawker Hector

The Hawker Hector was intended as a replacement for the Hawker Audax in army co-operation squadrons, and entered service in 1937. During the early war years it was used for liaison and glider-towing purposes.

History and notes

Last of the many variants of the Hawker Hart to remain in first-line service with the RAF, the Hector was designed as a replacement for the Audax. The requirement was for an army co-operation aircraft of improved performance, and it was decided to utilise the Napier Dagger engine which had first been fitted experimentally to a Hart bomber in 1933. While basically a Hart, the Hector differed considerably in appearance. This was due, of course, primarily to the engine installation which, because of its increased height, changed completely the characteristic pointed nose of the Hart family. In addition, the alteration caused to the aircraft's centre of gravity by installation of this heavier engine was corrected by using an upper wing with a straight leading-edge, instead of the swept-back upper wing of the earlier members of the family. In all other respects, equipment and layout were generally similar to those of the Audax.

The first of the production Hectors made its initial flight on 14 February 1936, and orders for this aircraft were to total 178 by May 1936, when a decision was made that these should be built under sub-contract by Westland at Yeovil, Somerset. The first Westland-built production aircraft was delivered in February 1937, and all had been constructed and handed over to the RAF before the end of the year.

Hectors first entered service with No. 4 Squadron in February 1937, eventually equipping seven RAF squadrons on home bases. When, in 1938-9, these units began to receive the new Westland Lysander as a replacement aircraft, the Hectors were used to equip Auxiliary Air Force Squadrons Nos. 602, 612, 613, 614 and 615, and many remained in service with these units at the outbreak of World War II.

Hectors were used operationally by No. 613 Squadron, which despatched six of its aircraft to attack German troops near Calais, but the loss of two aircraft on this operation highlighted the fact that the Hectors had come to the end of their useful life in first-line service. Relegated to the role of glider tug, they were to give another two years of reliable service.

Specification

Type: two-seat army co-operation biplane
Powerplant: one 805-hp (600-kW) Napier Dagger III MS 'H' inline piston engine
Performance: maximum speed 187 mph (301 km/h) at 6,500 ft (1980 m); service ceiling 24,000 ft (7315 m); endurance 2 hours 25 minutes
Weights: empty 3,389 lb (1537 kg); maximum take-off 4,910 lb (2227 kg)
Dimensions: span 36 ft 11½ in (11.26 m); length 29 ft 9¾ in (9.09 m); height 10 ft 5 in (3.17 m); wing area 346 sq ft (32.14 m²)
Armament: one 0.303-in (7.7-mm) forward-firing machine-gun and one 0.303-in (7.7-mm) Lewis gun on flexible mount in aft cockpit, plus underwing racks for supply containers or two 112-lb (51-kg) bombs
Operator: RAF

Hawker Fury I/II

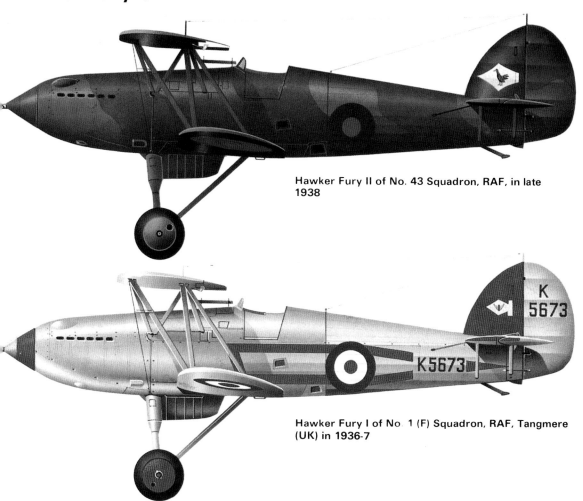

Hawker Fury II of No. 43 Squadron, RAF, in late 1938

Hawker Fury I of No. 1 (F) Squadron, RAF, Tangmere (UK) in 1936-7

History and notes

Development of the Hawker Fury biplane fighter stemmed back as early as 1927, but its advance into production was undoubtedly accelerated by the entry into service of the Hart day-bomber. A most attractive aeroplane which had, for a biplane, very clean lines, the Fury proved to be the RAF's first fighter able to exceed a speed of 200 mph (322 km/h) when it entered service with No. 43 (Fighter) Squadron in May 1931. An unequal-span single-bay biplane, the Fury had well staggered wings of composite construction with metal spars, ribs of wood, and fabric covering. The fuselage was a steel and light alloy structure, with metal panels forward and fabric covering aft; tail unit structure was similar, but with all-fabric covering. Landing gear was of the fixed tailskid type, and the basic powerplant was a 525-hp (391-kW) Rolls-Royce Kestrel IIS.

Like the Hart, however, the Fury appeared with a variety of powerplants, either for test purposes or specified by foreign purchasers, and these engines included the Armstrong Siddeley Panther, Bristol Mercury, Hispano-Suiza 12Nb or 12X, Lorraine Petrel,

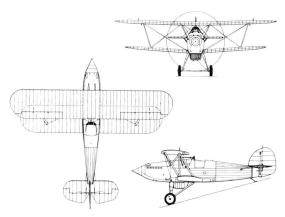

Hawker Fury I

and Pratt & Whitney S2B1-G Hornet. Initial production of Fury Is totalled about 160 aircraft, including those built to satisfy export orders, but in 1937 higher-performance Fury IIs began to enter RAF service, first with No. 25 Squadron. This version had been

Hawker Fury I/II

Hawker Fury (licence-built by Zmaj in Yugoslavia) of the Yugoslav air force in 1939

The Hawker Fury II differed from the Fury I in having a Kestrel engine offering some 20% more power and in being fitted with wheel spats. However, some export Fury IIs were fitted with neat cantilever main legs.

developed from the Fury I, but differed primarily by having a more powerful Rolls-Royce Kestrel VI engine, increased fuel tankage for the bigger capacity power-plant and, for RAF aircraft, spatted main wheels. As will be appreciated, this increased performance had not been achieved without cost: in this case there was a reduction of some 43 per cent in range, despite increased fuel capacity.

Both versions appeared attractive to other nations, and examples were supplied to Norway, Persia, Portugal, South Africa, Spain, and Yugoslavia.

The Fury IIs which were manufactured for the RAF, totalling 98, were used to equip six squadrons pending entry into service of the Hawker Hurricane which, in 1937, was under development. Furies remained in first line service until replaced by Hurricanes in 1939, and after the outbreak of war some Fury IIs continued to operate in a training role. Three squadrons of these fighters were used by the South African Air Force in

East Africa during the early stages of the World War II, and Yugoslav Furies were in combat in 1941.

Specification

Type: single-seat biplane fighter
Powerplant (Fury II): one 640-hp (477-kW) Rolls-Royce Kestrel VI inline piston engine
Performance: maximum speed 223 mph (359 km/h) at 16,500 ft (5030 m); service ceiling 29,500 ft (8990 m); range 270 miles (435 km)
Weights: empty 2,734 lb (1240 kg); maximum take-off 3,609 lb (1637 kg)
Dimensions: span 30 ft 0 in (9.14 m); length 26 ft 9 in (8.15 m); height 10 ft 2 in (3.10 m); wing area 252 sq ft (23.41 m²)
Armament: two 0.303-in (7.7-mm) forward-firing synchronised machine-guns
Operators: Persia, Portugal, RAF, SAAF, Spain, Yugoslavia

Hawker Fury I/II

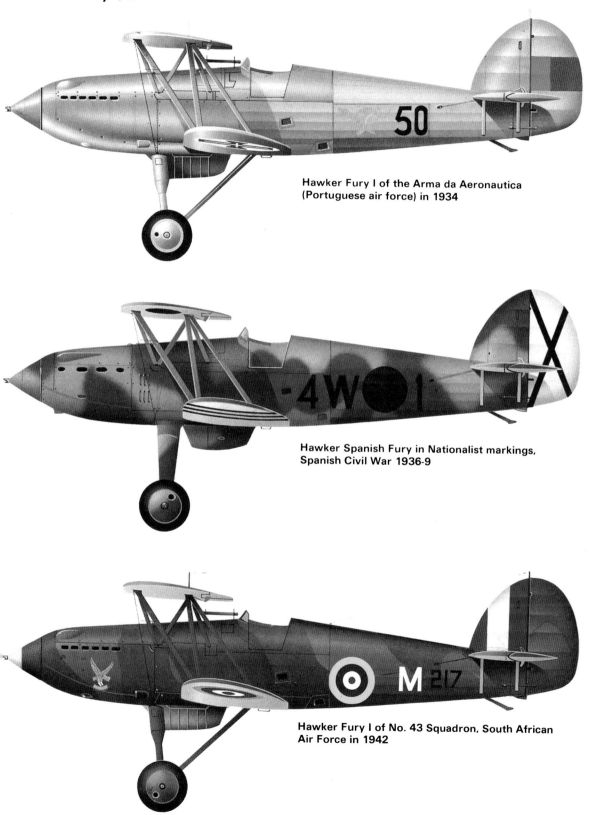

Hawker Fury I of the Arma da Aeronautica (Portuguese air force) in 1934

Hawker Spanish Fury in Nationalist markings, Spanish Civil War 1936-9

Hawker Fury I of No. 43 Squadron, South African Air Force in 1942

Hawker Nimrod

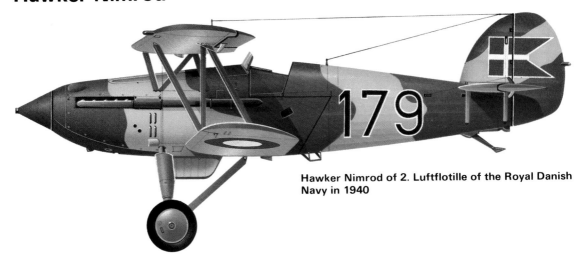

Hawker Nimrod of 2. Luftflotille of the Royal Danish Navy in 1940

History and notes

From 1924 to 1932 the Fairey Flycatcher, with its apparently 'cocked-up' aft fuselage, had the distinction of being the only fleet fighter in service with the Fleet Air Arm. However, with a top speed of only 133 mph (214 km/h) at sea level, a performance which deteriorated with altitude, it was realised that steps needed to be taken to procure a fighter of improved capability. As early as 1926 an Air Ministry specification had outlined the requirement, and Hawker Engineering offered as its contender a radial-engined biplane named the Hoopoe. This was not acceptable, but from it, out of the Fury, came a clean-looking biplane known unofficially at first as the Norn.

This was to become the Nimrod, generally similar in appearance to the RAF's Fury, the first production example of which was flown on 14 October 1931, and during 1932 Nimrod Is replaced Flycatchers in FAA Flights Nos. 402, 408 and 409. Subsequently, in 1933, these aircraft came into the possession of No. 800 Squadron on board HMS *Courageous*, and Nos. 801 and 802 Squadrons (HMS *Furious* and *Glorious* respectively). Production of an improved Nimrod II began in September 1933, with initial deliveries to the FAA being made in March 1934: these had arrester gear and, progressively, more powerful engines and tail surfaces of increased area. Many of the 57 Nimrod Is were later modified to Mk II standard. It is interesting to note that the first three Nimrod IIs had a basic structure of stainless steel, but the remaining 27 production examples reverted to Hawker's conventional structure of light alloy and steel.

Hawker were not successful in drumming up any significant export orders for the Nimrod. One was supplied to Japan, one to Portugal, and two to Denmark, in which last country they were known as Nimrodderne. The Royal Danish Naval Dockyard planned to licence-build an additional 10 examples of this aircraft, but there appears to be no conclusive evidence that this took place.

The FAA's Nimrods had been relegated to training and communications duties at the outbreak of World

Hawker Nimrod I of No. 800 Squadron, Fleet Air Arm. The naval equivalent of the Hawker Fury, the Nimrod I (57 built) was superseded by the Nimrod II with the more powerful Kestrel V engine.

War II, but continued in service until declared obsolete in July 1941. The Danish Nimrodderne remained in service until the time of the German invasion in April 1940 but, fortunately for the pilots of these by now totally obsolete naval fighters, the German onslaught was too swift for the Nimrodderne to be called upon to participate.

Specification

Type: single-seat carrier-based fighter
Powerplant (Nimrod II): one 608-hp (453-kW) Rolls-Royce Kestrel VFP inline piston engine
Performance (landplane): maximum speed 193 mph (311 km/h) at 14,000 ft (4265 m); cruising speed 115 mph (185 km/h); service ceiling 28,000 ft (8535 m); endurance 1 hour 40 minutes at 10,000 ft (3050 m)
Weights (standard production): empty 3,115 lb (1413 kg); maximum take-off 4,059 lb (1841 kg)
Dimensions: span 33 ft 6¾ in (10.23 m); length 26 ft 6½ in (8.09 m); height 9 ft 10 in (3.00 m); wing area 301 sq ft (27.96 m²)
Armament: two 0.303-in (7.7-mm) forward-firing synchronised machine-guns, plus provision for four 20-lb (9-kg) bombs to be carried beneath wings.
Operators: Danish Navy, RN

Hawker Henley

History and notes

Air Ministry Specification P.4/34, issued in February 1934, detailed the requirement for a light bomber which could also be deployed in a close-support role. High performance was required, with a maximum speed of around 300 mph (483 km/h), and the contenders for this demand were Fairey, Gloster and Hawker Aircraft.

With high performance paramount, and with only a modest requirement in respect of bomb load, it seemed logical to the Hawker design team to evolve an aircraft somewhat similar in size to the Hurricane. This latter aeroplane was then in an advanced design stage, and if at least some assemblies could be common to both there would not only be some economies, but also certain production advantages. Thus the Henley, as this aircraft was to become known, had outer wing panels and tailplane that were built from identical jigs. The wings, however, did not have four machine-guns in each outer panel as did those of the Hurricane. The other common area was in respect of powerplant, for with no great difference in size the Rolls-Royce Merlin, then being developed and already selected for installation in the Hurricane, offered the best power/weight ratio allied to minimum frontal area. Landing gear was of the retractable tailwheel type, the cantilever fabric-covered monoplane wing was mid-set, and accommodation differed considerably from that of the Hurricane by providing for a pilot and an observer/air gunner.

Construction of a prototype began in mid-1935, but with all priorities going to the Hurricane, it was not until 10 March 1937 that it was first flown, powered by a Merlin 'F' engine. Subsequently this aircraft was provided with light alloy stressed-skin wings and a Merlin I engine, and testing was to confirm the excellence of its overall performance. It was at this point that the Air Ministry decided it no longer had a requirement for a light bomber, and the Henley was ordered into production as a target tug, with 200 to be built under sub-contract by Gloster Aircraft. The second prototype was thus modified for this revised role, being provided with a propeller-driven winch to haul in the drogue cable after air-to-air firing sorties. The modified aircraft first flew on 26 May 1938.

Designated Henley III, production aircraft entered service first with Nos. 1, 5 and 10 Bombing and Gunnery Schools, as well as with the Air Gunnery Schools at Barrow, Millom and Squires Gate. It was soon discovered that unless restricted to an unrealistically low tow speed, the rate of engine failure was unacceptably high. This resulted in the Henley's withdrawal from this role, and its relegation to an even less suitable task, that of towing larger drogue targets with anti-aircraft co-operation units and squadrons. As might have been expected, the number of engine failures increased and, unfortunately, several Henleys were lost in accidents which resulted after the engine cut out and the drogue could not be released quickly enough.

This situation was brought to an end in mid-1942,

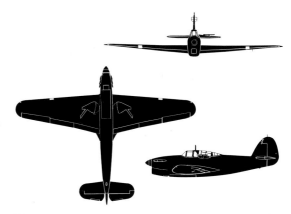

Hawker Henley TT.III

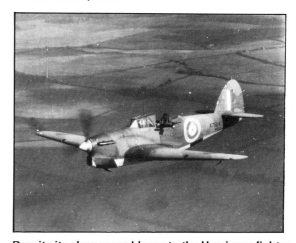

Despite its clear resemblance to the Hurricane fighter, the Hawker Henley was in fact designed as a light bomber. In 1937, however, the Henley was ordered into production in the vital role of high-speed target-tug.

with the Henleys withdrawn from service as Boulton Paul Defiants were adopted for target towing, and purpose-built Miles Martinets came into use.

Specification

Type: two-seat target tug
Powerplant: one 1,030-hp (768-kW) Rolls-Royce Merlin II or III inline piston engine
Performance: maximum speed (with air-to-air target) 272 mph (438 km/h) at 17,500 ft (5335 m), (with ground-to-air target) 200 mph (322 km/h); cruising speed 235 mph (378 km/h) at 15,000 ft (4570 m); service ceiling 27,000 ft (8230 m); range 950 miles (1529 km)
Weights: empty 6,010 lb (2726 kg); maximum take-off 8,480 lb (3846 kg)
Dimensions: span 47 ft 10½ in (14.59 m); length 36 ft 5 in (11.10 m); height 14 ft 7½ in (4.46 m); wing area 342 sq ft (31.77 m²)
Armament: none
Operator: RAF

Hawker Hurricane

History and notes

Few members of the British public could have been aware that a significant new fighter aircraft had joined the ranks of the RAF when, in December 1937, the first production examples of the Hawker Hurricane I were delivered to No. 111 Squadron at RAF Northolt. It was not until two months later, during February 1938, that this news became common, and exciting, knowledge when banner headlines announced, on 11 February, that one of these new Hurricane fighters had more than lived up to its name on the previous afternoon. Piloted by Sqn Ldr J.W. Gillan, commanding officer of No. 111 Squadron, this aircraft had been flown from Turnhouse, Scotland, to Northolt, a distance of 327 miles (526 km), in 48 minutes at an average speed of almost (409 mph (658 km/h).

The impact of this news story was not then diluted by the information that such a high speed had been recorded only because of an exceptionally fast tail wind. This bald, unadulterated statement of fact achieved maximum effect, doubtlessly intended, and served the dual purpose of, firstly, encouraging the British people by intimating that a new and revolutionary fighter was available for the defence of the country and, secondly, providing propaganda for consumption by the German people and their leaders, propaganda which sought to offset the achievements of the German Bf 109 designed by Willy Messerschmitt. This later aircraft had created headlines of its own in the summer of 1937, winning climb, dive, speed and team race competitions, as well as the international Circuit of the Alps race, at the international flying meeting held at Zurich in late July. But having regard to the fact that a Bf 109, with a specially supercharged engine, had captured the world speed record for landplanes on 11 November 1937, at a speed of 379.38 mph (610.55 km/h) it is doubtful if Germans would have believed or been impressed by the British news.

The subject of all this excitement, the Hurricane, stemmed back as far as 1933 when Hawker's chief designer, Sydney Camm, discussed with the Air Ministry's Directorate of Technical Development the prospects for a monoplane fighter. This needs explanation for today's reader as, despite the fact that monoplane racing seaplanes involved in the Schneider Trophy contests had achieved speeds up to 340 mph (547 km/h), and that the Italian Macchi MC.72 monoplane seaplane had established a world speed record of 423.82 mph (682.07 km/h) on 10 April 1933, the British Air Ministry then had little confidence in the integrity of the monoplane structure.

Hawker Aircraft decided to design a monoplane fighter based on the Fury biplane, using as its powerplant the Rolls-Royce Goshawk engine. As development of the design progressed, the Goshawk became supplanted by the Rolls-Royce P.V.12, a private venture engine which led directly to the Merlin, and Hawker began construction of a prototype around which the Air Ministry Specification F.36/34 had been drawn up. As first flown, on 6 November 1935, this prototype had

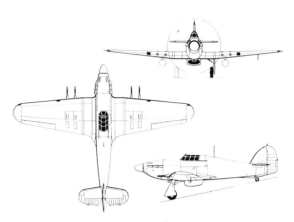

Hawker Hurricane IIC (dashed lines: optional underwing bombs)

retractable tailwheel type landing gear, a strut-braced tailplane, conventional Hawker-structure fuselage with fabric covering, a new two-spar monoplane wing covered with fabric, and a powerplant comprising a 990-hp (738-kW) Rolls-Royce Merlin 'C' engine driving a two-blade fixed-pitch propeller.

Official trials began in February 1936, when the most optimistic high-speed performance predictions were comfortably exceeded, and on 3 June 1936 an initial order for 600 production aircraft was issued to Hawker. At the end of the month the new fighter was named the Hurricane. Hawker had in fact anticipated the production contract, and plans for the construction of 1,000 examples had already been initiated when the Air Ministry order was received. This, however, called for installation of the Merlin II engine, causing some delay as it was necessary to redesign related items such as controls, mountings, and nose cowlings, but Hawker's advance preparations made possible the first flight of a production Hurricane I on 12 October 1937.

As mentioned at the beginning of this entry, the Hurricane I began to enter service with No. 111 Squadron at Northolt, Middlesex, which had one flight operational in December 1937 and was completely re-equipped by the end of the following month. Soon afterwards, Nos. 3 and 56 Squadrons became equipped, and by the end of 1938 about 200 Hurricanes had been delivered to the RAF's Fighter Command. The early production aircraft differed little from the prototype, except for the installation of the 1,030-hp (768-kW) Merlin II engine. The aircraft initially had individual exhaust stubs for each of the engine's 12 cylinders, but triple ejector exhaust manifolds on each side were soon to become standardised. Other early variations were to be found in the propeller installation, the Watts two-blade propeller being replaced first by a de Havilland three-blade variable-pitch unit and later by a de Havilland or Rotol three-blade constant-speed type.

No doubts existed that the Hurricane was anything but an important and essential aircraft to reinforce the expansion of the RAF, and plans were made in late

Hawker Hurricane

Hawker Hurricane I of No. 56 Squadron, RAF, North Weald (UK) in 1939

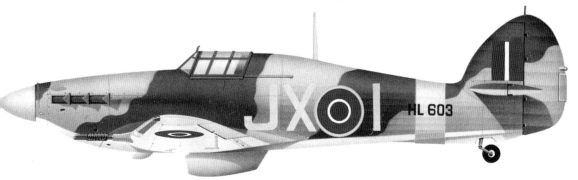

Hawker Hurricane IIC of No. 1 Squadron, RAF, in 1942

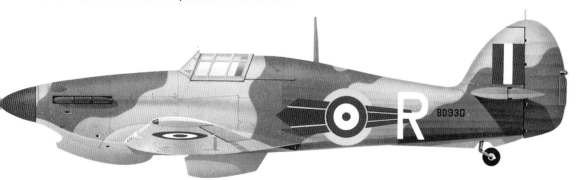

Hawker Hurricane IIB of No. 73 Squadron, RAF, Western Desert in 1942

Hawker Hurricane IID of No. 6 Squadron, RAF, North Africa in 1942

Hawker Hurricane

Hawker Hurricane IIDs prepare for take-off in the Western Desert. Armed with a pair of mighty 40-mm anti-tank cannon under the wings, Mk IIDs were cumbersome but potent destroyers of Axis armour.

1938 for additional construction to be undertaken by Gloster Aircraft at Hucclecote, Gloucestershire. This latter company's first production aircraft was to make its initial flight on 27 October 1939, and in little over 12 months Gloster had completed 1,000 Hurricanes, a figure that was to reach 1,850, plus 1,924 by Hawker, before later versions superseded the Hurricane I in production. Before that happened, however, the fabric-covered wing had been replaced by one with metal stressed skin, and other progressively introduced improvements had included the Merlin III engine, a bullet-proof windscreen, and some armour protection for the pilot.

Despite the pressure of its production programme for the RAF, Hawker had found time and space to cope with modest production orders covering 24 aircraft and a production licence for Yugoslavia, followed by aircraft for Belgium, Iran, Poland, Romania and Turkey: Belgium also negotiated a production licence for construction to be carried out by Avions Fairey, but only two Belgian-built Hurricanes had been completed and flown before the German invasion. Arrangements were also completed for Hurricanes to be built in Canada by the Canadian Car and Foundry Co., the first production aircraft flying on 9 January 1940. Canadian aircraft were at first generally similar to the British-built Hurricane I, but later differed by having the Packard-built Merlin engine.

At the outbreak of World War II 19 RAF squadrons were fully equipped with Hurricanes, and within a short time Nos. 1, 73, 85 and 87 Squadrons had been despatched to bases in France. Not inappropriately, a Hurricane of No. 1 Squadron was the first RAF aircraft to destroy a German machine over the Western Front in World War II. This victory came on 30 October 1939 when Pilot Officer P.W. Mould shot down a Dornier Do 17 over Toul, but in this 'phoney' period of the war these squadrons had comparatively little to do until the German push westward in May 1940. Immediately, six more Hurricane squadrons were flown to France, followed shortly after by two more squadrons, but these were an inadequate number to stem the flood of German arms, armour and aircraft. Post-Dunkirk accounting showed that almost 200 Hurricanes had been lost, destroyed or so severely damaged that they had to be abandoned. It represented a major disaster for the RAF, for this number of aircraft amounted to about a quarter of its total strength in first-line fighters.

Fortunately for the UK, and the RAF, the anticipated invasion of the British Isles by Germany failed to materialise, and there was a breathing space during which the squadrons of Fighter Command were able to reinforce their numbers. On 8 August 1940, which is regarded officially as the opening date of the Battle of Britain, the RAF could call upon 32 squadrons of Hurricanes and 19 squadrons of Supermarine Spitfires. But despite the débâcle at Dunkirk and the resulting fighter famine in Britain, three Hurricane squadrons were transferred overseas. These comprised No. 261 Squadron sent to support the island of Malta, and Nos. 73 and 274 Squadrons which, suitably 'tropicalised' by the substitution of a larger coolant radiator and a small-particle filter for the engine air intake (to minimise sand ingestion), began operations in the Western Desert.

It had been appreciated at an early date that the basic Hurricane had considerable development poten-

Hawker Hurricane

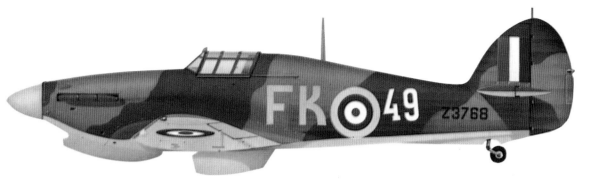

Hawker Hurricane IIB of No. 81 Squadron, RAF, Vaenga (USSR) in autumn 1941

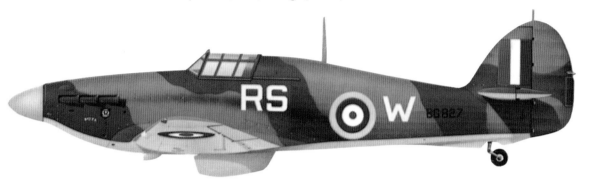

Hawker Hurricane IIB of No. 30 Squadron, RAF, Ceylon in late 1942

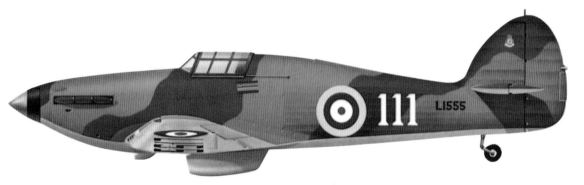

Hawker Hurricane I of No. 111 Squadron, RAF, Northolt (UK) in 1937

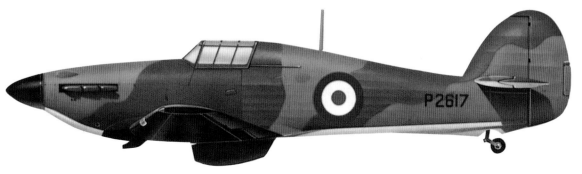

Hawker Hurricane I

Hawker Hurricane

A Hawker Hurricane IID tank-buster swoops in during a firing pass with its pair of underwing 40-mm Vickers 'S' cannon against an Axis armoured vehicle in the Western Desert during 1942.

tial, leading first to the introduction of a Merlin XX engine in a Hurricane I airframe under the designation Hurricane IIA Srs 1. Generally similar, except for a slightly lengthened fuselage, was the Hurricane IIA Srs 2, this representing an interim change on the production lines to make possible the installation of newly-developed and interchangeable wings. Thus, with a wing housing no fewer than 12 0.303-in (7.7-mm) machine-guns and with provision for the carriage of two 250-lb (113-kg) or two 500-lb (227-kg) bombs beneath the wings the designation became Mk IIB. The Hurricane IIC was generally similar, but the 12 wing-mounted machine-guns were replaced by four 20-mm cannon. When the Hurricane's life as a fighter had virtually come to an end, in 1942, the introduction of yet another wing was to rejuvenate this remarkable aircraft as the IID. The new wing carried two 40-mm Rolls-Royce B.F. or Vickers Type S anti-tank guns, plus one harmonised 0.303-in (7.7-mm) machine-gun for each anti-armour weapon to assist in aiming. The Hurricane IID 'tank buster' was to prove a potent weapon, highly effective against German armour in North Africa and when opposing more lightly armoured Japanese fighting vehicles in Burma.

The success of these wing variations led to the final production version, the Hurricane IV (early examples of this version were designated IIE), which introduced the 1,620-hp (1208-kW) Merlin 24 or 27 engine, and a 'universal wing' to make the Mk IV a highly-specialised ground-attack aircraft. This wing carried two 0.303-in (7.7-mm) machine-guns to assist in sighting the other weapons, which could include two 40-mm anti-tank guns, two 250-lb (113-kg) or 500-lb (227-kg) bombs, or smoke curtain installations, ferry or drop tanks, or

eight rocket projectiles with 60-lb (27-kg) warheads. This last weapon, first proposed in late 1941, had been tested on a Hurricane in February 1942. When used operationally on the Hurricane IV, this was the first of all Allied aircraft to deploy air-to-ground rockets, leading to newspaper headlines which claimed that the Hurricane 'packed a punch equivalent to the broadside from a destroyer'. Such fire power meant that the little Hurricane was a giant in capability, extending its operational life beyond the end of World War II, for it was not until January 1947 that the RAF's last Hurricane squadron, No. 6, received replacement aircraft.

Hurricane production in Canada had, like that in Britain, grown considerably in proportions from the initial line of Hurricane Is. The introduction of the 1,300-hp (969-kW) Packard-built Merlin 28 engine and Hamilton Standard propellers brought a designation change to Hurricane X. This model was generally similar to the British-built IIB with the 12-gun wing, and while small numbers of these were supplied to Britain, the majority was retained for use by the Royal Canadian Air Force. The Hurricane XI which followed was developed specifically for RCAF requirements, but differed from the Mk X primarily in having RCAF rather than RAF military equipment. Major production version from Canadian sources was the Hurricane XII, this introducing the 1,300-hp (969-kW) Packard-built Merlin 29. Initially, this was provided with the 12-gun wing; subsequently, the four-cannon and 'universal' wings became available. The final land-based version to emanate from Canada was the Mk XIIA, identical to the XII except for having an eight-gun wing.

Hawker Hurricane

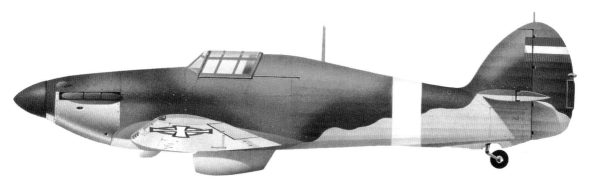

Hawker Hurricane I (Yugoslav-built by Zmaj at Zeman) of the Royal Yugoslav air force in April 1941

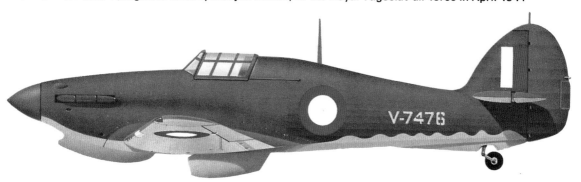

Hawker Hurricane I of Nos. 2 & 3 Communications Flights, Royal Australian Air Force

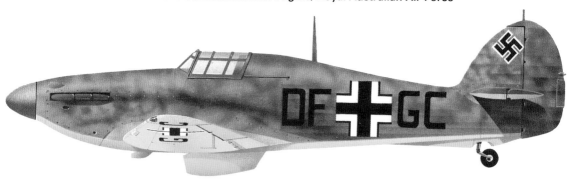

Hawker Hurricane of unknown identity tested at Magdeburg by the Luftwaffe

Hawker Hurricane I of No. 85 Squadron, RAF, Debden and Croydon (UK) in August 1940

Hawker Hurricane

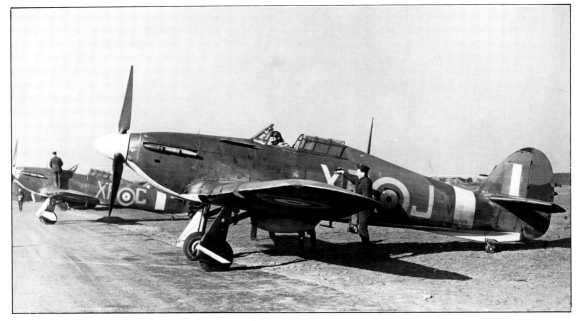

The Hawker Hurricane I squadrons were the mainstay of Fighter Command's strength in 1939 and 1940. Seen here are a pair of Hurricanes from No. 71 Squadron in late 1940 or early 1941.

In addition to the Hurricanes which went to other countries before the war, wartime production was to supply almost 3,000 of these aircraft to Russia, although as a result of convoy shipping losses not all reached their destination. Other wartime deliveries, most made at a time when it was difficult to spare a single aircraft, went to Egypt (20), Finland (12), India (300), Irish Air Corps (12), Persia (1), and Turkey (14), and total production in Britain and Canada amounted to more than 14,000 aircraft.

Undoubtedly one of the great fighter aircraft of World War II, it is difficult to highlight the capabilities of this remarkable aircraft without using a host of tired adjectives or clichés. In the Battle of Britain Hurricanes destroyed more enemy aircraft than all other defences, air or ground, combined. Even this statement must be put in perspective, for there was an early appreciation that the maximum speed of the Hurricane put it at a distinct disadvantage when confronted by the Messerschmitt Bf 109. Consequently, the Spitfires tangled with the Bf 109s, enabling the Hurricanes to battle against the German bombers which sought initially to destroy the RAF's fighter airfields and Britain's vital radar installations. 'Hurribombers' fought from Malta, carried out anti-shipping operations in the English Channel, and caused havoc to Axis columns in the Western Desert. 'Tank busting' Hurricanes ranged far and wide in practically every operational theatre. One fighter, flown by Flt Lt J.B. Nicholson of No. 249 (Fighter) Squadron, during that eventful late summer of 1940, helped earn for its gallant pilot the only Victoria Cross to be awarded to a member of Fighter Command. This occurred on 17 August when, with his Hurricane badly damaged and wreathed in flames, the

wounded and severely burnt Nicholson succeeded in destroying the attacking Messerschmitt Bf 110 before baling out, to be rescued and survive his wounds.

It is not really surprising, therefore, that for many years after the end of World War II, a lone Hurricane had the honour of leading the RAF fly-past over London, flown each year to commemorate victory in the Battle of Britain. Some 23 Hurricanes have been preserved: these comprise five Mk Is, 14 Mk IIs, two Mk IVs, one Mk X and one Mk XI. The RAF's Historic Aircraft Flight has two of the Mk IIs.

Specification

Type: single-seat fighter/fighter-bomber

Powerplant (Mk IIB): one 1,280-hp (954-kW) Rolls-Royce Merlin XX inline piston engine

Performance: maximum speed 342 mph (550 km/h) at 22,000 ft (6705 m); maximum cruising speed 296 mph (476 km/h) at 20,000 ft (6100 m); long-range cruising speed 212 mph (341 km/h); service ceiling 36,500 ft (11 125 m); range with internal fuel 480 miles (772 km); range with maximum internal plus external fuel 985 miles (1585 km)

Weights: empty 5,500 lb (2495 kg); maximum take-off 7,300 lb (3311 kg)

Dimensions: span 40 ft 0 in (12.19 m); length 32 ft 2½ in (9.82 m); height 13 ft 1 in (3.99 m); wing area 257.5 sq ft (23.92 m²)

Armament: 12 0.303-in (7.7-mm) forward-firing machine-guns, plus two 250-lb (113-kg) or 500-lb (227-kg) bombs

Operators: Belgium, Eire, Finland, (Italy), (Luftwaffe), Netherlands, Persia, RAAF, RAF, RCAF, RNZAF, SAAF, Soviet Union, Turkey

Hawker Hurricane

Hawker Hurricane I of No. 501 Squadron, RAF, Gravesend (UK) in August 1940

Hawker Sea Hurricane

Hawker Canadian Hurricane X completed as Sea Hurricane in 1941

History and notes

The early success of the Hawker Hurricane fighter in RAF service meant that the Royal Navy was keen to acquire numbers of these aircraft to help in the Battle of the Atlantic which, in early 1940, was depicted statistically by a steeply rising graph of shipping losses. A large proportion of such losses resulted far from shore, in areas where land-based aircraft could not provide air cover for Allied convoys. Thus German long-range patrol aircraft were able to range freely, spotting convoys far out at sea, and calling in and directing U-boat packs to attack them.

An interim measure gave birth to the 'Hurricat' a converted Hurricane carried by CAM-ships (Catapult Aircraft Merchantmen). Mounted on and launched from a catapult at the ship's bows, the Hurricane was flown off on what was usually a one-way flight: after providing defence for the convoy there was nowhere for the FAA or RAF pilot to land, which meant that he was obliged to bale out, or ditch his aircraft as near as possible to the convoy, hoping that he would be picked up. The provision of long-range drop tanks beneath the wings, introduced in August 1941 after the CAM-ships had been provided with more powerful catapults for the higher gross weight, improved the situation a little.

Hurricanes converted for the above role needed only the addition of catapult spools, and fifty Mk I landplanes so modified were designated Sea Hurricane IAs. They were followed by about 300 Mk Is converted to Sea Hurricane IB configuration, these having catapult spools plus a V-frame arrester hook; in addition 25 Mk IIA Srs 2 aircraft were similarly modified as Sea Hurricane IBs or Hooked Hurricane IIs. Their initial role was a considerable improvement on CAM-ship deployment, for from October 1941 they began to go to sea aboard MAC-ships, these being large merchant ships which had received the addition of a small flight deck. They carried on deck (for there was no hangar accommodation) a small number of fighter and ASW aircraft, which were able to operate from and to the mini-carriers. Sea Hurricane ICs, introduced in February 1942 were, once again, conventional Mk I conversions with catapult spools and arrester hook: they had, however, the four-cannon wing of the land-based Hurricane IIC. Last of the Sea Hurricanes from British

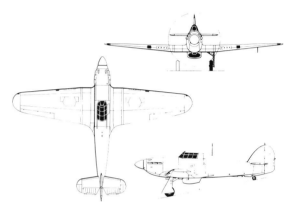

Hawker Sea Hurricane IB

sources was the Mk IIC, which was intended for conventional carrier operations and, consequently, was without catapult spools. They introduced also to navy service the Merlin XX engine, and carried FAA radio equipment. Last of the Sea Hurricane variants was the Mk XIIA, of which a small number were converted from Canadian-built Mk XIIs, and these were used operationally in the North Atlantic and Mediterranean, operating with some success mostly from light carriers and the ubiquitous escort carriers.

Specification

Type: single-seat carrier-based fighter
Powerplant (Mk IIC): one 1,280-hp (954-kW) Rolls-Royce Merlin XX inline piston engine
Performance: maximum speed 342 mph (550 km/h) at 22,000 ft (6705 m); maximum cruising speed 292 mph (470 km/h) at 20,000 ft (6100 m); long-range cruising speed 212 mph (341 km/h); service ceiling 35,600 ft (10 850 m); range with internal fuel 460 miles (740 km); range with maximum internal and external fuel 970 miles (1561 km)
Weights: empty 5,880 lb (2667 kg); maximum take-off 8,100 lb (3674 kg)
Dimensions: span 40 ft 0 in (12.19 m); length 32 ft 3 in (9.83 m); height 13 ft 1 in (3.99 m); wing area 257.5 sq ft (23.92 m²)
Armament: four 20-mm forward-firing cannon
Operators: RN, Royal Canadian Navy

Hawker Typhoon

Hawker Typhoon IB of No. 198 Squadron, RAF, in summer 1944

History and notes

Although, meteorologically speaking, the Hawker Typhoon was little more than an unreliable breeze in its early days, there is no doubt that by the summer of 1944 it had become the strongest wind in Hawker's inventory, as any German survivors of their action at the Falaise gap can testify.

Design of this aircraft had been initiated in 1937 by Sydney Camm, who anticipated that the Air Ministry would shortly be seeking a successor to the Hawker Hurricane. Nevertheless, this interest probably came a little earlier than even he had expected with the issue of Air Ministry Specification F.18/37. This called for a 12-gun interceptor to be powered by either a Rolls-Royce Vulture or a Napier Sabre, both 24-cylinder engines, and with much of the basic design work com-

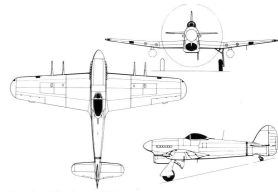

Hawker Typhoon IB (later production with bubble canopy)

An armourer prepares to hoist the first of two underwing bombs onto its attachment points on a Hawker Typhoon IB of No. 175 Squadron of the 2nd Tactical Air Force. Other crew work on the cockpit and engine.

Hawker Typhoon

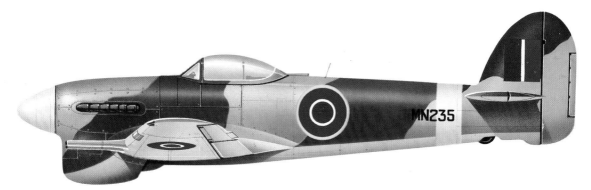

Hawker Typhoon IB in 1943

pleted it was decided to proceed with the final design of two fighters. One was to be powered by the Vulture: this ultimately became known as the Tornado but, like other Vulture-engined projects, was to become the subject of extensive redesign when further development of the Vulture engine was abandoned by Rolls-Royce.

The Sabre-engined version was to become known as the Typhoon and it, in its turn, was to suffer serious development problems, primarily as a result of its chosen powerplant. This, however, was to survive the teething troubles, for the Napier company was able to devote more effort to its development than Rolls-Royce could spare for the Vulture, for the latter were committed to the production and improvement of the

Merlin engine in unprecedented numbers. The Merlin had to have every priority, for so much depended on it.

The Typhoon prototype was flown for the first time on 24 February 1940, and it seems likely that the Hawker design team must have felt that they had laid an egg which, instead of hatching as the light, high-flying hawk that they had anticipated, had cracked apart to reveal an ugly duckling in which nobody seemed to be interested. This was inevitable, of course, in the traumatic period of the war in which its early flight programme took place, for within 10 weeks of the prototype's first flight the Germans had started their attack against western Europe. Within no time at all the UK had its back to the wall, and the only interest shown by the Air Ministry was for the manufacture

RAF armourers prepare to load a pair of 1,000-lb (454-kg) bombs onto the shackles under the wings of a Hawker Typhoon IB fighter-bomber. Rockets could be carried in lieu of bombs.

Hawker Typhoon

Hawker Typhoon IB of No. 440 Squadron, Royal Canadian Air Force, Goch (Germany) in March 1945

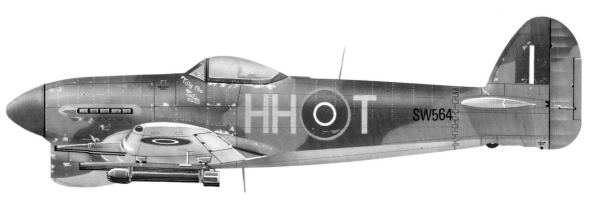

Hawker Typhoon IB of No. 175 Squadron, RAF, Celle (Germany) in April 1945

and delivery of every possible example of the Hurricane, Supermarine Spitfire and Merlin engine. This was considered essential to mount a spirited defence against the anticipated invasion of Britain, which then seemed the inevitable corollary to German occupation of the Low Countries and France.

Adding to the difficulties of the times, and selection of a powerplant which was then both unorthodox and new, Hawker were discovering a few problems of their own. The first major one came on 9 May 1940, for a routine test of the first prototype nearly ended in disaster when the fuselage suffered a structural failure in flight, and there was a loss of a month before investigation and remedial action put the prototype back on the flight line. This aircraft had a 12-gun wing, and was to be designated in production form as the Typhoon Mk IA, the first production example being flown on 27 May 1941. This aircraft had been built by Gloster Aircraft at Hucclecote, the company been given responsibility for construction of the Typhoon from the outset, with the parent company scheduled to manufacture only a token batch.

A little over three weeks before this latter event, on 3 May 1941, the second prototype had been flown. This had different armament, the wing housing four 20-mm cannon, and production aircraft in this configuration were to be designated Typhoon Mk IB. Early production aircraft were almost entirely Mk IAs, with

occasional Mk IBs coming off the line, but ultimately the cannon armament was regarded as the more important and was produced in greater numbers.

In this form the Typhoon was a cantilever low-wing monoplane of all-metal construction, the wing having Frise-type ailerons and split trailing-edge flaps. The fuselage was of what had then become standard Hawker construction, with the centre-region built up of steel tubes and the aft fuselage a monocoque stressed-skin structure. The tail unit was a conventional cantilever structure, and the wide-track landing gear of the retractable tailwheel type. In its later developed form for ground-attack, the pilot had the protection of armour fore and aft, plus a bullet-proof windscreen.

The first production examples began to enter RAF service in September 1941, initially with No. 56 (Fighter) Squadron, and Typhoons were delivered also to the Air Fighting Development Unit. Away from the Gloster incubator where, understandably, the new chicks had been treated with every care, it was soon discovered that the Typhoon's problems had by no means been eradicated. As increasing numbers were delivered to the RAF, so there was a corresponding escalation of the accident rate. This was not confined to service units, however, for a number of Gloster's test pilots were killed in accidents, and it was suggested at the Air Ministry that the type should be withdrawn from service.

Hawker Typhoon

In the low-level role where it excelled, the Hawker Typhoon IB used its quartet of 20-mm cannon, supplemented by eight 60-lb (27-kg) rocket projectiles (illustrated) or two 1,000-lb (454-kg) bombs.

This did not happen, however, for Hawker was able to discover the cause of the problem: fatigue failure at a rear fuselage joint had been responsible for the loss of the complete tail unit of an alarming number of aircraft. But even the elimination of this failing was not to represent the end of the aircraft's teething troubles, for high-speed buffeting and aileron reversals were being experienced, together with continuing engine failures. But by the end of 1942 the worst was over, and the RAF was able to take a less jaundiced look at its new interceptor.

However enthusiastic pilots might be about this or that aspect of the Typhoon's capabilities, there was unanimous agreement that it had an abysmal rate of climb and very disappointing high-altitude performance. The Typhoon's forte was high speed at low altitude, for in this segment of the flight envelope it was supreme among all Allied fighters. These factors had encouraged its deployment in a low-level interception role in late 1941, when German use of the high-speed Focke-Wulf Fw 190 to make hit-and-run attacks against Britain's south and east coast military installations and strategic targets was becoming rather more than a nuisance. The Typhoon quickly showed its capability in this role when No. 609 Squadron took its aircraft to RAF Manston in November 1941, and within a week had destroyed four Fw 190s.

This early and highly successful use of the Typhoon in a low-level role was to encourage further development along the same lines, despite the fact that at that time the cause of mounting Typhoon losses had not been determined. Once this problem was out of the way, and the early and unreliable Sabre I engine replaced by the much improved 2,180-hp (1626-kW) Sabre IIA, it became possible to utilise the growing potential of this aircraft to the full. By the end of 1942 the Typhoon could no longer be regarded purely as a defensive aircraft, for it had become equipped to serve most effectively in an offensive role, thanks to its ability to carry two 250-lb (113-kg), 500-lb (227-kg), or 1,000-lb (454-kg) bombs on underwing racks. These weapons, in conjunction with four wing-mounted 20-mm cannon, were to make the Typhoon an important fighter-bomber, and towards the end of 1942 No. 609 Squadron pioneered the use of these aircraft in a night intruder role. From that period, used primarily by day, but also by night, Typhoons in service with Nos. 174, 181, 245 and 609 Squadrons ranged over France and the Low Countries, playing havoc with German communications. Their low-level, high-speed capability provided a considerable degree of immunity from both German fighters and ground weapons.

During 1943, following an extended series of trials and development, the Hurricane had become the first Allied aircraft to be armed with rocket projectiles, using them operationally for the first time on 2

Hawker Typhoon

Hawker Typhoon IB of No. 3 Squadron, RAF, West Malling (UK) in early 1943

Hawker Typhoon IB of No. 247 Squadron, RAF, Colombes (France) in June 1944

September 1943. Similarly equipped, the Typhoon was to realise its full potential, and by the end of 1943 was operating in conjunction with fighter-bomber squadrons based along Britain's south coast, their combined efforts limiting very considerably German coastal shipping. Even more effective were the low-level attacks which these units mounted almost continuously in the early months of 1944, before D-Day, using the most efficient combination of rockets, bombs and guns to harass German communications by day and night. The aim was not only to attack and eliminate if possible the trains or vehicles moving on rail or road, but also to destroy or damage bridges, tunnels and major junctions. At the height of this campaign up to 150 locomotives were being destroyed each month, and in their first few months of such operations No. 609 Squadron accounted for 100 locomotives for the loss of only two aircraft. The resulting chaotic conditions on D-Day, when it was only with extreme difficulty that the Germans could move troops and essential supplies in the areas behind the Normandy beach-heads, were to prove just how successful this cross-Channel interdiction had been.

There was to be little change in the Typhoon during the last year of war in Europe, other than progressive improvements in the installed powerplant. As mentioned above, the Sabre I had been displaced by the Sabre IIA, and this in turn was to be followed by the

2,200-hp (1641-kW) Sabre IIB, and finally the 2,260-hp (1685-kW) Sabre IIC. Propellers could be either three- or four-blade units of the constant-speed type, supplied by de Havilland or Rotol. Variants were meagre in number, comprising a single NF.Mk IB night fighter converted from a fighter-bomber in late 1941, and equipped with AI Mk VI interception radar, and a small quantity of tactical reconnaissance aircraft. These latter, produced in two versions during 1944, were both designated Typhoon FR.Mk. IB. One carried two vertical cameras and retained its full four-cannon armament, the other substituted a forward-facing ciné recorder for the port inner cannon. When production ended in 1944, more than 3,200 Typhoons had been built, all but about 20 by Gloster Aircraft. They had all been delivered to the RAF, but some were allocated for use by RCAF and RNZAF units operating alongside the RAF in Europe.

By D-Day, utilisation of the Typhoon was at its peak, with no fewer than 26 squadrons serving in the 2nd Tactical Air Force, and these were to play a significant role in the break-out from Caen. Their contribution to the German débâcle at the Falaise gap was little short of horrific, the results best described perhaps by the pen of a Canadian official reporter who commented: 'Burned out tanks and vehicles in incredible numbers lined and blocked every road and track. Dead soldiers and dead horses, by hundreds and thousands, lay on

Hawker Typhoon

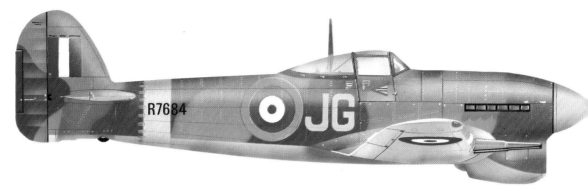

Hawker Typhoon IB of Wg Cdr John Grandy, CO of the Duxford Wing (Nos. 56, 266 & 609 Squadrons, RAF) in June 1942

Hawker Typhoon IB of Flg Off. L.W.F. Stark of No. 609 Squadron, RAF, Manston (UK) in early 1943

Designed to replace the Hurricane as an interceptor, the Hawker Typhoon IB was dogged initially by poor altitude performance and some structural defects, but made its name as a superlative ground-attack aircraft.

the roadways and in the ditches. Bulldozers had to clear a way through the human and mechanical debris for our advancing columns . . . "

Such had become the capability of a 'Hurricane-sized' fighter, so unreliable at the time of its operational debut that it had almost been withdrawn from service. None, however, were to remain in operational use for any considerable time after VE-Day, being replaced by Hawker Tempests.

Specification

Type: single-seat fighter-bomber
Powerplant: one 2,180-hp (1626-kW) Napier Sabre IIA horizontal H piston engine
Performance: maximum speed 374 mph (602 km/h) at 5,500 ft (1675 m), and 405 mph (652 km/h) at 18,000 ft (5485 m); long-range cruising speed 254 mph (409 km/h); service ceiling 34,000 ft (10 365 m); range with maximum weapon load 510 miles (821 km)
Weights: empty 8,800 lb (3992 kg); maximum take-off 11,400 lb (5171 kg)
Dimensions (late production): span 41 ft 7 in (12.67 m); length 31 ft 11½in (9.74 m); height 15 ft 4 in (4.67 m); wing area 279 sq ft (25.92 m²)
Armament (Mk IB): four 20-mm cannon in wings, plus up to eight 60-lb (27-kg) rocket projectiles or two 1,000-lb (454-kg) bombs on underwing racks
Operators: RAF, RCAF, RNZAF

Hawker Tempest

Hawker Tempest II of No. 33 Squadron, RAF, Germany in 1947

Hawker Tempest II of No. 54 Squadron, RAF, Chilbolton (UK) in 1946

History and notes

The Hawker Typhoon proved a disappointment in its intended role as an interceptor, although it was to distinguish itself later as a fighter-bomber, particularly when armed with rocket projectiles. Its rate of climb and performance at altitude were relatively poor, and in 1941 it was suggested that remedial action might be taken in the form of a new, thinner wing, elliptical in planform. The radiator was to be moved from beneath the engine to the wing leading-edges, and the Napier Sabre EC.107C was specified. As the new wing would be some 5 in (0.13 m) thinner than that of the Typhoon, the inclusion of an additional fuselage fuel tank was needed to replace the wing-tank capacity lost.

The design study, originally referred to as the Typhoon II, was submitted to the Air Ministry, and on 18 November 1941 two prototypes were ordered to Specification F.10/41. There were major changes, however, compared with the earlier aircraft, resulting in the name change to Tempest in early 1942. After cancellation of the Hawker Tornado programme, the alternative engine installations planned for that aircraft were, instead, applied to the Tempest. Thus the two original prototypes became the Tempest I with Sabre IV and Tempest V with Sabre II, and four more were ordered. Two Tempest IIs were to have the 2,520-hp (1879-kW) Bristol Centaurus, and two Tempest IIIs the Rolls-Royce Griffon IIB, becoming Tempest IVs

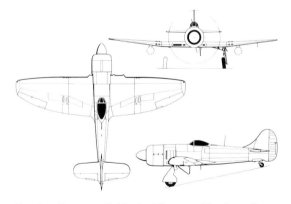

Hawker Tempest II (dashed line on side view: fin profile of prototype; dashed line on front view: optional underwing bombs)

when re-engined with the Griffon 61. Only one Griffon-engined aircraft was completed, in fact, as one of the prototype Hawker Furies.

Before any of the prototypes could be flown, however, the Air Ministry placed contracts for 400 Tempest Is, although these were later transferred to other versions. The prototype Tempest I, its lines not spoilt by the beard radiator of the Typhoon, was flown on 24 February 1943, and later achieved a maximum speed of 466 mph (750 km/h) at 24,500 ft (7470 m) with the

161

Hawker Tempest

The radial-engined counterpart of the inline-engined Tempest V, the Hawker Tempest II entered service just after the war. Performance of the two was roughly comparable, apart from the Tempest II's superior range.

Sabre IV's supercharger in FS (high) gear. The engine programme suffered from technical problems and delays, however, and the Tempest I was dropped.

The first of the Tempest prototypes to fly had been that of the Mk V, flown by Philip Lucas on September 1942. Retaining the Typhoon's chin radiator, it was fitted originally with a standard Typhoon tail unit, but the lengthened fuselage necessitated the addition of a fairing to the leading-edge of the fin, and an increase in tailplane chord. The first of 805 Tempest Vs was flown from Langley on 21 June 1943, one of the initial production batch of 100 Series 1 aircraft which had four 20-mm British Hispano Mk II cannon, whose barrels protruded from the leading-edge of the wing. The remaining Tempest Vs had short-barreled Mk V cannon, completely contained in the wings. In 1945, one Mk V was fitted with a 40-mm 'P' gun under each wing, similar to the 40-mm cannon installation of the Hawker Hurricane IID. After the war had ended some were converted for use as TT.5 target tugs.

An order for 500 of the Centaurus-powered Tempest IIs was placed in October 1942, once again before the first flight of the prototype. This first flight took place on 28 June 1943, the aircraft being powered by a Mk IV engine, which was superseded by the 2,520-hp (1879-kW) Mk V in the production aircraft that were built

under sub-contract by the Bristol Aeroplane Company at its Weston-super-Mare factory. The first Bristol-built aircraft flew on 4 October 1944, but only 36 were completed before production was transferred back to Hawker, the parent company manufacturing a further 100 F.II fighters and 314 FB.II fighter-bombers with underwing racks for bombs or rockets. In 1947 India ordered 89 tropicalised Tempest IIs from RAF stocks, and in the following year Pakistan ordered 24 similar aircraft although, unlike the Indian aircraft, they retained the fuel transfer system fitted to RAF Mk IIs.

The third and last production version of the Tempest was the F.VI with the 2,340-hp (1745-kW) Napier Sabre V engine, the result of a trial installation in the Tempest V prototype which was first flown in this configuration on 9 May 1944. Increased radiator frontal area necessitated the transfer of carburettor intakes to the wings, and the installation of an additional oil cooler in the starboard wing root. Intended for service in the Middle East, 142 tropicalised Tempest VIs were built. As in the case of the Mk V, some were converted as TT.6 target tugs.

RAF service commenced in April 1944, when 50 Tempest Vs were delivered to Newchurch, Kent, where the first Tempest Wing was formed within No. 85 Group, under the command of Wing Commander

Hawker Tempest

Hawker Tempest V of No. 486 (New Zealand) Squadron, RAF, Venlow (Netherlands) in January 1945

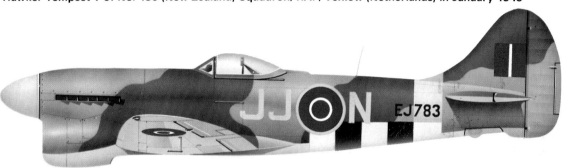

Hawker Tempest V of No. 274 Squadron, RAF, in spring 1945

Hawker Tempest VI

Hawker Tempest V of No. 501 Squadron, RAF, Hawkinge (UK) in 1944-5

Hawker Tempest

Another classic design from Sydney Camm, the Hawker Tempest V was essentially a Typhoon with a number of aerodynamic improvements, principally a thinner wing of elliptical planform and a longer fuselage.

R.P.Beaumont, DSO, DFC. The component squadrons were Nos. 3 and 486 Squadrons, Royal New Zealand Air Force, joined by No. 56 Squadron in June. The wing was active during the build-up to the Normandy invasion, but on 13 June the first V-1 flying bomb fell at Swanscombe in Kent, and the Tempests were among aircraft tasked to combat the menace. Their success can be measured by the fact that of 1,847 bombs destroyed by fighters between June 1944 and March 1945, 258 were disposed of by No. 3 Squadron and kills confirmed for No. 486 totalled 223½. Top-scoring Tempest pilot against V-1s was Sqdn Ldr J. Berry of No. 501 Squadron at Hawkinge, with 61⅓. Until the end of war in Europe, Tempest Vs flew 'cab rank' patrols in support of ground forces, moving up to airfields in France and Belgium as the Germans fell back. In addition, they engaged in combat the Luftwaffe's Messerschmitt Me 262 jet fighters, 20 of which were destroyed before VE-Day.

Although plans were made for 50 Tempest IIs to be sent to the Far East in May 1945, to operate with Tiger Force against the Japanese, the war in the Pacific ended before these aircraft were ready for service. Wing Cdr Beaumont was to have commanded the wing, and it was he who flew the leading aircraft in the Victory Fly Past over London on 8 June 1946, No.

54 Squadron at Chilbolton having re-equipped with the type in November 1945. It was to be the only home-based Mk II unit, the others serving in Germany, Hong Kong, India, and Malaya. The Tempest VI was also too late to see wartime service, although this mark was flown later by squadrons in Germany and the Middle East. The Tempest II remained operational with squadrons in the Middle East until they were replaced by de Havilland Vampires during 1949.

Specification

Type: single-seat fighter/fighter-bomber
Powerplant (Mk V): one 2,180-hp (1626-kW) Napier Sabre IIA inline piston engine
Performance: maximum speed 426 mph (686 km/h) at 18,500 ft (5640 m); service ceiling 36,500 ft (11 125 m); maximum range 1,530 miles (2462 km)
Weights: empty 9,000 lb (4082 kg); maximum take-off 13,540 lb (6142 kg)
Dimensions: span 41 ft 0 in (12.50 m); length 33 ft 8 in (10.26 m); height 16 ft 1 in (4.90 m); wing area 302 sq ft (28.06 m²)
Armament: four 20-mm cannon, plus two 500-lb (227-kg) or two 1,000-lb (454-kg) bombs, or rocket projectiles
Operators: RAF, RNZAF

Hawker Tornado

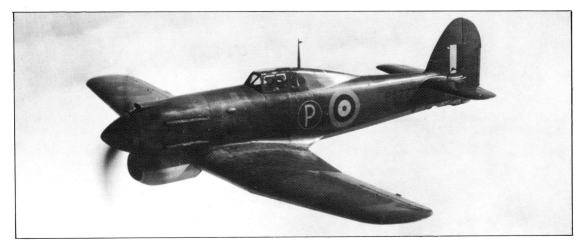

The specification that led to the great Typhoon also spawned another Hawker design, the Tornado powered by the Rolls-Royce Vulture. The first prototype had a ventral radiator, while the second had a chin radiator.

History and notes

Hawker's proposals for a Hurricane replacement comprised two alternative projects, one with a Napier Sabre engine, known initially as the Type N, and the other with a Rolls-Royce Vulture, referred to as Type R. The former later became the Typhoon and the latter the Tornado, both developed to Air Ministry Specification F.18/37 which called for a high performance single-seat fighter with 12 0.303-in (7.7-mm) machine-guns. It was to have a minimum speed of 400 mph (644 km/h) at 15,000 ft (4570 m), and a service ceiling of 35,000 feet (10 670 m).

Two prototypes of each design were ordered on 3 March 1938, both structurally similar, the major differences being dictated by the characteristics of the respective engines. The front fuselage of the Tornado was extended by 1 ft (0.30 m), the wings fitted three inches (0.08 m) lower on the fuselage, and the radiator located beneath the fuselage; the general appearance was, therefore, very similar to that of the Hurricane.

The first prototype was moved from Kingston to Langley for completion and its first flight was made on 6 October 1939, the pilot being P.G.Lawrence. Flight trials revealed airflow problems around the radiator, which was relocated to a chin position, and the aircraft was test-flown in its new configuration on 6 December. Later changes included increased rudder area, and the installation of a Rolls-Royce Vulture V engine.

The second prototype, completion of which was delayed by concentration on Hurricane production, featured the chin radiator, additional window panels in the fairing behind the cockpit, and four 20-mm cannon in place of the 12 machine-guns. Its first flight was made on 5 December 1940, powered by a Vulture II, although as in the case of the first machine, a Vulture V was later installed.

Five hundred production aircraft were ordered in late 1939, and sub-contracted to Avro at Manchester; only one was actually completed and flown, at Woodford, on 29 August 1941. Shortly afterwards the

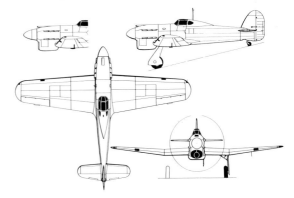

Hawker Tornado 2nd prototype (scrap view: nose of single production Tornado I used for trials of Rotol contra-rotating propeller unit)

Vulture programme was abandoned, closely followed by cancellation of the Tornado order. One other Tornado, the third prototype, was flown on 23 October 1941, powered by a 2,120-hp (1581-kW) Bristol Centaurus CE.4S engine, and this was the progenitor of the Hawker Tempest II.

Specification

Type: single-seat fighter
Powerplant: one 1,980-hp (1476-kW) Rolls-Royce Vulture V inline piston engine
Performance: maximum speed 398 mph (641 km/h) at 23,000 ft (7010 m); service ceiling 34,900 ft (10640 m)
Weights: empty 8,377 lb (3800 kg); maximum take-off 10,668 lb (4839 kg)
Dimensions: span 41 ft 11 in (12.78 m); length 32 ft 10 in (10.01 m); height 14 ft 8 in (4.47 m); wing area 283 sq ft (26.29 m²)
Armament: none fitted, but with provision for four 20-mm cannon in outer wing panels
Operator: RAF (evaluation only)

Hawker Sea Fury

The Hawker Sea Fury was the epitome of the Camm design philosophy, its clean lines and powerful Centaurus engine offering sparkling performance allied with good armament and first-class handling characteristics.

History and notes

Intended originally as a smaller, lighter version of the Hawker Tempest, to meet the requirements of Specification F.6/42, the Hawker Fury fighter was developed to the joint Air Ministry/Admiralty requirements of Specifications F.2/43 and N.7/43. Hawker was to design and develop the land-based version, and Boulton Paul to undertake the conversion of the naval aircraft.

By December 1943, six prototypes had been ordered: one was to be powered by a Bristol Centaurus XII, two with the Centaurus XXII, and two with the Rolls-Royce Griffon; the sixth was to be a test airframe. The first to fly was the Centaurus XII-powered aircraft, which made its maiden flight on 1 September 1944, followed by the Griffon 85-engined second prototype on 27 November; the latter was later re-engined with a Napier Sabre VII.

Although production contracts had been placed in April 1944 for 200 aircraft for the Royal Air Force, and a similar number for the Fleet Air Arm, including 100 to be built by Boulton Paul, the RAF order was cancelled at the war's end. Development of the Sea Fury continued, however, the first prototype having flown on 21 February 1945, powered by a Centaurus XII. This aircraft was fitted with an arrester hook, but retained non-folding wings; the first fully-navalised aircraft was the Centaurus XV-powered second prototype, which flew on 12 October.

The Boulton Paul contract had been cancelled in January 1945, and of the 100 Sea Furies that remained on order the first 50 were completed as Mk X fighters. The first of these was flown on 7 September 1946, and the third undertook trials aboard HMS *Victorious* during the winter of 1946-7, prior to the type entering service with Nos. 778, 802, 803, 805 and 807 Squadrons.

In May 1948 No. 802 Squadron was the first to receive the Sea Fury FB.11, of which 615 were built to

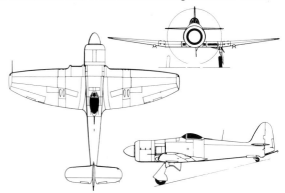

Hawker Sea Fury FB.11

British contracts, including 31 and 35 aircraft for the Royal Australian and Royal Canadian Navies respectively.

Specification

Type: single-seat carrier-based fighter-bomber
Powerplant: one 2,480-hp (1849-kW) Bristol Centaurus 18 radial piston engine
Performance: maximum speed 460 mph (740 km/h) at 18,000 ft (5485 m); service ceiling 35,800 ft (10 910 m); range 700 miles (1127 km) with internal fuel
Weights: empty 9,240 lb (4191 kg); maximum take-off 12,500 lb (5670 kg)
Dimensions: span 38 ft 4¾ in (11.70 m); length 34 ft 8 in (10.57 m); height 15 ft 10½ in (4.84 m); wing area 280 sq ft (26.01 m²)
Armament: four 20-mm cannon in wings, and racks for 12 60-lb (27-kg) rockets, or two 1,000-lb (454-kg) bombs under the wings
Operators: RAF (evaluation only), RN

Miles M.3B Falcon Six

History and notes

The first true cabin aircraft designed by F.G.Miles, the M.3 Falcon made its first flight on 12 October 1934 and the following March was flown from Darwin to Lympne by H.L. Brook, establishing a solo record for the trip of under eight days.

While the prototype was a three-seater, the first production example seated four in a wider cabin. A number of variants of the basic aircraft were flown under the names M.3A Falcon Major and M.3B Falcon Six, and two of the latter were built for the Royal Aircraft Establishment, Farnborough, to test wing sections. The RAE later acquired a third aircraft from the Netherlands.

Total production of the various Falcons amounted to 36, of which six were impressed for military service in World War II. Half of these survived to return to civilian ownership, and one of the RAE aircraft was used postwar to test the wing of the Miles M.52 supersonic project, in which version it was known as the Gilette Falcon.

Specification

Type: three/four-seat communications aircraft
Powerplant: one 200-hp (149-kW) de Havilland Gipsy Six inline piston engine
Performance: maximum speed 180 mph (290 km/h); cruising speed 160 mph (257 km/h); range 560 miles (901 km)
Weights: empty 1,550 lb (703 kg); maximum take-off 2,650 lb (1202 kg)
Dimensions: span 35 ft 0 in (10.67 m); length 25 ft 0 in (7.62 m); height 6 ft 6 in (1.98 m); wing area 174 sq ft (16.16 m²)
Armament: none
Operators: RAE, RAF

Miles M.11A Whitney Straight

History and notes

In the mid-1930s Whitney Straight, then a young and wealthy aviation and motor racing enthusiast, and much later deputy chairman of British Overseas Airways Corporation, approached F.G.Miles to initiate the design of a new lightplane for club use. This was envisaged as a side-by-side two-seat cabin monoplane which both realised would give a greater degree of comfort than contemporary open cockpit aircraft.

The result was the M.11, named Whitney Straight, and flown on 14 May 1936 in prototype form. Its all-round good qualities ensured immediate production, with only minor modifications to the landing gear and windscreen, and the asking price was a competitive £985.

In the two years of production, 50 Whitney Straights were built for civilian customers and several were used for experimental purposes; the second production aircraft was a test-bed for the 135-hp (101-kW) Villiers Maya engine, the prototype at one time had a Menasco Pirate, and another aircraft used a 140-hp (104-kW) de Havilland Gipsy Major II with a variable-pitch propeller. Experiments with auxiliary aerofoil flaps on the prototype gave useful data for later Miles aircraft, such as the M.28, Messenger and Gemini.

Although no new Whitney Straights were supplied to the services, a number were impressed during World War II, including 23 for the RAF (21 in the UK and two in India); three were similarly acquired by the Royal New Zealand Air Force.

Specifications

Type: two-seat communications aircraft
Powerplant: one 130-hp (97-kW) de Havilland Gipsy Major inline piston engine
Performance: maximum speed 145 mph (233 km/h); range 570 miles (917 km)
Weights: empty 1,275 lb (578 kg); maximum take-off 1,896 lb (860 kg)
Dimensions: span 35 ft 8 in (10.87 m); length 25 ft 0 in (7.62 m); height 6 ft 6 in (1.98 m); wing area 187 sq ft (17.37 m²)
Armament: none
Operators: RAF, RNZAF

A successful pre-war lightplane, the Miles Whitney Straight appealed to the RAF as a light communications type, and 20 were impressed. Such a fate befell G-AERV which became EM999.

Miles M.14 Magister

Miles Magister of an RAF training unit in 1940

History and notes

Following the success of the Miles Hawk Trainer on the civil market and in the Elementary Flying Training School operated by Phillips & Powis (later Miles Aircraft), the Air Ministry produced Specification T.40/36 for a development of the Hawk to be built as an elementary trainer for the RAF. The new aircraft was to make history as the first low-wing trainer adopted by that service, and it also cut across the contemporary Air Ministry policy to use only metal aircraft, by being of wooden construction with plywood covering.

Changes to the basic design of the Hawk Trainer included larger cockpits and provision of blind flying equipment, and production began to a new specification, T.37/37; the first M.14 Magister was christened on 20 March 1937, and displayed at Woodley by F.G.Miles.

Deliveries to the RAF began in May 1937, and early production aircraft were virtually identical to the prototype. Problems were encountered early in the Magister's life when a series of crashes followed failure to recover from a spin. The prototype, which had been flown to the Aircraft and Armament Experimental

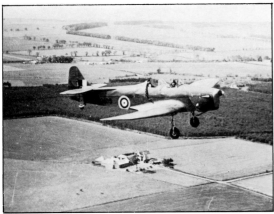

The Miles Magister was the RAF's first monoplane trainer, entering service in October 1937. It remained in use throughout the war, and no fewer than 16 Elementary Flying Training Schools were equipped with the type.

Establishment, Martlesham Heath, for spinning trials, was lost in this way on its first flight from the test establishment, the pilot escaping by parachute.

Modifications to cure the problem included the raising of the position of the tailplane, the redesign of the rear fuselage and decking, and the fitting of anti-spin strakes. When these did not prove sufficient a new rudder of increased area and higher aspect ratio was fitted and this cured the fault. The modifications were incorporated in all subsequent Magisters, these being designated M.14A. Although landing gear fairings were fitted as standard on new aircraft they were usually removed in service, presumably to avoid mud clogging the wheels.

Production ran from 1937 to 1941, and at its peak reached 15 per week. The Air Ministry contract covered 1,229 aircraft, but some of these were exported; there were also additional aircraft built for overseas orders. Countries receiving Magisters for military use included Egypt (42), New Zealand (2), Eire (15) and Turkey (4), and this last country also built 100 under licence. In addition to military orders, a number of civil M.14s were supplied before the war, and many ex-RAF Magisters came back on to the civil market as Hawk Trainer IIIs after the war had ended.

In RAF service the Magister proved an excellent trainer, its low-wing layout being particularly useful for fighter pilot training, and several RAF Magisters were used for experimental purposes during the war. When a German invasion of Britain was expected, in June 1940, racks to carry eight 25-lb (11-kg) bombs were fitted to about 15 aircraft; some de Havilland Tiger Moths were similarly adapted.

In 1941, the Air Ministry asked Miles to experiment with an auxiliary aerofoil surface, or wing, to see if it was feasible that such a device could be used to carry bombs and thereby increase the bomb load of medium bombers. Towed behind a Magister, the idea was found to be practicable, but the advent of larger bombers rendered it unnecessary.

Another interesting experiment involved the trials of landing gear legs and wheels which could be castored. This was then considered desirable to simplify

Miles M.14 Magister

cross-wind landings on the new runways which were beginning to appear, replacing the earlier all-grass airfields on which a landing could be made from any direction.

Magisters served with many Elementary Flying Training Schools, the Central Flying School, and in all RAF commands; the type also saw service with the British Army and Fleet Air Arm. With the army its work included glider pilot training and co-operation with ground forces. Many Magisters were used as squadron 'hacks', and for general communications duties, and it is recorded that some 40 Fighter Command squadrons each had a Magister on strength.

The Magister lingered on in RAF service until about 1948, when the last were put up for disposal.

Specification
Type: two-seat elementary trainer
Powerplant: one 130-hp (97-kW) de Havilland Gipsy Major I inline piston engine
Performance: maximum speed 132 mph (212 km/h) at 1,000 ft (305 m); cruising speed 123 mph (198 km/h); service ceiling 18,000 ft (5485 m); range 380 miles (612 km)
Weights: empty 1,286 lb (583 kg); maximum take-off 1,900 lb (862 kg)
Dimensions: span 33 ft 10 in (10.31 m); length 24 ft 7½ in (7.51 m); height 6 ft 8 in (2.03 m); wing area 176 sq ft (16.35 m²)
Armament: none
Operators: Egypt, Eire, RAF, RNZAF, Turkey

Miles M.16 Mentor

History and notes
Developed from the Miles M.7 Nighthawk, the M.16 Mentor was produced to meet Air Ministry Specification 38/37 for a three-seat cabin communications monoplane with a 200-hp (149-kW) engine. Among its other duties, the Mentor was to be capable of carrying out instrument and radio training by day or night. Full dual controls were specified, together with blind-flying instruments, landing lights and radio.

The prototype flew on 5 January 1938, proving to be heavier and more sluggish than the Miles M.7 Nighthawk which had preceded it, but was submitted for trials, and orders for 45 were placed for supply to the RAF.

Like the Magister, the Mentor was provided with anti-spin strakes and, following the prototype's testing, a taller rudder similar to that of the Magister was fitted. Used by the RAF for communications and train-ing, only one Mentor survived the war, being sold to a civil owner in 1947, but this was destroyed in a crash on 1 April 1950.

Specification
Type: three-seat training and communications aircraft
Powerplant: one 200-hp (149-kW) de Havilland Gipsy Six 1 inline piston engine
Performance: maximum speed 156 mph (251 km/h) at sea level; service ceiling 13,800 ft (4205 m)
Weights: empty 1,978 lb (897 kg); maximum take-off 2,710 lb (1229 kg)
Dimensions: span 34 ft 9½ in (10.60 m); length 26 ft 1¾ in (7.97 m); height 9 ft 8 in (2.95 m); wing area 181 sq ft (16.81 m²)
Armament: none
Operator: RAF

Miles M.17 Monarch

History and notes
An improved model of the Miles M.11 Whitney Straight, the M.17 Monarch flew on 21 February 1938. Designed by George Miles, the new aircraft had three seats and a deeper windscreen than its forerunner. The outer wing panels were interchangeable with those of the Magister, and a number of other standard Miles parts were used.

Extensive demonstrations, both at home and abroad, aroused considerable interest, but with Master and Magister production in full swing there was little space available for the Monarch to be built, and only 11 were laid down before World War II broke out.

Five Monarchs were impressed for RAF service, this number including one Belgian civil aircraft which had been flown to the UK in May 1940 when Belgium was invaded. Used as communications aircraft by the RAF, and by several manufacturers including Phillips & Powis, Rolls-Royce and Vickers Armstrongs, four of the Monarchs survived the war and were returned to civil ownership.

Specification
Type: three-seat communications aircraft
Powerplant: one 130-hp (97-kW) de Havilland Gipsy Major inline piston engine
Performance: maximum speed 140 mph (225 km/h) at sea level; cruising speed 125 mph (201 km/h); service ceiling 17,400 ft (5305 m); range 620 miles (998 km)
Weights: empty 1,390 lb (630 kg); maximum take-off 2,150 lb (975 kg)
Dimensions: span 35 ft 7 in (10.85 m); length 25 ft 11¾ in (7.92 m); height 8 ft 9¼ in (2.67 m); wing area 180 sq ft (16.72 m²)
Armament: none
Operator: RAF

Miles M.20

A magnificent extemporisation, the Miles M.20 utility fighter was developed in nine weeks from Master and other 'off the shelf' parts, but despite adequate performance and good armament did not find favour.

History and notes

Sixty-five days from beginning of design to first flight of a new fighter sounds impossible today, when gestation periods of aircraft are measured in years rather than days, but this astonishing feat was achieved with the Miles M.20. The intention was to evolve a fighter of all-wood construction, which could be manufactured at high speed in the UK and Canada, to supplement the RAF's Hawker Hurricanes and Supermarine Spitfires in the inevitable struggle following German occupation of Western Europe.

Miles had been given authority by Lord Beaverbrook, Minister of Aircraft Production, to proceed with the design against Specification F.19/40, and Walter Capley was in charge of the team. The whole concept was based on speed of production and, where possible, standard Miles Master parts were used. A fixed spatted landing gear was fitted, all hydraulics being eliminated, and the extra space which this provided in the wings enabled 12 Browning 0.303-in (7.7-mm) machine-guns to be installed, plus 5,000 rounds of ammunition and 154 Imperial gallons (700 litres) of fuel. Offering double the range and ammunition of the Spitfire and Hurricane, its speed of 350 mph (563 km/h) was between that of these two in-service fighters. A far superior field of vision was provided by the bubble canopy, and the 1,300-hp (969-kW) Rolls-Royce Merlin XX engine was the same as that used in the Halifax and Lancaster.

The prototype M.20 was flown for the first time by Tommy Rose on 14 September 1940, and testing proved the new fighter to be satisfactory. But the Battle of Britain was nearing its end by that time, and as the RAF still had fighters in reserve the M.20 was not needed. During the winter of 1940 the aircraft was damaged when, unable to stop on the icy grass runway at Woodley, it went through a fence and into a sandpit.

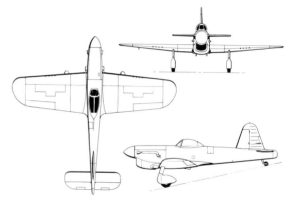

Miles M.20 Mk II

There was some revival of interest when Specification N.1/41 for a new naval fighter was issued, and a second M.20 prototype was built and underwent service trials, but no order was forthcoming.

Specification

Type: single-seat fighter

Powerplant: one 1,300-hp (969-kW) Rolls-Royce Merlin XX inline piston engine

Performance: maximum speed 350 mph (563 km/h) at 20,600 ft (6280 m); service ceiling 31,400 ft (9570 m); range 870 miles (1400 km)

Weights: empty 5,870 lb (2663 kg); maximum take-off 7,758 lb (3519 kg)

Dimensions: span 34 ft 7 in (10.54 m); length 30 ft 1 in (9.17 m); height 12 ft 6 in (3.81 m); wing area 234 sq ft (21.74 m²)

Armament: 12 fixed forward-firing 0.303-in (7.7-mm) machine-guns in outer wing panels

Operator: RAF, RN (for evaluation only)

Miles M.25 Martinet

The Miles Martinet was the RAF's first target-tug to be designed as such, and offered markedly superior performance to such types as the Westland Wallace. Between 1942 and 1945 more than 1,700 were built.

History and notes

For a number of years, target towing for the British services was carried out by obsolete aircraft adapted for the purpose, but in 1941 F.G.Miles was approached by the Air Ministry with a request to evolve an aircraft specifically for this purpose. Specification 12/41 was issued, and the prototype M.25 flew on 24 April 1942, to be followed shortly after by the second prototype.

The Martinet, as this excellent little tug became named, was based on the Miles Master II but had a longer nose than the trainer, this being necessary to compensate for the weight of target-towing equipment which considerably altered the position of the centre of gravity; the cockpit enclosure also differed; and the winch could be either wind-driven or motorised. Stowage was provided for six flag and sleeve drogue targets. Construction followed normal Miles practice, with a wooden structure covered in plywood.

As Martinet production began the type superseded the Master on the line at Woodley, and between 1942 and 1945 more than 1,700 were built. They continued to serve for some years after the war until replaced by faster aircraft.

In 1943 the Air Ministry awarded a contract to Miles for a radio-controlled pilotless version of the Martinet. Built to Specification Q.10/43, and the Miles designation M.50, this variant was known as the Queen Martinet, and following successful tests with the prototype a production contract for 65 was awarded, of which 11 were new and the remainder conversions of M.25 target tugs. Entering service during 1946, these replaced biplanes such as the Queen Bee and Queen Wasp, then in service with the RAF and Royal Navy, and demonstrated a 30 per cent increase in speed over the latter.

Another version of the standard Martinet was a glider tug, in which the standard target-towing gear was replaced by somewhat heavier equipment to make it suitable for its new role. Apart from deletion of the winch, the only external difference was removal of the lower part of the rudder to prevent it from fouling the tow cable.

The Air Ministry had ordered into production a turboprop-powered trainer, the Boulton Paul Balliol, but to guard against extended delay in delivery of its powerplant Miles proposed a development of the Martinet. In 1946 the company built two prototypes of an M.37 trainer version of the Martinet; in these the instructor's cockpit (to the rear) was raised well above the level of that of the pupil forward, and fitted with a clear vision teardrop canopy. It was not, however, awarded a production contract as the Boulton Paul Balliol was then nearing completion.

Six surplus Martinets received civil registrations after the war; four were sold to Sweden where they were operated by the civil target-towing company, Svensk Flygtjärst, while the other two were broken up for spares in the UK in 1948.

Specification

Type: two-seat target tug
Powerplant: one 870-hp (649-kW) Bristol Mercury XX or XXX radial piston engine
Performance: maximum speed 240 mph (386 km/h) at 5,800 ft (1770 m); cruising speed 199 mph (320 km/h) at 5,000 ft (1525 m); range 694 miles (1117 km)
Weights: empty 4,640 lb (2105 kg); maximum take-off 6,750 lb (3062 kg)
Dimensions: span 39 ft 0 in (11.89 m); length 30 ft 11 in (9.42 m); height 11 ft 7 in (3.53 m); wing area 242 sq ft (22.48 m²)
Armament: none
Operator: RAF, RN

Miles M.28

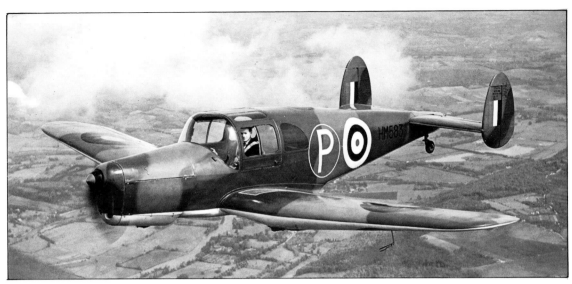

The Miles Mercury was conceived as an economical replacement for the Whitney Straight and Monarch (M.11 and M.17), and is here seen in prototype form. It was not ordered into production during World War II.

History and notes

The Miles M.28 had originally been projected in 1939 as a replacement for the Miles M.11 Whitney Straight and M.17 Monarch, but on the outbreak of war the scheme was shelved, only to be revived in 1941 when a requirement for a new trainer and communications aircraft arose.

Design work was carried out as a private venture, by Ray Bournon under the direction of George Miles, and the M.28 followed the usual Miles practice of wooden construction. Many features were introduced that were not then found on training aircraft, including retractable landing gear, wing trailing-edge flaps, constant-speed propeller and enclosed cabin side-by-side seating.

As a communications aircraft the M.28 had four seats, and according to the manufacturer's figures, with these filled it could have a still air range of 500 miles (805 km), a top speed of 160 mph (257 km/h) and cover 20 miles (32 km) per Imperial gallon (4.5 litres) of fuel, impressive figures even today.

George Miles first flew the M.28 on 11 July 1941. It proved to have light and effective controls, although the low aspect ratio wing gave a marked rate of sink which could be turned to advantage in that, with its slow approach speed, the landing run was very short.

Only six M.28s were built because of Miles' other wartime production commitments. They were fitted with a variety of engines, No. 1 having a 130-hp (97-kW) de Havilland Gipsy Major I, No. 2 a 140-hp (104-kW) Gipsy Major IIA, Nos. 3, 5 and 6 a 150-hp (112-kW) Blackburn Cirrus Major III (also fitted at a later date to No. 2) and No. 4 a 145-hp (108-kW) Gipsy Major IIA. The first four were built respectively in 1941, 1942, 1943 and 1944, while the remaining two flew in 1947 and 1946.

M.28 No. 3 was built to a Ministry of Aircraft Pro-

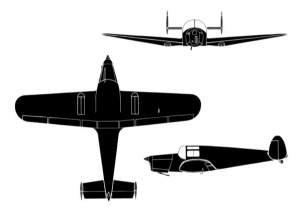

Miles M.28 Mercury

duction order for evaluation as a triple-control trainer, this differing in some respects from the other aircraft, for its layout put two pupils side-by-side in the front seats with the instructor seated centrally behind them.

Specification

Type: two-seat trainer/four-seat communications aircraft

Powerplant: one 150-hp (112-kW) Blackburn Cirrus Major III inline piston engine

Performance: maximum speed 159 mph (256 km/h); cruising speed 152 mph (245 km/h); range 408 miles (657 km)

Weights: empty 1,658 lb (752 kg); maximum take-off 2,500 lb (1134 kg)

Dimensions: span 30 ft 8 in (9.35 m); length 24 ft 0 in (7.32 m); height 8 ft 4 in (2.54 m); wing area 162 sq ft (15.05 m²)

Armament: none

Operator: RAF (for evaluation only)

Miles M.33 Monitor

History and notes

The first Miles aeroplane to employ composite wood and metal construction, the M.33 Monitor was built to Specification Q.9/42 for a twin-engined target tug capable of towing at not less than 300 mph (483 km/h) at 20,000 ft (6100 m). It was to have an endurance of about 3½ hours, and was required to be able to fly at only 90 mph (145 km/h) when streaming targets. A most unusual item of the specification called for the capability of being accommodated in standard packing cases when dismantled.

Despite issuing the specification, the Air Ministry was not then convinced of the need for a twin-engined target tug, and Miles' project was rejected as suitable engines were not available. Eventually, when the Ministry agreed on the twin formula, the 1,700-hp (1268-kW) Wright Cyclone was chosen and Miles received an order for 600 aircraft.

The prototype Monitor flew on 5 April 1944, only 15 months after the basic design had been agreed, but was subsequently destroyed in a crash near Woodley after a fire in one of the engine bays. Two further prototypes followed, but as the end of the war was in sight the order was cut to 200, then to 50, and eventually cancelled after 20 Monitors had been completed.

By this time it had been decided that the aircraft would not go to the RAF, but to the Royal Navy as the Monitor TT.Mk II. Ten were delivered to serve briefly with the Fleet Requirements Unit, but were soon replaced by Mosquito TT.39s.

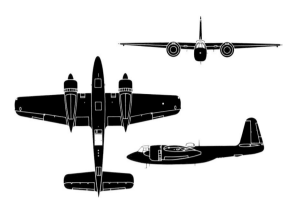

Miles Monitor II

Specification

Type: two-seat high-speed target tug
Powerplant: two 1,700-hp (1268-kW) Wright Cyclone R-2600-31 radial piston engines
Performance: maximum speed 330 mph (531 km/h) at 15,000 ft (4570 m); cruising speed 265 mph (426 km/h) at 15,000 ft (4570 m); service ceiling 29,000 ft (8840 m); maximum range 2,750 miles (4426 km)
Weights: empty 15,850 lb (7189 kg); maximum take-off 21,075 lb (9559 kg)
Dimensions: span 56 ft 3 in (17.15 m); length 47 ft 8 in (14.53 m); height 14 ft 3 in (4.34 m); wing area 500 sq ft (46.45 m²)
Armament: none
Operator: RN

With the Miles Monitor the British finally acquired a target-tug able to operate at speeds comparable with those of current fighters, but the 20 built for the RAF were in the event used only by the Fleet Air Arm.

Miles M.35

History and notes
Among the collection of projects which emerged from Miles during World War II, two of the strangest were the M.35 and M.39 tandem-wing aircraft, and while most of the projects did not materialise, these two were built and flown.

The M.35 was conceived as a layout practicable for a carrier-based fighter, the pilot being in the extreme nose with the pusher engine mounted behind the rear wing. With the availability of lift from two wings, span could be short and there would be no need for wing-folding.

Designed by Ray Bournon under the direction of George Miles, and built in secrecy, the M.35 was completed and flown in six weeks, using landing gear and rudders from a Miles Magister. On 1 May 1942 it flew (following taxying trials) with George Miles at the controls, but proved to be very unstable, a situation which later wind-tunnel tests showed could be largely cured, so the tandem-wing layout was proved feasible.

A proposal for a tandem-wing naval fighter was submitted but not accepted.

Specification
Type: single-seat tandem-wing research aircraft
Powerplant: one 130-hp (97-kW) de Havilland Gipsy

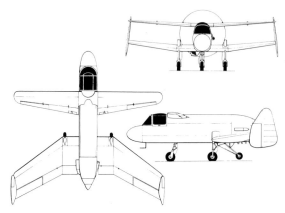

Miles M.35

Major inline piston engine
Performance: no data available
Weights: empty 1,456 lb (660 kg); maximum take-off 1,850 lb (839 kg)
Dimensions: span 20 ft 5 in (6.22 m); length 20 ft 4 in (6.20 m); height 6 ft 9 in (2.06 m); wing area 134.50 sq ft (12.50 m²)
Armament: none
Operator: UK (for evaluation only)

Miles M.38 Messenger

History and notes
At the private request of certain army officers in June 1942, George Miles designed and built the prototype of an air observation post (AOP) aircraft. The requirements were an ability to carry two people, a radio, armour plating and other military equipment. At the same time, it had to be suitable for operation from small, tree-surrounded fields in all weathers, be maintained in the field by unskilled staff, and have the capability of being flown by pilots of limited experience.

There is little doubt that this was just the sort of challenge on which George Miles thrived; he took the prototype M.28 fuselage and its engine, to which he added a larger one-piece wing with non-retractable external aerofoil flaps, and a large tailplane with endplate fins and rudders, third central fin and rudder being added later. To produce the required ground angle for the short landing and take-off characteristics, a stalky, fixed landing gear was adopted, and the powerplant was given a fine-pitch propeller.

Within three months of the initial approach, George Miles flew the prototype M.38 on 12 September 1942, subsequently allowing an AOP squadron to test fly it. The M.38 was an instant success, proving capable of fulfilling all the army's requirements. At this juncture officialdom stepped in and, not for the first time, Miles was reprimanded for not obtaining government authority before building the aircraft. So strong was the feeling of the Ministry of Aircraft Production on this matter that the M.38 was not ordered for the AOP

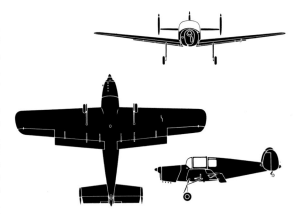

Miles Messenger

squadrons; but in the following year Miles received a small production order against Specification 17/43 for the type to be used for VIP communications work under the name Messenger. A total of 21 was built, 11 at Reading and 10 at Newtonards, Northern Ireland. Among the VIPs to receive personal Messengers were Field Marshal Sir Bernard Montgomery and Marshal of the RAF Lord Tedder.

Miles continued to experiment with the prototype Messenger in a number of ways. One idea was to operate the aircraft in an anti-submarine role, using a 60ft (18.29 m) square deck aboard a small merchant ship, which would be provided with simple arrester

Miles M.38 Messenger

gear. The scheme was tested successfully at Woodley, using a simulated deck and with nets to stop the aircraft should its hook fail to engage the bungee cord arrester. The Messenger's ability to carry two depth charges was also proved by the carriage of similarly weighted ballast in the form of five passengers plus the pilot. Even so, no further action was taken by the authorities to implement the scheme.

In 1944 one Messenger was fitted with a 150-hp (112-kW) Blackburn Cirrus Major engine and retractable flaps, under the designation M.48, but the modification had little effect on performance and was not taken any further.

Nineteen of the 21 Messengers that had been built survived the war, and were released for civil use; at the same time production for the civil market was initiated. By January 1948, when production came to an end, a total of 92 Messengers (21 military and 71 civil) had been built; one more was assembled in 1950. With their wooden construction few survive today, but one is still flying in the UK, painted to represent Montgomery's aircraft.

Specification
Type: four-seat liaison and VIP communications aircraft
Powerplant: one 140-hp (104-kW) de Havilland Gipsy Major inline piston engine
Performance: maximum speed 116 mph (187 km/h);

The Miles Messenger was developed to an army specification for an air observation post (AOP) aircraft, but the 21 production examples were used by the RAF for light communications and liaison with three passengers.

cruising speed 95 mph (153 km/h); service ceiling 14,000 ft (4265 m); range 260 miles (418 km)
Weights: empty 1,518 lb (689 kg); maximum take-off 1,900 lb (862 kg)
Dimensions: span 36 ft 2 in (11.02 m); length 24 ft 0 in (7.32 m); height 9 ft 6 in (2.90 m); wing area 191 sq ft (17.74 m²)
Armament: none
Operator: RAF

Miles M.39B

History and notes
Encouraged by his experiments in the belief that the tandem-wing layout would work, George Miles conceived a heavy bomber, the M.39, to be powered by three turbojet engines, or in its initial form with two high-altitude Rolls-Royce Merlin 60s or Bristol Hercules VIIIs.

A five-eighths scale model of the bomber was built and designated M.39B, flying for the first time on 22 July 1943 with George Miles at the controls. Powered by two 140-hp (104-kW) de Havilland Gipsy Major engines, the aircraft was stable and had normal handling characteristics, unlike the M.35.

Flight trials continued on a private venture basis, but in 1944 the Ministry of Aircraft production said they wished to buy the M.39B and would continue flight trials at the Royal Aircraft Establishment, Farnborough, to speed up the programme. The reverse happened when an RAE pilot forgot to lower the undercarriage and made a belly landing, necessitating return to Miles for repairs. Shortly afterwards the aircraft was blown on to its back at the RAE by the slipstream of another aircraft running up, so back it went to Miles for extensive repairs.

All the work, however, came to nothing, and the M.39B was returned to Miles at the end of its RAE tests, subsequently being broken up.

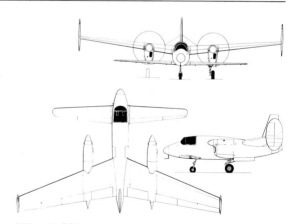

Miles M.39B

Specification
Type: two-seat tandem-wing research aircraft
Powerplant: two 140-hp (104-kW) de Havilland Gipsy Major IC inline piston engines
Performance: maximum speed 164 mph (264 km/h)
Weights: empty 2,405 lb (1091 kg); maximum take-off 2,800 lb (1270 kg)
Dimensions: span 37 ft 6 in (11.43 m); length 22 ft 2 in (6.76 m); height 9 ft 3 in (2.82 m); wing area 249.20 sq ft (23.15 m²)
Armament: none
Operator: UK (for evaluation only)

Miles Master (M.9, M.19, M.24 and M.27)

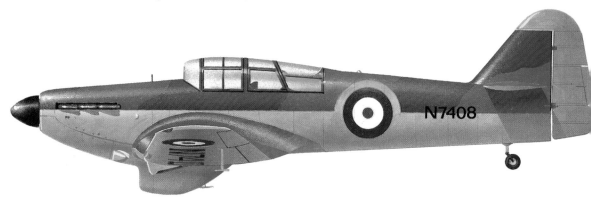

Miles Master I of an RAF training unit in 1940

History and notes

By the mid-1930s the RAF had begun to take delivery of its first high-performance monoplanes, and it became clear that a trainer with similar performance characteristics would be required. F.G.Miles therefore designed a low-wing monoplane trainer around the 745-hp (556-kW) Rolls-Royce Kestrel XVI engine used in the Hawker Fury and Hart biplanes. Rolls-Royce had acquired a large financial interest in Phillips & Powis, primarily to ensure a continuing market for the Kestrel engine, and the new aircraft acquired the same name. Of wooden construction, this trainer was of exceptionally clean design, and Miles duly submitted it to the Air Ministry. It was turned down as being premature but Miles, undeterred, pressed on with construction as a private venture. The Kestrel flew first on 3 June 1937 and proved to have an exceptional performance, with a top speed of almost 300 mph (483 km/h), a mere 20 mph (32 km/h) less than the Hawker Hurricane, which had an engine giving an additional 350 hp (261 kW).

With the failure of another trainer project which had been ordered by the Air Ministry, and with nothing else in prospect, an official order was placed on 11 June 1938 to Specification 16/38. This was for the M.9 development of the Kestrel, to be named Master, and the £2 million contract was then the largest ever awarded by the Air Ministry for a training aircraft.

The Ministry demanded a considerable number of modifications to the Kestrel design to meet their requirements. Changes were made to the windscreen, cabin top, rear fuselage and tail unit, the radiator was moved back from its position beneath the engine to below the wing centre-section, and the engine was changed to the derated 715-hp (533-kW) Kestrel XXX. Not surprisingly, the changes were made at a considerable cost to performance, the Master I having a top speed 70 mph (113 km/h) below that of the Kestrel; even so, it was still the best training aircraft of its day, and had handling characteristics similar to those of the Hurricane and Supermarine Spitfire. Like the Kestrel, it was of wooden construction, covered with plywood.

The first of 900 M.9A Master Is flew on 31 March 1939, but only seven had entered service by the

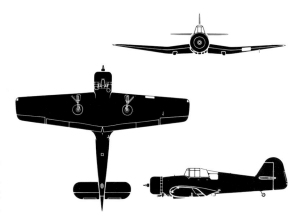

Miles Master III

outbreak of World War II. A sliding canopy soon replaced that of hinged design fitted on early aircraft, and in 1942 the round wingtips were removed in favour of square-cut tips, reducing the span by 3 ft 2 in (0.97 m) to 39 ft (11.89 m). A popular feature with pilots was the provision of a hand control box of Miles design: mounted on the port side of the cockpit, this incorporated controls for throttle, mixture, propeller, landing gear, trailing-edge flaps, landing lights, and elevator and rudder trim tabs, all easily accessible to the left hand.

A number of Master Is were converted to single-seat configuration and equipped with six 0.303-in (7.7-mm) Browning machine-guns at the time of the Battle of Britain. Intended for use in dire emergency, none of these M.24 Modified Master Is were, however, used in anger. In addition to use in a training role, Master Is were also attached to squadrons for ferrying pilots.

Before the Master I entered production, Miles was asked by the Air Ministry to modify an airframe to take the 870-hp (649-kW) Bristol Mercury XX engine as stocks of the Rolls-Royce Kestrel, then no longer in production, were unlikely to be adequate to meet total production requirements. With the Miles designation M.19, the Mercury-engined Master made its first flight in November 1939 and undertook service trials during the same month. In this form it became the M.19

Miles Master (M.9, M.19, M.24 and M.27)

The Miles Master was the most significant indigenously designed advanced trainer used by the RAF in World War II, and is seen here in the form of an M.27 Master III powered by the Pratt & Whitney Wasp Junior.

Master II, and was 16 mph (26 km/h) faster than its predecessor.

At this point the Ministry found that there were no stocks of Mercury engines available, so another powerplant, the 825-hp (615-kW) Pratt & Whitney Wasp Junior, was installed in a modified airframe and flown as the M.27 Master III in 1940. This was some 10 mph (16 km/h) slower than the Master II, but otherwise satisfactory. By the time it had completed its trials, however, the Ministry had discovered stocks of Mercury engines, so the Master II and III were both put into production. Assembly lines at Woodley and South Marston built the Mk II, while the Mk III was only built at the latter factory. A total of 1,698 Master IIs was built, plus 602 Mk IIIs, before the two production lines became occupied with other types: Miles Martinets at Woodley and Spitfires at South Marston. By the time production had been completed, 1,748 Master IIs and 602 Master IIIs (excluding prototypes) had been built for the RAF.

All variants of the Master had an instructor's seat in the rear cockpit, which could be raised to provide a better view over the head of the pupil in the front seat for take-off and landing. Interconnected with the seat-raising mechanism was a hinged panel in the cockpit canopy which was raised automatically to provide a windscreen for the instructor.

Master IIs were used for a variety of experiments in addition to their normal training role. One was fitted with underwing rockets to assess its suitability as an armed trainer, and in 1942 a requirement arose to replace the Hawker Audax and Hector biplane in the light glider-tug role. Within five days of the request being made by the Air Ministry, Miles delivered a Master II for service trials; it had been modified to incorporate a towing hook in the rear fuselage with a release mechanism in the cockpit. The trials were completely successful and a number of other airframes were similarly converted to tow Hotspur gliders.

In addition to the RAF orders, a number of Master IIs were supplied to overseas military customers, including 26 to Egypt, 18 to Turkey, and one to Portugal. One aircraft was transferred to the US Air Force, and one Master III went to the Irish Air Corps. Many Master IIs were shipped to South Africa.

Specification

Type: two-seat advanced trainer
Powerplant (Mk II): one 870-hp (649-kW) Bristol Mercury XX radial piston engine
Performance: maximum speed 242 mph (389 km/h) at 6,000 ft (1830 m); service ceiling 25,100 ft (7650 m); range 393 miles (632 km)
Weights: empty 4,293 lb (1947 kg); maximum take-off 5,573 lb (2528 kg)
Dimensions: span 39 ft 0 in (11.89 m); length 29 ft 6 in (8.99 m); height 9 ft 3 in (2.82 m); wing area 235 sq ft (21.83 m²)
Armament: provision for one fixed forward-firing Vickers 0.303-in (7.7-mm) machine-gun and practice bombs
Operators: Egypt, Eire, RAF, SAAF, Turkey

Percival Proctor

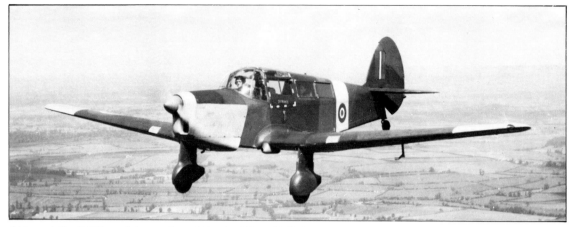

Although the RAF bought a number of Percival Vega Gulls for communications duties before the war, it was as the Proctor that the type was more widely produced (1,143) as a radio-trainer and liaison aircraft.

History and notes

Developed from the pre-war Vega Gull, fifteen of which had been acquired by the Royal Air Force for communications duties and for the use of overseas air attachés, the Percival Proctor was designed to Air Ministry Specification 20/38 as a communications and radio training aircraft. The prototype made its first flight on 8 October 1939, and was the first of more than 1,100 military examples to be produced during the war years for the RAF and Fleet Air Arm.

The initial production version was the P.28 Proctor I (247 built), a three-seat communications aircraft, followed by the P.30 Proctor II (175) and P.34 Proctor III (437), both of which were radio trainers without dual controls. Named originally Preceptor, and designed to Specification T.9/41, the P.31 Proctor IV had a longer, deepened fuselage to accommodate four, including trainee radio operators who were provided with operational standard equipment. The increase in capacity made this an effective communications aeroplane, and many were later fitted with dual controls. An experimental Proctor IV with a 250-hp (186-kW) de Havilland Gipsy Queen engine was used as a personal transport by Air Vice Marshal Sir Ralph Sorley. Some 258 Proctor IVs were built and powered, as in the case of the earlier marks, by the 210-hp (157-kW) Gipsy Queen II engine.

Most Proctors built during the war were manufactured under sub-contract by F. Hills and Sons of Manchester, the result of the involvement of the Percival factory at Luton with sub-contract manufacture of Airspeed Oxfords and de Havilland Mosquitoes. Hills share comprised 25 Mk Is, 100 Mk IIs, 437 Mk IIIs and 250 Mk IVs.

At the end of World War II, more than 200 Proctor Is, IIs and IIIs were prepared for disposal to civil buyers, but some Mk IVs remained in service with communications squadrons until 1955, when surviving aircraft were similarly sold on the civil market. In 1945, however, three Proctor IVs had been furnished to civil standards to meet an expected postwar demand from

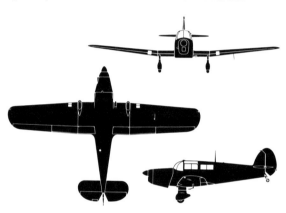

Percival Proctor IV

charter companies and flying clubs, leading to the introduction of the Proctor 5. One hundred and fifty of this version were built, and of these four were supplied to the RAF, for use by air attachés, under the designation Proctor C.5. A single Proctor 6 floatplane was built in 1946 for the Hudson's Bay Company in Canada.

Specification

Type: three/four-seat radio trainer and communications aircraft

Powerplant: one 210-hp (157-kW) de Havilland Gipsy Queen II inline piston engine

Performance: maximum speed 160 mph (257 km/h); cruising speed 140 mph (225 km/h) at 3,000 ft (915 m); service ceiling 14,000 ft (4265 m); range 500 miles (805 km)

Weights: empty 2,370 lb (1075 kg); maximum take-off 3,500 lb (1588 kg)

Dimensions: span 39 ft 6 in (12.04 m); length 28 ft 2 in (8.59 m); height 7 ft 3 in (2.21 m); wing area 202 sq ft (18.77 m²)

Armament: none

Operators: RAF, RN

Percival Q.6 Petrel

History and notes

Edgar Percival's first twin-engined aircraft was the Type Q, designed as a Q.4 four-seat executive transport with a crew of two, and powered by de Havilland Gipsy Major engines; or as a six-seat Q.6 feederliner with 205-hp (153-kW) Gipsy Six engines. Only the Q.6 was built, and the prototype was first flown at Luton by Captain Percival on 14 September 1937.

Of wooden construction with plywood and fabric covering, the aircraft initially had fixed tailwheel type landing gear, the main units in streamlined fairings beneath the engine nacelles. The Q.6 entered production in 1938, and 27 aircraft were completed, including four with retractable landing gear. The first of the latter was used for landing gear trials at Martlesham Heath in June 1938, and after completion of these tests, although built to the order of Captain P.G.Taylor, the renowned Australian pilot and navigator, the aircraft was delivered not to him but to Vickers-Armstrong Ltd.

Government users included Egypt, with two camouflaged aircraft, while the Royal Air Force received seven new Q.6s, to which the service name Petrel was applied. The Petrel was ordered under Air Ministry Specification 25/38 for communications duties and the last of the RAF order was delivered in March 1940. By May 1940 the nine civil-registered Q.6s which were based in Great Britain had been impressed for use by the RAF and the Royal Navy, serving with station flights and communications squadrons. Two aircraft were impressed at Heliopolis in February 1940 and December 1941.

One Q.6 was used by Vickers as a civil aircraft throughout the war, but in 1946 four impressed machines which had survived hostilities were assembled with many other requisitioned aircraft at No. 5 Maintenance Unit at Kemble for sale to civil buyers. Three of the seven RAF Petrels also found their way onto the British civil register in 1946 and 1947.

Specification

Type: four/six-seat communications aircraft or feederliner
Powerplant: two 205-hp (153-kW) de Havilland Gipsy Six inline piston engines
Performance: maximum speed 195 mph (314 km/h); cruising speed 175 mph (282 km/h); service ceiling 21,000 ft (6400 m); range 750 miles (1207 km)
Weights: empty 3,500 lb (1588 kg); maximum take-off 5,500 lb (2495 kg)
Dimensions: span 46 ft 8 in (14.22 m); length 32 ft 3 in (9.83 m); height 9 ft 9 in (2.97 m); wing area 278 sq ft (25.83 m²)
Armament: none
Operators: RAF, RN

The RAF bought eight Percival Q.6s as communications aircraft with the name Petrel. At least another 12 civil Q.6s were impressed, and the USSR took over two Q.6s of the Lithuanian National Airline in 1940.

Saro A.27 London

Saro London II of No. 240 Squadron, RAF, Calshot/Invergordon/Sullow Voe/Pembroke Dock (UK) in 1939/40

History and notes

Between the wars the flying boat reigned supreme for coastal patrol work with the RAF, and the Saro London, together with its contemporary, the Supermarine Stranraer, were the last of the biplane flying boats to see service before replacement by the Short Sunderland. Twenty-nine Londons were still in service at the outbreak of World War II.

The prototype London, built to Specification R.24/31, flew in 1934 and the type was ordered into production in the following March. Deliveries began in 1936 and the first ten aircraft were designated Mk Is. Construction Nos. 11 to 48 (the final production London) were all Mk IIs, which differed in having 915-hp (682-kW) Bristol Pegasus X engines, driving four-bladed propellers, in place of the Mk I's 820-hp (611-kW) Pegasus IIIs with two-bladed propellers.

First service deliveries, between April and September 1936, were to No. 201 Squadron, replacing Supermarine Southamptons at Calshot; further batches were delivered in October 1936 to No. 204 Squadron at Mount Batten, Plymouth, also replacing Southamptons. More were delivered to the same squadron at Mount Batten the following year to replace Blackburn Perths, and in 1938 the Londons supplanted Supermarine Scapas of No. 202 Squadron at Malta.

No. 204 Squadron used five Londons on a long-

The Saro London II differed only slightly from the London I, and 29 Londons were in service in 1939. The type at the time served with three Coastal Command squadrons, one in the Mediterranean and two in the UK.

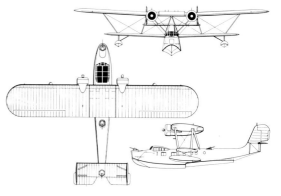

Saro London II

distance training flight to New South Wales and back between December 1937 and May 1938, with external overload fuel tanks to increase their range to 2,600 miles (4184 km).

Nos. 201, 202 and 240 Squadrons were still operating Londons in first-line service at the outbreak of war, but they were retired early in 1941 when replaced by Consolidated Catalinas, some Londons going to the Royal Canadian Air Force.

Specification

Type: six-seat general reconnaissance flying boat
Powerplant (Mk II): two 915-hp (682-kW) Bristol Pegasus X radial piston engines
Performance: maximum speed 155 mph (249 km/h) at 6,250 ft (1905 m); cruising speed 129 mph (208 km/h); service ceiling 19,900 ft (6065 m); range 1,100 miles (1770 km)
Weights: empty 11,100 lb (5035 kg); maximum take-off 18,400 lb (8346 kg)
Dimensions: span 80 ft 0 in (24.38 m); length 56 ft 9½ in (17.31 m); height 18 ft 9 in (5.72 m); wing area 1,425 sq ft (132.38 m²)
Armament: three 0.303-in (7.7-mm) Lewis guns (one each in nose, dorsal and tail positions), plus up to 2,000 lb (907 kg) of bombs
Operators: RAF, RCAF

Saro S.36 Lerwick

Intended as a medium-range counterpart to the long-range Sunderland, the Saro Lerwick proved to have dismal water and air handling characteristics, and the 21 built served operationally for only a few months.

History and notes

Designed to Specification R.1/36, the Saro S.36 Lerwick was intended to serve alongside the Short Sunderland in RAF Coastal Command. The first three aircraft were used for trials, completed in 1938, and these revealed that the Lerwick was unstable on the water and in the air.

The deficiencies were sufficient, in the opinion of the pilots and crews who flew the machine, to render it unfit for service use, and a series of modifications were made, including the fitting of auxiliary fins; these improved the performance, but were subsequently replaced by a larger fin and rudder.

Trials continued and revealed that the Lerwick had a vicious stall and its performance in roll and yaw was still not satisfactory. However, as the war had by now begun and aircraft were required urgently, production started and the type first entered service with No. 209 Squadron at Oban towards the end of 1940, replacing Short Singapores. One aircraft was soon lost, sinking on 6 December, and another went just over three months later.

The last of 21 Lerwicks was delivered to the RAF in May 1941, the same month in which No. 209 Squadron re-equipped with Consolidated Catalinas. A few Lerwicks served with No. 4 Operational Training Unit at Invergordon, and three others carried out service trials with No. 240 Squadron. The type was withdrawn from operational service in May 1941 and declared obsolete the following year as soon as adequate numbers of more acceptable patrol flying-boats became available from home production and Lend-Lease.

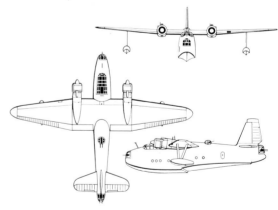

Saro Lerwick I

Specification

Type: six-seat reconnaissance flying boat
Powerplant: two 1,375-hp (1025-kW) Bristol Hercules II radial piston engines
Performance: maximum speed 216 mph (348 km/h) at 4,000 ft (1220 m); cruising speed 166 mph (267 km/h); service ceiling 14,000 ft (4265 m)
Weight: maximum take-off 33,200 lb (15 059 kg)
Dimensions: span 80 ft 10 in (24.64 m); length 63 ft 7½ in (19.39 m); height 20 ft 0 in (6.10 m); wing area 845 sq ft (78.50 m²)
Armament: seven 0.303-in (7.7-mm) machine-guns (one in nose turret, two in dorsal turret and four in tail turret), plus up to 2,000 lb (907 kg) of bombs
Operator: RAF

Short S.19 Singapore III

Short Singapore III of No. 203 Squadron, RAF, Aden in 1940

History and notes

Largest of the RAF's prewar biplane flying boats still in service at the outbreak of World War II, the Short S.19 Singapore III was powered by two tractor and two pusher Rolls-Royce Kestrel engines, mounted in back-to-back pairs.

Development of the Singapore's basic design began with the Mk I of 1926, and was followed by the Mk II of 1930 which did not go into production. The Mk III was Short's submission to Specification R.3/33; four development aircraft were ordered and the first flew in July 1934. This batch underwent trials at the Marine Aircraft Experimental Establishment, Felixstowe, and following the completion of these a production order was issued against a new Specification, R.14/34. Contracts followed in batches, and production ceased with the 37th aircraft in June 1937.

The four development aircraft were delivered to squadrons for operational training, and the first production Singapore III flew in March 1935. Deliveries began to No. 230 Squadron at Pembroke Dock in April 1935, and other Singapores went to Nos. 203, 205, 209 and 210 Squadrons.

Nineteen Singapores were still in service at the outbreak of World War II, and continued in operational use until replaced by Sunderlands.

Specification

Type: six-seat general reconnaissance flying boat
Powerplant: four 560-hp (418-kW) Rolls-Royce Kestrel inline piston engines
Performance: maximum speed 145 mph (233 km/h) at 2,000 ft (610 m); cruising speed 105 mph (169 km/h); service ceiling 15,000 ft (4570 m); range 1,000 miles (1609 km)
Weights: empty 18,420 lb (8355 kg); maximum take-off 27,500 lb (12 474 kg)
Dimensions: span 90 ft 0 in (27.43 m); length 76 ft 0 in (23.16 m); height 23 ft 7 in (7.19 m); wing area 1,834 sq ft (170.38 m²)
Armament: three 0.303-in (7.7-mm) Lewis guns (one each in nose, dorsal and tail positions) plus up to 2,000 lb (907 kg) of bombs
Operators: RAF, RNZAF

The last of Short's biplane flying boats, the Singapore III was a classic of its type. Production reached 37, and these boats equippped six home and three overseas squadrons. The RNZAF also had four Singapores.

Short S.25 Sunderland

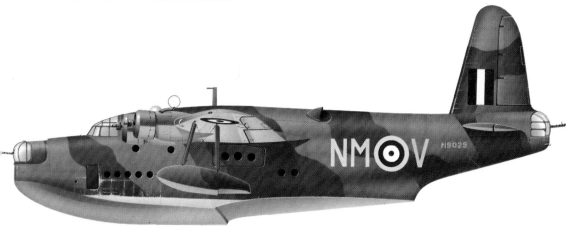

Short Sunderland I

History and notes

From the 'Empire' (C class) flying boats with which Imperial Airways had established many of their long-distance commercial air routes during the 1930s, Short Brothers developed their S.25 military general reconnaissance flying boat to Air Ministry Specification R.2/33, revised in March 1936 as Specification R.22/36 to cover an initial production order for 21 Sunderlands. The prototype was flown from the River Medway at Rochester, on 16 October 1937, its power-operated nose and tail turrets being the first fitted to a British flying boat.

A total of 90 Sunderland Is was built, with 1,010-hp (753-kW) Bristol Pegasus XXII engines, and with one 0.303-in (7.7-mm) Vickers 'K' gun in each of two beam positions, supplementing the two 0.303-in Brownings in the nose turret and four similar weapons in the tail. The Sunderland II, introduced in August 1941, had a power-operated dorsal turret in place of the beam guns. Twenty-three were built at Rochester, 15 at Short Brothers and Harland's Belfast factory, and five under sub-contract by Blackburn Aircraft at Dumbarton, the last-named company having previously built 15 Mk Is.

Air-to-Surface Vessel (ASV) Mk II radar was fitted to early Sunderlands, identified by the four vertical masts rising from the top of the hull and by the two rows of four transmitting loops on each side of the fuselage. The equipment was also fitted to the Mk III, of which the first production example flew on 15 December 1941. It retained the 1,065-hp (794-kW) Pegasus XVIII engines of the Mk II, but featured a revised planning bottom, with a shallow forward step. Mk III production totalled 456 aircraft, of which 71 were built at Belfast, 35 at the Short factory at Windermere, 170 by Blackburn and the rest at Rochester.

The Sunderland IV, evolved to meet the requirements of Specification R.8/42 for a more powerful, more heavily armed flying boat for operation in the Pacific theatre, resulted in two Bristol Hercules-powered prototypes, but this version differed to the extent that it was virtually a different aeroplane and

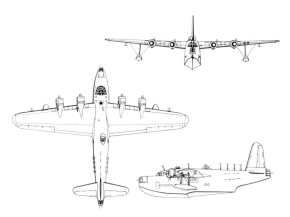

Short Sunderland III

was thus renamed Seaford, so that the last production version was the Mk V.

Introduced in March 1944, the Sunderland V was powered by four 1,200-hp (895-kW) Pratt & Whitney Twin Wasp radial engines, introduced to overcome the problem of engine wear which had resulted from the need to run the Pegasus engines almost continuously at full power. ASV Mk IVC radar, introduced on late production Mk IIIs, was standard equipment for the Mk V, the scanners being located in blisters outboard of the outer float bracing wires under the wings. Construction of the Mk V totalled 150, with 47 built at Belfast, 43 at Rochester and 60 at Dumbarton. A number of Mk IIIs were later converted to Mk V standard.

The first operational Sunderland squadron was No. 230, then based at Seletar, Singapore, with Short Singapores. Initial deliveries were made in June 1938, the aircraft being ferried out by No. 210 Squadron from Pembroke Dock, and re-equipment was completed in December. Withdrawn to Koggola, Ceylon, in February 1940, the squadron operated from bases in North Africa, Egypt and East Africa before returning to the Far East in May 1945, finally taking up residence at its old home base at Seletar on 1 December.

A magnificent shot of a Short Sunderland V planing 'on the step'. The aircraft illustrated is a machine of No. 201 Squadron. Comprehensively equipped with defensive and offensive armament, and provided with the latest ASV Mk VIC radar with split scanners in radomes under each wing, the Sunderland V posed a formidable threat to U-boats, the more so as it was armed with four fixed forward-firing machine-guns in the nose (the two ports on the left-hand side of the aircraft can just be seen under the nose turret) to counter the efforts of German AA guns located on conning towers.

Short S.25 Sunderland

Short Sunderland III in southern Pacific markings

At home, No. 228 Squadron gave up its Supermarine Stranraers for Sunderlands in November 1938 at Pembroke Dock, joining No. 210 Squadron as one of three home-based RAF Sunderland squadrons that were operational when war broke out. The third was No. 204, which replaced its Saro Londons in June 1939 at Mount Batten, Plymouth. Coastal Command's first U-boat kill was recorded on 31 January 1940, when a Sunderland of No. 228 Squadron sighted *U-55*, which was promptly scuttled. A little over two months later, on 3 April, a Sunderland demonstrated its remarkable defensive power to the Germans, to whom it became known as the 'Flying Porcupine', when it beat off an attack by six Junkers Ju 88s, destroying one, forcing another to land in Norway, and driving off the remaining four.

Other squadrons based in the UK included Nos. 119, 201 and 246, while Commonwealth units operating in Britain included Nos. 10 and 461 Squadrons, Royal Australian Air Force, the former having received its first Sunderland at Pembroke Dock on 11 September 1939, while the latter was formed at Mount Batten on 25 April 1942. Nos. 422 and 423 Squadrons Royal Canadian Air Force were equipped with Sunderlands, initially at Oban, from December and July 1942 respectively. Formed at Oban in February 1943, No. 330 Squadron was a Norwegian-manned Sunderland unit, later based at Sullom Voe.

In March 1941 No. 95 Squadron moved to Freetown, Sierra Leone, to operate its Sunderlands over the South Atlantic, in which theatre it was joined by No. 204 at Bathurst, the Gambia, in August 1941; by No. 270 at Apapa, Nigeria, in December 1943; and by No. 490 Squadron, Royal New Zealand Air Force at Jui, Sierra Leone, in May 1944. At Dakar Aéronavale *Flottille* 7E became No. 343 Squadron, Royal Air Force, in November 1943, and was re-equipped with Sunderlands.

Over the Indian Ocean Sunderlands shared patrol duties with Consolidated Catalinas and Consolidated Liberators, flying with No. 230 Squadron from Dar es Salaam in January 1943. No. 209 Squadron was another East African-based unit which converted to Sunderlands at Kpevu, Kenya, in February 1945, moving to Koggala, Ceylon in July 1945, these joining No. 205 which had converted from Catalinas the previous month, and replacing No. 230 which had moved on to Akyab, Burma. VJ-Day found No. 230 Squadron at Redhills Lake, Madras, together with No. 240 Squadron which had formed there on 1 July 1945.

After the war had ended the Sunderland force was run down, and by June 1948, when the Berlin Airlift started, only Nos. 201 and 230 Squadrons and No. 235 Operational Conversion Unit were available for use. Between June and December their aircraft carried almost 4,800 tons (4877 tonnes) of freight from Hamburg to Berlin's Havel See. All British-based Sunderland operations ceased with the disbandment of Nos. 201 and 230 Squadrons on 28 February 1957. In the Far East the Sunderland was not retired until 1959.

Specification

Type: 10-seat long-range maritime reconnaissance-bomber flying boat

Powerplant: four 1,200-hp (895-kW) Pratt & Whitney R-1830-90B Twin Wasp radial piston engines

Performance: maximum speed 213 mph (343 km/h) at 5,000 ft (1525 m); cruising speed 133 mph (214 km/h) at 2,000 ft (610 m); service ceiling 17,900 ft (5455 m); range 2,690 miles (4329 km) with 1,668 lb (757 kg) of bombs

Weights: empty 36,900 lb (16 738 kg) maximum take-off 65,000 lb (29 484 kg)

Dimensions: span 112 ft 9½ in (34.38 m); length 85 ft 3½ in (26.00 m); height 34 ft 6 in (10.52 m); wing area 1,687 sq ft (156.72 m²)

Armament: ten 0.303-in (7.7-mm) machine-guns (four fixed forward firing, two in bow turret, and four in tail turret) and two 0.50-in (12.7-mm) machine-guns (one each in port and starboard beam positions) plus up to 4,960 lb (2250 kg) of bombs, mines, or depth charges

Operators: RAAF, RAF, RCAF, RNZAF

Short S.45 Seaford

History and notes

For service in the Pacific the Air Ministry required a more powerful, more heavily armed flying boat than the Short Sunderland, and specification R.8/42 was met by a new Short design, known originally as the Sunderland V but later renamed Seaford, with the company designation S.45.

Gross weight rose to 75,000 lb (34 019 kg) and a number of structural improvements were incorporated to compensate for this; these included a strengthened wing and enlarged horizontal tail surfaces. The hull was also modified, its beam being increased by 1 ft (0.30 m) by the introduction of flared chines, and the step was deepened. Overall length was increased by 3 ft 3 in (0.99 m). Armament comprised two 0.50-in (12.7-mm) machine-guns in a Brockhouse turret in the bow, and two 0.303-in (7.7-mm) machine-guns in the nose decking. Two 20-mm cannon were mounted in a Boeing B-17 dorsal turret, and the Martin tail turret contained a pair of 0.50-in guns, two more of which were located in beam positions. A bomb load could also be carried in a fashion similar to that of the Sunderland.

The first of two prototypes, powered by four 1,680-hp (1253-kW) Bristol Hercules XVII engines, was flown on 30 August 1944 and 30 production aircraft, with 1,720-hp (1283-kW) Hercules XIXs, were also ordered. Of these only six were completed. In April and May 1946 No. 201 Squadron carried out operational trials with the Seaford, in co-operation with the Marine Aircraft Experimental Establishment at Felixstowe, but the programme was cancelled and the completed machines were converted as 39-passenger aircraft for BOAC, acquiring the designation Solent 3. A seventh Solent 3 was a conversion of the second production Seaford, which had been evaluated by BOAC in 1946,

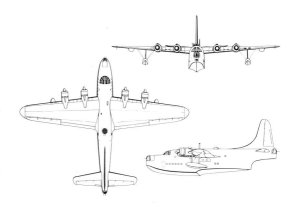

Short Seaford I

leading to an order for 12 30-passenger Solent 2s which was delivered in 1948.

Specification

Type: long-range maritime patrol flying boat
Powerplant (Seaford): four 1,720-hp (1283-kW) Bristol Hercules XIX radial piston engines
Performance: maximum speed 242 mph (389 km/h); range 3,100 miles (4989 km)
Weights: empty 45,000 lb (20 412 kg); maximum take-off 75,000 lb (34 019 kg)
Dimensions: span 112 ft 9 in (34.37 m); length 88 ft 7 in (27.00 m); wing area 1,487 sq ft (138.14 m²)
Armament (intended): two 20-mm cannon in dorsal turret, four 0.50-in (12.7-mm) machine-guns (two each in bow and tail turrets) and two 0.303-in (7.7-mm) machine-guns in nose decking
Operator: RAF (evaluation only)

Designed under the name Sunderland IV, the Short Seaford was essentially an up-engined and more heavily armed version of the Sunderland designed for operations in the Pacific. Only 10 were built for limited service.

Short S.26 'G' Class

History and notes

Imperial Airways' requirements for a long-range mail and passenger-carrying flying boat, to fly between Foynes in Ireland and New York without refuelling, met with a response from Short Brothers in the form of an enlarged 'C' Class (Empire) flying boat, designated S.26 'G' Class. It closely resembled the earlier aircraft, but incorporated the knife-edge rear step, and enlarged flight deck with provision for a flight engineer, both features of the Short Sunderland. Four 1,380-hp (1029-kW) Bristol Hercules IVC radial engines were installed and 3,600 Imperial gallons (16365 litres) of fuel in the wing tanks gave a maximum cruising range of 3,200 miles (5150 km).

The British flag carrier ordered three such boats, named *Golden Hind*, *Golden Fleece* and *Golden Horn*, and the first was launched on 17 June 1939, making its first flight, in the hands of John Parker, on 21 July. It was handed over to Imperial Airways on 24 September, but the outbreak of war earlier that month resulted in all three being taken over by the Air Ministry for long-range maritime reconnaissance duties under the designation S.26M. Armour plating was added to protect crew positions and fuel tanks, and universal carriers were added beneath the wings to carry up to eight 250-lb (113-kg) bombs. A flare chute was provided in the floor of the rear fuselage, and smoke and flame floats and reconnaissance flares could be carried. Two Boulton Paul A Mk II turrets, each with four 0.303-in (7.7-mm) machine-guns, were fitted dorsally, together with a third in the tail, this last necessitating redesign of the tail cone.

The second and third aircraft were delivered to Blackburn Aircraft Ltd at Dumbarton in August 1940 for completion, being joined by the first machine on 17 September, after it had completed evaluation at the Marine Aircraft Experimental Establishment, Helensburgh. ASV (Air to Surface Vessel) radar was installed and all three were issued to G Flight of No. 119 Squadron at Bowmore, Loch Indaal, Islay from March 1941. In June they were attached to No. 10 Squadron, the Royal Australian Air Force Sunderland unit based at Mount Batten, Plymouth, for long-range supply flights to Gibraltar and the Middle East. On 20 June the former *Golden Fleece* suffered double engine failure off Cape Finistère and was lost when forced to

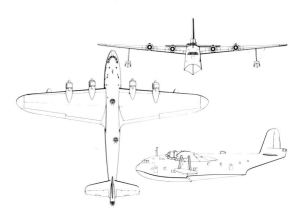

Short S.26M 'G' Class

land in a heavy swell; the survivors were picked up by a U-boat. The remaining two S.26Ms were slightly damaged in separate incidents and repaired by BOAC at Hythe during July and August, and although redelivered to the RAF they were transferred to BOAC when No. 119 Squadron was disbanded at Pembroke Dock on 6 December 1941.

With turrets and other military equipment removed, and with civil markings but retaining military camouflage, the two 'G' Class boats were, for the first time, furnished internally for the carriage of 40 passengers. On 18 July 1942 a service was opened between Poole and Lagos, via Foynes, Lisbon, Bathurst, Freetown and Accra. *Golden Horn* crashed into the River Tagus at Lisbon, on 9 January 1943 as the result of an engine fire, and *Golden Hind* was later flown to East Africa. It opened a service from Kisumu on Lake Victoria, Kenya, to the Seychelles, via Mombasa, Pamanzi and Madagascar, the route being extended to Ceylon via the Maldive Islands on 28 November. After the war *Golden Hind* flew a weekly BOAC service from Poole to Cairo from 30 September 1946 to 21 September 1947, after which it was sold and eventually scrapped in May 1954.

Specification

Type: long-range maritime patrol and transport flying boat

Powerplant: four 1,380-hp (1029-kW) Bristol Hercules IVC radial piston engines

Performance: maximum speed 209 mph (336 km/h) at 5,500 ft (1675 m); cruising speed 180 mph (290 km/h) at 7,500 ft (2285 m); range 3,200 miles (5150 km)

Weights: empty 37,705 lb (17 103 kg); maximum take-off 74,500 lb (33 793 kg)

Dimensions: span 134 ft 4 in (40.94 m); length 101 ft 4 in (30.89 m); height 37 ft 7 in (11.46 m); wing area 2,160 sq ft (200.66 m²)

Armament: 12 0.303-in (7.7-mm) machine-guns (in one tail and two dorsal turrets), plus up to 2,000 lb (907 kg) of bombs

Operators: RAAF, RAF

In 1940 the three Short 'G' Class flying-boats, scaled-up versions of the 'C' Class boats and intended for transatlantic mail service, were impressed as maritime-reconnaissance aircraft with powerful armament.

Short S.29 Stirling

Short Stirling I Series 1 of No. 7 Squadron, RAF, in early 1941

History and notes

The Short S.29 Stirling was the RAF's first four-engine monoplane bomber to enter service, and the first to be used operationally in World War II. Ironically, since it was also the first to be withdrawn from service, it was the only one of the three bombers to be designed from the outset with four engines, both the Avro Lancaster and Handley Page Halifax originating as twin-engine projects.

Specification B.12/36 drew submissions from Armstrong Whitworth, Shorts and Supermarines, and two prototypes were ordered from each of the two latter companies. In the event, the Supermarine aircraft were destroyed in an air raid before completion, so Short's design was left with a clear field. An initial production order for 100 was given to Shorts at Rochester, and another 100 were ordered from Short & Harland's new Belfast factory. It was decided to build a half-scale wooden research aircraft, powered by four 90-hp (67-kW) Pobjoy Niagara engines, to test the aerodynamic qualities of the design, and this flew at Rochester on 19 September 1938. It was later re-engined with 115-hp (86-kW) Niagaras and made well over 100 flights before being scrapped in 1943.

It was only natural that, as Britain's pre-eminent flying boat builder, Shorts should consider using the Sunderland wing design, but an Air Ministry requirement that the span should not exceed 100 ft (30.48 m), so that the aircraft could be housed in standard RAF hangars, meant that the wing had to be shortened, and the high altitude performance suffered accordingly.

The prototype Stirling made its first flight on 14 May 1939, but was written off when a brake seizure caused the landing gear to collapse on landing; hardly an auspicious start to its career. Seven months later the second prototype flew, powered like the first with 1,375-hp (1025-kW) Bristol Hercules II engines. The first production Stirling, flown on 7 May 1940, had 1,595-hp (1189-kW) Hercules XIs, and deliveries to the RAF began in August 1940, when No. 7 Squadron at Leeming began to replace its Wellingtons with the first of the new four-engined bombers. The Stirling was 'blooded' on the night of 10/11 February 1941, when three aircraft from No. 7 Squadron attacked oil storage tanks at Rotterdam.

Stirling orders then stood at 1,500 aircraft, and

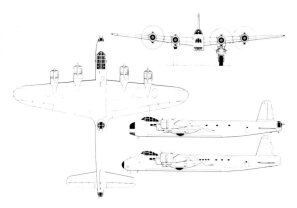

Short Stirling III (lower side view: Stirling C Mk V)

contracts for manufacture were extended to cover Austin Motors at Longbridge, Birmingham, and Rootes at Stoke-on-Trent; Stirling production eventually spread to more than 20 factories, but was initially very slow as priority had been allocated to fighter construction. Another factor which held up early production was the destruction of a number of Stirlings on the assembly lines, when the Rochester and Belfast factories were bombed in August 1940.

However, production eventually got into its stride, and by the end of 1941 more than 150 Stirlings had been completed. In service the Stirling was to prove popular with its crews and very manoeuvrable—a useful attribute when it was attacked by German fighters, and one which earned it the contemporary nickname 'the fighter bomber'. One Stirling of No. 218 Squadron, returning from a night raid in June 1942, survived attacks from four German night fighters and destroyed three, before returning battered but safe to its base.

Plans to build Stirlings in Canada were made in 1941, but although a contract for 140 was placed it was later cancelled. This was to have been the Mk II, powered by 1,600-hp (1193-kW) Wright Cyclone R-2600 engines, and two prototypes were built as conversions from Mk Is. They were followed by three production aircraft, but this variant was not adopted as the supply of Hercules engines was proving sufficient for requirements.

The Stirling III had 1,635-hp (1219-kW) Hercules VI

Short S.29 Stirling

The Short Stirling was the first of the RAF's trio of four-engined heavy bombers to enter service in World War II. Operationally, the type was hampered by its lack of ceiling, resulting from too short a wing span.

or XVI engines; apart from their minimal extra power, the main advantage of this powerplant was that it was far easier to maintain. The Mk III was given a new dorsal turret, of flatter profile, to replace the angular model of the Mk I, and some internal changes were made.

Stirling production peaked at 80 aircraft a month by mid-1943, and the last to be built as bombers were completed in the autumn of 1944.

As deliveries of the Halifax and Lancaster built up, so the Stirlings began to be withdrawn for other tasks. They had two main drawbacks: an inability to attain the operating altitude of around 20,000 ft (6100 m) achieved by the newer bombers, and a bomb bay which could not be adapted to carry the ever larger bombs that were being designed. Bomber Command's last oper-

ational Stirling sortie was flown by No. 149 Squadron, on 8 September 1944, and at the peak of their use 13 squadrons had been equipped in the bombing role (Nos. 7, 15, 75, 90, 101, 149, 166, 199, 214, 218, 513, 622 and 623). Total production of bomber versions amounted to 1,759, of which 712 were Mk Is and 1,047 Mk IIIs.

From the beginning of 1944 the Stirling's main role became that of glider tug and transport with RAF Transport Command, under the designation Mk IV.

Two Stirling IIIs served as prototypes for the new version, and were first flown in 1943. Retaining the Mk III's engines, the Mk IV had nose and dorsal turrets removed and the apertures faired over. Glider towing equipment was fitted in the rear fuselage, but the tail turret was retained.

Short S.29 Stirling

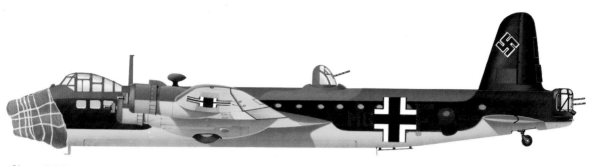

Short Stirling I shot down over Holland and partially repaired for Luftwaffe evaluation

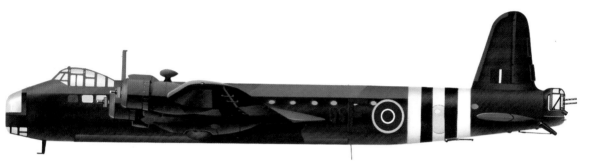

Short Stirling IV of No. 620 Squadron, RAF, in June 1944

Short Stirling V of No. 196 Squadron, RAF, in 1944

Short Stirling I Series 3 of No. 149 Squadron, RAF, Mildenhall (UK) in early 1942

Short S.29 Stirling

Short Stirling I Series 2 of No. 7 Squadron, RAF, Oakingham (UK) in spring/early summer 1943

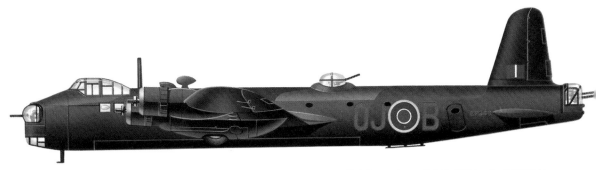

Short Stirling I (with Mk III dorsal turret) of No. 149 (East India) Squadron, RAF, Mildenhall (UK) in January 1942

The Stirling proved efficient in its new roles, with Nos. 190 and 622 Squadrons from Fairford and Nos. 196 and 299 from Keevil, towing Airspeed Horsa gliders to Normandy on D-Day, 6 June 1944. Stirling IVs were also used for the airborne landings at Arnhem and the March 1945 attack across the Rhine. Other squadrons to use this version included Nos. 138, 161, 171, 295, 570, 620 and 624.

As a glider tug, the Stirling IV could cope with one Hamilcar or two Horsas in the assault role, or up to five Hotspurs on a ferry flight or for training. Less well known were the operations of Nos. 138 and 161 (Special Duties) Squadrons, flying for the Special Operations Executive (SOE) from Tempsford, near Cambridge. They had the task of supplying arms to the Resistance in occupied countries, and No. 624 Squadron engaged in similar work in the Mediterranean area, operating from Blida in North Africa. Total production of the Mk IV was 450.

The last production version was the Mk V unarmed transport, first flown from Rochester in August 1944. It could carry up to 40 troops (20 if they were fully equipped paratroops), or 12 stretchers and 14 seated casualties. The lengthened nose hinged open, and there was a 9 ft 6 in x 5 ft 1 in (2.90 x 1.55 m) loading door in the right-hand side of the rear fuselage with portable loading ramps. Two jeeps with trailers, or a jeep with a field gun, trailer and ammunition could be carried.

Production of the Stirling V was undertaken at Belfast, and ended with the 160th aircraft in November 1945. The Mk Vs served with Nos. 46, 48, 158, 242 and 299 Squadrons until Avro Yorks replaced them.

Twelve Stirling Vs were converted during 1947 by Airtech Ltd at Thame, for a Belgian civil operator. Six were cargo aircraft and the other six had seats for 36 passengers.

Official figures for the RAF Stirling show that they made 18,440 sorties, dropped 27,821 tons (28 268 tonnes) of bombs and laid 20,000 mines for the loss of 769 aircraft.

Specification

Type: seven/eight-seat heavy bomber
Powerplant (Mk III): four 1,650-hp (1230-kW) Bristol Hercules XVI radial piston engines
Performance: maximum speed 270 mph (435 km/h) at 14,500 ft (4420 m); ceiling 17,000 ft (5180 m); range 2,010 miles (3235 km) with 3,500 lb (1588 kg) of bombs or 590 miles (950 km) with 14,000 lb (6350 kg) of bombs
Weights: empty 43,200 lb (19 595 kg); maximum take-off 70,000 lb (31 751 kg)
Dimensions: span 99 ft 1 in (30.20 m); length 87 ft 3 in (26.59 m); height 22 ft 9 in (6.93 m); wing area 1,460 sq ft (135.63 m²)
Armament: eight 0.303-in (7.7-mm) machine-guns (two each in nose and dorsal turrets, and four in tail turret), plus up to 14,000 lb (6350 kg) of bombs
Operator: RAF

Supermarine Stranraer

Supermarine Stranraer of No. 240 Squadron, RAF in 1939

History and notes

Air Ministry Specification R.24/31 called for a twin-engined general-purpose coastal reconnaissance flying boat, and Supermarine's submission was a biplane known originally as the Southampton V, although it clearly owed more to its immediate predecessor, the Scapa, than to the 1925-vintage Southampton. Of all-metal construction, with fabric-covered wings, the Stranraer was larger than the Scapa, with an extra bay in the wings and a lengthened fuselage with an open gun position in the tail.

The prototype Southampton V, renamed Stranraer in August 1935, was powered by two Bristol Pegasus IIIM engines, each driving two-blade wooden propellers, but these were replaced by Pegasus Xs with three-blade Fairey-Reed metal propellers for production machines. In August 1935 17 were ordered to Specification R.17/35, and a further six in May of the following year. In 1936 No. 228 Squadron at Pembroke Dock was the first Royal Force Squadron to receive the Stranraer, and the type was still in service at the outbreak of war in September 1939. Nos. 201 and 209 Squadrons at Invergordon used the aircraft until the summer of 1940, when they were re-equipped respectively with Short Sunderlands and Saro Lerwicks.

The Stranraer was also built under licence by Canadian Vickers, the initial Royal Canadian Air Force order for seven aircraft being later increased to 40. Production began in 1938, and eight were in the RCAF inventory when the war started. The last Canadian-built Stranraer was delivered in 1941.

The RCAF's No. 5 (General Reconnaissance) Squadron received its first Stranraers in November 1938 and, after redesignation as a bomber reconnaissance squadron on 31 October 1939, operated Canadian east coast anti-submarine patrols from bases in Nova Scotia. No. 4 Squadron, in British Columbia, performed a similar role off the west coast, later joined by Nos. 6, 7 and 9 Squadrons, the last being the ultimate squadron to retire its Stranraers which were withdrawn in April

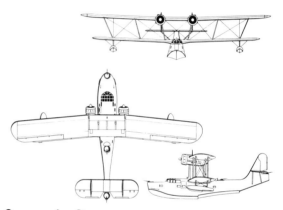

Supermarine Stranraer

1944 on replacement by Consolidated Cansos. The Stranraer was used briefly by No. 117 (Auxiliary) Squadron in the autumn of 1941, and from October 1941 to November 1942 by No. 13 Operational Training Squadron to train flying boat crews.

Specification

Type: six-seat general reconnaissance flying boat
Powerplant: two 875-hp (652-kW) Bristol Pegasus X radial piston engines
Performance: maximum speed 165 mph (266 km/h) at 6,000 ft (1830 m); cruising speed 105 mph (169 km/h); service ceiling 18,500 ft (5640 m); range 1,000 miles (1609 km)
Weights: empty 11,250 lb (5103 kg); maximum take-off 19,000 lb (8618 kg)
Dimensions: span 85 ft 0 in (25.91 m); length 54 ft 10 in (16.71 m); height 21 ft 9 in (6.63 m); wing area 1,457 sq ft (135.36 m²)
Armament: three 0.303-in (7.7-mm) Lewis guns (one each in nose, dorsal and tail positions) plus up to 1,000 lb (454 kg) of bombs
Operators: RAF, RCAF

Supermarine Walrus

Inelegant by any standards, the Supermarine Walrus amphibian was a vital part of the UK's war effort: though useful for gunnery spotting, the 'Shagbat' is best remembered for its service as an air-sea rescue aircraft.

History and notes

Designed by R.J.Mitchell, and produced by Supermarine as a private venture, the Seagull V was a very different flying boat from its similarly-named predecessor, the Seagull III. It had a hull of metal instead of wood, a pusher rather than a tractor powerplant, an enclosed cockpit for the crew of two, and was stressed for catapult launch from warships. The prototype Seagull V was flown by chief test pilot J. 'Mutt' Summers on 21 June 1933, and 24 were ordered for the Royal Australian Navy. The first aircraft sailed with HMAS *Australia* in September 1936, the second was allocated to HMAS *Sydney*, while others were issued to No. 1 Seaplane Training Flight and No. 101 Flight.

The prototype was flown to the Marine Aircraft Experimental Establishment at Felixstowe on 29 July 1933, for Air Ministry trials, and 12 aircraft were ordered to Specification 2/35 in May 1935, being given the name Walrus in August. The first two were completed in March 1936, and initially delivered to Felixstowe; others were used for pilot training at Calshot and observer training at Lee-on-Solent.

Further orders for the Walrus I, with the 620-hp (462-kW) Bristol Pegasus IIM2 engine, were placed in 1936 to Specification 37/36. A total of 287 was built by Supermarine before production was transferred to Saunders Roe Ltd at East Cowes, Isle of Wight, thus enabling the Supermarine factory to concentrate on Spitfire production. When production ceased in January 1944, Saunders Roe had built 453 Walrus IIs with 775-hp (578-kW) Bristol Pegasus VI engines, a wooden

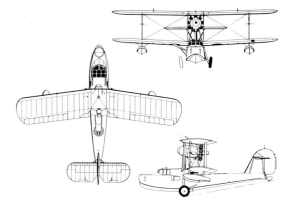

Supermarine Walrus II

hull, and a tailwheel replacing the skid of the Mk I.

The third production Walrus was possibly the first to be allocated to a specific ship, serving aboard HMS *Achilles*, then with the Royal Navy's New Zealand Division. Interestingly, after she had been transferred to the Royal New Zealand Navy, *Achilles* and her sister ship HMNZS *Leander* unloaded five aircraft in New Zealand in 1942, to equip the Seaplane Training Flight of the Royal New Zealand Air Force, preparing pilots for conversion to Catalinas.

In the UK the Admiralty had equipped many of its battleships, battle-cruisers and cruisers with the Walrus by the time war broke out, and in January 1940 these catapult flights were combined as No. 700

Supermarine Walrus

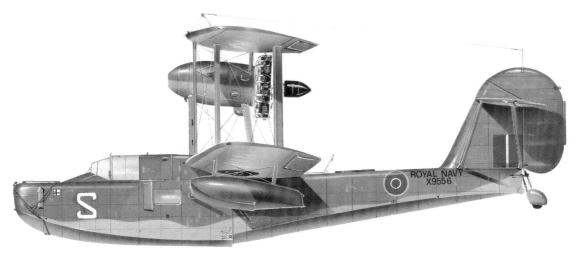

Supermarine Walrus I of the Fleet Air Arm, in 1941-3

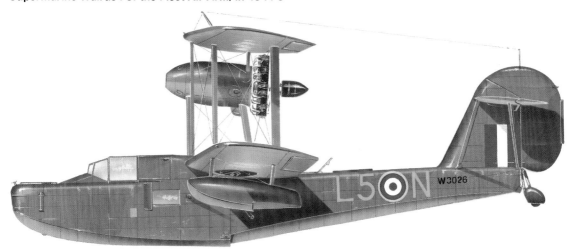

Supermarine Walrus I, about 1940-1

Squadron, Fleet Air Arm. This was gradually run down during 1943, and finally disbanded on 24 March 1944. Not all Fleet Air Arm operations were from ships, however, and by 10 September 1939 No. 710 Squadron was flying coastal patrols from Freetown, Sierra Leone, watching for German commerce raiders.

Affectionately known as the 'Shagbat', the Walrus was used by the Royal Navy for ship-to-shore communication flights, spotting for its parent ship's guns, and in an attack role using its capacity to carry 760 lb (345 kg) of bombs or depth-charges on underwing racks.

Late in 1941 the RAF began to form specialist air-sea rescue squadrons, and the Walrus became the mainstay of many of these life-saving units. Four Middle East and seven home-based squadrons flew the type and, of these, No. 277 alone rescued 598 survivors. Landings were often made in mine-infested waters or under enemy fire, and the Walrus established an enviable reputation for reliability and its ability to withstand damage.

Specification
Type: four-seat spotter-reconnaissance or air-sea rescue aircraft
Powerplant (Mk II): one 775-hp (578-kW) Bristol Pegasus VI radial piston engine
Performance: maximum speed 135 mph (217 km/h) at 4,750 ft (1450 m); cruising speed 95 mph (153 km/h) at 3,500 ft (1065 m); service ceiling 18,500 ft (5640 m); range 600 miles (966 km)
Weights: empty 4,900 lb (2223 kg); maximum take-off 7,200 lb (3266 kg)
Dimensions: span 45 ft 10 in (13.97 m), folded 17 ft 11 in (5.46 m); length 37 ft 3 in (11.35 m); height 15 ft 3 in (4.65 m); wing area 610 sq ft (56.67 m²)
Armament: one 0.303-in (7.7-mm) Vickers 'K' or Lewis machine-gun in bow position, and one or two similar weapons on flexible mount in midships position, plus up to 760 lb (345 kg) of bombs or depth charges on underwing racks
Operators: Eire, RAAF, RAF, RN, RNZAF

Supermarine Sea Otter

Designed to succeed the Walrus, the Supermarine Sea Otter had aerodynamic improvements and a more powerful engine driving a tractor propeller, and production of 290 examples lasted from 1943 to 1946.

History and notes

The last of Supermarine's biplane amphibians, the Sea Otter was intended as a replacement for the Supermarine Walrus, designed to fulfil the requirements of Specification S.7/38. The Sea Otter had an improved all-metal hull, with better hydrodynamic performance which, with the additional benefit of cleaner lines and a more powerful 855-hp (638-kW) Bristol Mercury XXX engine, endowed the aircraft with the ability to lift heavier loads off the water (at a maximum overload weight of 10,830 lb/4912 kg), and to operate over greater distances from base. The prototype made its first flight in August 1938 and Specifications S.14/39 and S.12/40 were written to cover development, modifications including shorter wing-tip float struts, a deeper engine nacelle for the tractor power unit, and trials with various types of propeller.

Production aircraft were the responsibility of Saunders Roe at East Cowes, Isle of Wight, who built 290 Sea Otters between 30 July 1943, when the first machine flew, and July 1946. The air-sea rescue Sea Otter II entered service with RAF Coastal Command squadrons towards the end of 1943, the last biplane type to enter the RAF inventory. Bases included Beccles and Martlesham Heath in East Anglia, Hawkinge in Kent and St Eval in Cornwall. In addition, Sea Otters flew with the air-sea rescue service during the 1944-5 Burma campaign.

Sea Otter Is entered service with the Fleet Air Arm in November 1944 when six were delivered to Lee-on-Solent, later embarking in the escort carrier HMS *Khedive* with No. 1700 Squadron which, by the end of the war, had been assigned to the East Indies Fleet, based at Trincomalee, Ceylon. No. 1701 Squadron, formed in February 1945, was attached to the Pacific Fleet based in Australia and later in Hong Kong, while

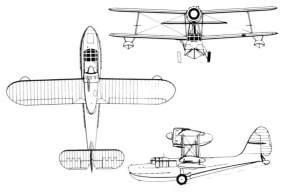

Supermarine Sea Otter II

Mediterranean duties were undertaken by No. 1702 Squadron formed in June 1945.

Specification

Type: three/four-seat carrier-based or shore-based communications or air-sea rescue amphibian
Powerplant: one 855-hp (638-kW) Bristol Mercury XXX radial piston engine
Performance: maximum speed 150 mph (241 km/h) at 5,000 ft (1525 m); cruising speed 100 mph (161 km/h); service ceiling 16,000 ft (4875 m); range 565-725 miles (909-1167 km)
Weights: empty 6,805 lb (3087 kg); maximum take-off 10,000 lb (4536 kg)
Dimensions: span 46 ft 0 in (14.02 m); length 39 ft 5 in (12.01 m); height 16 ft 2 in (4.93 m); wing area 610 sq ft (56.67 m²)
Armament: one 0.303-in (7.7-mm) Vickers 'K' gun in a bow position, and two similar weapons amidships
Operators: RAF, RN

Supermarine Spitfire

Supermarine Spitfire I of Sqn Ldr Henry Cozens, CO of No. 19 Squadron, RAF, Duxford (UK) in October 1938

Supermarine Spitfire I, the sole example acquired by the Armée de l'Air (French air force) in late 1939

History and notes

As the Royal Air Force entered the 1930s, Air Ministry thinking still centred on biplane fighters. Despite this, Supermarine designer R.J.Mitchell's submission to Air Ministry Specification F.7/30 was of monoplane configuration, an open-cockpit single-seater with a cranked wing, fixed landing gear, and a Rolls-Royce Goshawk engine. Four machine-guns were included, one on each side of the lower fuselage and one in each undercarriage fairing.

Mitchell was not satisfied with this aircraft, however, his mind being absorbed by the implications of Specification F.5/34, which demanded eight guns, an enclosed cockpit, and retractable landing gear. For this Mitchell evolved a rather small machine, to be powered by a Rolls-Royce P.V.12 (Merlin) engine, and with the armament located in the wings. The latter were elliptical in planform, and were to become a distinctive feature of the aircraft, a prototype of which was ordered in January 1935 to Specification F.37/34.

Given the Supermarine type number 300, this machine was powered initially by a 990-hp (738-kW) Merlin 'C' engine, and Captain J. 'Mutt' Summers flew it for the first time on 5 March 1936 at Eastleigh aerodrome, Southampton. The Type 300 soon displayed superb handling qualities and performance, achieving a level speed of almost 350 mph (563 km/h), and on 3 June 310 Mk I aircraft were ordered to Specification F.16/36. This represented the first of nearly 23,000 of all marks, developed largely by Joe Smith, who

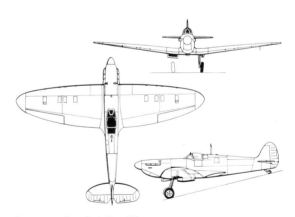

Supermarine Spitfire IIA

succeeded Mitchell on the latter's death on 11 June 1937.

These early Spitfire Is, the first of which flew on 14 May 1938, were powered by a 1,030-hp (768-kW) Rolls-Royce Merlin II, driving a two-blade fixed-pitch wooden propeller. Ejector exhaust stubs were introduced, as well as a tailwheel in place of the prototype's skid. Only four of the planned eight 0.303-in (7.7-mm) machine-guns were installed as a result of supply shortages, and trailing-edge flaps and landing gear were raised and lowered manually. Improvements were introduced quickly, including a bullet proof windscreen, a bulged canopy, armour plating behind the engine, hydraulics

197

Supermarine Spitfire

A fine flying shot of a Supermarine Spitfire VB of No. 603 (Polish) Squadron. The sky band round the rear fuselage was introduced in December 1940, and the yellow leading-edge stripes in September 1941.

for actuation of flaps and landing gear, and a Merlin II engine driving a three-blade variable-pitch de Havilland metal propeller. The eight-gun aircraft were designated Spitfire IA, and 30 Mk IBs, with two machine-guns and one 20-mm cannon in each wing, were delivered in 1940 for operational trials. The drum feed for the cannon tended to jam, however, and the aircraft were withdrawn. A total of 1,566 Spitfire Mk Is was built, including 50 manufactured by Westland Aircraft Ltd.

The second production Spitfire I became the prototype Mk II, powered by a 1,175-hp (876-kW) Merlin XII, and 920 were built subsequently. Of these 750 were Mk IIAs, with eight machine-guns, and 170 Mk IIBs with the same armament as the Mk IB. In this latter installation the cannon were belt-fed and turned on their sides, clearance being provided by a blister in the upper surface of the wing. Mk II aircraft used by the air-sea rescue squadrons were designated Spitfire IIC.

Converted from a Spitfire I, the prototype Mk III was a structurally strengthened version with clipped wings, a retractable tailwheel, jettisonable hood, improved windscreen, additional armour plating, and powered by a 1,280-hp (954-kW) Merlin XX. The second prototype was re-engined with a Rolls-Royce

Griffon IIB to become the Mk IV, later redesignated Mk XX to avoid confusion with the Spitfire P.R.IV, which was an unarmed Merlin 46-engined aircraft, introduced in September 1941, and carrying one oblique and two vertical cameras. Spitfire P.R.IV production totalled 229.

With strengthened longerons to take the 1,470-hp (1096-kW) Merlin 45, the Mk V was built in three main versions: Mk VA with eight 0.303-in (7.7-mm) machine-guns, Mk VB with two 20-mm cannon and four guns, and the Mk VC with the 'universal' wing which could take the armament of either Mk VA or VB, or four 20-mm cannon, in addition to one 500-lb (227 kg) or two 250-lb (113 kg) bombs. Increased endurance was provided by a 115- or 175-Imperial gallon (523- or 796-litre) drop tank beneath the fuselage. Production comprised 94 Mk VAs, 3,923 Mk VBs and 2,447 Mk VCs. From 1943 some were converted for low-altitude work as L.F.Vs, with clipped wings and 1,585-hp (1182-kW) Merlin 45M engines.

For high-altitude interception of German bombers, Supermarine developed the Spitfire VI, essentially a Mk VB with a pressure cabin, extended wingtips and a Merlin 47 engine. One hundred of these interim high-altitude fighters were built, pending introduction of

Supermarine Spitfire

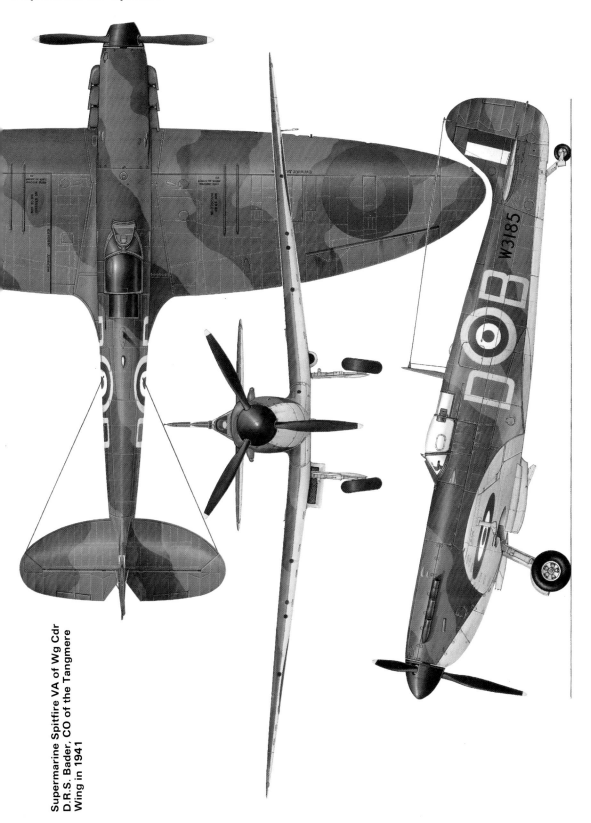

Supermarine Spitfire VA of Wg Cdr
D.R.S. Bader, CO of the Tangmere
Wing in 1941

Supermarine Spitfire

A pair of Supermarine Spitfire IXs patrol over Italy. The Spitfire IX was based on the Mk VC airframe but introduced a two-speed, two-stage Merlin engine (Merlin 60 series) with a four-blade Rotol propeller.

the definitive Spitfire H.F.VII, first flown in April 1942. This mark was the first to be designed for the longer, more powerful two-stage Merlin 60 series engine. A redesigned cooling system was included, resulting in the addition of a second radiator under the port wing, to match that originally fitted to starboard. The Universal wing, with 14-Imperial gallon (63.6-litre) leading-edge tanks, was used while other improvements included a double-glazed canopy and the retractable tailwheel developed for the Mk III. Some 140 were built, later aircraft with a pointed broad-chord rudder.

The Spitfire IX was another interim type, pending development of the Mk VIII, although it was built in greater numbers than any other single mark. The total of 5,665 included 4,010 L.F.IXs, 1,255 F.IXs and 400 H.F.IXs. Externally identical, these variants were basically Mk VC airframes with Merlin 66, Merlin 61 and Merlin 70 engines respectively. In later examples the 20-mm cannon in each wing was relocated in the bay formerly occupied by the two 0.303-in (7.7-mm) machine-guns, and a 0.50-in (12.7-mm) gun installed in the original position of the 20-mm weapon.

With the exception of the pressure cabin, the changes featured in the Mk VII were also incorporated in the Mk VIII, built in the same L.F., F. and H.F.

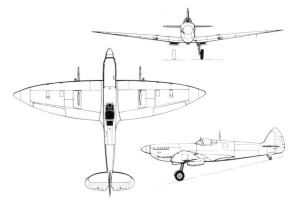

Supermarine Spitfire F.VII

versions as the Mk IX, although the wings were respectively clipped, standard, and with extended tips. Introduced in June 1943, Mk VIIIs included 1,225 L.F. VIIIs, 267 F.VIIIs and 160 H.F.VIIIs, all tropicalised with a Vokes air intake filter.

Spitfire P.R.Xs, of which 16 were manufactured, were based on the Mk IX but with pressure cabins and Merlin 64 (later Merlin 77) engines. The unpressurised

Supermarine Spitfire

Supermarine Spitfire IIB of No. 603 (Polish) Squadron, RAF, Northolt (UK) in August 1941

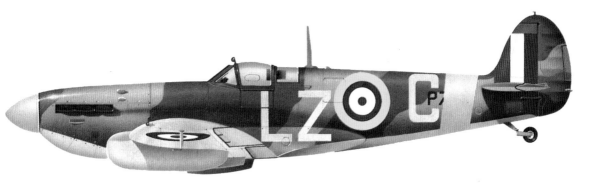

Supermarine Spitfire IIA of No. 66 Squadron, RAF, in 1941 with port-wing long-range tank installation

Supermarine Spitfire IIA of Sqn Ldr D.O. Finlay, CO of No. 41 Squadron, RAF, Hornchurch (UK) in December 1940

Supermarine Spitfire VB of the 334th Fighter Squadron, 4th Fighter Group, US 8th Air Force, Debden (UK) in late 1942/early 1943

Supermarine Spitfire

Supermarine Spitfire VB fighter-bombers of No. 417 Squadron prepare for a mission over the Western Desert. The Spitfires' smooth nose contours are spoiled by the Vokes particle-filters for the carburettors.

and low-level reconnaissance Mk XIIIs, 18 of which were converted from Mk Vs, were powered by 1,620-hp (1208-kW) Merlin 32s. Most numerous of the photographic reconnaissance Spitfires based on the Mk IX was the Spitfire P.R.XI, which was unpressurised and powered initially by the Merlin 61. A total of 471 was built, these having additional fuel tanks in the leading-edge of the wings, and an underfuselage slipper tank which conferred a range in excess of 2,000 miles (3219 km).

The final Merlin-engined Spitfire was the Mk XVI, basically similar to the Mk IX, but powered by the Packard-built Merlin 266 of 1,705 hp (1271 kW). Built in two versions, with clipped or standard wings, and with the mixed 20-mm and 0.303-in (7.7-mm), or 20-mm and 0.50-in (12.7-mm), armament schemes, the Mk XVI was modified later in the production run by the introduction of a cut-down rear fuselage and a rear-view bubble canopy. Production totalled 1,054 by August 1944, when the last was delivered.

It will be recalled that the second of the Mk III prototypes had been re-engined with a Rolls-Royce Griffon IIB, being redesignated eventually Mk XX. It was then fitted with clipped wings to become the prototype Mk XII. Production Mk XIIs were based on

the Mk VC or Mk VII airframes (50 of each), and were powered by the Griffon III or IV engine, necessitating the use of the broad-chord fin and rudder.

Further development flying with eight Griffon-powered Mk VIIIs led to the introduction of the Spitfire XIV, another interim version. This used the Mk VIII airframe fitted with the 2,050-hp (1529-kW) Griffon 65 engine, driving a five-blade Rotol propeller. The chord of the fin was increased even more than that of the Mk XII, and later aircraft had the cut-down rear fuselage and clear-view hood of the Mk XVI. Some 527 Spitfire XIVs were built, mostly with the 20-mm and 0.50-in (12.7-mm) armament scheme, together with 430 F.R.XIVs with clipped wings and a camera mounted in the rear fuselage.

The Mk XVIII had structurally strengthened wings and fuselage, with improved landing gear, to permit operation at a higher gross weight. This was to take advantage of additional fuel tankage comprising 26½ Imperial gallons (120 litres) in the wings and 66 Imperial gallons (300 litres) in the fuselage. Production comprised 100 F.XVIIIs and 200 F.R.XVIIIs.

The combination of Mk XIV airframe with modified Mk VC wings identified the last of the RAF's unarmed photographic reconnaissance Spitfires, the P.R.XIX.

Supermarine Spitfire

Supermarine Spitfire VC of No. 1435 Squadron, RAF, Luqa (Malta) in October 1942

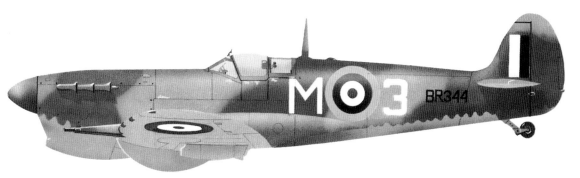

Supermarine Spitfire VC flown from USS "Wasp" to Malta in May 1942

Twenty pre-production aircraft had Griffon 65 engines and were unpressurised, but 205 production Mk XIXs, powered by Griffon 66s, had pressure cabins and further increases in wing tankage to bring total fuel capacity to 172 Imperial gallons (782 litres).

Built with the Mk IV/Mk XX prototype to Specification F.4/41, a second machine, powered by the Griffon 61, was used to develop features incorporated in the Mk XXI, of which the first production example appeared in March 1945, some later machines having were made, in particular to the wing, with fuel capacity increased by the installation of 18-Imperial gallon (82-litre) tanks in the wings; additionally, strengthened landing gear was introduced. Only 122 of a planned production run of 1,500 were completed. With a cut-down rear fuselage and bubble canopy, the Mk 22 appeared in march 1945, some later machines having Griffon 85s driving contra-rotating propellers. The second prototype Spitfire 22 had a pointed wing of 40 ft 6 in (12.34 m) span and an armament of six 20-mm cannon, bringing a designation change to Mk 23.

A total of 278 Spitfire F.22s was built and some, together with 54 uncompleted Mk 22 airframes, were to become F.24s. This mark introduced the tail unit developed for the Supermarine Spiteful, an extra fuselage fuel tank, and armament changes including four 20-mm cannon and underwing launchers for rocket projectiles. The last was completed at the Eastleigh factory in October 1947, bringing the total of Spitfires built for the RAF to 20,351.

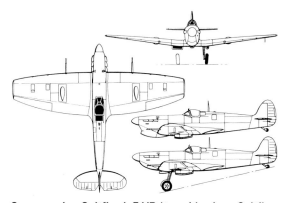

Supermarine Spitfire L.F.VB (top side view: Spitfire F.VC)

Produced in such numbers, and with the distinction of being the only Allied fighter in production at the outbreak of war to remain in continuous manufacture throughout hostilities, the Spitfire saw service with literally hundreds of Allied units, including US and Russian squadrons.

The Spitfire Mk I entered RAF service with No. 19 Squadron at Duxford in July 1938, and by the outbreak of war nine Spitfire squadrons were operational. A Spitfire of No. 603 Squadron claimed the first German aircraft to be destroyed over Britain in World War II, the victim being a Heinkel He 111 shot down over the Firth of Forth on 16 October 1939. On 8 August 1940,

Supermarine Spitfire

Supermarine Spitfire VBs of No. 417 Squadron patrol at medium altitude. Some 24 Middle East squadrons flew the Mk V, together with 72 home-based and four Far Eastern squadrons. Production totalled 6,464.

shortly before the Battle of Britain reached its climax, Fighter Command's order of battle included 19 Spitfire I squadrons, six of them in the hard-pressed south-east sector of No. 11 Group.

Spitfire IIs had achieved operational status by December 1940, and were among aircraft which carried out 'Rhubarb' sweeps over occupied Europe, being joined by the Mk V which entered service with No. 92 Squadron in February 1941. The first Spitfires to be released for service overseas were 15 Mk VBs, flown to Malta from HMS *Eagle* in the Mediterranean on 7 March 1942. The first Spitfires to reach the Middle East were tropicalised Mk VBs with air intake filters under the nose, delivered to No. 145 Squadron at Helwan in May 1942, while No. 54 Squadron at Darwin received the first Pacific theatre Mk Vs in February 1943. The first P.R.IV reached No. 69 Squadron in Malta in March 1942, having entered service in Britain, in August 1941, with No. 1 PRU.

On 22 April 1942, No. 616 Squadron at Kingscliffe received the first of the high-altitude Mk VIs, intended to counter high-flying German reconnaissance bombers. They were passed on to meteorological reconnaissance units when replaced by Mk VIIs, first flown by No. 124 Squadron in January 1943. The tropicalised Mk VII

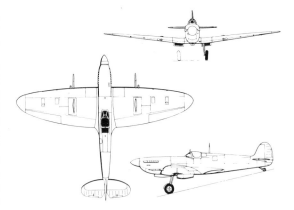

Supermarine Spitfire F.IXC

entered service with No. 145 Squadron in Italy in the summer of 1943, and with No. 155 Squadron over Burma in December. The Mk IX had meanwhile reached its first unit, No. 64 Squadron at Hornchurch in July 1942, while the P.R.XI flew its first sortie with No. 541 Squadron in November 1942. This unit also operated the P.R.XIII from 1943, although this mark

Supermarine Spitfire

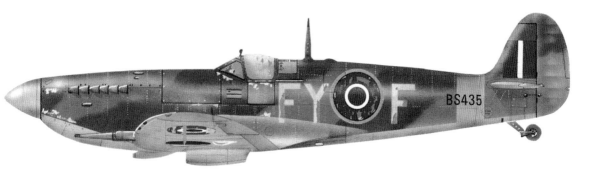

Supermarine Spitfire IX of No. 611 Squadron, Auxiliary Air Force, in 1944

Supermarine Spitfire IX of No. 340 (Free French) Squadron, RAF, in 1943

Supermarine Spitfire IX of No. 402 Squadron, Royal Canadian Air Force in early 1943

Supermarine Spitfire VB of the 309th Fighter Squadron, 31st Fighter Group, US 8th Air Force, High Ercall and Westhampnett (UK) in summer 1942

Supermarine Spitfire

Supermarine Spitfire L.F.VB in flight. The style of fuselage lettering indicates this to be a wing commander's aircraft with the pilot's initials in place of the unit code. Note the open radiator shutter.

was used largely for training, and conducted the first P.R.X. sortie on 11 May 1944.

The Griffon-engined Spitfire XII was issued to Nos. 41 and 91 Squadrons at Hawkinge in the spring of 1943 and its high-altitude counterpart, the Mk XIV, to No. 610 Squadron in January 1944. On 4 October a No. 401 Squadron Spitfire XIV claimed the first Messerschmitt Me 262 to be shot down by an Allied fighter. The Mk XVI saw wartime service, principally with 2nd Tactical Air Force squadrons, as did the Mk XVIII in the Middle and Far East. No. 542 first used the P.R.XIX operationally on 24 May 1944 and it was a similar aircraft, of No. 81 Squadron in Malaya, which flew the last RAF operational Spitfire mission on 1 April 1954.

Specification

Type: single-seat interceptor fighter/fighter-bomber
Powerplant (Mk XIV): one 2,050-hp (1529-kW) Rolls-Royce Griffon 65 inline piston engine
Performance: maximum speed 448 mph (721 km/h) at 26,000 ft (7925 m); cruising speed 362 mph (583 km/h); service ceiling 43,000 ft (13105 m)
Weights: empty 6,700 lb (3039 kg); maximum take-off 10,280 lb (4663 kg)
Dimensions: span 36 ft 10 in (11.23 m); length 32 ft

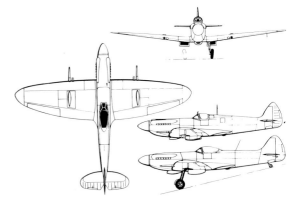

Supermarine Spitfire F.XIVE (top side view: Spitfire F.XII)

8 in (3.86 m); wing area 244 sq ft (22.67 m²)
Armament: two 20-mm cannon and two 0.50-in (12.7-mm) machine-guns, plus provision for one 500-lb (227-kg) bomb or rocket projectiles
Operators: Egypt, FAF, FFAF, Greek Air Force, ICoAF, Portugal, RAAF, RAF, RCAF, RNZAF, SAAF, Soviet Union, Turkey, USAAF

Supermarine Spitfire

Supermarine Spitfire VIII of the 308th Fighter Squadron, 31st Fighter Group, US 12th Air Force, Tunisia in early 1943

Supermarine Spitfire L.F.VB of No. 40 Squadron, South African Air Force, Italy in August 1943

Supermarine Spitfire VC of 308th Fighter Squadron, 31st Fighter Group, US 12th Air Force, Tunisia in mid-1943

Supermarine Spitfire VC of No. 54 Squadron, RAF, Australia in 1943

Though unmistakeably Spitfires, these Mk 21s have hardly a single part common to any of the Merlin-engined versions, and in particular introduced a completely redesigned wing. In turn this type served as the basis for the even more advanced marks of Seafire.

Supermarine Seafire

History and notes

Following the success of the Hawker Sea Hurricane in carrierborne operations, the decision was taken to go ahead with a naval version of the Supermarine Spitfire. A Spitfire VB, fitted in late 1941 with an arrester hook beneath the fuselage, was flown on to HMS *Illustrious* for compatibility trials. While the Spitfire's narrow track landing gear made it more difficult to operate aboard carriers than the Hurricane, the concept was proved and work began on converting a number of existing Spitfires, the name Seafire being chosen for the modified aircraft.

Air Service Training at Hamble undertook the conversion in 1942, and others were modified by Supermarine on the production line. About 140 Spitfire Vs were involved, and were designated Seafire IBs. Additionally, 48 new Seafire IBs were built by Cunliffe-Owen Aircraft.

All Seafire IBs had fixed wings, some being clipped as on the Spitfire VB, and the type of wing fitted depended on the mark of Spitfire converted. The B wing had two 20-mm cannon and four 0.303-in (7.7-mm) machine-guns, while the C could have four 20-mm cannon; the latter was not common, however, because of the weight penalty imposed by the heavier armament and ammunition.

Following the Mk IB came 372 Seafire IICs, similar to the earlier mark but using the C wing and having provision for catapult spools. This variant was built in two versions, by Supermarine (262) as the F.IIC and by Westland (110) as the L.IIC, the latter being a low-altitude version. A sub-variant, the LR.IIC, carried F.24 cameras for photo-reconnaissance work.

Seafire IIC deliveries began in June 1942, when 12 were received by No. 807 Squadron. These, together with Seafires delivered to No. 801 Squadron in September, were embarked on HMS *Furious* until February 1943, participating in the Allied invasion of North Africa in November 1942. By the end of 1942 six squadrons had received Seafires, the others being Nos. 808, 880, 884 and 887. During 1943 Nos. 809, 886, 894,

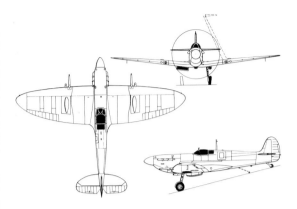

Supermarine Seafire III

895, 897 and 899 Squadrons were equipped, while Nos. 833, 834, 842 and 879 Squadrons operating from escort carriers each received six Seafires.

The next variant, the Seafire III, introduced a manually folding wing, folding upwards from just inboard of the cannon, with the wingtips folding downwards. This enabled Seafires to be moved on carrier lifts, and made deck handling in general considerably easier. The Seafire III prototype was a converted IIC, and the new mark went into production in 1943, a total of 1,220 being built between November 1943 and July 1945, 870 by Westland and 350 by Cunliffe-Owen.

The Seafire III was built in three versions, fighter (F.), low-altitude fighter (L.) and low-altitude reconnaissance (LR.), the last having vertical and oblique cameras like the LR.IIC. A 30-Imperial gallon (136-litre) flush-fitting drop tank could be fitted beneath the fuselage to increase the range from 465 to 725 miles (748 to 1167 km).

Not surprisingly, considerable numbers of Seafires took part in operations in the Mediterranean. In September 1943 the Allied forces landed in the Gulf of Salerno, naval air support being provided by the fleet carriers HMS *Formidable* and *Illustrious* and four escort carriers, operating eight Seafire squadrons totalling 76 aircraft; additionally the repair and maintenance carrier HMS *Unicorn* was pressed into temporary service and had three squadrons of Seafires, a total of 30.

With only a light wind blowing and the carriers operating 1,000 yards (915 m) apart, conditions for the Seafires were unfavourable and an unusually large number of deck-landing accidents occurred. Many propeller tips were damaged when the Seafires' noses dipped slightly as the hooks picked up the arrester wires, and on the escort carrier HMS *Hunter* 19 such incidents in three days exhausted the ship's stock of spare propellers. The only course of action was to crop the damaged propellers, and 6 inches (0.15 m) were cut off each blade, an effective remedy which subsequently became standard practice.

Seafire III deliveries began in March 1944 to No. 899

A Supermarine Seafire F.IIC of No. 885 Squadron, Fleet Air Arm. The Mk IIC entered service in late 1942 in three versions: F.IIC fighter, L.IIC low-altitude fighter and LR.IIC reconnaissance fighter.

Supermarine Seafire

Deck crew of various categories prepare a quartet of Supermarine Seafire IICs for launch. Though based on the Spitfire VC, the Mk IIC was the first Seafire version to be built as such, rather than converted.

Squadron at Belfast, and in July the squadron embarked on the escort carrier HMS *Khedive* for the Mediterranean, its 26 Seafires joining Nos. 807, 809 and 879 Squadrons of No. 4 Naval Fighter Wing at Malta. All took part in the invasion of southern France in August 1944.

Meanwhile, other Seafire squadrons had seen active service in the Allied invasion of northern France in June 1944, with Nos. 808, 885, 886 and 897 Squadrons operating from shore bases alongside two Spitfire squadrons as part of the 2nd Tactical Air Force. The Seafires returned to Fleet Air Arm command the following month.

By 1945, Seafires were operational in the Far East, eight squadrons flying from six carriers. By VJ-Day 12 Seafire squadrons were in first-line service, eight of them with Mk IIIs and four with IICs. All were powered by various marks of Rolls-Royce Merlin engine giving between 1,340 and 1,640 hp (999 and 1223 kW).

As powerplant of the Spitfire changed from the Merlin to the Rolls-Royce Griffon, it was a natural progression for the Seafire to be similarly equipped, and three prototypes were built to Specification N.4/43, all flying in 1944. This first Griffon variant was designated the Mk XV, and production orders were placed for 384, Westland building 250 and Cunliffe-Owen 134. Increased fuel capacity in internal wing tanks was provided, and from the 51st aircraft a new 'sting' type arrester hook was mounted at the bottom of the rudder, replacing the V-type hook used on earlier Seafires. Rocket-assisted take-off gear was

standardised from the 75th aircraft. No. 802 Squadron at Arbroath was the first to receive Seafire XVs, in May 1945.

A later variant, the Seafire XVII, was basically a refined version of the XV with a clear-view bubble canopy, a cut-down rear fuselage and greater fuel capacity, with a 33-Imperial gallon (150-litre) tank in the rear fuselage, but this version did not enter service until after the war had ended. It was the longest lived of the post-war variants, which also included the final Seafire marks, the 45, 46 and 47, all being Griffon-engined naval versions of the Spitfire 21, 22 and 24 respectively.

Specification

Type: single-seat carrier-based fighter
Powerplant (Mk III): one 1,470-hp (1096-kW) Rolls-Royce Merlin 55 inline piston engine
Performance: maximum speed 352 mph (566 km/h) at 12,250 ft (3735 m); cruising speed 218 mph (351 km/h) at 20,000 ft (6100 m); service ceiling 33,800 ft (10300 m); range 465 miles (748 km), or 725 miles (1167 km) with drop tank
Weights: empty 5,400 lb (2449 kg); maximum take-off 7,100 lb (3221 kg)
Dimensions: span 36 ft 8 in (11.18 m); length 30 ft 0 in (9.14 m); height 11 ft 2 in (3.40 m); wing area 242 sq ft (22.48 m²)
Armament: two 20-mm cannon and four 0.303-in (7.7-mm) machine-guns in wings, plus provision for 500 lb (227 kg) of bombs
Operator: RN

Supermarine Spiteful/Seafang

History and notes

With its Spitfire stretched to the design's ultimate limit, Supermarine welcomed the chance to tender for Air Ministry Specification F.1/43 for a follow-on design. The result was the Supermarine Type 371, later named Spiteful.

The new aircraft's ancestry was immediately obvious, the tail surfaces in particular being virtually identical to those of the Spitfire 24, but the rest of the airframe was completely new. Most original feature was the square-cut laminar-flow wing (later adapted for the Supermarine Attacker) with very low drag radiators which, together with the very clean lines of the whole airframe, enabled the aeroplane to attain a speed of 475 mph (764 km/h) and an initial rate of climb of 4,750 ft (1448 m) per minute.

A major departure from Spitfire design was the decision to use wide-track inward-retracting landing gear. This was a most desirable improvement, but was necessary in any case, as the outer panels of the laminar wing were too shallow to accept outward retracting main units.

Like the later Spitfires, the Spiteful used the Rolls-Royce Griffon engine. The three marks of Spiteful proposed were the F.14 with a Griffon 65, driving a Rotol five-blade constant-speed propeller; the F.15 with a Griffon 89 or 90, driving two three-blade contra-rotating Rotol propellers; and the F.16 with a Griffon 101 with a three-stage blower, again driving a Rotol five-blade propeller. This last version on one occasion attained a speed of 494 mph (795 km/h).

Three prototype Spitefuls were built, and the first flight was made in June 1944 by Vickers Armstrong's test pilot, Jeffrey Quill. A batch of 67 was ordered but later cancelled, then further orders were placed, revising a contract for Spitfire F.21s to Spitefuls.

The first production aircraft was completed in March 1945, while the sixth was the first to be delivered to the RAF, in November 1946. The production line turned out its 17th and last Spiteful on 17 January 1947, after outstanding orders had been cancelled in favour of jets. Three were delivered to service test establishments, three were retained by the manufacturers for development work, and the rest went into store at Brize Norton.

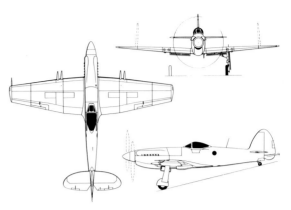

Supermarine Seafang 32

While the Seafire was the naval derivative of the Spitfire, it was natural to seek a similar partner to the Spiteful and, to Specification N.5/45, the Seafang appeared. Basically a Spiteful with deck landing hook in its original form, the Seafang was ordered in May 1945, to the tune of two prototypes and 150 production aircraft — an optimistic order as things turned out. The first Seafang to fly was a production F.31, which came off the assembly line after the fifth Spiteful and was sent to the Royal Aircraft Establishment at Farnborough on 15 January 1946.

At this time the Admiralty had not decided whether the Seafang represented a sufficient advance in performance over the Seafire FR.47, but after considerable vacillation it was decided to abandon Seafang production and only 18 were completed: eight F.31s with Griffon 61 engines, and 10 F.32s with Griffon 89s and contra-rotating propellers as on the Spiteful F.15. The F.32s also featured hydraulically operated folding wings and increased fuel tankage. Only 11 Seafangs were flown; the other seven aircraft were delivered in dismantled condition and never flew.

The Seafang had the same measurements as the Spiteful, with the exception of the extra 14 in (0.36 m) of the arrester hook protruding below the rudder.

Specification

Type: single-seat fighter
Powerplant (Spiteful F.16): one 2,375-hp (1771-kW) Rolls-Royce Griffon 65 inline piston engine
Performance: maximum speed 475 mph (764 km/h) at 28,500 ft (8685 m); service ceiling 43,000 ft (13105 m); range 564 miles (908 km) or 1,315 miles (2116 km) with drop tanks
Weights: empty 7,350 lb (3334 kg); maximum take-off 10,200 lb (4627 kg)
Dimensions: span 35 ft 6 in (10.82 m); length 32 ft 4 in (9.86 m); height 13 ft 5 in (4.09 m); wing area 210 sq ft (19.51 m²)
Armament: four 20-mm cannon in wings, plus provision for underwing rockets or two 1,000-lb (454-kg) bombs
Operators: RAF, RN

The ultimate expression of the Spitfire design philosophy, the Supermarine Spiteful was built only in very small numbers. Illustrated is the first Spiteful F.14, capable of 483 mph (777 km/h) at altitude.

Vickers Vildebeest

History and notes

In the period between the two world wars, the RAF operated a number of types of large single-engine biplanes, the Vickers Vildebeest being a typical example. Its origins went back to 1926, when Vickers tendered to Specification 24/25 for a torpedo-bomber to replace the Hawker Horsley. An Air Ministry order for a prototype was received, and as the Vickers Type 132 it flew from the company's Brooklands Airfield, Weybridge, in April 1928, powered by a 460-hp (343-kW) Bristol Jupiter VIII geared engine, later going to the Aircraft and Armament Experimental Establishment at Martlesham Heath for competitive trials with the Blackburn Beagle. Following these it was tested on floats at the Marine Aircraft Experimental Establishment at Felixstowe.

Initial problems were concerned mainly with engine cooling, and several versions of the Jupiter were tried without encouraging results. Eventually, a second prototype was built as a private venture: this flew from Brooklands in August 1930, powered by a geared Armstrong Siddeley Panther IIA engine, but its performance was, if anything, worse.

Finally, the 660-hp (492-kW) Bristol Pegasus became the standard Vildebeest powerplant, and with successful trials at last behind it the type was accepted, nine aircraft being ordered to revised Specification 22/31. In 1932 Vickers signed a licensing agreement under which 25 Vildebeests, with 600-hp (447-kW) Hispano Suiza 12Lbr engines, were built by CASA at Madrid for service with the Spanish navy.

Deliveries to the RAF began in 1933, when No. 100 Squadron at Donibristle received a batch of the first production Vildebeests, having had one aircraft for familiarisation for several months. The squadron moved subsequently to Singapore, and the type was to remain in service in the Far East well into World War II.

Further contracts followed, and improved marks of Vildebeest entered service. The Mk II, ordered in December 1933, was fitted with a 635-hp (474-kW) Pegasus IIM3 engine, but when 30 had been built a modification was requested by the Air Ministry to a new specification, 15/34. A third crew member position was required and the rear cockpit was redesigned. In this form the aircraft was designated Mk III. Production aircraft were delivered to Nos. 22 and 36 Squadrons during 1935-6 and 12 were ordered for the Royal New Zealand Air Force, another 15 being diverted later from the RAF order. The RNZAF Vildebeests had folding wings.

The final production version was the Mk IV, 56 of which were ordered in December 1936 with 825-hp (615-kW) Bristol Perseus VIII sleeve-valve engines, the first such engine to enter RAF service. Performance was considerably improved, and the first Vildebeest Mk IVs were delivered to No. 42 Squadron in 1937, remaining in service until replaced by Bristol Beauforts in 1940. The last Vildebeest IV was delivered in November 1937, and total production of the Mks I to IV amounted to 194.

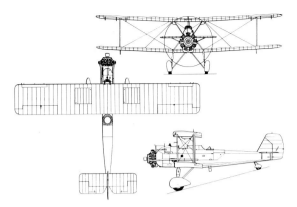

Vickers Vildebeest III

Though totally obsolete by the end of 1941, Vickers Vildebeest torpedo-bombers were used by Nos 36 and 100 Squadrons against Japanese warships in Malayan waters, operating against overwhelming opposition.

At the outbreak of World War II about 100 Vildebeests were still in service, and the Singapore-based aircraft with Nos. 36 and 100 Squadrons operated against the Japanese until Singapore fell in 1942.

Specification

Type: two/three-seat torpedo-bomber
Powerplant (Mk IV): one 825-hp (615-kW) Bristol Perseus VIII radial piston engine
Performance: maximum speed 156 mph (251 km/h) at 5,000 ft (1525 m); service ceiling 19,000 ft (5790 m); range 1,625 miles (2615 km)
Weights: empty 4,724 lb (2143 kg); maximum take-off 8,500 lb (3856 kg)
Dimensions: span 49 ft 0 in (14.94 m); length 37 ft 8 in (11.48 m); height 14 ft 8 in (4.47 m); wing area 728 sq ft (67.63 m²)
Armament: one fixed forward-firing 0.303-in (7.7-mm) machine-gun and one Lewis gun in rear cockpit, plus one 18-in (457-mm) torpedo or 1,000 lb (454 kg) of bombs
Operators: RAF, RNZAF

Vickers Vincent

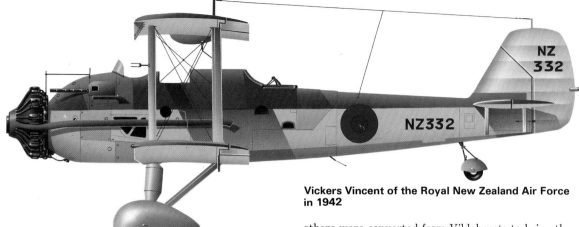

Vickers Vincent of the Royal New Zealand Air Force in 1942

History and notes

A need to replace the Westland Wapiti and Fairey IIIF general-purpose biplanes led the Air Ministry to order a modified version of the Vickers Vildebeest to Specification 21/33. A tour of RAF stations in the Middle East and Africa in 1932-3 by a converted Vildebeest had shown that the type would be a suitable replacement, and 51 were ordered on 8 December 1933 under the name Vincent. In place of the torpedo, the Vincent carried a long-range fuel tank beneath the fuselage, and other special equipment included message pick-up gear and pyrotechnics.

The first production Vincent, converted from a Vildebeest Mk II to the revised Specification 16/34, was seen for the first time in public at the 1935 RAF Display at Hendon. However, initial deliveries of production aircraft had been made to No. 8 Squadron at Aden in late 1934, eventually replacing the Fairey IIIFs then in service with Bristol Blenheims.

Total Vincent production was 171, and a number of others were converted from Vildebeests to bring the total to almost 200. More than 80 were still in service at the beginning of World War II, and Vincents saw action with No. 244 Squadron in Iraq in 1941, being replaced eventually by Bristol Blenheims.

Specification

Type: three-seat general-purpose biplane
Powerplant: one 660-hp (492-kW) Bristol Pegasus IIM3 radial piston engine
Performance: maximum speed 142 mph (229 km/h) at 4,920 ft (1500 m); service ceiling 17,000 ft (5180 m); range 625 miles (1006 km), or 1,250 miles (2012 km) with long-range tank
Weights: empty 4,229 lb (1918 kg); maximum take-off 8,100 lb (3674 kg)
Dimensions: span 49 ft 0 in (14.94 m); length 36 ft 8 in (11.18 m); height 17 ft 9 in (5.41 m); wing area 728 sq ft (67.63 m²)
Armament: one 0.303-in (7.7-mm) forward-firing machine-gun and one Lewis gun in rear cockpit, plus up to 1,000 lb (454 kg) of bombs
Operators: RAF, RNZAF

Derived from the Vildebeest by the deletion of torpedo gear and the addition of a long-range tank under the fuselage, the Vickers Vincent was intended to replace the Westland Wapiti and Fairey IIIF.

Vickers Valentia

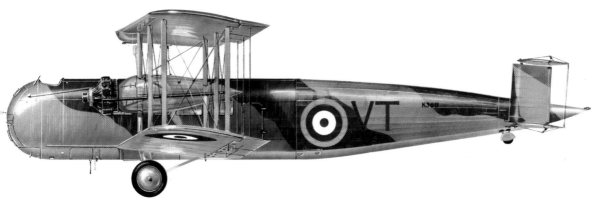

Vickers Valentia I of No. 216 Squadron, RAF, in 1939

History and notes

The Vickers Vimy biplane, which was originated to play a significant role in World War I, materialised too late to take part in that conflict. It is remembered especially for three great pioneering flights: from west to east across the North Atlantic, and from the UK to Australia and to South Africa. It must also be regarded as the sire of the Virginia bomber, and the Victoria and Valentia troop transports.

The last of this line, the Valentia, was derived in the early 1930s from the need to improve on the performance of the Victoria, which in its original Mk III production form had first entered service in 1925. The Victorias were equipped with Napier Lion engines, long-serving and reliable powerplants which had originated in 1917 with a take-off rating of about 300 hp (224 kW). The evolutionary process of development had almost doubled this rating, for the Lion XIBs that powered this Type 169 Victoria Mk V each produced a maximum of 570 hp (425 kW).

The Bristol Pegasus radial engine was chosen for trial installation in a Victoria Mk V, and this led to an initial order for 11 Pegasus-powered aircraft which became designated Victoria Mk VI. However, to take full advantage of the additional power available from the Pegasus engines, plans were made for the airframe structure to be strengthened for operation at a higher gross weight, which resulted in reinforcement of the wing, provision of strut-braced rather than wire-braced landing gear, and the introduction of wheel-brakes and a tailwheel instead of a tailskid. Testing of a trial conversion, powered by 660-hp (492-kW) Pegasus IIL3 engines, brought the decision that this basic powerplant should be introduced retrospectively for in-service aircraft, as well as being used for new production machines. Thus Victoria Mk Vs with the new engines installed, but without structural strengthening, were designated Victoria VI. New production aircraft (28 built) and conversions (54), which included both the new engines and the structural changes, became designated Valentia I.

Equipped to accommodate a crew of two and a total of 22 troops, Valentias first entered service with No. 70 Squadron in the Middle East during 1934; in the

An improved version of the Victoria troop-carrier, the Vickers Valentia served with one India and three Middle East squadrons. Some 54 were converted from Victorias, while another 28 were built as such.

following year No. 216 Squadron began to receive these improved aircraft, and they remained in operational use with these units until 1940 and 1941 respectively. A version with Pegasus IIM3 engines, which offered improved high altitude/temperature performance, was supplied in 1938 for service with one flight of No. 31 Squadron which was then based at Lahore, India. Valentias of this squadron took part in the evacuation of Habbaniyah during the Iraqi rebellion of 1941.

Specification

Type: troop transport
Powerplant: two 635-hp (474-kW) Bristol pegasus IIM3 radial piston engines
Performance: maximum speed 120 mph (193 km/h) at 5,000 ft (1525 m); service ceiling 16,250 ft (4955 m); range 800 miles (1287 km)
Weights: empty 10,994 lb (4987 kg); maximum take-off 19,500 lb (8845 kg)
Dimensions: span 87 ft 4 in (26.62 m); length 59 ft 6 in (18.14 m); height 17 ft 9 in (5.41 m); wing area 2,178 sq ft (202,34 m²)
Armament (optional): up to 2,200 lb (998 kg) of bombs on underwing racks
Operator: RAF

Vickers Wellesley

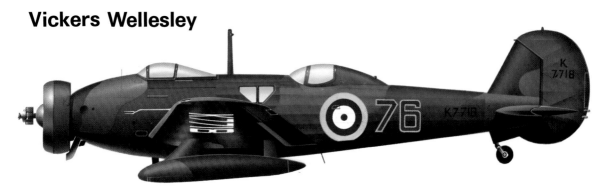

Vickers Wellesley of No. 76 Squadron, RAF, Finningley (UK) in 1937

History and notes

Like many other successful aircraft, the Vickers Wellesley started life as a private venture. Its most radical feature was the use for the first time in a heavier-than-air craft of the geodetic construction devised by Barnes Wallis, to give maximum strength for minimum weight.

The origin of the Wellesley was somewhat unusual, stemming from Specification G.4/31 for a general-purpose biplane. Vickers built a biplane to this specification, and this aircraft flew on 16 August 1934; on 19 June 1935 the company flew its private venture monoplane, which had been designed to meet the same specification. Comparison of the performance of the two aircraft showed the monoplane to be far superior, and the proposed order for 150 biplanes was changed to 96 monoplanes, these to be named Wellesley.

The first production aircraft, to the new specification 22/35, flew at Brooklands on 30 January 1937, and was delivered to the RAF on 18 March for trials at the Aircraft and Armament Experimental Establishment, Martlesham Heath. The second Wellesley went to No. 76 Squadron at Finningley for service trials, and this unit was the first to be re-equipped with the new aircraft. Further production orders followed, and a total of 176 Wellesleys was built. Other UK squadrons to receive the type included Nos. 35, 77, 148 and 207, and more than 100 served overseas with Nos. 14, 45, 47 and 223 Squadrons in Aden, Asmara, East Africa, Egypt, Nairobi, Sudan and Transjordan.

In 1938 a world long distance record flight of 7,162 miles (11526 km), made in just over 48 hours, was established by two Wellesleys of the RAF Long Range Development Flight: their route was from Ismailia, Egypt, to Darwin, Australia. A third aircraft reached Kupang, but with fuel capacity getting low it was considered prudent for it to land there; after refueling it completed the flight to Darwin.

Mk I Wellesleys had separate canopies for the two cockpits, but the Mk II featured a continuous canopy. Novel features were the extremely long span wing and the underwing bomb carriers with a capacity of up to 1,000 lb (454 kg) each. These were also each capable of carrying two 250-lb (113-kg) depth charges, and Wellesleys were used for anti-submarine patrols in 1942 by No. 47 Squadron operating from Egypt.

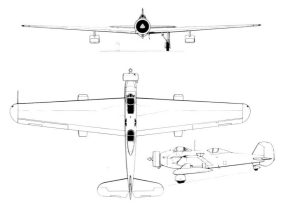

Vickers Wellesley I

Wellesleys had been replaced in Bomber Command by Handley Page Hampdens, Armstrong Whitworth Whitleys and Vickers Wellingtons by the outbreak of World War II, and those still overseas were replaced between 1941 and 1944 by Bristol Blenheims, Bristol Beauforts and Martin Marylands. Notable wartime efforts were the bombing of Addis Ababa by Wellesleys of No. 223 Squadron from Perin Island in August 1940, the bombing of Massana by No. 14 Squadron from Port Sudan in June 1940, and shipping reconnaissance by No. 202 Group up into 1941.

Specification

Type: two-seat general-purpose bomber
Powerplant (Mk I): one 950-hp (708-kW) Bristol Pegasus XX radial piston engine
Performance: maximum speed 228 mph (367 km/h) at 19,680 ft (6000 m); cruising speed 188 mph (303 km/h); service ceiling 33,000 ft (10 060 m); range 1,110 miles (1786 km)
Weights: empty 6,369 lb (2889 kg); maximum take-off 11,100 lb (5035 kg)
Dimensions: span 74 ft 7 in (22.73 m); length 39 ft 3 in (11.96 m); height 12 ft 4 in (3.76 m); wing area 630 sq ft (58.53 m²)
Armament: one 0.303-in (7.7-mm) forward-firing machine-gun, one Vickers gun in rear cockpit, plus up to 2,000 lb (907 kg) of bombs
Operator: RAF

Vickers Wellington

Vickers Wellington IA of No. 37 Squadron, RAF, Aqir (Palestine) in April 1941

Vickers Wellington IC of No. 150 Squadron, RAF, Newton (UK) in winter 1940-1

History and notes

Building upon the experience gained from Barnes Wallis' geodetic structural concept, which had been used in the airframe of the Wellesley, Vickers adopted such construction when tendering for a prototype contract to Air Ministry Specification B.9/32. This called for an aircraft capable of delivering a bomb load of 1,000 lb (454 kg) and with a range of 720 miles (1159 km). These requirements were surpassed by the Vickers proposal, which was for a mid-wing medium day bomber with two Rolls-Royce Goshawk engines and retractable landing gear, able to carry more than 4,500 lb (2041 kg) of bombs, and having a maximum range of 2,800 miles (4506 km).

The prototype B.9/32, with two 915-hp (682-kW) Bristol Pegasus X engines, and having a Supermarine Stranraer fin and rudder assembly, was completed at Weybridge in May 1936. It was first flown by Vickers' chief test pilot, J. 'Mutt' Summers, on 15 June. Later that month, it was exhibited at the 1936 Hendon Air Display, with nose and tail cupolas covered to prevent details of its still-secret constructional method being revealed. After initial manufacturer's testing the aircraft was flown to the Aircraft and Armament Experimental Establishment at Martlesham Heath for official trials. Near there, on 19 April 1937, with tests almost concluded, the prototype crashed after elevator overbalance in a high-speed dive resulted in inversion and structural failure.

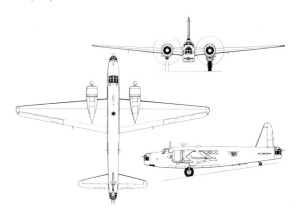

Vickers Wellington IC

On 15 August 1936, however, the Air Ministry had placed an order for 180 Wellington Mk Is to Specification B.29/36. These were required to have a re-designed and slightly more angular fuselage, a revised tail unit, and hydraulically operated Vickers nose, ventral and tail turrets. The first production Wellington Mk I was flown on 23 December 1937, powered by Pegasus X engines. In April 1938, however, the 1,050-hp (783-kW) Pegasus XVIII became standard for the other 3,052 Mk Is of all variants built at Weybridge, or at the Blackpool and Chester factories which were established to keep pace with orders.

Vickers Wellington

Armourers prepare the fuses of 500-lb (227-kg) bombs before moving the bomb train under the fuselage of a Vickers Wellington bomber. After a poor start in day missions, the Wellington came of age in night raids.

Initial Mk Is totalled 181, of which three were built at Chester. These were followed by 187 Mk IAs with Nash and Thompson turrets and strengthened landing gear with larger main wheels. Except for 17 Chester-built aircraft, all were manufactured at Weybridge. The most numerous of the Mk I variants was the Mk IC, which had Vickers 'K' or Browning machine-guns in beam positions (these replacing the ventral turret), improved hydraulics, and a strengthened bomb bay beam to allow a 4,000-lb (1814-kg) bomb to be carried. Of this version 2,685 were built (1,052 at Weybridge, 50 at Blackpool and 1,583 at Chester), 138 of them being delivered as torpedo-bombers after successful trials at the Torpedo Development Unit, Gosport.

Many of the improvements incorporated in the Mks IA and IC were developed for the Mk II, powered by 1,145-hp (854-kW) Rolls-Royce Merlin X engines as an insurance against Pegasus supply problems. The prototype was a conversion of the 38th Mk I, and this made its first flight on 3 March 1939 at Brooklands. Although range was reduced slightly, the Wellington II offered improvements in speed, service ceiling and maximum weight, the last rising from the 24,850 lb (11 272 kg) of the basic Mk I to 33,000 lb (14 969 kg). Weybridge built 401 of this version.

With the Wellington III a switch was made to Bristol Hercules engines, the prototype being the 39th Mk I airframe with Hercules HEISMs, two stage super-chargers and de Havilland propellers. After initial problems with this installation, a Mk IC was converted to take two 1,425-hp (1063-kW) Hercules III engines driving Rotol propellers. Production Mk IIIs had 1,590-hp (1186-kW) Hercules XIs, and later aircraft were fitted with four-gun FN.20A tail turrets, doubling the fire power of the installation in earlier marks. Two were completed at Weybridge, 780 at Blackpool and 737 at Chester.

The availability of a number of 1,050-hp (783-kW) Pratt & Whitney Twin Wasp R-1830-S3C4-G engines, ordered by but not delivered to France, led to development of the Wellington IV. The prototype was one of 220 Mk IVs built at Chester, but on its delivery flight to Weybridge carburettor icing caused both engines to fail on the approach to Brooklands, and the aircraft made a forced landing at Addlestone. The original Hamilton Standard propellers proved very noisy and were replaced by Curtiss propellers.

For high-altitude bombing Vickers was asked to investigate the provision of a pressure cabin in the Wellington: the resulting Mk V was powered by two turbocharged Hercules VIII engines. Service ceiling was increased from the 23,500 ft (7165 m) of the Mk II to 36,800 ft (11 215 m). The cylindrical pressure chamber had a porthole in the lower nose position for the bomb-aimer, and the pilot's head projected into a small pressurised dome which, although offset to port, provided little forward or downward view for landing. Two prototypes were built in Vickers' experimental

Vickers Wellington

Vickers Wellington IC of No. 301 (Polish) Squadron, RAF, Syerston (UK) in winter/spring 1941

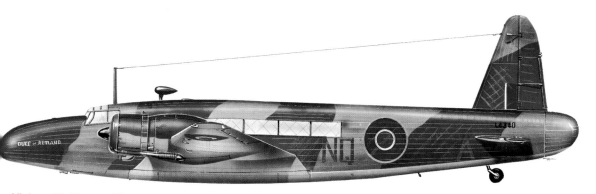

Vickers Wellington IC transport conversion of No. 24 Squadron, RAF, Hendon (UK) in 1942

shop at Foxwarren, Cobham, to Specification B.23/39 and one production machine, to B.17/40, was produced at the company's extension factory at Smith's Lawn, Windsor Great Park.

The Wellington VI was a parallel development, with 1,600-hp (1193-kW) Merlin 60 engines and a service ceiling of 38,500 ft (11 735 m), although the prototype had achieved 40,000 ft (12 190 m). Wellington VI production totalled 63, including 18 re-engined Mk Vs, all assembled at Smith's Lawn. Each had a remotely-controlled FN.20A tail turret, and this was locked in position when the aircraft was at altitude.

Intended originally as an improved Mk II with Merlin XX engines, the Wellington VII was built only as a prototype, and was transferred to Rolls-Royce at Hucknall for development flying of the Merlin 60s.

First Wellington variant to be developed specifically for Coastal Command was the GR.VIII, a general reconnaissance/torpedo-bomber version of the Pegasus XVIII-engined Mk IC. Equipped with ASV (Air to Surface Vessel) Mk II radar, it was identified readily by the four dorsal antennae and the four pairs of transmitting aerials on each side of the fuselage. A total of 271 torpedo-bombers for daylight operation was built at Weybridge, together with 65 day bombers, and 58 equipped for night operation with a Leigh searchlight in the ventral turret position. In these last aircraft the nose armament was deleted and the position occupied by the light operator.

The designation Mk IX was allocated to a single troop-carrying conversion of a Wellington IA, but the Mk X was the last of the bomber variants and the most numerous. It was based on the Mk III, but had the more powerful 1,675-hp (1249-kW) Hercules VI or XVI engine with downdraught carburettor, and was identified externally from earlier marks by the long carburettor intake on top of the engine cowling. Internal structural strengthening, achieved by the use of newly-developed light alloys, allowed maximum take-off weight to raise to 36,000 lb (16 329 kg). Production was shared between Blackpool and Chester, with totals of 1,369 and 2,434 respectively. After withdrawal from first-line service with Bomber Command, Mk Xs were among many Wellingtons flown by Operational Training Units. After the war a number were converted by Boulton Paul Aircraft as T.10 crew trainers, with the nose turret faired over.

Making use of the experience gained with the Wellington VIII torpedo-bombers, the GR.XI was developed from the Mk X, using the same Hercules VI or XVI engines. It was equipped initially with ASV Mk II radar, although this was superseded later by centrimetric ASV Mk III. This latter equipment had first been fitted to the GR.XII, which was a Leigh Light-equipped anti-submarine version. Weybridge built 105 Mk XIs and 50 Mk XIIs, while Blackpool and Chester respectively assembled 75 Mk XIs and eight Mk XIIs, but with 1,735-hp (1294-kW) Hercules XVII engines.

Vickers Wellington

The Vickers Wellington I was the RAF's most important bomber at the beginning of World War II, but soon had to become a night bomber after some catastrophic loss rates in daylight raids against Germany.

Weybridge was responsible for 42 Mk XIIIs and 53 Mk XIVs, Blackpool for 802 XIIIs and 250 Mk XIVs, and Chester for 538 Mk XIVs.

A transport conversion of the Mk I, the C.IA, was further developed as the C.XV, while the C.XVI was a similar development of the Mk IC. They were unarmed, as were the last three basic versions which were all trainers. The T.XVII was a Mk XI converted by the RAF for night fighter crew training with SCR-720 AI (Airborne Interception) radar in a nose radome. Eighty externally similar aircraft, with accommodation for instructor and four pupils and based on the Mk XIII, were built at Blackpool as T.XVIIIs. Finally, RAF-converted Mk Xs for basic crew training were designated T.XIXs. In total 11,461 Wellingtons were built, including the prototype, and the last was a Blackpool-built Mk X handed over on 25 October 1945.

The fourth production Wellington Mk I was the first to reach an operational squadron, arriving at Mildenhall in October 1938 for No. 99 Squadron. Six squadrons, of No. 3 Group (Nos. 9, 37, 38, 99, 115 and 149) were equipped by the outbreak of war, and among units working up was the New Zealand Flight at Marham, Norfolk, where training was in progress in preparation for delivery to New Zealand of 30 Wellington Is. The flight later became No. 75 (NZ) Squadron, the first Dominion squadron to be formed in World War II. Sergeant James Ward of No. 75 later became the only recipient of the Victoria Cross while serving on

Wellingtons, the decoration being awarded for crawling out on to the wing in flight to extinguish a fire, during a sortie made on 7 July 1941.

On 4 September 1939, the second day of the war, Wellingtons of Nos. 9 and 149 Squadrons bombed German shipping at Brunsbüttel, sharing with the Bristol Blenheims of Nos. 107 and 110 Squadrons the honour of Bomber Command's first bombing raids on German territory. Wellingtons in tight formation were reckoned to have such outstanding defensive firepower as to be almost impregnable, but after maulings at the hands of pilots of the Luftwaffe's JG 1, during raids on the Schillig Roads on 14 and 18 December, some lessons were learned. Self-sealing tanks were essential, and the Wellington's vulnerability to beam attacks from above led to introduction of beam gun positions. Most significantly, operations switched to nights.

Wellingtons of Nos. 99 and 149 Squadrons were among aircraft despatched in Bomber Command's first attack on Berlin, which took place on 25/26 August 1940; and on 1 April 1941, a Wellington of No. 149 Squadron dropped the first 4,000-lb (1814-kg) 'block-buster' bomb during a raid on Emden. Of 1,046 aircraft which took part in the Cologne raid during the night of 30 May 1942, 599 were Wellingtons. The last operational sortie by Bomber Command Wellingtons was flown on 8/9 October 1943.

There was, however, still an important role for the Wellington to play with Coastal Command. Maritime

Vickers Wellington

Finished in Coastal Command colouring, the maritime reconnaissance role of this Vickers Wellington is attested by the transmitting and receiving antennae of the ASV Mk II radar on the fuselage top and sides.

operations had started with the four DWI Wellingtons: these had been converted by Vickers in the opening months of 1940 to carry a 52-ft (15.85-m) diameter metal ring, which contained a coil that could create a field current to detonate magnetic mines. Eleven almost idential aircraft, with 48-ft (14.63-m) rings, were converted by W.A. Rollason Ltd at Croydon, and others on site in the Middle East.

No. 172 Squadron at Chivenor, covering the Western Approaches, was the first to use the Leigh Light-equipped Wellington VIII operationally, and the first attack on a U-boat by such an aircraft at night took place on 3 June 1942, with the first sinking recorded on 6 July. From December 1941 Wellingtons were flying shipping strikes in the Mediterranean, and in the Far East No. 36 Squadron began anti-submarine operations in October 1942.

In 1940 the entry of the Italians into World War II resulted in Wellingtons being sent out from Great Britain to serve with No. 205 Group, Desert Air Force. No. 70 Squadron flew its first night attack on 19 September, against the port of Benghazi, and as the tide of war turned during 1942 and 1943, units moved into Tunisia to support the invasions of Sicily and Italy, operating from Italian soil at the close of 1943. The last Wellington bombing raid of the war in southern Europe took place on 13 March 1945, when six aircraft joined a Consolidated Liberator strike on marshalling yards at Treviso in northern Italy.

In the Far East, too, Wellingtons served as bombers with No. 225 Group in India, Mk ICs of No. 215 Squadron flying their first operational sortie on 23 April 1942. Equipped later with Wellington Xs, Nos. 99 and 215 Squadrons continued to bomb Japanese bases and communications until replaced by Liberators in late 1944, when the Wellington units were released for transport duties.

After the war the Wellington was used principally for navigator and pilot training, Air Navigation Schools and Advanced Flying Schools until 1953.

Specification

Type: long-range night bomber
Powerplant (Mk III): two 1,500-hp (1119-kW) Bristol Hercules XI radial piston engines
Performance: maximum speed 235 mph (378 km/h) at 15,500 ft (4725 m); service ceiling 19,000 ft (5790 m); range 1,540 miles (2478 km) with bomb load of 4,500 lb (2041 kg)
Weights: empty 18,650 lb (8459 kg); maximum take-off 29,500 lb (13381 kg)
Dimensions: span 86 ft 2 in (26.26 m); length 60 ft 10 in (18.54 m); height 17 ft 5 in (5.31 m); wing area 840 sq ft (78.04 m²)
Armament: eight 0.303-in (7.7-mm) machine-guns (two in nose, four in tail turret, and two in beam positions), plus up to 4,500 lb (2041 kg) of bombs
Operators: RAAF, RAF, RCAF, RNZAF

Vickers Warwick

Vickers Warwick III with cargo pannier, early 1945

History and notes

The failure of the Rolls-Royce Vulture engine effectively killed both the Vickers Warwick and the Avro Manchester, but at least the latter entered service and was subsequently the basis of the highly successful Lancaster. The Warwick, on the other hand, flew in prototype form with Vultures, but teething troubles were so prolonged that the Warwick had been superseded by the new four-engined bombers before it could enter production.

Designed to Specification B.1/35, and intended to be complementary to the Wellington, the Warwick got off to a bad start because of policy changes and some doubts on the form of geodetic construction. It was not until 13 August 1939 that the Vulture-powered prototype flew. The unreliability of this engine compelled a change, and the second prototype flew with a Bristol Centaurus powerplant in April 1940.

Delay in delivery of these engines in quantity necessitated another change of powerplant, this time to American Pratt & Whitney Double Wasps of 1,850 hp (1380 kW), and in this form the Warwick Mk I entered production, the first aircraft flying from Brooklands on 1 May 1942. By then it was far too late to consider the aircraft as a bomber, and in January 1943

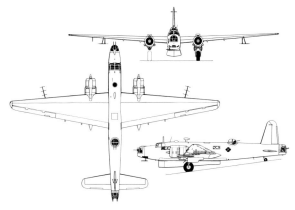

Vickers Warwick ASR.I

the decision was made to convert the type for air-sea rescue work, carrying an airborne lifeboat beneath the fuselage. This became the Warwick ASR.I, and the first three were delivered in August 1943 to No. 280 Squadron at Langham, Norfolk, where they replaced Ansons.

Early Warwick ASR.Is, known as Stage A aircraft, carried a Mk I lifeboat and Lindholme rescue equip-

A Vickers-Armstrong Warwick ASR.I of No. 282 Squadron, RAF Coastal Command, carrying a Mk 1A lifeboat under the fuselage in the air-sea rescue role. This aircraft was burnt out in January 1946.

Vickers Warwick

Designed as a Wellington replacement, the promising Vickers Warwick was delayed by specification changes, and entered service only in 1943. Illustrated is a postwar maritime-reconnaissance GR.V with undernose radar.

ment; later versions (Stage B aircraft), had provision for ASV radar and a Frazer-Nash tail turret, but had no camera mounting. The final (Stage C) version could be operated at higher all-up weights. Total production of ASR Warwicks amounted to 275, and 16 B.Is were also built.

A BOAC requirement for a long-range transport led in 1942 to an order for 14 Warwick transports. Designated C.Is, these came from the Weybridge production line, with nose and tail turrets replaced by blunt fairings, and all military equipment was removed. The first Warwick C.I flew on 5 February 1943, powered by Pratt & Whitney Double Wasp R-2800s, and following tests at Boscombe Down the type entered service with BOAC on its Middle East routes. The Warwick C.Is served with the airline until 1944, when they were transferred to RAF Transport Command and operated by No. 167 Squadron at Holmsley South.

A further transport development was the Warwick III, which was basically similar to the C.I but had a large, fixed ventral pannier. In cargo configuration a 6,710-lb (3044-kg) payload could be carried, or alternatively 24 men and equipment; in a VIP role 8 to 10 passengers could be accommodated. One hundred Warwick IIIs were built and served mainly in the Mediterranean area with Nos. 46 and 47 Groups of RAF Transport Command, before being withdrawn in 1946.

Bristol Centaurus engines became available in 1943, and the opportunity was taken to develop the Warwick in the general-reconnaissance role as the GR.II, and

133 were built to serve with Coastal Command squadrons at home and in the Middle and Far East. The GR.II had a single nose gun in place of the two-gun turret of earlier versions, and a mid-upper turret was added.

The last production Warwick was the GR.V, generally similar to the GR.II, but with beam guns in place of the mid-upper turret. A radar scanner beneath the nose also housed the Leigh Light, an airborne searchlight intended primarily for anti-submarine operations.

The first GR.V flew at Brooklands in April 1944, and service trials were carried out at Hullavington. Deliveries began to No. 179 Squadron at St Eval in 1945 and 212 were built, but this mark was too late to see war service.

Specification

Type: seven-seat general-reconnaissance aircraft
Powerplant (GR.II): two 2,500-hp (1864-kW) Bristol Centaurus VI radial piston engines
Performance: maximum speed 262 mph (422 km/h) at 2,000 ft (610 m); service ceiling 19,000 ft (5790 m); range 3,050 miles (4908 km)
Weights: empty 31,125 lb (14118 kg); maximum take-off 51,250 lb (23247 kg)
Dimensions: span 96 ft 8½ in (29.48 m); length 68 ft 6 in (20.88 m); height 18 ft 6 in (5.64 m); wing area 1,006 sq ft (93.46 m²)
Armament: six 0.303-in (7.7-mm) machine-guns (one each in nose and dorsal turrets, and four in tail turret), plus up to 12,250 lb (5557 kg) of bombs
Operator: RAF

Vickers Windsor

Designed to provide better performance than the Lancaster in the long-range bomber role, the Vickers Windsor had many interesting features, but suffered from protracted development and was cancelled in 1945.

History and notes

The Barnes Wallis geodetic construction, introduced on the Vickers Wellesley and used later on the Vickers Wellington and Vickers Warwick, was highly successful. To exploit its physical characteristics fully, however, a very big aeroplane was desirable.

Vickers' designer, Rex Pierson, used geodetics in evolving a four-engined bomber to meet Specification B.13/36, but the Short Stirling was awarded the contract. Another opportunity came with Specification B.1/39, but this was again unsuccessful, and it was not until the submission to Specification B.5/41 that the Vickers tender was accepted.

The requirement was for a high-altitude heavy bomber with pressurised crew compartment, and an ability to fly at 345 mph (555 km/h) at 31,000 ft (9450 m). Two prototypes of the new bomber were ordered, but changes resulted in a new specification, B.3/42, being drawn up. Vickers designated their design the Type 447, and the name Windsor was given to the aircraft. Various armament trials were carried out on a Warwick prototype, and the first Windsor flew from Farnborough, where it had been assembled, on 23 October 1943. It attained a speed of 302 mph (486 km/h) at 25,000 ft (7620 m), and had completed almost 34 hours of flight testing before being written off in a forced landing, caused by problems with a propeller constant-speed unit. The second prototype, Type 457, contained armour plating and other modifications, and flew from Wisley on 15 February 1944, demonstrating similar performance to the first aircraft. This aircraft was grounded in June 1946, and broken up.

A third Windsor, Type 480, was flown on 11 July 1944, with some further changes incorporated. This aircraft was fitted later with defensive barbettes in the outboard engine nacelles, each barbette having two remotely-controlled rear-firing 20-mm cannon.

Trials for these were carried out by a Lancaster, but although further tests continued for some 10 months, the Windsor programme was cancelled on 15 March 1946, with the third aircraft finishing its days as an

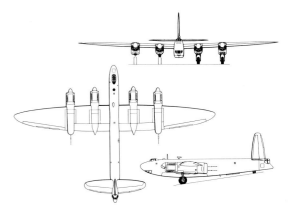

Vickers Windsor (dashed lines: proposed armament of twin 20-mm Hispano cannon in each outer engine barbette)

instructional airframe. A fourth Windsor, originally Type 471 but later changed to Type 483, was almost complete when the programme finished.

Specification

Type: heavy bomber
Powerplant (Type 447): four 1,635-hp (1219-kW) Rolls-Royce Merlin 65 inline piston engines
Performance: maximum speed 317 mph (510 km/h) at 23,000 ft (7010 m); service ceiling 27,250 ft (8305 m); range 2,890 miles (4651 km) with 8,000-lb (3629-kg) bomb load
Weights: empty 38,606 lb (17511 kg); maximum take-off 54,000 lb (24494 kg)
Dimensions: span 117 ft 2 in (35.71 m); length 76 ft 10 in (23.42 m); height 23 ft 0 in (7.01 m); wing area 1,248 sq ft (115.94 m²)
Armament: two 0.303-in (7.7-mm) machine-guns in nose turret and two rear-firing 20-mm cannon in each outboard engine nacelle, plus up to 12,000 lb (5443 kg) of bombs
Operator: RAF (for evaluation only)

Westland Wapiti

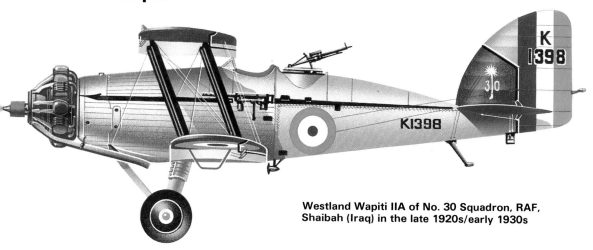

Westland Wapiti IIA of No. 30 Squadron, RAF, Shaibah (Iraq) in the late 1920s/early 1930s

History and notes

The first Westland design to achieve quantity production, the Wapiti was built to replace the ageing de Havilland D.H.9A: when, in 1926, the Air Ministry decided to invite competitive tenders for this new aircraft, it was stipulated that as many D.H.9A parts as possible should be used.

Westland had built over 400 D.H.9As and rebuilt more than another 150, so were well placed to produce a successor. The prototype Wapiti, flown in early 1927, had standard D.H.9A wings, ailerons, interplane struts and tail unit, with a new fuselage 5½ in (0.14 m) wider and 12 in (0.30 m) deeper than that of the original de Havilland aircraft. Powerplant was the 420-hp (313-kW) Bristol Jupiter VI. Early tests indicated that a larger fin and rudder were needed, and when these had been fitted the prototype went to the Aircraft and Experimental Establishment, Martlesham Heath, for trials.

A first batch of 25 Wapiti Mk Is was ordered to Specification F.26/27, these being required for service trials with No. 84 Squadron in Iraq, and intended to replace their D.H.9As. Like the prototype, they had the Jupiter VI engine, and the wings and rear fuselage were of wooden construction. Ten Mk IIs followed, to Specification 16/31, and all-metal construction was featured from this mark which had the 460-hp (343-kW) Jupiter VI. The Mk IIA, introduced in 1931, had the 550-hp (410-kW) Jupiter VIII, and a batch of 35 similarly powered Mk Vs followed. The last RAF version was the Mk VI dual-control trainer, introduced in 1932, and of which 16 were built. Wapiti production ended in August 1932, after 517 had been constructed for the RAF. Overseas customers included Australia, China and South Africa, 27 being licence-built in this last country.

Many sub-variants were flown with a variety of engines, some being tested on floats, and the prototype Wapiti Mk V, provided with an enclosed cabin, was flown over Mount Everest in April 1933.

At the outbreak of World War II, Wapitis remained

Production of the Westland Wapiti for the RAF totalled some 500 in five marks. This inelegant but worthy general-purpose biplane served with 10 home bomber and 11 overseas bomber/army co-operation squadrons.

in use in India with Nos. 5, 27 and 60 Squadrons, while others were serving in the Royal Canadian Air Force and South African Air Force.

Specification

Type: two-seat general-purpose biplane
Powerplant (Mk IIA): one 550-hp (410-kW) Bristol Jupiter VIII radial piston engine
Performance: maximum speed 135 mph (217 km/h) at 5,000 ft (1525 m); cruising speed 110 mph (177 km/h); service ceiling 20,600 ft (6280 m); range 360 miles (579 km)
Weights: empty 3,180 lb (1442 kg); maximum take-off 5,400 lb (2449 kg)
Dimensions: span 46 ft 5 in (14.15 m); length 32 ft 6 in (9.91 m); height 11 ft 10 in (3.61 m); wing area 468 sq ft (43.48 m²)
Armament: one 0.303-in (7.7-mm) machine-gun firing forward on side of fuselage and one Lewis gun in rear cockpit, plus up to 580 lb (263 kg) of bombs
Operators: China, RAAF, RAF, RCAF, SAAF

Westland Wallace

Basically a Wapiti with aerodynamic improvements and a Bristol Pegasus radial in a neat Townend cowling, the Westland Wallace served until 1943. The 68 Wallace Is were conversions, the other 104 being newly built.

History and notes

With the success of its Wapiti assured, Westland went ahead with a private venture development in 1931. Designated P.V.6, the prototype was of all-metal construction, and of generally similar configuration to the Wapiti. However, the fuselage was lengthened by 1 ft 8 in (0.51 m), and spatted landing gear, wheel brakes, and a cowled 655-hp (488-kW) Bristol Pegasus IV engine were introduced.

Duly impressed by a much improved performance, the Air Ministry ordered 12 Wapitis converted to the new standard against Specification 19/32. The name Wallace was chosen for the new type. These Mk I aircraft were fitted with 570-hp (425-kW) Bristol Pegasus IIM3 engines and were delivered to No. 501 Squadron at Filton in early 1933. Another 56 Wapitis were converted to Wallace Mk I standard, and in 1935 the Wallace Mk II appeared with an enclosed cabin and 680-hp (507-kW) Pegasus IV engines.

Contracts for 75 Wallace Mk IIs to Specification G.31/35 were placed in June 1935, and a further 29 were ordered the following February, the last Wallace leaving Westland's factory in October 1936.

Most Wallaces served with Auxiliary Air Force Squadrons Nos. 501, 502, 504, 608 and 610, while others replaced Hawker Horsleys at Biggin Hill with the Anti-Aircraft Co-operation Flight. As more modern types entered service the Wallaces began to be withdrawn, but 83 were still in use at the outbreak of World War II, many as target tugs, and they continued to serve in this role until about 1943, fulfilling an important if unglamorous role until finally replaced by monoplane types capable of performing more comparably with later combat aircraft.

Specification

Type: two-seat general-purpose biplane
Powerplant (Mk II): one 680-hp (507-kW) Bristol Pegasus IV radial piston engine
Performance: maximum speed 158 mph (254 km/h) at 15,000 ft (4570 m); cruising speed 135 mph (217 km/h); service ceiling 24,100 ft (7345 m); range 470 miles (756 km)
Weights: empty 3,840 lb (1742 kg); maximum take-off 5,750 lb (2608 kg)
Dimensions: span 46 ft 5 in (14.15 m); length 34 ft 2 in (10.41 m); height 11 ft 6 in (3.51 m); wing area 488 sq ft (45.34 m²)
Armament: one 0.303-in (7.7-mm) forward-firing machine-gun and one Lewis gun in rear cockpit, plus up to 580 lb (263 kg) of bombs
Operator: RAF

Westland Lysander

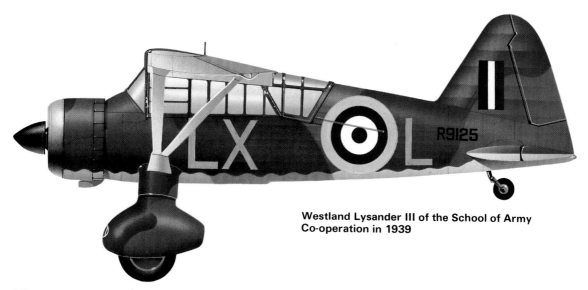

Westland Lysander III of the School of Army Co-operation in 1939

History and notes

British army co-operation aircraft used between the wars were largely conversions of existing airframes. In 1934, however, the Air Ministry issued Specification A.39/34, for a new aircraft to replace the Hawker Hector biplane which was then used for the purpose. In June 1935 Westland tendered for, and won, a contract covering two prototypes which the company designated P.8, the name Lysander being adopted subsequently. The first prototype underwent taxiing trials at Yeovil on 10 June 1936, before being taken by road to Boscombe Down, where it made its first flight on 15 June, in the course of which it returned to Yeovil. Minor modifications were made and the prototype was shown at the SBAC Display at Hatfield at the end of June, and on 24 July it went to the Aircraft and Armament Experimental Establishment at Martlesham Heath for a week to undertake handling evaluation.

A production order for 144 aircraft was placed in September, and the second prototype flew on 11 December 1936, spending much of its time at Martlesham before going to India in 1938, for tropical trials with No. 5 Squadron. Deliveries to the RAF began in June 1938, when No. 16 Squadron at Old Sarum received its first aircraft to replace the Hawker Audax then in service. The School of Army Co-operation was also based at Old Sarum, and its pilots received instruction on the Lysander from squadron personnel.

During 1939, 66 Lysander Mk Is were completed: of these No. 16 Squadron received 14, the School of Army Co-operation nine, while other deliveries were made to No. 13 Squadron at Odiham, No. 26 at Catterick and No. 4 at Wimborne, the Lysanders in all cases replacing Hawker Hectors. On the outbreak of war there were seven Lysander squadrons, the others being No. 2, and the Auxiliary Air Force's squadrons Nos. 613 and 614. By this time most of the home-based squadrons had replaced their 890-hp (664-kW) Bristol

Mercury XII-powered Mk Is with Mk IIs. These had the 905-hp (675-kW) Bristol Perseus XII engine, which offered a slightly better performance at altitude. Many of the Mk Is were sent overseas, for service in Egypt, India and Palestine. A total of 116 Mk Is was followed on the production line by 442 Mk IIs, and it was with this latter mark that Nos. 2, 4, 13 and 26 Squadrons moved to France in 1940.

As the German attack mounted, No. 4 Squadron moved to Belgium, but such was the fury of the onslaught that 11 Lysanders were lost between 10 and 23 May, some being eliminated on the ground. One of the squadron's Lysander crews destroyed a Bf 110 during a running battle with six Messerschmitts, but managed to return to base; on 22 May an aircraft of No. 2 Squadron accounted for a Henschel Hs 126 with its front gun and a Junkers Ju 87 with the rear gun. By then the end of French resistance was near, and the Lysander squadrons were withdrawn to the UK, although some sorties were still made over the battle area to drop supplies to Allied forces. Such an operation was decimated when, of 16 Lysanders and Hectors sent out on a supply sortie over Calais, 14 aircraft and crews failed to return. In all, some 118 Lysanders and 120 crew members were lost over France and Belgium between September 1939 and May 1940, almost 20 per cent of the aircraft sent out from the UK.

The heavy fighting on the continent, and severe losses incurred by army co-operation units, indicated that the old concept of this type of operation was outdated, particularly when air superiority had not been achieved. Accordingly, Lysanders were withdrawn from the UK-based squadrons, which began to re-equip in early 1941 with Curtiss P-40 Tomahawks.

Overseas, Lysanders had replaced Audaxes in No. 208 Squadron in Egypt in April 1939, and the squadron's new aircraft saw action in the Western Desert alongside Hawker Hurricanes of the same squadron which were being used for tactical reconnaissance. The squadron

Westland Lysander

Though it gave its crew excellent fields of view in the army co-operation role, the Westland Lysander was too large and slow to operate against enemy air superiority. This aircraft is from No. 54 OTU.

later took part in the Greek campaign, its Lysanders being replaced by Tomahawks in 1942.

No. 6 Squadron at Ramleh, Palestine, operated a variety of aircraft, and was using Hawker Hardies and Gloster Gauntlets when it received its Lysanders in February 1940. These were supplemented and later replaced, in 1942, by various marks of Hurricane and Bristol Blenheim IVs.

In September 1941 No. 28 Squadron at Ambala, India, was the first squadron in the area to receive Lysanders, replacing Audaxes. The squadron subsequently took its new aircraft to Burma, and operated in ground-attack bombing and tactical reconnaissance roles before being withdrawn to India in March 1942; in December of that year it converted to Hurricanes, becoming a fighter squadron. The last squadron to use Lysanders in action was No. 20, in Burma during late 1943 before receiving Hurricanes as replacements.

Although withdrawn from first-line service, Lysanders continued in operation for a variety of other roles:

as target tugs, air-sea rescue aircraft and, least publicised at the time, with the Special Operations Executive. Nos. 138 and 161 Squadrons, using a mixed bag or aircraft which included Lysanders, maintained contact with resistance groups in occupied Europe, dropping supplies and agents, and bringing agents back to the UK. It was in these night operations in occupied territory that the Lysander really came into its own, being able to use its remarkable short landing and take-off capabilities to the utmost in the small fields marked out by the resistance. Lysander Mk IIIs and IIIAs were used for this work, 367 of the former and 347 of the latter being built, powered by the 870-hp (649-kW) Bristol Mercury XX or XXX engines.

Final production variant was the TT.IIIA target tug, of which 100 were built. Figures for total Lysander production vary, as a number of aircraft were cancelled, but around 1,650 were built, including 225 under licence in Canada.

A batch of 26 Mk IIs was supplied to the Turkish air

Westland Lysander

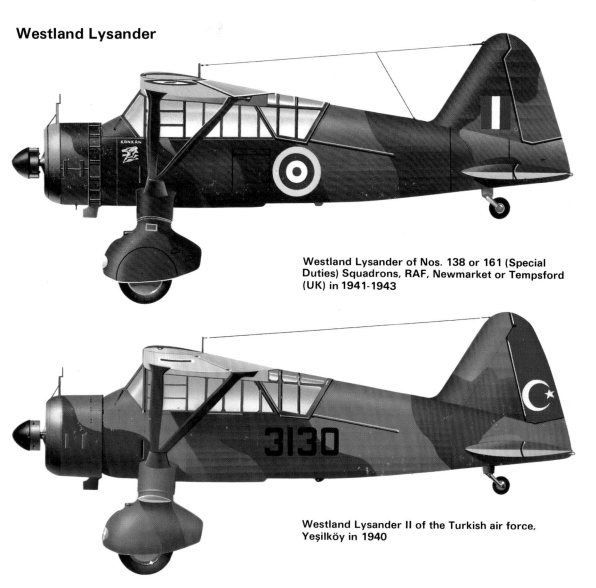

Westland Lysander of Nos. 138 or 161 (Special Duties) Squadrons, RAF, Newmarket or Tempsford (UK) in 1941-1943

Westland Lysander II of the Turkish air force, Yeşilköy in 1940

force, 20 to Egypt, six to the Irish Air Corps, nine to Finland, eight to Portugal and several to France. Three went to the USAF, and others to the South African Air Force.

Several Lysanders were used for experimental purposes, the most unusual being a tandem-wing conversion with twin fins and rudders and a Boulton Paul gun turret mock-up. This was intended as a home-defence beach strafer, but fortunately was not needed. Another Lysander was fitted with a completely new wing designed by Blackburn. Intended for research purposes only, this Steiger wing was swept forward 9°, and used full-span slats and flaps to provide high lift.

At the end of the war Canada was the only country to have a large Lysander population, some of which remained in service until the early 1960s. Several have survived, due to the activities of the preservation groups, and remain in airworthy condition in both Canada and the UK.

Specification

Type: two-seat army co-operation aircraft
Powerplant (Mk III): one 870-hp (649-kW) Bristol Mercury XX or XXX radial piston engine
Performance: maximum speed 212 mph (341 km/h) at 5,000 ft (1525 m); service ceiling 21,500 ft (6555 m); range 600 miles (966 km)
Weights: empty 4,365 lb (1980 kg); maximum take-off 6,318 lb (2866 kg)
Dimensions: span 50 ft 0 in (15.24 m); length 30 ft 6 in (9.30 m); height 14 ft 6 in (4.42 m); wing area 260 sq ft (24.15 m²)
Armament: two forward-firing 0.303-in (7.7-mm) machine-guns in wheel spats, two 0.303-in (7.7-mm) guns on mounting in rear cockpit, plus light bombs on stub wings attached to spats
Operators: Egypt, Eire, FAF, FFAF, Finland, Portugal, RAAF, RAF, RCAF, SAAF, Turkey, USAAF

Westland Whirlwind

Westland Whirlwind I of No. 263 Squadron, RAF, Exeter (UK) in 1941 (also plan and front views on opposite page)

Westland Whirlwind of No. 263 Squadron, RAF, in winter 1941-2

History and notes

After a long series of rather staid biplanes, the choice of Westland to produce a high-speed fighter must have seemed somewhat unlikely, but the company tendered against Specification F.37/35 and in January 1939 won a production contract for 200 aircraft.

The first of two prototype Westland Whirlwinds flew on 11 October 1938, but the Air Ministry lowered a security curtain around the new fighter which was not to be raised until August 1941. This caused considerable amusement, since a French technical paper had published drawings in 1938, and there was every reason to suppose that the Germans knew about the Whirlwind.

The new type was interesting on several accounts: it was the RAF's first twin-engined fighter, and had low-altitude performance that was better than that of any contemporary single-seat fighter. Furthermore, its four 20-mm nose-mounted cannon gave a weight of fire of 600 lb (272 kg) per minute, which conferred firepower superior to that of any other fighter in the world.

Production deliveries began to No. 263 Squadron at Drem in July, 1940, and the squadron settled down to eliminate the inevitable bugs in a new airframe and

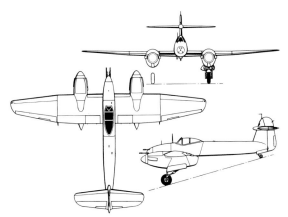

Westland Whirlwind

engine—the Rolls-Royce Peregrine. Troubles were also experienced with the cannon but the squadron scored its first confirmed success with the destruction of an Arado Ar 196 floatplane on 8 February 1941, although a Whirlwind pilot was lost.

Deliveries were slow, as a result of a shortage of engines, and only eight Whirlwinds had been received

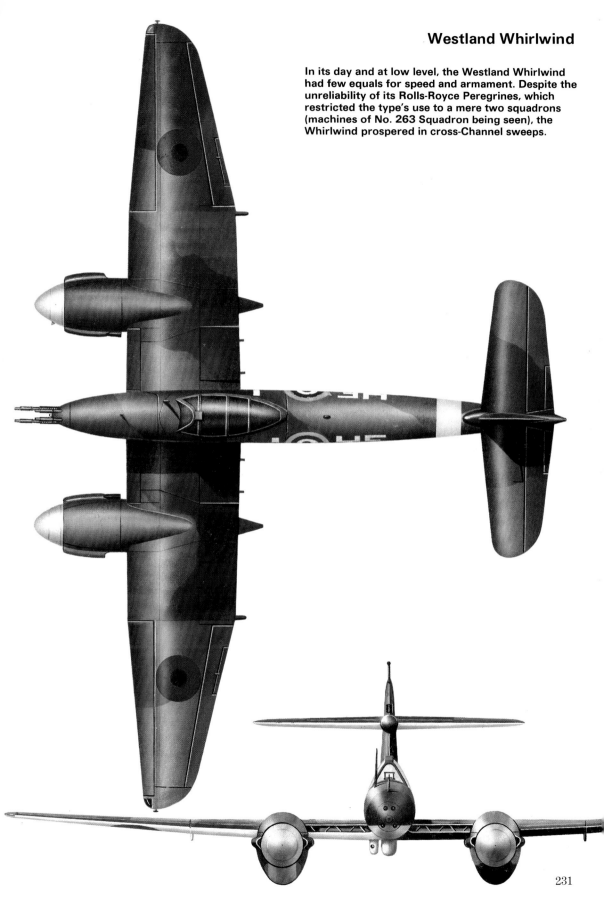

Westland Whirlwind

In its day and at low level, the Westland Whirlwind had few equals for speed and armament. Despite the unreliability of its Rolls-Royce Peregrines, which restricted the type's use to a mere two squadrons (machines of No. 263 Squadron being seen), the Whirlwind prospered in cross-Channel sweeps.

This Whirlwind I, one of a production total of 114, was retained by Westland Aircraft and registered as G-AGOI in late 1945. The rest saw action chiefly as target of opportunity bombers over northern Europe in 1941-2.

Westland Whirlwind

A powerful long-range fighter-bomber, the Westland Whirlwind was dogged by the unreliability of its Rolls-Royce Peregrine engines. Only 112 were built, serving with Nos 137 and 263 (illustrated) squadrons.

by the RAF at the end of 1940. No. 137 was the second (and only other) squadron to be equipped with Whirlwinds; it was formed at Charmy Down on 20 September 1941 with a nucleus of No. 263 Squadron personnel.

While the new fighter proved to have excellent performance at low altitude, it was at a distinct disadvantage when fighter against fighter combat began to move to higher altitudes, and it was necessary to restrict Whirlwind operations to a lower level where, for a time, the type proved useful for light bombing operations and fighter sweeps.

It had become obvious by 1940 that the Whirlwind had its drawbacks, engine unreliability being high on the list, while high landing speed restricted the number of airfields it could use. The initial order for 200 was cut to 112, and a second order for 200 was cancelled, with the last production aircraft off the line flying in January 1942. In June 1943 No. 137 Squadron was re-equipped with rocket-firing Hawker Hurricane IVs, while No. 263 gave up its Whirlwinds for Hawker Typhoons in December of that year.

Some experimental work had taken place with Whirlwinds: the second prototype undertook night-fighting trials with No. 25 Squadron, a Blenheim Mk IF unit, between May and July 1940; the first prototype was tested with an armament of 12 Browning 0.303-in (7.7-mm) machine-guns; and another had a 37-mm cannon installed.

One Whirlwind survived the war, being used under civil markings as a Westland hack during 1946-7, before being dismantled in the latter year.

Specification

Type: single-seat long-range fighter-bomber
Powerplant: two 885-hp (660-kW) Rolls-Royce Peregrine inline piston engines
Performance: maximum speed 360 mph (579 km/h) at 15,000 ft (4570 m); service ceiling 30,000 ft (9145 m)
Weights: empty 8,310 (3769 kg); maximum take-off 11,388 lb (5166 kg)
Dimensions: span 45 ft 0 in (13.72 m); length 32 ft 9 in (9.98 m); height 11 ft 7 in (3.53 m); wing area 250 sq ft (23.23 m²)
Armament: four 20-mm cannon in nose, plus up to 1,000 lb (454 kg) of bombs
Operator: RAF

Westland Welkin

Designed to combat high-altitude German raids, the Westland Welkin followed the design philosophy pioneered by the Whirlwind, but with longer wings. Only 67 were built, but none was ever used on an operational mission.

History and notes

Soon after the outbreak of World War II the Air Ministry, aware of the existence of the Junkers Ju 86P high-altitude reconnaissance aircraft, issued Specification F.4/40 for a cannon-armed high-altitude single-seat fighter which would be able to operate at an altitude of 40,000 ft (12190 m).

Westland accepted the challenge and its obvious problems: a large wing span was needed, and a pressure cabin was necessary for the pilot. Made of bullet-resisting light alloy, this cabin was a self-contained unit attached to the wing front spar, and incorporated an atmosphere valve to correct the air pressure automatically for any given height.

A revised Specification, F.7/41, was issued for the prototype Welkin, which flew on 1 November 1942. A second flew later with modified fin and rudder, and production began early the following year, the first of 67 production aircraft flying in September 1943. Since the apparent high-altitude threat did not materialise in any numbers, the Welkin contract was cancelled and no aircraft were delivered to squadrons.

A considerable amount of high-altitude flight was carried out, including tests with liquid oxygen for injection into modified engines to increase performance at high altitude; trials were discontinued, however, because of the difficulty of handling liquid oxygen.

In 1944 Westland flew a two-seat night fighter version, the Welkin Mk II, which had a lengthened nose to take AI Mk VIII airborne interception radar, and the front cockpit moved forward to give space for a rearward-facing observer's seat. The pilot's windscreen was lowered, and dihedral was increased on the outer wing panels. Developed to Specification F.9/43, the Welkin Mk II was not ordered, and the sole example ended its days as a radar test-bed.

Although not used operationally, the Welkin provided much useful data on high-altitude flight. It was

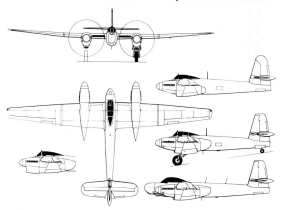

Westland Welkin (bottom side view: Welkin Mk II)

said to be heavier than the original estimates and 15 to 20 mph (24 to 32 km/h) slower than expected. It was also slower than the Mosquito NF.30 which was about to enter service, although it was more stable at extreme heights than the latter, and could attain a higher altitude.

Specification

Type: single-seat high-altitude day/night fighter
Powerplant (Mk I): two 1,250-hp (932-kW) Rolls-Royce Merlin 76/77 inline piston engines
Performance: maximum speed 387 mph (623 km/h) at 26,000 ft (7925 m); service ceiling 44,000 ft (13410 m); range 1,200 miles (1931 km)
Weights: empty 12,610 (5720 kg); maximum take-off 17,500 lb (7938 kg)
Dimensions: span 70 ft 0 in (21.34 m); length 41 ft 7 in (12.67 m); height 15 ft 9 in (4.80 m); wing area 460 sq ft (42.73 m²)
Armament: four 20-mm cannon in nose
Operator: RAF (for evaluation only)

INDEX

A

A.27 (Saro London) **180**
A.W.29 (Armstrong Whitworth) **96**
A.W.38 (Armstrong Whitworth Whitley) **16-20, 122**
A.W.41 (Armstrong Whitworth Albemarle) **21**
AS.5 (Airspeed Courier), **8**
AS.6 (Airspeed Envoy) **9, 10**
AS.10 (Airspeed Oxford) **10-11, 13**
AS.30 (Airspeed Queen Wasp) **12**
AS.45 (Airspeed Cambridge) **13**
AS.51 (Airspeed Horsa) **14-15**
AS.58 (Airspeed Horsa) **14-15**
Airspeed AS.5 Courier **8**
Airspeed AS.6 Envoy **9**
Airspeed AS.10 Oxford **10-11, 13**
Airspeed AS.30 Queen Wasp **12**
Airspeed AS.45 Cambridge **13**
Airspeed AS.51 Horsa **14-15**
Airspeed AS.58 Horsa **14-15**
Albacore (Fairey) **100-101, 104**
Albatross (de Havilland D.H.91) **75, 76**
Albemarle (Armstrong Whitworth A.W.41) **21**
Anson (Avro 652A) **25-27**
Armstrong Whitworth A.W.29 **96**
Armstrong Whitworth A.W.38 Whitley **16-20, 28, 122**
Armstrong Whitworth A.W.41 Albemarle **21**
Audax (Hawker) **98, 136, 137, 138, 139**
Auster series **71**
Avro 504 **22**
Avro 621 Tutor **22, 23**
Avro 626 Prefect **23**
Avro 652A Anson **25-27**
Avro 679 Manchester **24, 28**
Avro 683 Lancaster **24, 28-32, 34, 127, 189**
Avro 685 York **32, 33**
Avro 694 Lincoln **34**

B

B-6 (Blackburn Shark) **35**
B-24 (Blackburn Skua) **36, 37**
B-25 (Blackburn Roc), **37**
B-26 (Blackburn Botha), **38**
B-37 (Blackburn Firebrand), **39**
Barracuda (Fairey), **104-105**
Battle (Fairey) **96-99**
Beaufighter (Bristol 156), **61-67, 68, 69**
Beaufort (Bristol 152) **38, 57-60, 61**
Beagle (Blackburn B.T.1) **211**
Bisley (Bristol 160) **56**
Blackburn B-6 Shark **35**
Blackburn B-24 Skua **36, 37**
Blackburn B-25 Roc **37**
Blackburn B-26 Botha **38**
Blackburn B-37 Firebrand **39**
Blackburn B.T.1 Beagle **211**

Blenheim (Bristol 142M, 149 and 160), **47-56, 61, 68**
Bolingbroke (Bristol 149) **52-54, 57**
Bombay (Bristol 130) **46**
Botha (Blackburn B-26) **38**
Boulton Paul P.82 Defiant **40-42, 145**
Brigand (Bristol 164) **69**
Bristol Type 105 Bulldog **43-45, 110, 113**
Bristol Type 130 Bombay **46**
Bristol Type 142M Blenheim **47-56, 61, 68, 135**
Bristol Type 149 Blenheim/Bolingbroke **47-56, 68, 77**
Bristol Type 150 **57**
Bristol Type 152 Beaufort **38, 57-60, 61**
Bristol Type 155 **21**
Bristol Type 156 Beaufighter **61-67, 68, 69**
Bristol Type 160 Blenheim/Bisley **47-56, 68**
Bristol Type 163 Buckingham **68, 70**
Bristol Type 164 Brigand **69**
Bristol Type 166 Buckmaster **70**
Buckingham (Bristol 163) **68, 70**
Buckmaster (Bristol 166) **70**
Bulldog (Bristol 105) **43-45**

C

CG-4A (Waco Hadrian) **14**
Cambridge (Airspeed AS.45) **13**
Courier (Airspeed AS.5) **8**

D

D.H.60T (de Havilland Moth Trainer), **72**
D.H.82 (de Havilland Tiger Moth) **72-73**
D.H.86 (de Havilland Express) **74**
D.H.89 (de Havilland Dragon Six/Dragon Rapide) **74**
D.H.89M (de Havilland Dominie) **25, 72**
D.H.91 (de Havilland Albatross) **75, 76**
D.H.95 (de Havilland Flamingo) **76**
D.H.98 (de Havilland Mosquito) **68, 77-84**
D.H.103 (de Havilland Hornet/Sea Hornet) **85**
de Havilland Queen Bee **12**
de Havilland D.H.60T Moth Trainer **72**
de Havilland D.H.82 Tiger Moth **72-73**
de Havilland D.H.86 Express **74**
de Havilland D.H.89 Dragon Six/Dragon Rapide **74**
de Havilland D.H.89M/Dominie **25, 72**
de Havilland D.H.91 Albatross **75, 76**
de Havilland D.H.95 Flamingo **76**
de Havilland D.H.98 Mosquito **68, 77-84**
de Havilland D.H.103 Hornet/Sea Hornet **85**
Defiant (Boulton Paul P.82) **40-42**
Demon (Hawker) **135**
Dominie (de Havilland D.H.89M) **25, 72**
Dragon Six/Dragon Rapide (de Havilland D.H.89) **74**

E

E.28/39 (Gloster) **118**
Envoy (Airspeed AS.6) **9, 10**
Express (de Havilland D.H.86) **74**

F

F.9/37 (Gloster) **117**
Fairey IIIF **88, 214**

Fairey Albacore **100-101, 104**
Fairey Barracuda **104-105**
Fairey Battle **96-99**
Fairey Firefly **106-107**
Fairey Flycatcher **144**
Fairey Fox **86, 135**
Fairey Fulmar **102-103, 106**
Fairey Gordon **88**
Fairey Seafox **87**
Fairey Seal **88, 89**
Fairey Swordfish **88-95, 100, 104**
Falcon Six (Miles M.3B) **167**
Firebrand (Blackburn B-37) **39**
Firefly (Fairey) **106-107**
Flamingo (de Havilland D.H.95) **76**
Flycatcher (Fairey) **144**
Fox (Fairey) **86, 135**
Fulmar (Fairey) **102-103, 106**
Fury (Hawker biplane) **141-143, 146**
Fury (Hawker monoplane) **166**

G

'G' Class (Short S.26) **188**
G.41 (Gloster Meteor) **119-121**
Gauntlet (Gloster SS.19) **110-112, 113**
General Aircraft G.A.L.48 Hotspur **108**
General Aircraft G.A.L.49 Hamilcar **109**
Gladiator (Gloster SS.37) **113-116**
Gloster E.28/39 **118**
Gloster F.9/37 **117**
Gloster G.41 Meteor **119-121**
Gloster SS.19 Gauntlet **110-112, 113**
Gloster SS.37 Gladiator **113-116**
Gordon (Fairey) **88**

H

H.P.50 (Handley Page Heyford) **18, 125**
H.P.52 (Handley Page Hampden) **122-123, 124**
H.P.52 (Handley Page Hereford) **122, 124**
H.P.54 (Handley Page Harrow) **125-126**
H.P.55 (Handley Page) **127**
H.P.56 (Handley Page) **24, 127, 128**
H.P.57 (Handley Page Halifax) **24, 28, 127-131, 189**
Hadrian (Waco CG-4A) **14**
Halifax (Handley Page H.P.57) **24, 28, 127-131, 189**
Hamilcar (General Aircraft G.A.L.49) **109**
Hampden (Handley Page H.P.52) **122-123**
Harrow (Handley Page H.P.54) **125-126**
Hereford (Handley Page H.P.52) **122, 124**
Heyford (Handley Page H.P.50) **18, 125**
Handley Page H.P.50 Heyford **18, 125**
Handley Page H.P.52 Hampden **122-123, 124**
Handley Page H.P.52 Hereford **122, 124**
Handley Page H.P.54 Harrow **125-126**
Handley Page H.P.55 **127**
Handley Page H.P.56 **24, 127, 128**
Handley Page H.P.57 Halifax **24, 28, 127-131, 189**
Hardy (Hawker) **138**
Hart (Hawker) **96, 132-134, 135, 136, 137, 138, 140, 141**
Hartebeeste (Hawker) **137**

Harvard (North American) **13**
Hawfinch (Hawker) **43**
Hawker Audax **98, 136, 137**
Hawker Demon **135**
Hawker Fury (biplane) **141-143, 146**
Hawker Fury (monoplane) **166**
Hawker Hardy **138**
Hawker Hart **96, 132-134, 135, 136, 138, 139, 140, 141**
Hawker Hartebeeste **137**
Hawker Hawfinch **41**
Hawker Hector **140, 225**
Hawker Henley **145**
Hawker Hind **139**
Hawker Hoopoe **144**
Hawker Horsley **211**
Hawker Hotspur **41**
Hawker Hurricane **40, 145, 146-153, 154, 155, 165**
Hawker Nimrod **134, 144**
Hawker Osprey **134**
Hawker Sea Fury **166**
Hawker Sea Hurricane **102, 154**
Hawker Tempest **161-164, 165, 166**
Hawker Tornado **156, 161, 165**
Hawker Typhoon **155-160, 161, 165**
Hector (Hawker) **140, 225**
Henley (Hawker) **145**
Heyford (Handley Page H.P.50) **18**
Hind (Hawker) **139**
Hoopoe (Hawker) **144**
Hornet (de Havilland D.H.103) **85**
Horsley (Hawker) **211**
Hotspur (General Aircraft G.A.L.48) **108**
Hotspur (Hawker) **41**
Hurricane (Hawker) **40, 145, 146-153, 154, 155, 156**

L

Lancaster (Avro 683) **24, 28-32, 34, 127, 189**
Lerwick (Saro S.36) **181**
London (Saro A.27) **180**
Lysander (Westland) **227-229**

M

M.3B (Miles Falcon Six) **167**
M.9 (Miles Master) **13, 176-177**
M.11A (Miles Whitney Straight) **167, 172**
M.14 (Miles Magister) **168-169**
M.16 (Miles Mentor) **169**
M.17 (Miles Monarch) **169, 172**
M.19 (Miles Master) **13, 176-177**
M.20 (Miles) **170**
M.24 (Miles Master) **13, 176-177**
M.25 (Miles Martinet) **145, 171**
M.27 (Miles Master) **13, 176-177**
M.28 (Miles Mercury) **172**
M.33 (Miles Monitor) **173**
M.35 (Miles) **174**
M.38 (Miles Messenger) **174-175**
M.39B (Miles) **175**

Magister (Miles M.14) **168-169**
Manchester (Avro 679) **24, 28**
Martinet (Miles M.25) **145, 171**
Master (Miles M.9, M.19, M.24 and M.27) **13, 176-177**
Mentor (Miles M.16) **169**
Mercury (Miles M.28) **172**
Messenger (Miles M.38) **174-175**
Meteor (Gloster G.41) **119-121**
Miles M.3B Falcon Six **167**
Miles M.9 Master 13 **176-177**
Miles M.11A Whitney Straight **167, 172**
Miles M.14 Magister **168-169**
Miles M.16 Mentor **169**
Miles M.17 Monarch **169, 172**
Miles M.19 Master **13, 176-177**
Miles M.20 **170**
Miles M.24 Master **13, 176-177**
Miles M.25 Martinet **145, 171**
Miles M.27 Master **13, 176-177**
Miles M.28 Mercury **172**
Miles M.33 Monitor **173**
Miles M.35 **174**
Miles M.38 Messenger **174-175**
Miles M.39B **175**
Monarch (Miles M.17) **169, 172**
Monitor (Miles M.33) **173**
Mosquito (de Havilland D.H.98) **68, 77-84**
Moth Trainer (de Havilland D.H.60T) **72**

N

Nimrod (Hawker) **134, 144**
North American Harvard **13**

O

Osprey (Hawker) **134**
Oxford (Airspeed AS.10) **10-11, 13**

P

P.82 (Boulton Paul Defiant) **40-42, 145**
PT-24 (de Havilland) **73**
Percival Petrel **179**
Percival Proctor **178**
Percival Q.4 **179**
Percival Q.6 **179**
Percival Vega Gull **178**
Petrel (Percival) **179**
Prefect (Avro 626) **23**
Proctor (Percival) **178**

Q

Q.4 (Percival) **179**
Q.6 (Percival) **179**
Queen Bee (de Havilland) **12**
Queen Wasp (Airspeed AS.30) **12**

R

Roc (Blackburn B-25) **37**

S

S.19 (Short Singapore III) **182**

S.25 (Short Sunderland) **181, 182, 183-186**
S.26 (Short 'G' Class) **188**
S.29 (Short Stirling) **189-192**
S.36 (Saro Lerwick) **181**
S.45 (Short Seaford) **187**
SS.18 (Gloster) **110**
SS.19 (Gloster) **110**
SS.19B (Gloster Gauntlet) **110, 113**
SS.37 (Gloster Gladiator) **113-116**
Saro A.27 London **180**
Saro S.36 Lerwick **181**
Sea Fury (Hawker) **166**
Sea Hornet (de Havilland D.H.103) **85**
Sea Hurricane (Hawker) **102, 154, 210**
Sea Otter (Supermarine) **196**
Seafang (Supermarine) **196**
Seafire (Supermarine) **102**
Seaford (Short S.45) **187**
Seafox (Fairey) **87**
Seagull (Supermarine) **194**
Seal (Fairey) **88, 89**
Shark (Blackburn B-6) **35**
Short S.19 Singapore III **182**
Short S.25 Sunderland **181, 182, 183-186**
Short S.26 'G' Class **188**
Short S.29 Stirling **127, 189-192**
Short S.45 Seaford **187**
Singapore (Short S.19) **182**
Skua (Blackburn B-24) **36, 37**
Southampton (Supermarine) **193**
Spiteful (Supermarine) **212**
Spitfire (Supermarine) **40, 148, 197-209, 210**
Stirling (Short S.29) **127, 189-192**
Stranraer (Supermarine) **180, 193**
Sunderland (Short S.25) **181, 182, 183-186**
Supermarine Sea Otter **197**
Supermarine Seafang **210**
Supermarin Seafire **102, 210-211**
Supermarine Seagull **194**
Supermarine Southampton **193**
Supermarine Spiteful **212**
Supermarine Spitfire **40, 148, 197-209, 210**
Supermarine Stranraer **180, 210**
Supermarine Walrus **194-195, 196**
Swordfish (Fairey) **88-95, 100, 104**

T

Taylorcraft Auster series **71**
Tempest (Hawker) **161-164, 165, 166**
Tiger Moth (de Havilland D.H.82) **72-73**
Tornado (Hawker) **156, 161, 165**
Tutor (Avro 621) **22, 23**
Type 105 (Bristol Bulldog) **43-45, 110, 110, 113**
Type 130 (Bristol Bombay) **46**
Type 142M (Bristol Blenheim) **47-56, 68, 77, 135**
Type 149 (Bristol Bolingbroke/Blenheim) **47-56, 57, 68**
Type 150 (Bristol) **57**
Type 152 (Bristol Beaufort) **38, 57-60**
Type 155 (Bristol) **21**
Type 156 (Bristol Beaufighter) **61-67, 68, 69**

Type 160 (Bristol Bisley/Blenheim) **47-56, 68**
Type 163 (Bristol Buckingham) **68, 70**
Type 164 (Bristol Brigand) **69**
Type 166 (Bristol Buckmaster) **70**
Type 504 (Avro) **22**
Type 621 (Avro Tutor) **22, 23**
Type 626 (Avro Prefect) **23**
Type 652A (Avro Anson) **25-27**
Type 679 (Avro Manchester) **24**
Type 683 (Avro Lancaster) **24, 28-32, 34, 189**
Type 685 (Avro York) **32, 33**
Type 694 (Avro Lincoln) **34**
Typhoon (Hawker) **155-160, 161, 165**

V

Valentia (Vickers) **46, 215**
Vega Gull (Percival) **178**
Vickers **271, 122**
Vickers Valentia **46, 215**
Vickers Vildebeest **213, 214**
Vickers Vincent **214**
Vickers Virginia **125**
Vickers Warwick **127, 222-223**
Vickers Wellesley **216, 217**
Vickers Wellington **122, 217-221**

Vickers Windsor **224**
Vildebeest (Vickers) **211, 212**
Vincent (Vickers) **212**

W

Waco CG-4A Hadrian **14**
Wallace (Westland) **226**
Walrus (Supermarine) **194-195, 196**
Wapiti (Westland) **213, 225**
Warwick (Vickers) **127, 222-223**
Wellesley (Vickers) **216, 217**
Welkin (Westland) **235**
Wellington (Vickers) **122, 217-221**
Westland Lysander **227-229**
Westland Wallace **226**
Westland Wapiti **214, 225**
Westland Welkin **235**
Westland Whirlwind **230-235**
Whirlwind (Westland) **230-235**
Whitley (Armstrong Whitworth A.W.38) **16-20, 28**
Whitney Straight (Miles M.11A) **167, 172**
Windsor (Vickers) **224**

Y

York (Avro 685) **32, 33**

Picture Acknowledgements

We are grateful to the following organisations for
their help in supplying photographs for this book.

Imperial War Museum: 1, 5, 10, 11, 30, 57, 58, 62, 64,
84, 90, 108, 131, 132, 148, 150, 155, 190, 200, 202, 204,
206, 218, 220, 221
Fox Photos: 16, 52, 94, 123, 156, 198, 211
Military Archive & Research Service: 32
Popperfoto: 73, 78, 82, 105, 185
RAF Museum, Hendon: 23, 136, 139, 144, 208, 222, 232